Henry Adams:

SCIENTIFIC HISTORIAN

by WILLIAM H. JORDY

ARCHON BOOKS   1970

Copyright, 1952, by Yale University Press
Reprinted 1970 with permission
in an unaltered and unabridged edition

ISBN: 0-208-00828-4
Library of Congress Catalog Card Number: 77-114423
Printed in the United States of America

TO SAL

who was the most patient of all

Action frustrated, intellect unrealized, artistry qualified, life not lived: such is the quadruple nature of the "failure" chronicled in *The Education of Henry Adams*. As it happened, Adams' notion of a science of history affected in one way or another every aspect of his multiple complaint. Not that he developed a coherent idea of scientific history; nor should the reader of this volume expect that I have found one. This book inquires rather into an attitude of mind, a purpose stated elsewhere but best reinforced at the outset. It attempts to explain how an unusually sensitive man quite casually and most ambiguously—that is, more by temperament than logic—embraced the cause of scientific history; how ultimately by his imagination he fused his predilections for science and history, and art as well, into the failure celebrated in the *Education*.

So much by way of introduction. As for the pleasant task of thanking those who have contributed to my research, let me start at the beginning. My introduction to Henry Adams occurred in the thirties when Carlton Qualey, then teaching history at Bard College, suggested that no undergraduate should leave college without reading the *Education*. Under his sympathetic guidance and that of George Genzmer, whose seminar in writing was an especial delight, I first ventured into the intricacies of Adams' paradoxical thought. There followed graduate work, the army, a return to graduate work, and more by chance than design I found myself again at work on Adams. Throughout the initial period of research on this book Samuel Flagg Bemis, Ralph H. Gabriel, Leonard W. Labaree, Norman Holmes Pearson, and David M. Potter were generous with both time and suggestions, first as my teachers before I submitted a much reduced version of this manuscript as a doctoral dissertation, later as advisers of a less official character. From the beginning, too, Bernhard Knollenberg has offered advice and encouragement. For assistance on special problems of a historical nature I am indebted to Hajo Holborn, Richard

Barnes, Sumner Crosby, Raymond Walters, and Anthony N. B. Garvan; to the latter, as editor of the *American Quarterly*, I owe thanks for permission to reprint most of Chapter I. On scientific questions the instruction of Lynde P. Wheeler, Jared K. Morse, Henry Margenau, Joseph Gregory, Richard Flint, J. I. Tracey, Benjamin Owen, Albert Conrad, Lester Lichty, and Karl Waagé proved immensely helpful. I am particularly grateful to G. Evelyn Hutchinson, who read the three chapters on Adams' use of science and corrected at least my most glaring blunders. In addition to the aid of these individuals on specific problems, I must also acknowledge the courteous assistance of Stewart Mitchell and Stephen Riley at the Massachusetts Historical Society, of George Strong at the Western Reserve University Library, and of Wayne Andrews at the New York Historical Society.

To the late Henry Adams, a descendant of my subject, I am indebted for the use of certain papers in the Henry Adams estate. For a similar privilege in respect to the estate of John Torrey Morse, Jr., I am indebted to his daughter Miss Charlotte Morse. David Randall and R. V. Coleman, both of Charles Scribners' Sons, assisted me with documents on the *History* in the possession of the firm, while Mrs. Ward Thoron and Miss Aileen Tone very kindly contributed some of their personal recollections of Henry Adams.

At one time, when I rashly believed that I could finish this work in the fall of 1948, Ernest Samuels courteously permitted me to read the galleys of *The Young Henry Adams* in advance of its publication. Of other Adams scholars who have assisted with specific problems, I must mention Harold Dean Cater and Max I. Baym. My greater indebtedness to them—and of course to other scholars—appears in my footnotes.

For permission to print excerpts from Henry Adams' writings I must, first of all, acknowledge the cooperation of Houghton, Mifflin Company, the publishers of *Mont-Saint-Michel and Chartres*, *The Education of Henry Adams*, the two-volume *Cycle of Adams Letters, 1861–1865, Letters of Henry Adams* (again two volumes, and all four edited by Worthington C. Ford), and finally *Henry Adams and his Friends*, edited by Harold Dean Cater. The Macmillan Company has permitted the reprinting of excerpts from *The Degradation of the Democratic Dogma;* the estate of Henry James an excerpt from *Letters of William James*, edited by Henry James and published by the Atlantic Monthly Press.

As editor of the Yale Historical Publications, Lewis P. Curtis displayed a rare combination of discrimination, sympathy, and patience—the latter quality severely taxed by the many versions of this manuscript and parts of versions which he read. Miss Denise Hoesli and Mrs. Frank McMullan did yeoman duty for the Yale University Press on the styling, while Eugene Davidson offered encouragement when I most needed it and Norman Donaldson took a friend's as well as a publisher's interest in the manuscript from its inception. Edward Poitras assisted with the bibliography and other prickly bits of research. And finally—the inevitable last but not least—my gratitude for the considerable assistance of my wife Sarah Spock Jordy.

WILLIAM H. JORDY

Yale University
New Haven, Connecticut
March, 1952

I N THE footnotes I have used short titles for works by Henry Adams frequently cited, for the various collections of his letters together with the collection of his wife's letters edited by Ward Thoron, and for three recent volumes on Adams by Ernest Samuels, Robert A. Hume, and Max I. Baym. Page references to Adams' writings will serve for any of the most accessible trade editions with the exception of *Mont-Saint-Michel and Chartres*. A new printing of this work in 1936 altered pagination slightly, but the variation is not more than two or three pages from the pagination of the earlier editions which I have used. Starred items (*) refer to volumes in the Henry Adams library deposited in the Massachusetts Historical Society. When these volumes were written in other than English, and an English translation existed, I have cited the English edition but given the non-English version in brackets with the star inside the brackets, and the page reference corresponding to that of the English edition.

The following list contains the short titles used in the footnotes and in the index.

Baym: Max I. Baym. *The French Education of Henry Adams.* New York, Columbia University Press, 1951.

Cater: Harold D. Cater, ed. *Henry Adams and His Friends.* Boston, Houghton Mifflin, 1947.

Chartres: Henry Adams. *Mont-Saint-Michel and Chartres.* Boston and New York, published "by authority of the American Institute of Architects," Houghton Mifflin, 1913.

Cycle, 1 or 2: Worthington C. Ford, ed. *A Cycle of Adams Letters, 1861–1865.* Boston and New York, Houghton Mifflin, 1920.

Degradation: Henry Adams. *The Degradation of the Democratic Dogma.* New York, Macmillan, 1919. Ed. with Introduction by Brooks Adams.

Degradation: Letter: Henry Adams. "A Letter to American Teachers of History." In *Degradation,* pp. 137–263. Originally privately published. Washington, 1910. 1 vol.

Degradation: Rule: Henry Adams. "The Rule of Phase Applied to History." In *Degradation,* pp. 267–311. Written in 1909; in manuscript at Adams' death.

Degradation: Tendency: Henry Adams. "The Tendency of History." In *Degradation,* pp. 125–133. Originally published in *Annual Report of the American Historical Association for 1894.* Washington, Government Printing Office, 1895. Pp. 17–23.

Democracy: Henry Adams. *Democracy: An American Novel.* New York, Holt, 1880.

Education: Henry Adams. *The Education of Henry Adams, an Autobiography.* Boston and New York, Houghton Mifflin, 1918. Reprinted, New York, Modern Library, 1931.

Esther: Henry Adams. *Esther: A Novel.* New York, Holt, 1884. Reprinted, Robert E. Spiller, ed. Scholars' Facsimiles and Reprints, 1938.

Ford, 1 or 2: Worthington C. Ford, ed. *Letters of Henry Adams, 1858–1891,* Vol. 1; *1892–1918,* Vol. 2. Boston and New York, Houghton Mifflin, 1930, 1938.

Gallatin: Henry Adams. *The Life of Albert Gallatin.* Philadelphia and London, Lippincott, 1879.

"Great Secession Winter": Henry Adams. "The Great Secession Winter of 1860–61." *Proceedings of the Massachusetts Historical Society, 43* (1909), 656–687.

History: Henry Adams. *History of the United States of America during the First Administration of Thomas Jefferson.* New York, Scribners, 1889. 2 vols. *History . . . during the Second Administration of Thomas Jefferson.* 1890. 2 vols. *History . . . during the First Administration of James Madison.* 1890. 2 vols. *History . . . during the Second Administration of James Madison.* 1891. 3 vols. Reprinted in 4 vols., 9 books, New York, Boni, 1930.

Hume: Robert A. Hume. *Runaway Star, an Appreciation of Henry Adams.* Ithaca, Cornell University Press, 1951.

NAR: North American Review.

Randolph: Henry Adams. *John Randolph.* Boston, Houghton Mifflin, 1882.

Samuels: Ernest Samuels. *The Young Henry Adams.* Cambridge, Harvard University Press, 1948.

Thoron: Ward Thoron, ed. *The Letters of Mrs. Henry Adams.* Boston, Little, Brown, 1936.

CONTENTS

The historian must not try to know what
is truth, if he values his honesty;
for, if he cares for his truths, he is certain
to falsify his facts.

THE EDUCATION OF HENRY ADAMS

I. TWO TEMPERAMENTS IN HISTORY:
SCIENTIFIC AND LITERARY

S INCE Gibbon, the spectacle was almost a scandal. History had lost even the sense of shame. It was a hundred years behind the experimental sciences. For all serious purpose, it was less instructive than Walter Scott and Alexandre Dumas." Thus in 1905 Adams chided his fellow historians in the *Education*, about fifteen years after he had completed his massive study of the Jefferson and Madison administrations. Then he quickly made a few exceptions to his general condemnation: "Sir Henry Maine, Tylor, McLennan, Buckle, Auguste Comte, and the various philosophers who, from time to time, stirred the scandal, and made it more scandalous." [1]

The scandal to which Adams alluded was of course the notion that history was storytelling, while his mention of the experimental sciences suggested that history had meaning and validity only if it provided generalizations so comprehensive as to apply to more than a particular sequence of events. His statement thus reflected the battle waged between so-called literary and scientific historians during the nineteenth century, if indeed "battle" does not state the antagonism too strongly. For, despite the antipathy of one school for the work of the other, the battle was more a series of skirmishes among individuals than a concerted action. Actually, no less than three groups, inharmonious among themselves if not mutually incompatible, fought under the banner of scientific history.[2]

Most scientific historians sought a method of objectifying and presenting data so as, in the well-known phrase of Ranke, to reveal

1. *Education*, p. 301.
2. W. Stull Holt, "The Idea of Scientific History in America," *Journal of the History of Ideas, 1* (1940), 352–362, mentions only two kinds of scientific history, comparable to the first and third meanings given here. He does suggest, however, some of the characteristics included in the social science approach to scientific history.

history as it had actually happened. The other two factions felt that an impersonal method of analyzing data was in itself not enough; they strove also to approximate science by providing the kind of generalization which Adams demanded in his *Education.* Some held that these generalizations should come from the social sciences, usually from political science, economics, sociology, anthropology, psychology, or geography.[3] This group stemmed less from Ranke than from Comte and to some extent echoed the faith of the French philosopher that society could discover the laws under which it operated, the frequent implication being that such discovery promised social betterment. Hence the Comtian group was likely to approach history with some notion of reform, or at least with a sense of purpose so woefully lacking in the more pedantic followers of Ranke, who confused the master's insistence on the sacredness of the past with documented antiquarianism. The third faction among the scientific historians sought their generalizations in the natural and physical sciences. During the nineteenth century biological evolution provided the favorite analogies. To be sure, the latter two factions frequently merged. Evolutionary theories like those of Spencer drifted into the social sciences, while such followers of Comte as Buckle and Taine favored historical standards akin to those for the natural sciences.[4] But a distinction is necessary, since it was possible to separate the two approaches, while commitments varied depending on the choice.

Obviously any adjective bracketing such a diversity of interest challenged precise definition. Nevertheless, "scientific" did refer to a movement of some homogeneity in that it comprehended a broad trend away from what many came to consider the overem-

3. Geography is included among the social sciences because it was often grouped with them, especially during the first two decades of the twentieth century. To cite some random examples of this interest in geography in the United States: the influential volume by Ellen C. Semple, *American History and Its Geographical Conditions* (Boston and New York, Houghton Mifflin, 1903); the grant by the Carnegie Corporation in 1912 for the comprehensive atlas by Charles O. Paullin, *Atlas of the Historical Geography of the United States* (Washington, Carnegie Institution and American Geographical Society, 1932); the choice of the geographer Ellsworth Huntington as president of the American Historical Association in 1913; the prominent place given to geography in Frederick J. Teggart, *The Processes of History* (New Haven, Yale University Press, 1918); the stimulus of Frederick J. Turner's studies on the frontier and sectionalism.

4. On Comte's insistence on pluralism in method among the various fields of knowledge see Ernst Cassirer, *The Problem of Knowledge* (New Haven, Yale University Press, 1950), chap. xiv, which also discusses the failure of Buckle and Taine to preserve the methodological differences between the natural and social sciences. See Bibliography, Sec. G, on Comtism.

phasis on narrative by so-called literary historians like Macaulay, Michelet, and Prescott. But this movement for scientific history was more than protest. On its positive side it aimed to professionalize history and so paralleled a trend common to many other areas of knowledge during the nineteenth century. As Whitehead has observed, the great invention of the nineteenth century was that of perfecting the technique of invention so that science depended for its development no longer on the haphazard investigations of scattered geniuses but could be pressed with that rapidity and systematization which have made our technological civilization possible. Just so scientific historians meant to deliver history from the indiscriminate enthusiasms of the man of letters, to departmentalize it within the university. Hence the core of the movement was methodological. History required a method readily adapted to standardization, to institutionalization, and thereby to cooperation. These were the social accompaniments to new standards for historical objectivity which, in Ranke's vision, provided the methodological means for universal history.[5]

Considering the impact of science on the nineteenth century, it is not surprising that these qualities—standardization, institutionalization, cooperation, and objectivity—should suggest the adjective "scientific." Unfortunately the label tended to distract attention from the essence which it designated. The simple question "What is the nature of history?" acquired a conditioning query: "If history is a science, then what is its nature?" Once argument took this tack the idea of necessary generalization followed.

Thus a single misapplied adjective served the amorphous movement toward historical professionalization, a movement roughly contemporaneous in the United States with Adams' most productive years. Moreover, unlike that of most scientific historians, his activity touched on scientific history in the whole of its threefold meaning, as even the briefest biography reveals. Comte had been his youthful bible and reform a major interest almost to his fortieth year. When he returned to Harvard in 1870 for his brief tenure of teaching Adams was among the pioneers in this country to intro-

5. Alfred N. Whitehead, *Science and the Modern World* (New York, Macmillan, 1925), pp. 140–143. For general bibliography on trends in the teaching of history in America during the nineteenth century see below, p. 37, n. 39. For sympathetic accounts of Ranke's frequently misunderstood position in history, Cassirer, *op. cit.*, chap. xiii; Hajo Holborn, "The Science of History," *The Interpretation of History*, ed. Joseph R. Strayer (Princeton, Princeton University Press, 1943).

duce the scientific method (or what was also prevalently, if rather vaguely, termed the "German method") [6] into the American university. There he taught a course in medieval institutions at a time when the comparative study of institutions was seminal to the fields of sociology and anthropology. Before leaving Harvard Adams and his graduate students, in their joint authorship of *Essays in Anglo-Saxon Law*, produced an example of cooperative scholarship which was at the time of its publication in 1876 unparalleled in American graduate education.[7] The eighties saw the writing of his account of the Jefferson and Madison administrations. Finally published between 1889 and 1891, these nine volumes are generally considered the finest work of scientific history published in America during the nineteenth century, and at least among the finest down to the present day. In 1893 Adams was elected the tenth president of the American Historical Association, which was a major force in promoting professionalism in history. His presidential address of the following year, "The Tendency of History," marked a significant change in his career as scientific historian. Here ideas only casually foreshadowed coalesced into his well-known plea for a science of history based upon laws from the experimental sciences. For the remainder of his historical career Adams intermittently worked to perfect a scheme for history founded on the physical sciences. This project terminated in 1910 with his tentative pronouncement in *A Letter to American Teachers of History*, which he closed with the admission that reconciling history with the experimental sciences required "the aid of another Newton." [8]

Such, briefly, was his career in scientific history, a career desultorily pursued throughout forty of his eighty years, or roughly from 1870 to 1910. We may conveniently halve the four decades, allotting twenty years (up to the appearance of the final volume of his *History* in 1891) to his use of the scientific method in conventional historical studies along with his significant inter-

6. For Adams' comments on German history see immediately below; also *Education*, p. 302. As applied to teaching, the "German method" also referred to the seminar method of instruction, especially in graduate work.

7. *Essays in Anglo-Saxon Law* (Boston, Little, Brown, 1876), containing four essays, the first by Adams, the others being the doctoral dissertations of Adams' first three doctoral candidates; see below, p. 36. On the relation between institutional history and the early development of sociology and anthropology, Floyd N. House, *The Development of Sociology* (New York and London, McGraw-Hill, 1936), chap. xiii; Robert H. Lowie, *The History of Ethnographical Theory* (New York, Farrar & Rinehart, 1937), chaps. v, vi, vii.

8. *Degradation: Tendency*, p. 263.

est in generalizations from the social sciences; the next twenty to his hope that history might be fitted to laws from the physical sciences. When he went to Harvard in 1870 he was the third member of a three-man department of history which was probably, at the time, the most important in this country. Before he bowed from history, leaving final solutions to some unborn Newton, history had become a major department in every American college, and the principles of scientific history had triumphed. Or at least substantially triumphed.

By 1910 the so-called scientific method was firmly established in history, while the impact of the social sciences on history had just begun to be felt. In 1912, James Harvey Robinson published his essay "The New History," in which he proposed an end to purely narrative history, to the history of events, and to history with an excessively political bias. "The 'New History' is escaping from the limitations formerly imposed upon the study of the past. It will come in time consciously to meet our daily needs; it will avail itself of all those discoveries that are being made about mankind by anthropologists, economists, psychologists, and sociologists . . ." [9] This essay became a rallying point for the new historians. If its welcome to the social sciences seems excessively buoyant today, it is because the essay reflected the exuberance of discovery. The plethora of social, cultural, and other "interpretations" of history which has followed in the wake of this discovery of the social sciences has shifted the center of history decisively away from nineteenth-century predilections for narrative and "past politics." [10]

Only the third aspect of scientific history—that concerning the relation between history and the laws from the natural and physical sciences—has fared badly. Today even the word "scientific" is, implicitly if not explicitly, wreathed in apologetic punctuation.[11] In part this discomfiture with the scientific factor stems from the disillusionment with evolutionary theories of history; in part from attacks by the historical relativists against the notion

9. James Harvey Robinson, *The New History* (New York, Macmillan, 1912), p. 24. On "new" history see also below, pp. 242–246; see Bibliography, Sec. I.

10. The phrase is Edward Freeman's.

11. Charles A. Beard, "That Noble Dream," *American Historical Review, 41* (1935), pp. 76 f., suggests the term "historicism" (as an English translation of *Historismus*), although this term implies more than mere method. He has also, in "Written History as an Act of Faith," *American Historical Review, 39* (1934), 226, referred to the "empirical or scientific method." See Bibliography, Sec. H, on history.

that any method can eliminate subjective elements, thus yielding the past as it actually happened; in part from an increased awareness of the tremendous role played by irrational elements in history; and in part perhaps from a growing belief that history, dealing with man as it does, is after all rooted in the humanistic studies. So today "scientific" rarely accompanies "history," nor should it. The adjective has fallen into disrepute; but, for better or worse, what men once called scientific history has effected a major transformation in history, while Adams' historical career occupied the period of this transition.

He is the more interesting as a partisan of scientific history because he himself never really made the transition to professionalism. His *History* reflected the professional ideal in its rigorous dependence on the documents; but its urbanity, together with the urbane conditions of its creation, disclosed the man of the world, the cultivated man of experience, the gentleman-dilettante. Thus the *History* at once betokened the emerging history of the graduate school and reflected the distinguished literary tradition in American historiography exemplified by Prescott, Motley, George Bancroft, and Parkman. This awareness of literary values, with all that such awareness implied for his personality, saved Adams from a blind faith in science. Indeed he was that rarest of scientific historians who not only contributed significantly to the cause but never quite trusted the direction in which his studies led. When he eventually completed his scheme for subsuming history under the experimental sciences, all that was aesthetic and humane in his personality protested the result.

Hence his historical career illuminates not only the transition of a profession but the transition as well of a sensitive spirit who ultimately abandoned whatever certainties existed in the nineteenth century to embrace the uncertainties of our own.

Reared in a family highly conscious of history, Adams had imbibed history from youth. Only when he came to practice history in the seventies and eighties, first as teacher, then as gentleman historian at work on his account of the Jeffersonian period, did he need consciously to consider his historical ideals. Looked back on from a twentieth-century vantage point, these may seem less progressive than they were at the time. To Adams history demanded a strict dependence on the document with as little embellishment as possible, whether of rhetoric or conclusions. Moreover, history was scientific only if it dealt with the evolution of institutions or society rather than with specific heroes or episodes. Finally—and how pregnant for his later speculations—scientific history traced the slow development of some broad concept such as nationalism or democracy. Whatever the concept, it must be larger than its illustration in any particular country or set of circumstances, and hence capable of comparative treatment. Adams conceived of scientific history, then, as embracing a method, a subject matter, and a purpose. To translate this triad into terms savoring more of science: the historian's method should be as objective as possible; his subject matter impersonal in essence; his purpose that of discovering principles applicable to more than just the sample analyzed.

Not that Adams ever precisely formulated these ideas. Far from it. But among his chores at Harvard was that of editing the *North American Review*, in which he wrote a number of reviews of institutional histories. Fortunately, these make unmistakable his criteria for historical scholarship. He repeatedly upbraided American and, more especially, English historians for their failure to attain the caliber of scientific perfection in history allegedly achieved by the Germans.[12] Adams admired the "exact basis" [13] which some German historians had given to the study of institutions. But William Stubbs was scrupulously objective in his *Constitutional History of England;* he was interested in institutions. On what grounds, then, did Adams criticize the Englishman? "His History aims at the correct appreciation of facts, so far as they are at hand, rather than the development of an idea. He is the perfect editor; he would be an admirable lexicographer; but as an historian he will infallibly be voted dull." [14] As for Edward Freeman, he fell below Stubbs. Although Freeman had read the German historians, he failed to understand both the method and aims of the German institutionalists. In another comparison of the historical accomplishments of the two countries Adams noted that England could not show work "equally thorough and equally broad." Except "perhaps" for Austin and Sir Henry Maine, the English had not developed a "faculty for comparison and criticism, for minute analysis and sweeping generalization." [15] Although

12. Samuels, p. 230. *NAR, 114* (1872), 193, 195, 197, 198 f.; *118* (1874), 416 f.; *119* (1874), 236 f.; *120* (1875), 179 f.
13. *NAR, 118* (1874), 425.
14. *Ibid., 119* (1874), 235.
15. *Ibid., 114* (1872), 195, 198 f.

Adams praised Maine's *Ancient Law* more highly than the work of any other English institutionalist, even this volume suffered because it treated Roman law as "the pure, typical, legal history, to be illustrated rather than to be used for illustration, to be studied as the end rather than to be used as a subject for classification." [16] With Adams the sweeping generalization, so large as to influence many periods and many places, went hand in hand with minute analysis; else history risked becoming mere lexicography or, as he said of the works of both Stubbs and George Bancroft, mere "facts." [17]

Only the trend of some broad principle gave history its continuity. This latter word appeared twice in Adams' reviews,[18] while the idea eventually grew to the obsession around which the speculations of his old age turned. In his early writings Adams' idea of continuity approximated the "germ" concept of institutional history later popularized at Johns Hopkins. In fact, he referred to the "germs" of institutions in his review of Stubbs [19] and implied that the most promising task of history was the recreation of the entire development of an institution or an idea from seed to ultimate luxuriance. How unorganic, if some segment of the trunk were missing. If, for instance, one part of the continuous evolution of the idea of popular government should escape the historian's attention, like the "clew offered by the hundred [a county subdivision over which an Anglo-Saxon court presided]," then "the English judicial constitution [became] a confused jumble of words." Even as Adams wrote this sentence for the July, 1874, number of the *North American* [20] he looked forward to a selected group of Harvard graduate students who would meet with him for the first time that autumn for a seminar in which they would fit the "clew offered by the hundred" into a continuity tracing the idea of a popular judicial system from the ancient Teutonic courts to comparable institutions on the British Isles, and thence, by implication, into the judicial procedure of modern England. And when, some thirty years later, Adams exempted a few historians from his sweeping condemnation in the *Education*, he ex-

16. *Ibid., 118* (1874), 391; also p. 397.
17. On Bancroft, Ford, *1*, 293. For other statements by Adams on scientific history, *NAR, 118* (1874), 391; *119* (1874), 233 f.; '*120* (1875), 178 ff.
18. *NAR, 114* (1872), 197; *119* (1874), 242. Holt, *op. cit., 1*, 354 f., discusses the idea of continuity but does not clearly relate this concept to his two categories for scientific history.
19. *NAR, 119'* (1874), 235.
20. *Ibid.*, p. 240.

cepted just those like Sir Henry Maine, who, despite his shortcomings, had conceived of history as an impersonal continuity; or like Comte, who had gone further than Maine in his search for scientific synthesis; or, finally, like Gibbon, whose picture of decline matched the mood and scale of Adams' ultimate pessimism.

So much for the affirmative aspects of Adams' early ideas on scientific history. They also had their negative side, for the scientific historian opposed what Adams variously called "romantic," "dramatic," or "heroic" history.[21] The essence of scientific history depended quite as much on what it opposed as on its positive criteria; but the task of nicely differentiating the two historical modes most important in American historiography toward the end of the nineteenth century is not easy. The one category overlaps the other, while the overlap indicates the superficiality of the division, as might be expected of a dichotomy which few historians tried to analyze. Consider, for example, a contrast which immediately occurs to mind: the emphasis on narrative in literary history, on source materials in scientific. Not only does the literary historian necessarily make use of documentation in his narrative, and the scientific historian some use of narrative, but Henry Adams' *History* provides an instance of superb narrative. Among the virtues of the *History* which the contemporary historian might ponder, none is more profitable than Adams' use of the document to progress his narrative. On the other hand, if Francis Parkman is esteemed for his narrative, few historians have expended more effort in their quest for documentation. As Edward Bourne has said of Parkman, he among all American historians best merged in himself two vital traditions influencing history during three-quarters of the nineteenth century: the one stemming from the "critical spirit and method" of Wolf and Niebuhr, the other from the "sympathetic contemplation of the past" inspired by Chateaubriand and Scott.[22]

So the simple dichotomy vanishes in complications, while the characteristics which Adams and Parkman shared in common as historians—notably their view of history as a literary profession

21. *History*, 9, 223–225, 241. See below, p. 34.
22. Edward G. Bourne, "Francis Parkman," *Essays in Historical Criticism* (New York, Scribners; London, Arnold, 1901), p. 277. John S. Bassett, *The Middle Group of American Historians* (New York, Macmillan, 1917), p. ix, did not know whether or not to include Parkman among the literary historians but arbitrarily decided on his exclusion. Criticizing this arbitrary decision, Carl Becker, "Labeling the Historians," *Everyman His Own Historian* (New York, Crofts, 1935), pp. 132–142, protests against the notion of literary and scientific historians.

and their mutual interest in narrative—relate the two in time and spirit. Yet who would deny that the succession of documents on Adams' pages and the flow of narrative on Parkman's do not reveal essential differences in tone, in temperament, and in purpose? The difference in purpose might suffice for an epistemological study, but contrasts in tone and temperament are also important, however tenuous, and especially significant in comprehending the inner compulsions which drove Henry Adams to explore all facets of scientific history in his lifetime quest of unity. If the cleavage between the scientific and literary modes of history results in some exaggeration, both tone and temperament involve differences of degree, not of classification. No contrast could be more appropriate than that between the two Bostonians, the more because both were, in a sense, transitional figures in history. One looked toward a waning tradition in American historiography. The other acknowledged the tradition but abandoned it to herald the future trend.

Those documents that Parkman used he buried within his narrative lest they mar its continuity. What Parkman sought to hide, his fellow Brahmin made conspicuous. Adams patched his pages with the writings of early national statesmen, isolating their words from his own analysis. If the two historians used archives differently, this dissimilarity suggested dissimilar attitudes toward history. For Parkman, who called Scott, Cooper, and Byron his favorite authors,[23] history afforded a canvas on which "to paint the forest and its tenants in true and vivid colors" and "to realize a certain ideal of manhood, a little medieval, but nevertheless good." [24] For Adams, exposed as he had been to law, diplomacy, and the German method, the "historian need only state facts in their sequence." Thus he stated his credo in the *History*. Some years later he gave more specific advice to the daughter of Abraham Hewitt, who contemplated a biography of her father. The historian ought "only to give a running commentary on the documents in order to explain their relation." [25]

Each emphasis—the one on narrative, the other on source materials—has, in the hands of a master, its own appeal. Parkman

23. Mason Wade, *Francis Parkman, Heroic Historian* (New York, Viking, 1942), pp. 224, 326 f., 329. Charles H. Farnham, *A Life of Francis Parkman* (Boston, Little, Brown, 1900), p. 199; see also pp. 186 and 347 f. for Parkman's lack of interest in theory and speculation.

24. Henry D. Sedgwick, *Francis Parkman* (Boston and New York, Houghton Mifflin, 1904), p. 329.

25. *History, 3*, 45. Jan. 7, 1904; Cater, p. 548.

carries the reader on his full flood of narrative as easily as the Mississippi once bore the explorers of imperial France toward its mouth. Hence we may read his work almost as we read a novel. Like his favorite authors Parkman portrayed the past as a sequence of unique phenomena removed in time from the experience of his readers. This romantic concept of history undoubtedly attracted Parkman to his theme, where the grandeur of the wilderness matched the epic proportions of his heroes. If the complexities of diplomatic negotiations could hardly have attracted Parkman, it was not completely impossible to portray the Jefferson administration as Adams himself once described it: ". . . freighted with hopes and aspirations owing to a sincere popular faith that could never be revived, and a freshness, almost a simplicity of thought that must always give to its history a certain indefinable popular charm, like old-fashioned music . . ." [26] But Adams viewed his subject from no such remote retrospect. On the contrary, he used the document as the means to recapture Jefferson's reactions at the very moment of their occurrence.

The reader seems to peer with Adams at Jefferson's activities from behind a drapery in the White House. We see Jefferson at the moment he receives a letter; with him we fairly puzzle a reply. Then, if time be further confounded, we cross Lafayette Square with Adams and there discuss what was seen, before setting off once more in quest of other unsuspecting statesmen. Thus Adams gave his *History* the immediacy of a laboratory demonstration. As his readers could always climb the Tower at Pisa and duplicate the essence of Galileo's experiment (if not, of course, the whole complex of circumstances surrounding it), so they could leaf the documents from the Jefferson administration and, Adams hoped, show what had actually happened. Rather, to go Ranke's ideal one better, Adams could show the past actually happening. Such a goal could only be imagined (let alone attained) provided the area of history was limited, as Adams essentially limited his *History* to politics, diplomacy, and battles.

Croce and his numerous followers have made much of the role of the imagination to create a "present in the past." [27] In Crocean

---

26. *Gallatin,* p. 391.

27. Of course the phrase "present in the past" as Croce used it meant two things. He not only referred to the necessary role of the imagination in recreating the past but simultaneously asserted that the past always reflected the particular present in which the historian wrote. Of the two meanings I have considered only the first here.

terms, Parkman doubtless created a present in the wilderness
which he portrayed. Yet Parkman's present, if such it may be
termed, was a personal synthesis of his research. Therefore Parkman's present did not evolve before the reader; it had already
evolved—and vanished—like the wilderness itself, or the "certain
ideal of manhood." True, once the reader had made his mental
leap backward through centuries, and once he had accepted Parkman's world, then Parkman's genius gave this world the immediacy
of life. Such immediacy could be called a present; but Parkman's
past was always past though he made it as vivid as the present.
For Adams present and past were both arbitrary points in a time
sequence. Adams laid the past bit by bit before his readers as the
scientist might perform an experiment. In this sequence of now,
now, now, history approached a laboratory demonstration. Although history need not always depend on Adams' method to be
labeled scientific, yet his method does give a sense of events occurring as though in an isolated system, apart from the personality of the historian. History occurred as if imprisoned in some
apparatus while not only Adams' readers but Adams himself
watched the process. This sense of the evolving nature of events
and of their evolving apart from the intervention of the historian
not only gave a scientific flavor to Adams' *History* but was also
essential to his artistry. For like science itself, scientific history
has its aesthetic elements, and few historians have surpassed
Adams' sensitivity in using the documents themselves as the ingredients for narrative.

Like the scientist, too, Adams demanded that his readers ac-
tively participate in his analysis, while Parkman sought their
passive immersion in his synthesis. Of course Parkman hoped to
stimulate his readers intellectually, and to this extent he also
sought an active audience; but, above all, he appealed to their
emotions. For it was the emotional aura of the intrepidity of man,
of the vastness of the wilderness, and of nostalgia for what could
never reappear which lingered with Parkman's reader. This emotional response depended on a cumulative image, which only accumulated if the reader passively yielded to Parkman's resonance.
Adams' *History* reversed the roles of historian and reader. The
more activity the historian forced on his readers, the more passively
he viewed his intermediate role between the sources and his audience. Like the natural scientist again, Adams merely set up the
experiment, so that the intelligent witness apparently watched the

conclusions emerge of their own accord. Of course Adams never believed that he could duplicate the precision of the experimental scientist for any but the simplest phenomena in history. He might have felt it possible, however, to approach the certainty of such inferential sciences as cosmology. The cosmologist could not produce planets at will any more than the historian could recreate the Jefferson administration in a bell jar. Yet each might inferentially arrive at what had actually happened. At least Adams seemed to reflect this belief when complaining in the *Education* that "He had even published a dozen volumes of American history for no other purpose than to satisfy himself whether, by the severest process of stating, with the least possible comment, such facts as seemed sure, in such order as seemed rigorously consequent, he could fix for a familiar moment a necessary sequence of human movement." [28]

Adams' scientific point of view, then, stemmed from his belief in the historical facts as hard cores of certainty existing outside the mind of the historian. The historian gathered his certainties. He arranged them; or rather he maintained that they suggested their own arrangement. His only function was that of providing the minimum of commentary required to explain their relation.[29] Only function! How casually Adams shrugged off the very element that makes his *History* what it is. But he typified the scientific approach in his emphasis on the historian's function as (to appropriate a metaphor often applied to Ranke) a transparent eyeball to the past.

Historical relativists have thoroughly attacked on epistemological grounds this view that history can unfold without the historian. Subjective elements occur in the historian's own predilections, in his choice and presentation of evidence, and in the past itself. This is no place to consider their critique of scientific history, except to note that the present dichotomy between subjectivists and objectivists in history is not quite the same as that which existed between scientific and literary historians during the nine-

28. *Education*, p. 382.

29. In other words, this point of view is represented by three of the five assumptions by which Beard, *American Historical Review*, *41*, 76, has very conveniently summarized the scientific position as described by Karl Heussi. First, history exists as an object or a series of objects outside the mind of the historian. Second, the historian can describe his externalized history completely objectively, as it actually occurred. Third, the historian can for purposes of research and writing divest himself of the least taint of prejudice. For a general bibliography on relativism versus scientism in history see Bibliography, Sec. H.

teenth century. To be sure, the scientific historian opposed the subjective elements in literary history; but his opposition defies cataloguing on epistemological grounds because the average literary historian did not argue in such terms. His was a feeling for history more than a method, a sympathy for the past rather than a theory of historical knowledge. Once scientific historians had crystallized their views into a theory as to how they could know the past with uniform certainty, then the relativists could, in their turn, revive the importance of historical sympathy. But they reopened the quarrel on an analytical plane differing from that of the nineteenth century. Once elevated to an epistemological level, the old argument became in many ways new. Because scientific historians of the nineteenth century tended to think in terms which present-day relativism attacks, relativism illuminates the scientific position. It does not really help to define the literary school, for literary historians never reasoned after the fashion of Croce, Heussi, Collingwood, Becker, or Beard. We must stick with the distinction between active and passive historian, generalized though it is: the one ardently projecting his imagination into his material, the other standing apart from his data to let the accumulation show what actually happened. Ill-defined as this dichotomy is, it reflects the empirical point of view of most practicing historians. After all, neither Adams nor Parkman was a philosopher of history.

Philosophers will have their revenge, for unanalyzed premises, no matter how brilliant, have a way of leading their adherents to disaster. Certainly Adams courted disaster in suggesting that the mere accumulation of evidence, scrupulously authenticated and logically arranged, would of itself reveal generalizations; in short, that the accumulation of data disclosed causation in history. Here was the heartbreak of scientific history for anyone who took the scientific metaphor as seriously as Adams.[30] The "severest process of stating" simply did not permit him to "fix for a familiar moment a necessary sequence of human movement." So he complained in the *Education* long after he had replaced the laborious method of his earlier research in history by cosmic formulas.

The idea that generalizations in the natural and physical

---

30. Refer again to Beard's succinct catalogue. His fourth assumption is that the events of history have some inner (perhaps causal) relation which the impartial historian can grasp by inquiry and accurately describe. Fifth, the substances of history can be grasped in themselves by purely rational or intellectual means; they are not permeated by any transcendent element like God, spirit, or materialism.

sciences emerge from the mere accumulation of data obviously misrepresents the scientific method, since the scientist has some generalization in mind before he sets up his experiment. So for that matter did Adams; but to confide his generalization to his readers would impose the mind of the historian on the past, which in itself is proof that history can never be scientific in the sense of the physical and natural sciences. The historical relativists have shown how the generalizations of the historian—or less formally, his predilections—condition his view of the past, and their case is only partially weakened by frequent overstatement which amounts to calling all generalization subjective, as though the data did not to a considerable extent suggest the patterns possible. At least the rationale of the relativist could have saved Adams his somewhat exaggerated despair over history in the *Education*. Even the inferential impersonality of the cosmologist's theories must elude the historian. The historical past must always prove too complex, too full of contradictions, for absolute generalization in a single formula. To select one fact while discarding a second, or to emphasize one aspect of a problem while minimizing another, implied a personal decision. When the historian generalized a series of such decisions as conclusions, he obviously interposed his own personality upon his research by admitting that the evidence became intelligible only through his intervention. If such intervention was necessary, then he immediately disproved his basic contention that the conclusions to any sequence of documents were implicit in its unfolding.

He therefore tended to adopt the habit—a curiously nonscientific habit, too—of offering no conclusions, or at least he seemed to offer none. Hence the works of some scientific historians, and none more than Adams', seem to have no real termination. As Adams stated in the *Education*, "History is a tangled skein that one may take up at any point, and break when one has unravelled enough . . ." [31] True, he furnished a prologue and an epilogue to the body of his *History*. Yet these sections, indicating the changes in American society between 1800 and 1817, were independent of his chapters on political events; so much so, in fact, that the transformation apparently occurred despite the fumbling policies of the Republican administration.[32] Moreover, both his opening and his concluding sections terminated in questions.

31. *Education*, p. 302.
32. See below, especially pp. 95–98, 110–113.

The traits of American character were fixed; the rate of physical and economical growth was established; and history, certain that at a given distance of time the Union would contain so many millions of people, with wealth valued at so many millions of dollars, became thenceforward chiefly concerned to know what kind of people these millions were to be. They were intelligent, but what paths would their intelligence select? They were quick, but what solution of insoluble problems would quickness hurry? They were scientific, and what control would their science exercise over their destiny? They were mild, but what corruptions would their relaxations bring? They were peaceful, but by what machinery were their corruptions to be purged? What interests were to vivify a society so vast and uniform? What ideals were to ennoble it? What object, besides physical content, must a democratic continent aspire to attain? For the treatment of such questions, history required another century of experience.

So Adams closed his ninth volume with the implication that the tangled skein of history needed much more unraveling before answers would appear.

This continuous nature of history provided another reason for the scientific historian to forgo ostensible conclusions. No particular history could be complete in itself. Each work merely linked a chain of evidence that stretched as far into the past as man could probe, as far into the future as he could prophesy. Adams knew that other scholars would comment on the documents from a period prior to Jefferson's inauguration; still others would investigate the sources subsequent to Madison's departure from the White House. "The fragment I did," he told a correspondent in 1899, almost a decade after his nine volumes had appeared, "was merely an Introduction to our history during the Nineteenth Century and was intended only to serve the future historian with a fixed and documented starting-point. The real History that one would like to write, was to be built on it, and its merits or demerits, whatever they might be, could be seen only when the structure, of which it was to be the foundation, was raised." [33]

This emphasis on the cooperative and cumulative function of human knowledge reflected the inclusive point of view of the scientist as opposed to the selective mentality of the artist. It was,

33. Oct. 6, 1899; Cater, p. 480.

as we have seen, an attitude basic to the professionalization of history. Standards of judgment so precise and so impersonalized that one historian could hope to furnish his successors with a fixed and documented starting point further implied that every historian might study any segment of the past with equal objectivity. In reality the scientific movement in history has intensified historical specialization by its rigorous demands for verification of data; but the neutral coloration of every fact about the past promised a cosmopolitanism in theory virtually impossible in practice. While in Egypt during the summer of 1873 for a vacation from his Harvard teaching, Adams advised a student,

> It matters very little what line you take provided you can catch the tail of an idea to develope with solid reasoning and thorough knowledge. America or Europe, our own century or prehistoric time, are all alike to the historian if he can only find out what men are and have been driving at, consciously or unconsciously. So much is this the case that I myself am now strongly impelled to write an Essay on Egyptian Law, for I have a sort of notion that I could draw out of that queer subject some rather surprising deductions . . .[34]

Other interests forbade the proposed inquiry, but his letter unmistakably revealed a scientific attitude toward history in its confident assertion that a single historian could learn what men are and have been driving at for any period in the past by a thorough knowledge of the evidence and by solid reasoning from the tail of an idea. At least such was Adams' faith in documents while he taught at Harvard. When he finally compared history to a skein that merely required unwinding, he added a regretful and highly important qualification: "but complexity precedes evolution." By the time he wrote his *Education*, however, all his early affirmations had turned equivocal.

Adams' ultimate dismay that history should prove too complex to reveal its simple continuity reflected the disillusionment of a scientific disposition—specifically, of a scientific mentality nurtured on nineteenth-century ideas of evolution and not yet reconciled to the complexities of physical environment which twentieth-century science readily admits. Had Adams viewed history with a literary bias his later chagrin need never have occurred. The literary historian did not pretend a cosmopolitan indifference to

34. Jan. 2, 1873; Ford, *1*, 237.

subject matter. In effect he embraced complexity in history. Patriotism inspired much literary history. The patriotism of a Bancroft for the United States implied the equal validity of history as seen by a patriotic Frenchman like Michelet or a patriotic Prussian like Treitschke. Only the ardently patriotic could fail to perceive this logic, while only the intensity of their ardor made what should have been relative appear as absolute. To Bancroft, Michelet, and Treitschke indifference to subject matter was unthinkable, for they purposely sought to evoke the sentiments of their readers to gain support for specific nations. As a patriot Adams compared favorably with these three. Yet in his *History* he did not laud the inevitable superiority of the United States to every other nation as such; rather he reserved his praise for what he conceived as the superiority of certain ideas and institutions larger than the geographical boundaries of any country but best observed in the United States. To this extent the United States served Adams as the test tube served the scientist. To this extent his kind of patriotism differed from that of the historian with literary inclination. Fine though the distinction might be in theory, and finer still in practice, this divergence in attitudes between the two schools accounts in large part for the greater emotional appeal of the one, the intellectual emphasis of the other.

If particularized patriotism, whether for nation or faction, curtailed the range of subject matter available to the literary historian, he might also limit himself by aims more narrowly artistic in character; for example, by a fondness for a specific setting or type of personality. Because Parkman yearned to "paint the forest in true and vivid colors," he forced himself to concentrate upon those periods in the past when the wilderness had played an important part in history. Seeking to portray a certain ideal of manhood, he had further reduced his choice of theme. The instinctive practice of Parkman may be translated into the sophistication of Crocean theory, emphasizing as it does that historians can recreate the past only insofar as they relive it in their minds. Each historian can therefore revive only that small span in time which catches his sympathy.

Since the literary historian purposely limited himself to a portion of the past, his work no longer represented a fragment of an endless continuity. Of course he realized that history was continuous; yet his desire for synthesis compelled him not only to point his data toward final conclusions but also to direct his narrative toward ultimate climax. Like the novelist he hoped for the conclusiveness of literature or, to return to Parkman's metaphor, the unity of a painting, completely self-contained within the limits of its arbitrary frame.

A specific sampling from Parkman and Adams will reveal more precisely just how they differed in their approach to history. Having described the assassination of La Salle, Parkman epitomized the valor of this adventurer in a wonderfully sonorous passage.

> It is easy to reckon up his defects, but it is not easy to hide from sight the Roman virtues that redeemed them. Beset by a throng of enemies, he stands, like the King of Israel, head and shoulders above them all. He was a tower of adamant, against whose impregnable front hardship and danger, the rage of man and of the elements, the southern sun, the northern blast, fatigue, famine, disease, delay, disappointment, and deferred hope emptied their quivers in vain. That very pride which, Coriolanus-like, declared itself most sternly in the thickest press of foes, has in it something to challenge admiration. Never, under the impenetrable mail of paladin or crusader, beat a heart of more intrepid mettle than within the stoic panoply that armed the breast of La Salle. To estimate aright the marvels of his patient fortitude, one must follow on his track through the vast scene of his interminable journeyings,—those thousands of weary miles of forest, marsh, and river, where, again and again, in the bitterness of baffled striving, the untiring pilgrim pushed onward towards the goal which he was never to attain. America owes him an enduring memory; for in this masculine figure she sees the heroic pioneer who guided her to the possession of her richest heritage.[35]

Here the historian had momentarily stepped aside to eulogize his hero. Few readers would want this eulogy omitted. The dignity of such a climax gave to Parkman's history the epic grandeur of his adventurers.

In all save one of the volumes comprising Parkman's series on "France and England in North America," such heroes served

35. *The Discovery of the Great West* (Champlain ed., Boston, Little, Brown, 1897), paragraph closing the chapter entitled "Assassination of La Salle." Later published as *La Salle and the Discovery of the Great West;* minor variations among editions.

as the focal point around which events revolved. Reviewing this ·
notable exception for the *North American*, Adams ranked *The
Old Régime in Canada* as the finest in a series which then lacked
three volumes of completion. He added that his was a critic's
estimate, not "that of the public." The public would perhaps find
"a more absorbing and consecutive interest" in previous volumes
where Parkman had allowed his "natural inclination and cast of
mind . . . to follow action rather than to meditate upon it, to
relate rather than to analyze, to describe the adventures of individuals rather than the slow and complicated movements of
society." Adams congratulated Parkman on having finally "entered a wider field of thought," one that dealt with "matters which,
if not themselves of the highest philosophical interest, are still on
one side at least illustrative of great and permanent principles
in political science." Later in the review Adams mentioned that
the French colonization of Canada showed "one of the few examples of a conservative triumph" in social history. Had Parkman
viewed his subject as an example capable of comparative analysis,
his study would have gained "philosophical interest," a case study
of "great and permanent principles" rather than an isolated, if
colorful, instance.[36] Parkman subsequently lapsed into his natural
inclination; but Adams characteristically responded to a gift of
the *Montcalm and Wolfe* without so much as a mention of the
dramatic battle for Quebec. He observed only the "curious fact"
of the "sterility" of French colonization.[37] Neither the hero nor
the heroic held much interest for Adams, who closed his four
volumes on Jefferson with an economy contrasting strongly with
Parkman's eulogy of La Salle.

Having reproduced a letter from Jefferson to his former secretary of war, in which the Virginian acknowledged his fatigue
with public office, Adams continued,

> A week afterward Jefferson quitted Washington forever. On
> horseback, over roads impassible to wheels, through snow
> and storm, he hurried back to Monticello to recover in the
> quiet of home the peace of mind he had lost in the disappoint-
> ments of his statesmanship. He arrived at Monticello March
> 15, and never again passed beyond the bounds of a few adja-
> cent counties.

With a sigh of relief which seemed as sincere and deep as

36. *NAR, 120* (1875), 175, 178.
37. Dec. 21, 1884; Cater, p. 133.

his own, the Northern people saw him turn his back on the White House and disappear from the arena in which he had for sixteen years challenged every comer. In the Northern States few regrets were wasted upon his departure, for every mind was intent on profiting by the overthrow of his system; but Virginia was still loyal to him, and the citizens of his own county of Albemarle welcomed with an affectionate address his final return. His reply, dignified and full of grateful feeling, seemed intended as an answer to the attacks of partisan grossness and a challenge to the judgment of mankind:—

"The anxieties you express to administer to my happiness do of themselves confer that happiness; and the measure will be complete if my endeavors to fulfil my duties in the several public stations to which I have been called have obtained for me the approbation of my country. The part which I have acted on the theater of public life has been before them, and to their sentence I submit it; but the testimony of my native county, of the individuals who have known me in private life, to my conduct in its various duties and relations is the more grateful as proceeding from eye-witnesses and observers, from triers of the vicinage. Of you, then, my neighbors, I may ask in the face of the world, 'Whose ox have I taken, or whom have I defrauded? Whom have I oppressed, or of whose hand have I received a bribe to blind mine eyes therewith?' On your verdict I rest with conscious security." [38]

Appropriately the historian, who had merely strung the documents upon a thin strand of commentary, closed his account of Jefferson's presidency with Jefferson's own plea. As the famous Virginian had urged his neighbors to judge for themselves the record of the Republican administration, so the historian left his reader to evaluate the documents which he too had flung "in the face of the world." And, like Jefferson, Adams no doubt awaited a verdict with the same conscious security.

As a starting point, then, let the "scientific" bias with which Adams approached history be distinguished from the "literary" bent of Parkman by certain abbreviations marking the extremes of theory rather than the compromise of practice. Only through contrast do these attitudes assume their full significance, while

38. *History*, *4*, 472 ff. Adams' dismissal of Madison in the ninth volume is so matter of fact as to constitute an unfortunate anticlimax to the termination of the War of 1812.

this contrast applies in essence, if not in all details, to many more than these two historians.

Adams' scientific attitude	Parkman's literary attitude
Emphasis on source materials.	Emphasis on narrative.
An analytical progression.	A synthetical progression.
A primary appeal to the reader's intellect.	A substantial appeal to his emotions.
Active reader.	Passive reader.
Passive historian.	Active historian.
The past brought to the reader.	The reader transported into the past.
The evolution of society, institutions, or a concept larger than its exemplification.	The episodic quality of the hero or of specific events.
Generalizations (seemingly) implicit in the documents.	Generalizations explicit on the historian's pages.

Of course, this tabulation represents not absolutes but differences of degree.[39] In this instance degree is all important, for the historian's bent influenced his choice of subject, his method of research, the aesthetics of his composition, and, finally, his concept of what made historical investigation worth while.

Item by item, the differentiation between the two attitudes may seem slight; but as a complex the divergence is substantial. It increases enormously if the scientific attitude toward the conventional subject matter of history comes to embrace the idea of history subsumed under laws from the experimental sciences. In Adams' later speculation we see how enticing such laws can be, and how stimulating to the intellect, tracing as they do some broad pattern through the complications of the past. To this extent his search for laws was an aesthetic more than a scientific quest. Now pulled toward science, now toward art, he never reconciled this inmost conflict—a conflict complicated by the frustrations of his heritage.

To fit the pieces to some whole: this became his goal for history. In this sense his goal for history paralleled his wider quest in life. He failed in both. In the *Education* he asserted that the odds were from the start against his success in life. From the start the odds would also seem to oppose his finding the synthesis for which he sought in history.

39. For example, although Adams lauded the objectivity possible with source materials, he admitted, *NAR, 121* (1875), 222, that history "in the broad sense of absolute accuracy" could never be more than "approximately exact." If he affected the belief that every historian could write with equal objectivity on any segment of the past, he could not write on Alexander Hamilton; see below, p. 67 and n. 47.

II. THE EDUCATION OF A HISTORIAN

Adams' reputation in American history depends almost wholly on the activity of approximately fifteen years in his eighty-year life. Except for a few essays before his thirty-seventh birthday (and a vagrant piece for the *American Historical Review* in 1895 [1]), he accomplished his work in American history between 1874 and 1890. The first date marked the opening of his course in American colonial history at Harvard; the second, his completion of the *History*, the final volumes of which appeared in 1891. Although more than a quarter of a century remained to him, Adams never again (but for the fugitive exception noted) practiced in this field of his achievement.

The long preparation [2] had begun of course with the name itself, and with his family heritage. His early life might have shown the average uneventfulness of those of many other well-born Bostonians, except that he was able "to sit [in the Quincy church] behind a President grandfather, and to read over his head the tablet in memory of a President great-grandfather." [3] He never forgot these august ancestors and, while Henry was yet a young man, his father's distinguished diplomacy as United States minister to the Court of St. James's entitled Charles Francis to a prominent place in the son's mental gallery.

His father and his father's friends influenced his education as much as, or more than, either Master Dixwell's Latin School or Harvard University. The table talk of Richard Dana, Charles Sumner, and William Evarts emphasized contemporary politics; visits from Dr. John Palfrey and proofreading for his father's edition of John Adams' *Works* blended the politics of Henry's own youth with the accomplishments and convictions of his forebears. [4] Shelves of eighteenth-century literature in the paternal library

1. "Count Edward de Crillon," *American Historical Review, 1* (1895), 51–69.
2. Here given cursory treatment because of Samuels' excellent study.
3. *Education*, p. 15.
4. *Ibid.*, pp. 29, 31.

intensified this heritage, while classical and French literature gave it breadth. As an antidote to sober literature and serious conversation, the *Education* especially noted the joys of Thackeray, Dickens, Bulwer, Tennyson, Macaulay, Carlyle, and Scott. This catalogue could be extended, for books were the "source of life." [5] Looking back on these years Adams discovered that "As the children grew up, they exaggerated the literary and political interests." [6] From this boyhood environment of politics, history, and literature stemmed Adams' historical inclination.

The youth sheltered from the ungentlemanly tendencies in American life was equally insulated from contact with the mainstream when, after graduating from Harvard, he drifted to Europe in 1858 to study civil law in Berlin. Difficulties in language, coupled with the inhospitable Prussianism of the pedagogy and the lack (one is forced to believe) of a compelling interest in his subject, soon discouraged the affluent and vacillating student. For over a year he wandered aimlessly, yet observantly, touring Europe—an activity he plied tirelessly throughout much of his later life. His exposure to the German historical procedures at this time was of too perfunctory a nature to have substantially influenced his subsequent career. Adams' later experience with documents, while serving as private secretary to his father in the London legation, would prove more important for his *History;* so would his historical studies while teaching at Harvard, during the course of which he visited many of the leading continental and English scholars.[7] Yet his desire to study in Berlin already indicated a preference in scholarship. If the vagueness of the phrase "German historical method" as customarily applied to history seemed to suggest myth more than method, at least the myth adhered to the kind of history which Adams would one day write.

He returned home, determined (but still without enthusiasm) to study law in a more hospitable environment. His father's election as a congressman immediately on the son's return soon brought the erstwhile student of law to Washington, where he served as private secretary. For three months, until the session ended in March, 1861, Henry had his first glimpse at close range of American democracy. The fascination which he felt for Washington at

5. *Ibid.,* pp. 35, 39.
6. *Ibid.,* p. 35.
7. During his wedding trip to Europe, 1872–73. See Thoron, pp. 39 f.. 42: Samuels, pp. 238–242.

this time remained with him always. Adams finally became a "stable-companion to statesmen, whether they liked it or not." [8] He might very well have added "whether *he* liked it or not"; for despite global peregrinations, this descendant of statesmen inevitably returned to the only city he called home.[9]

Barely had the session of 1860–61 ended and the young student finally faced a tableful of law books in Quincy, Massachusetts, when the family whisked him from the American scene once more. Again he assumed the office of filial amanuensis—this time for seven years in the United States legation in London. Here the young clerk received firsthand knowledge of another impressive ingredient for the *History*. As his brief experience in Washington had brought him into direct contact with the American democratic process, so he now learned, as he could have from no other school, the analysis of documents. He learned to examine the components of history not only for what they said but for what they actually meant; from a word, a phrase, a contradiction to estimate the motives and emotions of the writer.

As he learned the intricacies of diplomacy the young Adams also steeped himself in Comtism, Darwinism, the liberal economics of John Stuart Mill, and the gamut of English and continental historians. Writing to Charles Francis, Jr., his elder brother, who was at the time an officer in the Union army, the student traced his scholarly ramblings: "So I jump from International Law to our foreign history, and am led by that to study the philosophic standing of our republic, which brings me to reflection over the advance of the democratic principle in European civilization, and so I go on till some new question of law starts me again on the circle." [10] Thus, even as he mastered both the method and the facts of history—his candles "seldom out before two o'clock in the morning" and his table "piled with half-read books and unfinished writing" [11]—he indicated his absorption with that broader concept of the past which has always marked the great historian. Seven years in London crystallized the diverse influences of early life into such a pattern that he at last perceived the practice of law was not to be for him. What vocation would he choose? His letters to Charles at this period—undoubtedly among the most

8. *Education*, p. 317.
9. *Ibid.*, pp. 317 f. See especially Ford, *1*, 320.
10. May 1, 1863; *Cycle*, *1*, 281 f.
11. July 23, 1863; *ibid.*, *2*, 62.

revealing that Henry ever wrote—showed his uncertainty. He told Charles that somehow "The great principle of democracy is still capable of rewarding a conscientious servant. And," prophetically, "I doubt me much whether the advance of years will increase my toleration of its faults." [12] A conscientious scholar might serve democracy, and scholarship had increasingly attracted him. A conscientious journalist might serve more directly, especially if he hoped to correct the flaws inherent in the great principle. As journalist he returned to America in 1868. The choice disclosed his unwillingness that society should drive an Adams to mere academic pursuits.

He had first tried his hand at journalism during those student travels in Europe which had superseded his short-lived plan to study civil law at the University of Berlin. These initial efforts had appeared in the *Boston Daily Courier* during the spring and summer of 1860 from accounts of European affairs irregularly addressed as letters to his older brother. Although he wrote these impressions in his early twenties, when caution is habitually held in low esteem, Henry indicated in his instructions to Charles the incompatibility of unsubstantial literary endeavor with that discrimination characteristic of the entire Adams family. In a roundabout manner he warned that his impressions would be recorded in letters "not written to be published but publishable in case they were worth it . . . Now, you will understand, I do *not* propose to write with the wish to publish at all hazards; on the contrary I mean to write private letters to you, as an exercise for myself, and it would be of all things my last wish to force myself into newspapers with a failure for my first attempt." [13] If his cautiousness indicated discrimination, Henry's dependence on his brother's judgment also proclaimed a lack of self-confidence which habitually sought a protective buffer against the world.[14] It was this want of self-assurance, an essential timidity, that later lent an element of heroism to Adams' brief career in reform journalism.

During the congressional session of 1860–61 Adams made further journalistic sorties. He wrote a series of unsigned "Letters from Washington" for the *Boston Daily Advertiser*, and when the

12. May 1, 1863; *ibid., 1,* 282.
13. Mar. 26, 1860; Ford, *1,* 59. On his scrupulosity in respect to substantial literary production see *ibid.,* p. 19.
14. See exchange of letters between the brothers in *Cycle* for the influence of Charles Francis, Jr., on Henry; see also letters to Charles in Ford, *1.* Samuels, pp. 57 ff., 66, 68 f., 75, 82 f., 91 f., 112–120, 146 f., 151, 176 f., 184.

Advertiser sent a staff correspondent to take over Adams' chores, he turned to an account of the "Secession Winter" for the *Atlantic Monthly.* The *Atlantic* never received this article since he discarded the manuscript for reasons of style after two months of labor [15]—an ominous portent for success in journalism. Equally ominous was a certain lack of immediacy in all of his journalism; current events became history under his pen.[16] Although he had participated as a spectator in the events of the Thirty-sixth Congress leading up to secession, his article lacked the vividness of immediate observation. He did not catch the passions of the moment beyond the intellectual passion of legislative debate. His account seemed rather a record for posterity than a piece of journalism. It was not surprising that an Adams able to view history in the making at close range should write with an eye to the possibility of future readers.[17] But more than a sense of the great moment gave Adams' journalism its historical flavor. His writing showed his preoccupation with historical parallels and continuity, with those "permanent principles" implicit in present events which might afford counsel for the future. Thus his "Secession Winter" closed in grand abstraction, the grander for the turgid rhetoric with which the young admirer of Burke swamped his moral.

> Where in all history is there to be found an instance of a power such as slavery has shown itself, peaceably ejected from the Government and forced to become rebels or submit? . . . Where else is or has there ever been that Government which could for five months remain inactive, while so vast a rebellion was developing itself under its very eyes, without breaking down into anarchy under the weight of its very inactivity? There does not exist and never has existed the Government which could maintain itself and the public peace; which could with wise and cautious patience bear and forbear, wait and endure, and stretch its elastic membranes beyond the limits of all creditability as ours has done during the past year. Nor, if strength is wanted, has any Government developed more than our own, when, at one stamp of his foot, the President

15. Eventually published in 1910 by Charles Francis Adams, Jr., as "The Great Secession Winter of 1860–61."

16. Samuels, pp. 193, 196. *Cycle, 1,* 34; his brother Charles recommended more "fresh enthusiasm" in Henry's articles and less "calmness and quaint philosophy."

17. Ford, *1,* 62.

called the whole nation to arms, and the bristling lines of bayonets poured down from every township in the North, to sustain the integrity of the Union.[18]

Before Adams left for England he had arranged for a second time to become a secret correspondent. Thirty-one unsigned letters were dispatched to the *New York Times* from June, 1861, until January, 1862, when the correspondence abruptly ceased as a result of the well-known blunder in respect to Henry's account, "A Visit to Manchester." This article, once more designed for the *Atlantic*, arrived too late for publication. Hence it appeared in the *Boston Daily Courier* along with the unfortunate attribution to "Mr. Henry Adams, the son of our Minister to Great Britain." Years later the *Education* revealed the scars of the secretary's embarrassment when the pro-Southern London *Times* and the *Examiner* sarcastically publicized this slip in anonymity.[19] Panicky at the possibility that his correspondence with the *Times* might be discovered, Adams ceased his propaganda activities altogether. A bolder man might have struck for independence. Adams drew back into the bosom of his family, to retain his niche at the legation.[20] For the remainder of his stay in London, from November, 1861, until he returned to the United States in July, 1868, journalism went into limbo. Posterity may owe the indiscreet editor of the *Courier* its gratitude. Had Adams pursued journalism too assiduously, history might have been forgotten.

Even before the exposé in the London *Times* Adams had thought of trying history. In October, 1861, he opened a letter to Palfrey, "You may remember that last spring you suggested at our house one day, certain historic doubts as to Capt. John Smith and Pocahontas. They interested me at the time very much . . ." and he added that he might "go on with the search." [21] After months of investigation and composition, followed by a period during which he decided not to publish, his first purely historical

18. "Great Secession Winter," p. 687.
19. *Education*, p. 120; Adams apparently forgot to mention that the *Examiner* attacked him, and he misstated when he claimed that the London papers did not know of his connection with the legation. *Cycle, 1*, 33–37, 43 f., 66 f., 104. Arthur W. Silver, ed., "Henry Adams' 'Diary of a Visit to Manchester,' " *American Historical Review, 51* (1945), 74–89. Samuels, pp. 116 f.
20. Samuels, pp. 117 f., 144. On the suggestion of his brother Charles that Henry cut himself off from the legation and become an independent journalist see below, p. 123.
21. Oct. 23, 1861; Cater, p. 8.

essay appeared as the leading article in the January, 1867, issue of the *North American*.[22]

Masquerading as a book review of original documents on the early colonization of Virginia recently edited by Charles Deane, the unsigned essay attacked the idea that Pocahontas had ever flung herself protectively on the most familiar target for a tomahawk in American history. For the exposé the neophyte historian compared two autobiographical accounts of Captain John Smith's adventures in Virginia, the first published in 1608 under the title *A True Relation*, the second in 1624 as *The Generall Historie*. Placing these two reminiscences side by side, Adams observed that Smith's dangers had accumulated terror and his achievements gained luster during the interval between versions. Furthermore, Smith apparently required sixteen years of cogitation before he recalled that Pocahontas had so nobly saved his life or, indeed, that she had even existed. In fact the captain's memory improved only after this Indian maiden became a brief sensation in London when John Rolfe brought her to the British capital.

As a historical exercise the subject possessed a compactness easily handled by the novice, the more so as Deane had already indicated some of the discrepancies existing between the two accounts by Smith. Adams manipulated a minimum number of documents to reach a clearly defined conclusion. The skill with which he later fused document and narrative appeared only tentatively in this deflation of Smith's heroics. But even in his first historical work Adams foreshadowed the polished causticity of his account of the Jefferson and Madison administrations. For example, he noted how historians had embroidered the Pocahontas legend with the passage of time.

> In the enthusiasm which her act has called out, language, and perhaps common sense, have been a little strained to cover her with attributes of perfection. Her beauty and wild grace, her compassion and disinterestedness, her Christian life and pure character, have been dwelt upon with warm affection, which is the more natural as the childhood of the nation has furnished little latitude to the imagination. One after another, all American historians have contented themselves with repeating the words of the Generall Historie, vying with each other in heap-

---

22. *NAR, 104* (1867), 1–30. For reprintings of this and other articles first published in the *NAR* see Samuels' bibliography of Adams' writings.

ing praises which no critics were cynical enough to gainsay,
now on the virtues of Pocahontas, and now on the courage and
constancy of Smith.[23]

Mimicking Burke or Gibbon, these periodic sentences contained
needless phrases like "now on the virtues of Pocahontas, and now
on the courage and constancy of Smith"—phrases introduced
solely to increase the sonorous roll of syllables. To the same end
Adams unnecessarily repeated a single idea through many variations. Yet, despite its pretensions, such a passage discloses elements
of Adams' mature historical style. His later irony is already apparent, tending toward the exaggeration of such a phrase as "vy-
ing with each other in heaping praises." Adams never wholly
curbed his tendency to exaggerate. Although checking himself in
the *History* from the obviousness of youthful exuberance, it was
not always easy, as copies of the private editions of the *History*
now in the Massachusetts Historical Society make clear. Serving
Adams as the final drafts of his volumes, these privately printed
versions reveal occasional warnings from George Bancroft; among
others, "not the style for history," "too serious for laughter," "the
assertion is too strong," "efface this. Nothing could be worse." Few
likewise would dispute the "Bah!" with which his brother Charles
greeted "Fulton was nearly ready with the steamboat which was
to tame the winds and turn the waters of the Mississippi backwards to their source." [24] Subdued in the *History*, this extrava-
gance of style would reappear in both the *Education* and the historical speculation of Adams' later life.

Although the essay on Smith disclosed some of Adams' besetting

23. *NAR, 104* (1867), 12.
24. Bancroft's comments refer to the italicized words in the following passages
as they appear in the privately printed editions of the *History* (Vols. 3 and 4 as
a single volume in 1885, Vols. 5 and 6 in 1888); page references, however, are
adjusted to the published edition. *History, 3,* 99: "As a result of the high tone
taken toward England in the winter of 1803–04, and as a result of the President's
intention *not to swallow so much* from the belligerents as President Washington
had done, the secretary's mildness . . ." Vol. *3,* 156, insert immediately after
the Gregg document: "Mr. Gregg's attitude, if not heroic, had at least a certain
shade of homely humor. Even Mr. Pitt, had he never laughed, *might well have been
amused.*" (In the privately printed editions Adams used "Mr." before all surnames.)
Vol. *4,* 161: ". . . Fulton's torpedoes would have amply protected New York . . ."
Vol. *4,* 265: "History cannot too often repeat that it has nothing to do with
law . . ." Vol. *4,* 321: ". . . third party. The rudest court in the backwoods of
Georgia could have produced no opinion more startling." For the location of the
exclamation by Charles Francis Adams, Jr., see Vol. *3,* 20. On Adams' exaggeration
see also Samuels, p. 224.

sins, it nevertheless revealed some of the virtues of his historical style. Already Adams worked for elegant balance, word against word, phrase against phrase, where one phrase flowed easily into the next, while all pointed toward the conclusion of the sentence. While at Harvard he particularly admonished his pupil Henry Cabot Lodge on sentence structure: the ordering of clauses, the need for variety among the sentences, and the virtues of economy in expression.[25] By the time he wrote his *History* Adams had polished his style until his longest sentences were terse arabesques, linear in their progression toward calculated climax, linear, too, in their effortless continuity. Effortless as the sentences seemed, they were infinitely complex, capable at once of the refinement needed to explain the subtlest motivation, the flexibility required for irony, or the restraint essential to dignity. To compare the *History* with the early essays is to see how, with time, Adams' efforts for succinctness and variety in his style had made him less self-consciously aware of the sentence as an entity. The rhythm and length of one sentence contrasted with that of its neighbors. Each played its part in moving the narrative toward some turning point in a chain of events, some generalization abruptly illuminating the complexities of the rigorous narrative and challenging the reader's attention as much by its unexpectedness as by its boldness. "Such an experience [as the Louisiana Purchase] was final; no century of slow and half-understood experience could be needed to prove that the hopes of humanity lay thenceforward, not in attempting to restrain the government from doing whatever the majority should think necessary, but in raising the people themselves till they should think nothing necessary but what was good." Or on the Chesapeake-Leopard affair, "For the first time in their history the people of the United States learned, in June, 1807, the feeling of a true national emotion." A final example, "With the repeal of the embargo ended the early period of United States history, when diplomatists played a part at Washington equal in importance to that of the Legislature or the Executive." [26] The periodic sentences remained, but Adams subordinated them to larger periods in his thought. As his style acquired precision in both argument and effect Adams attained the unique qualities in the style of the *History*, so nicely described by one critic as

25. Ford, *1*, 261 f., 269.
26. *History*, *2*, 130; *4*, 27; *7*, 895.

the limpid clarity and beauty, the classic restraint, the flashing brilliance of the prose; the lofty and tranquil impartiality, rigidly judicious without being abstract or impersonal; the serene philosophic approach which permeates the grave un-hurried pages of the volumes; the fine sense of balance and form that distinguishes the work of art from the mere com-pilation of historical facts; the splendid devotion to, the rigor-ous regard for, truth as the ultimate end of history.[27]

However much the style of the Smith essay suggests that of the *History*, probably none of Commager's adjectives unquali-fiedly applies to the early essay. The outstanding weakness of the essay lay in the attitude of its author toward the past. He felt himself rather superior to his materials. Through ruthless logic and an insistent appeal to evidence he could easily quash his puny victims, while decorating his remorselessness with wit. This urbane condescension toward the past might have precluded the breadth of mind essential for great history had not his early writing also revealed—"The Secession Winter," for example—his enthusiasm for the larger themes of history. Only the superficial reader of Adams' account of the Jefferson administration will fail to sense the fervor which sustained the intellectuality of the volumes, to-gether with Adams' respect for the integrity of the past which prevented an ironic theme from degenerating into condescension.

Before the seven years of diplomacy drew to a close the private secretary had published two more articles in his capacity as journalist-historian. The sobriety of their titles, "British Finance in 1816" and "The Bank of England Restriction, 1797–1821," forewarned *North American* readers of their substantiality in content. Into his luggage the retiring functionary had tucked still another manuscript reviewing the tenth edition of Sir Charles Lyell's *Principles of Geology*.[28] A reflection of Adams' inquiries into geological uniformitarianism, this article appeared during the autumn following his return. Logically, perhaps, the journalist, who had steadily tended toward history, should immediately have plunged into the more academic field. But earlier ambitions died hard. Free of the legation, he scuttled history and reverted to jour-nalism.

27. Henry S. Commager, Introduction to *History* (Boni ed.), *1*, xv. On Adams' early style see also Samuels, pp. 156 f.

28. The three articles appeared in the *NAR, 104* (1867), 354–386; *105* (1867), 393–434; *107* (1868), 465–501.

The youth was no longer young. He was thirty. Some twenty years in Boston, then two in Europe, a few months in Washington, and the balance in the legation—the first three decades of his life, if measured by tangible accomplishment, showed little more than a B.A. degree from Harvard, a handful of newspaper clippings, and the four essays published in the *North American*.

The next two years in the national capital reinforced earlier impressions of democracy. Although the meticulous journalist dispatched contributions to the *Nation* and the *New York Post*, his most important writings continued to go to the quarterlies. Among the latter was his first published account of a congressional session.[29] Modeling this essay on similar analyses of parliamentary debate by Lord Robert Cecil, Adams planned it as the first of a series which he hoped would establish the "annual 'Session' [as] an institution and a power in the land." [30] The 1870 version merited the journalist's confidence in the trenchancy of his pen, since its condemnation of the incompetency and corruption of the Grant administration made it a campaign tract.[31] Turning to other duties in 1870, Adams necessarily relinquished the reporter's method of establishing himself as a "political authority"; [32] but these two chapters on lawmaking forecast the brilliant congressional dissections in his *History*.

Not until the first year of a new decade did the still unsettled Adams enter on the last lap in the long preparation culminating in the *History*. In the autumn of 1870 a short, balding assistant professor with fashionably pointed beard opened his lectures on the Middle Ages at Harvard. In the *Education* Adams thus defined his position within President Eliot's hierarchy: "Professor Gurney was one of the leading reformers, and had tried his hand on his own department of History. The two full Professors of History—Torrey and Gurney, charming men both—could not cover the ground. Between Gurney's classical courses and Torrey's modern ones, lay a gap of a thousand years, which Adams was expected to fill." [33] "Historian" at last, Adams still clung to jour-

29. "The Session," *NAR, 108* (1869), 610–640. His first account of a congressional session, as contrasted with his first *published* account, was "Great Secession Winter," which went unpublished until 1910.

30. May 17, 1869; Ford, *1,* 158. *Education*, p. 258.

31. "The Session," *NAR, 111* (1870), 29–62; reprinted by the National Democratic Executive Committee in 1872.

32. *Education*, p. 258.

33. *Ibid.*, p. 300.

nalism—but as an editor. He had come to Harvard with the understanding that a portion of his duties involved the editorship of the *North American*. Without this editorship and pressure from both family and Harvard, he would doubtless have refused to abandon his career in journalism. Even so he left Washington reluctantly.[34] Once released from his five-year contract, he probably more than half intended to return. As it happened, this academic-editorial existence in Cambridge marked a permanent retreat from the life of more practical-minded men. More or less accidentally, and more against his will than not, Adams found himself a historian.

The recent discovery at Western Reserve University of Charles Thwing's notebook covering Adams' lectures on medieval institutions provides a means to reconstruct the broad outlines of this famous course.[35] Thwing took the course, open only to juniors and seniors with advanced standing, the third time that Adams gave it, in 1874–75. Inside the marbleized cardboard cover of his notebook Thwing had scribbled the books basic for Adams' lectures: Sir Henry Maine's *Ancient Law* and *Village Communities*, John F. McLennan's *Primitive Marriage*, and the *Lex Salica*. The first page opened boldly:

Three methods of studying history.

We can almost hear the scorn with which the assistant professor dismissed the first method.

First,—The Romantic method
Walter Scott,—

The notes abruptly hurried to more fruitful methods, with the occasional illiteracy common to lecture notes.

Second—the constitutional method.
The usual method— The term is like that

34. Adams was so reluctant to leave Washington that he turned down the first offer that he become editor of the *NAR*, as he refused the intitial suggestion that he become an assistant professor; Samuels, pp. 203 ff. On his reluctance to leave Washington see Cater, pp. 44 f.; Ford, *1*, 193 ff.; *Education*, pp. 293 f., 296 f.

35. Thwing later served as the president of Western Reserve. Mary E. Streeter and Wrayton Gardner discovered Thwing's notebook among his effects. It is now deposited in the Western Reserve University Library. On the front of the notebook appears the legend "History 300" ("History III" was the designation for Adams' course in the Harvard Catalogue; Samuels, p. 340); centered on the inside front cover, among other writing, "Lectures—Medieval Institutions/ Prof. Henry Adams/ 1874–5." In quoting from this notebook unimportant words crossed out and sometimes altered above have not been indicated.

international law vague. International
law does not exist: law implies a
sanction, this has none. It has no
power to enforce principles—. So the
term constitution is vague— By the time it
is agreed what a constitution really is, it
begins to change— No three persons agree
what the constitution of the U.S. is or means—
Third—the legal method— It is studied
from the point of view of the law—
Thus this course—

A line skipped, then the notes show that Adams plunged into the
well-known concept of the Indo-European origin of European
"races."

Two of these races, the Roman and the German, had "con-
tended for supremacy in Europe. From these struggles came
modern Europe———" The strength of Roman law was its "*scientific*" development, as opposed to the too metaphysical quality
of the Greek. Yet, as Adams pointed out somewhat later in his
lectures, the Greek tradition gave to Roman law a formal character lacking in the "common sense" development of law in northern Europe. The strength of German law lay in the development
of democratic institutions: "whole theory of German law is—
it is administered by people & for the people. It is popular."
Here, of course, Adams introduced his juniors and seniors to the
central theme of his graduate seminar, offered for the first time
during the very year in which Thwing labored through the undergraduate lectures. The beginnings of Roman law—and of Egyp-
tian, Greek, and Hebrew as well—were "pervaded with the re-
lig[ious] idea," much more so than the German law. At this point
Thwing misspelled the bibliographical reminder, "Comptes pos.
[itivistic] philosophy excellent chapter on fetish worship & its
growth." Maine had started with the "wrong basis" in his belief
that "European law not *divine* law but *human*." Thus the first of
Adams' many criticisms of Maine. The lecturer moved on to a
definition of law, how law emerged from popular custom, and
how, with time, customary law was codified.

The class crawled through Maine from cover to cover, stopping
first at one page, then another further on, for questioning, elaboration, criticism, and perhaps discussion, although Thwing's

notebook does not clearly reveal evidence of the discussions for which Adams' class in American history at least was famous. The notes seem to possess too assured an air to be the products of student intelligence; moreover, if disconnected, they nevertheless reveal none of the desultory quality of notes taken during a discussion. But the format of the course would certainly have permitted and even encouraged discussion. Like most students Thwing may have economized on note taking by waiting for professional comment.[36] In any event the notebook opens with reference after reference from the *Ancient Law* and only occasional material from *Village Communities* or McLennan's *Primitive Marriage.* About halfway through the year the emphasis of the course shifted from Roman to German law, the transition made by a brief dissection of German society largely from Caesar and Tacitus, much as the later *History* opened with a description of American society in 1800, derived in large part from the impressions of foreign travelers. Finally, the pages of the *Lex Salica* terminated the sessions with the same relentless analysis with which they had begun. Comparisons between Roman and Salic law corrected what Adams, in one of his reviews for the *North American,* had regarded as the deplorable tendency of English legal historians, except "perhaps" for Austin and Maine, to concentrate exclusively on a single legal system.[37]

The presumed discussions in the lecture room and the use of the *Lex Salica* as source material gave undergraduates a taste of the more rigorous program which Adams had planned for graduate students. Having met the latter for the first time during the academic year 1874–75, Adams wrote in June, 1876, of the "unalloyed satisfaction" of "baking [his first] batch of doctors of philosophy" and, incidentally, three of the first four doctorates in government granted by Harvard.[38] This seminar is generally credited among the pioneer attempts to introduce to the American graduate school what was then frequently called the German

36. In his course in medieval institutions Adams may have relied more on direct questions than discussion (Samuels, pp. 212 f.); but certainly the one method would have spilled over into the other. Robert Grant, *Fourscore Years* (Boston and New York, Houghton Mifflin, 1934), p. 87, noted that both Gurney and Adams taught "after the then new method of lectures with outside work by the class."

37. See above, p. 7.

38. June 30, 1876; Ford, *1,* 292. The new Ph.D.'s were Henry Cabot Lodge, Ernest Young, and J. Laurence Laughlin. The first doctorate in government went to Charles L. B. Whitney in 1873.

seminar method,[39] by which term most historians of the late nineteenth century seemed to mean merely the study of source materials
by small groups of students; had Adams used the term at all, he
would also have implied the comparative study of institutions.
From Adams' seminar came *Essays in Anglo-Saxon Law* in 1876,
wherein the newly baked Ph.D.'s and their mentor traced English
democracy to its origins in ancient Teutonic institutions. Although the Teutonic theory of the origin of English institutions,
so widely held at the time, is now discredited, the four *Essays*
still contain valuable contributions in detail.[40] What is more,
Herbert Baxter Adams, who later introduced the same type of
cooperative research monographs at Johns Hopkins, pronounced
the *Essays* "the first really original researches in History by
Harvard students." [41]

Even as he instituted his graduate seminar, Adams also began
his momentous shift from medieval to American history. While
Thwing pored over Maine and the *Lex Salica*, twenty-seven other
juniors and seniors listened to lectures on the "Colonial History
of America to 1789." Doubtless the pedantries of "Sac" and
"Soc," later to be satirized in the *Education*,[42] conjoined with an
irresistible fascination for American politics to draw Adams into
his new orbit. In 1876–77 the prosperous assistant professor trans-
ferred his course in American colonial history to Lodge by personally subsidizing his former pupil, while he himself undertook
the history of the United States from 1789 to 1840. Shortly
thereafter Adams must have begun serious work on a selection
of Federalist documents from the early national period, which
was published in Boston in 1877 as *Documents Relating to New
England Federalism, 1800–1815*. The Gallatin papers came into
his hands during the same year.[43] Inevitably his parallel study of

39. On Adams' role as a pioneer in American education see Herbert Baxter
Adams, *The Study of History in American Colleges and Universities*, United States
Bureau of Education, Circular of Information No. 2 (Washington, Government
Printing Office, 1887), sections on Henry Adams, Charles K. Adams, and Johns Hopkins. Michael Kraus, *A History of American History* (New York, Farrar & Rinehart, 1937), pp. 307, 312. The work of John W. Burgess at Columbia became important after 1880. Samuels, pp. 208–218, discusses Adams' teaching methods; he
also gives the bibliography on Adams' teaching and a list of the courses taught by
Adams, pp. 339 ff., nn. 3, 4.

40. Samuels, pp. 247–258, has an excellent discussion of the *Essays in Anglo-
Saxon Law*.

41. H. B. Adams, *op. cit.*, p. 36.

42. *Education*, p. 368.

43. Ford, *1*, 300.

the first fifteen years in the nineteenth century from two historical points of view must have suggested the ultimate large-scale account. Gallatin, of course, was inextricably entwined with his superior; and indeed in 1877 Adams already leafed the substantial literary remains of our most philosophic president.[44]

Meanwhile Adams' final fling at journalism provides further insight into his aspirations as a reformer. Grantism, so eruditely attacked from Washington in the "Session" pieces and in other articles, received a flurry of indignant attacks in the pages of Boston's august quarterly while Adams filled the *North American* editorship, but not quite the flurry for which he had hoped. In entering upon his editorial duties Adams confided to one correspondent that he had not lost interest in reform. "On the contrary, as editor I am deeper in [politics] than ever, and my party is growing so rapidly that I look forward to the day when we shall be in power again as not far distant." [45] Despite this optimism, Adams realized his attempt to make the *North American* a reform journal only with difficulty: in the beginning because of the unwillingness of reformers to contribute, then for a while because he apparently did not press his initial enthusiasm. But from 1874 until 1876, when both he and Lodge (his assistant editor) left the *North American*,[46] Adams again took up his project, this time with more success. He wheedled enough reform contributions to give his quarterly the tinge he sought. His final issue he thoroughly saturated with his brand of politics.

Aside from a sheaf of book reviews the busy editor-professor had little time for personal contribution. He composed, in fact, only one major article on Harvard antiquarianism and a long review of Von Holst's *The Constitutional and Political History of the United States*, written jointly with Lodge,[47] prior to that essay which resulted in the abrupt end of his editorial responsibilities. Of his final issue Adams wrote, "Both parties are impossibly corrupt and the public thoroughly indifferent." Then he

44. *Ibid.*, p. 303.

45. Nov. 19, 1870; *ibid.*, p. 198.

46. Samuels, pp. 225 f. Adams was responsible for the issues of the *NAR* dated January, 1871, through October, 1876, exclusive of those from January, 1873, through January, 1874, when he took a year's leave of absence from Harvard (during the academic year 1872–73) for his wedding trip to Egypt and Europe. Although he returned to his classes in September, 1873, he resumed his responsibility for the *NAR* only with the April, 1874, issue; *ibid.*, p. 242. Actually Adams departed for his wedding trip before completing the issue for October, 1872; *ibid.*, pp. 344 f., n. 2.

47. "Harvard College," *NAR, 114* (1872), 110–147; the review of Von Holst's history, *NAR, 123* (1876), 328–361.

added, "Of course I must have my little say, and I have devoted
the whole October number of the *North American* to a review of
the field. The result is sickening. But I consider my October
number a historical monument . . ." [48] On Adams' monument his
publishers engraved an epitaph to the effect that the editors had
"retired" from the management of the magazine "on account
of a difference of opinion with the proprietors as to the political
character of this number." Wishing to free himself of editorial
chores which had finally become onerous, Adams had broadened
a difference of opinion into a breach.[49]

The article so offensive to Osgood Republicanism was an
unsigned essay written jointly with his brother Charles under the title "The Independents in the Canvass." [50] It favored
(somewhat tentatively to be sure) Samuel J. Tilden over Rutherford B. Hayes. The featherweight argument that the Republicans
had been in office long enough finally tipped the balance away
from Hayes; while the Democrats might not do better, they could
not do worse. The article was particularly interesting in that it
mentioned the well-known meeting of two hundred Independents
held in New York on May 15, prior to the nominating conventions for the election of 1876. Adams was among the prime movers
of this gathering,[51] which attempted to mobilize sufficient reform
sentiment behind a single major party so that at least one candidate would stand in clear-cut opposition to Grantism. Carl Schurz
fatally split the solidarity of this nucleus when he led one half
behind Hayes' banners, while the remainder followed E. L. Godkin
to beat the drums for Tilden.

The disaffection of Schurz with the Tilden nomination marked
a turning point in Adams' life. At this time Adams had not only
been among the leaders in the organization of the Independent
movement but he had also considered the purchase, first, of the
Boston Daily Advertiser and, when this scheme collapsed, of the
Boston Post by a group of wealthy Independents, so that reform
sentiment might have its daily hearing.[52] Less than three months

48. Sept. 8, 1876; Ford, *1*, 299 f.
49. *Ibid.*, p. 300. Samuels, pp. 286 f. The publisher's announcement appeared
below the table of contents.
50. *NAR, 123* (1876), 426–467.
51. Ford, *1*, 266–284 *passim.* Samuels, pp. 280–285. Claude M. Fuess, *Carl
Schurz, Reformer* (New York, Dodd, Mead, 1932), pp. 215–236.
52. Samuels, pp. 281, 283. Ford, *1*, 279, n. 1, is in error; see letter to Francis
A. Walker cited below and compare with *ibid.*, p. 283. Later Adams owned stock
in the *New York Evening Post,* but his first letter referring to this stock is dated
1881; see Cater, pp. 109–140 *passim;* Ford, *1*, 349 f., 351, 356.

before the Independents met he wrote Francis Amasa Walker, with whom he had collaborated on an article [53] for the *North American* before they both turned to teaching, the one at Harvard, the other at Yale,

> I want to know what you think of a scheme of mine.
>
> The *Boston Post* is for sale. We here would like to buy it and make an independent paper of it . . .
>
> I have sounded some few gentlemen and I think I could raise the money ($150,000). But before going further, I must know what to do with the paper when bought . . .[54]

Adams then asked Walker to undertake the editorship of the *Post*, after confessing that he had already sounded Horace White and Charles Nordoff on the proposition. To convince the Yale professor, Adams added significantly, "Between ourselves the instruction of boys is mean work. It is distinctly weakening to both parties. I have reduced my pedagogic work to the narrowest dimensions and am working more and more back into active life."

Since his return from England Adams had attempted to wield political power behind the scenes, and had failed. Cajoled to Harvard before his annual "Session" articles could become a "power in the land," he had continued to flirt with the idea of an "active life" until for a few months in 1876 its attainment had seemed tantalizingly possible—only to vanish completely.

With the Independents hopelessly split, the plans for a liberal organ collapsed. Suppose that Schurz had supported Tilden? Suppose that Adams had been a prime backer in the establishment of a reform newspaper? Suppose that, as either a publisher or an editor, he had energetically joined in the campaign? Might he not have plunged so deeply into active life that he would never have produced his historical masterpiece?

As it happened, an active life was not for him. To Lodge he complained bitterly of Schurz.

> I cannot help laughing to think how, after all our labor and after we had by main force created a party for Schurz to

53. "The Legal Tender Act," *NAR, 110* (1870), 299–327. When Adams collaborated with him on this article for the *NAR* Walker was attached to the U.S. Bureau of Statistics. Later he supervised the censuses of 1870 and 1880. In 1873 he became professor of political science in the Sheffield Scientific School, Yale University, a post he left in 1881 to become president of the Massachusetts Institute of Technology.

54. Feb. 29, 1876; quoted in James P. Munroe, *A Life of Francis Amasa Walker* (New York, Holt, 1923), pp. 159 f.

lead, he himself . . . kicked us over in his haste to jump back to the Republicans. If he had taken the least pains to hold his friends together, I feel sure we would have spoken with effect . . . The leader who treats his followers in that way, is a mere will-o'-the-wisp . . . He can hereafter buy power only by devotion to party . . .[55]

Adams had worked hard at the task of establishing an independent political movement. Justifiably discouraged at the result, he made no effort to adjust to the new party situation. Instead, to Lodge, his coworker in the unsuccessful venture, he wrote on June 24, 1876, "Politics have ceased to interest me. I am satisfied that the machine can't be smashed this time . . . The Caucus and the machine will outlive me . . ."[56] In this mood he and Lodge (who was destined to show far more political fortitude than his erstwhile teacher) had put together their reform number of the *North American*, only to meet with opposition from their publisher. Disheartened in May by the collapse of his reform efforts, he was shortly thereafter brought to task for the "political character" of the October issue of his quarterly. Probably he could have retained his editorial post had he mended his ways; but the fascination of editorship had staled with its drudgery, especially with the prospect of an end to crusading—and, after all, really no cause for which to crusade! Quite suddenly the reform journalist found himself with neither cause nor journal. Further work along the line of what he had once fancied as his career demanded a new start with less chance of success than before. Only the hardiest personality could have started again, and only one willing to compromise far more than Adams could have done with the regular party organization.

He returned to Harvard for another semester of "mean work," which, now that it was settling into routine, doubtless seemed meaner than ever. Sometime during the spring of 1877, even as he negotiated with President Eliot about courses for the following autumn,[57] he had already begun to arrange the Gallatin papers which had just come into his hands. These papers, and what must have been a last-minute decision to throw off the boredom of teaching, led him to Washington following the commencement of 1877. Ultimately they also led to the *History*.

55. Sept. 4, 1876; Ford, *1*, 299.
56. *Ibid.*, p. 290.
57. See above, p. 37, n. 43.

At last Adams had attained something of that goal in life which he had so unerringly indicated for himself in the *Life-Book* of the class of 1858. "My immediate object is to become a scholar," the Harvard senior wrote, "and master of more languages than I pretend to know now. Ultimately it is most probable that I shall study and practise law, but where and to what extent is as yet undecided. My wishes are for a quiet and a literary life, as I believe that to be the happiest and in this country not the least useful." [58] The demands of scholarship ended his quest for active life. During the early eighties we occasionally see a glimmer of the old desire in Adams' letters.[59] Then in 1885 even the glimmer was snuffed. With his wife's suicide his life was "cut in halves." [60] Within a circle of friends—select, but cosmopolitan, and much larger than tradition often has it—Adams passed the three decades that remained to him withdrawn from the far larger circle of society into which an active life might well have led him.

58. George M. Elsey, "First Education of Henry Adams," *New England Quarterly, 14* (1941), 684; Samuels, pp. 51 f.

59. See immediately above, n. 52, for his interest in the editorial policies of the *New York Evening Post* during the early eighties; see also below, p. 268. His report on Cuba for Senator Don Cameron in 1896 is another indication of an interest in an active life after 1885. So is the draft of a circumlocutious speech on silver which Adams may have written for the same senator and which appears in an incomplete version, with emendations, in the Henry Adams' library at the Massachusetts Historical Society toward the end of a notebook on social research for the *History* entitled "Manners and Customs."

60. *Education,* p. 317.

III. THE HISTORY: ARTISTRY AND CHARACTERIZATION

WHEN Adams bade good-by to Boston he had completed his historical apprenticeship. He had read widely in history, taught history, written history. He had acquired knowledge of several languages. He had mastered the precise art of documentary analysis. He had observed firsthand both diplomats and legislators. Most important, the diverse influences had fused in the long foreground. He was ready for his massive historical accomplishment.

These years began so happily for Adams, were up to 1885 so intimately happy, then so poignant, that he left this segment of his life unmentioned in the *Education*. These were among the years, before his wife's death, when the Adams name opened archives to the copyists employed by the opulent historian. He pored over documents in Washington, London, Paris, and to a lesser extent Madrid. Then followed the months of composition when, as Adams once outlined a typical schedule to a correspondent, he wrote in his bold, square, almost painfully legible handwriting for five hours a day, rode along the Potomac with Mrs. Adams for two, and gave the remainder of his time to society [1]—the kind of leisure, unbroken by academic demands, which has produced most great history. At this time Henry Hobson Richardson, a classmate of Henry at Harvard, built adjoining houses for Adams and John Hay on Lafayette Square within sight of the White House. The construction was completed just before Mrs. Adams' death and she never moved in. Adams was left to finish the house as they had planned. [2]

1. Ford, *1*, 332 f., 346. For the years after his wife's death see *ibid.*, pp. 384, 391, for minor changes in Adams' schedule of work.
2. *Ibid.*, pp. 357 ff. *passim.* Cater, pp. 142 ff. *passim. Education*, p. 318. Ford, *1*, 364, indicates that considerable work was still going on in the interior of the new house in early November, 1885, although the Adamses had arrived in Washington from Beverly Farms on October 17 (Cater, p. 155) to make ready for the

There he concluded his *History*, and the setting might well epitomize the urbane atmosphere in which he wrote his nine volumes.[3] The library and study were at the front of the house and on the second floor. From both rooms windows opened over the park in Lafayette Square. Drawings and watercolors hung double-banked in the autumnal interiors. Most of them were doubtless collected during the honeymoon trip to Europe, since Mrs. Adams' letters of 1873 are full of their shopping for pictures, sculpture, carpets, vases, and bric-a-brac. "Henry has found and given me a charming little sketch in red and black crayon by Watteau—a girl lying asleep on a couch, bare feet, etc.; and we are pausing over a rough sepia sketch by Sir Joshua. What a pity the committee of the [Boston] Art Museum have not someone here to buy such things, which are only cheap by reason of the ignorance of the general public, but rising every day in price as taste is improving." Buying good drawings and watercolors which they could afford rather than the poor oils with which they must otherwise have suffered, they assembled a remarkable collection. In addition to the Watteau and perhaps the Reynolds, there were several Bonningtons, a Tiepolo sketch, other drawings in chalk, pencil, or wash by minor Italian masters, a little Rembrandt ink and wash. There were others too, but especially two Turners. One of the latter, a watercolor of the Rhone Valley, stood in an easel frame beside Adams' chair in the library and he never made ready for bed or travel without first veiling his prize with a bit

---

moving. Letters in Cater, pp. 156, 157, hint at the physical strain under which Mrs. Adams labored. Mrs. Ward Thoron states that Mrs. Adams never moved in. Marianna (Mrs. Schuyler) Van Rensselaer, *Henry Hobson Richardson* (Boston and New York, Houghton Mifflin, 1888), pp. 106–108, and Henry R. Hitchcock, *The Architecture of H. H. Richardson and His Times* (New York, Museum of Modern Art, 1936), pp. 270 f., pls. 121–123, give an architectural account of the house. There is a photograph of the exterior of the house in J. T. Adams, *Henry Adams* (New York, Boni, 1933), opp. p. 156.

3. For the description below I am indebted in largest part to the recollections of Mrs. Ward Thoron and Miss Aileen Tone. For the quotations below see Thoron, p. 112 (dated June 1, 1873); Ford, *1*, 364 (dated Nov. 4, 1885). Scattered comments in Thoron provide the best published source for information on the furnishings of the Adams house. By 1882 the Adams collection was sufficiently interesting to warrant a visit from Mrs. Schuyler Van Rensselaer, a perceptive critic of the period and the later biographer of Richardson; Thoron, p. 411. It should be added that the furnishings of the Washington house owed much (and perhaps most) to Mrs. Adams. When Adams later kept an apartment in Paris he furnished his rooms simply but elegantly with French antiques; significantly, Louis Seize was the only furniture mentioned in the description of his grandfather's house at Quincy in the *Education,* p. 11.

of Chinese brocade. A miscellaneous collection certainly, too casually brought together to warrant the name. Like the furniture,
the pictures had come to H Street because either he or Mrs.
Adams had liked them. He rarely spoke of them; indeed, he despised all talk of possessions. They simply belonged to the house.

His back to the fireplace in his study, Adams worked at a vast
kneehole table, facing double doors hung with the usual portieres.
Through the doors, which were never closed, he could look from
his chair across the width of the house to the library fireplace, the
"awful onyx tomb-stone," as he had written ruefully to Hay
when he first saw it. With time the awfulness of the onyx seemed
to have taken its place in the comfortable clutter. Unlike the adjoining house, which Richardson had designed for elaborate entertaining, Adams' was unpretentious and informal, partly owing
to the easy arrangement of its commodious rooms, partly to
Adams' struggle against the more excessive of Richardson's attempts to introduce carving and sumptuous materials into the
interiors, and partly to the comfortably heterogeneous furniture.
The quality of informality owed even more to Adams' mode of
entertaining when at home in the wide circle of his chosen acquaintances. Always urbane, he was casually so among his friends,
a quality contrasting strongly with his aloofness when outside
his circle. His phobia against going out after his wife's death
compelled his friends to come to him. His strong aversion to giving formal invitations, at least to those whom he knew best, meant
that close friends usually invited themselves, especially for lunch-
eon, which after the English custom Adams called breakfast.
When he was in Washington his table was customarily set for six,
and he rarely dined alone.

It is a mistake, then, to see him wholly in terms of his intellectualistic writing, worse to lift from his letters only such passages as make him a peevish misanthrope, hugging his eccentrici-
ties in solitude. To those few fortunate enough to get behind
the mask which Adams showed to the world, he was a fascinating
combination of intellect and imagination, adaptable to a wide
range of personalities and interests. He could talk with historians,
politicians, scientists, or aesthetes; yet he always bore his knowledge easily. He would abruptly dismiss intellectual matters to
immerse himself in some child's world or worry about gifts for
the nieces. He would suddenly quit his urban surroundings to
tramp with geologists in the Rockies. His cultivation was no sign

of effeteness. A vigor underlay his writing which neither the calculated style nor its frequent equivocality could hide; and certainly vigor characterized his conversation. The very unpredictability of his wide-ranging sympathies captivated his friends, while, to be sure, it also had its unpleasant aspects. Readily annoyed or bored, he could be abrupt to the point of well-bred rudeness. In short, he was a despot, ruling by force of personality within his private world. Imperious, he was also warm to those for whom he had affection, with a warmth rather sensed than seen. It was this emotional side of his nature which he damped most completely, as though fearing it might get out of check.

The complexity and the urbanity of the man appeared in the *History*; but the artistry of the nine volumes also owed something to the manner in which Adams had approached them. Writing to William James, Adams noted that "A few hundred men represent the entire intellectual activity of the whole thirteen hundred millions." [4] This letter referred to the world of 1882; but again among the last few pages of the *History* he applied the same formula to Jefferson's America. In a democratic nation "individuals were important chiefly as types." [5] As types Adams introduced the principal participants in Jefferson's administration, even essaying in his third chapter to connect, however tenuously, the society of each geographical section to the personalities of its favorite leaders. Indeed, it happened—unconsciously at first but doubtless quite purposely as he progressed—that he approached the *History* through a series of volumes emphasizing the contrasts among various personalities from various sections of the country.[6]

First of course New England. Published in 1877, his *Documents Relating to New England Federalism* centered on the most violent opposition to the two Republican presidents and the compromise position upheld by men like Rufus King and John Quincy Adams. The Gallatin papers, with *The Life of Albert Gallatin* appearing in 1879, depicted the practical public servant who rose as party leader in Congress "by the sheer force of ability and character, without ostentation and without the tricks of popularity." [7] Motivated by a practical nationalism which Adams

4. July 27, 1882; Cater, p. 122.
5. *History*, 9, 222.
6. By 1878 at the latest Adams foresaw his ultimate large-scale *History;* see Ford, *1*, 307.
7. *Gallatin*, p. 154.

found typical of the Middle States, Gallatin utilized the Treasury as Hamilton had done before him—to plan finance so as to design society. Visionary though Gallatin may have been, he proved the most realistic of the leading Republicans. It was Gallatin's balance sheet that almost realized Jefferson's democratic vista; it was Gallatin who favored preparations for war when, after the Chesapeake-Leopard affair, Adams believed, the United States could have afforded it best both financially and morally; it was Gallatin who opposed Jefferson's wasteful and futile gunboat program; Gallatin again who vainly advised a cautious policy which might have kept us out of the War of 1812; Gallatin who led the peace negotiations; and finally Gallatin who stepped aside to let the fourth Virginian enter the White House when, according to Adams, the honor justly belonged to the Pennsylvanian by virtue of both seniority and competence. In his correspondence Adams clearly revealed an affection for Gallatin which appeared only as guarded praise among the pages of the *History*.

> To do justice to Gallatin was a labor of love. After long study of the prominent figures in our history, I am more than ever convinced that for combination of ability, integrity, knowledge, unselfishness, and social fitness Mr. Gallatin has no equal. He was the most fully and perfectly equipped statesman we can show. Other men, as I take hold of them, are soft in some spots and rough in others. Gallatin never gave way in my hand or seemed unfinished. That he made mistakes I can see, but even in his blunders he was respectable.[8]

Or again Adams wrote to Lodge, shortly after the *Gallatin* had appeared,

> As for our estimates of Gallatin, I do not see that they materially differ. To my mind the moral of his life lies a little deeper than party politics and I have tried here and there rather to suggest than to assert it. The inevitable isolation and disillusionment of a really strong mind—one that combines force with elevation—is to me the romance and tragedy of statesmanship. The politician who goes to his grave without suspecting his own limitations, is not a picturesque figure; he is only an animal. That old beggar who was an Emperor somewhere,

8. Jan. 24, 1883; Cater, p. 125. For the early reviews of the *History* commenting on the significance of Gallatin see Bibliography, Sec. D.

and on his death-bed asked his weeping friends: "Have I not acted my part. well?"; that man was picturesque. Gallatin was greater, because he could and did refuse power when he found out what vanity it was, and yet became neither a cynic nor a transcendental philosopher.[9]

Nowhere in his correspondence occurred such glowing praise of either John or John Quincy Adams; and, indeed, the latter showed to disadvantage when measured against Gallatin in those chapters of the *History* discussing the negotiations leading to the Treaty of Ghent.[10]

John Randolph, appearing as Volume 16 in the "American Statesmen Series" in 1882, depicted yet another type. This was the Virginian who adamantly stuck to the original tenets of his party and section, even though the rest of the Republicans moved steadily toward Federalist nationalism and, in fact, moved far beyond it. Thus it happened that, largely by coincidence, Adams began his investigations with three of the most important subsidiary types in the Jefferson-Madison drama, namely, the opposition outside the party, the practical guiding spirit of the party, and the opposition within the party. Unfortunately, at least for drama, Randolph hardly held a respectable place as preceptor of the Republican tradition in Adams' eyes, since he finally displayed only "temper, without proving courage or forethought!" [11] Where Randolph became too abusive to remind Jefferson effectively of the ancient dogmas of his party, Adams himself gladly admonished the third president.

While working on his *Randolph* Adams also pondered a biography of Aaron Burr, the machine politician who sought compensation for neglect in activities suggesting treason. "Randolph is the type of a political charlatan who had something in him," Adams wrote the editor of the "American Statesmen Series." "Burr is the type of a political charlatan pure and simple, a

9. Oct. 6, 1879; Ford, *1*, 314.

10. *History, 9*, 15 ff., 28 ff., 44–53.

11. *Randolph*, p. 69. See also *History, 6*, 233 f., for Adams' views on the importance to leadership of temperance in debate. William C. Bruce, *John Randolph of Roanoke* (New York, Putnam, 1922), pp. v f., and throughout the footnotes, attacks Adams' own intemperance. John T. Morse, Jr., admitted late in life, when recalling his editorship of the "American Statesmen Series," that the choice of Adams for the life of Randolph was the single "real blunder" in his attempt to allot his subjects to sympathetic authors; "Incidents Connected with the American Statesmen Series," *Proceedings of the Massachusetts Historical Society, 64* (1931), 374.

very Jim Crow of melodramatic wind-bags. I have something to say of both varieties." [12] Hence Burr personified the antithesis of Gallatin. But when the historian suggested the addition of his Burr to the Houghton Mifflin galaxy, he met with the reply that Jefferson's vice-president was no "statesman." To this response the historian snorted, "Not bad that for a damned bookseller! He should live a while at Washington and know our *real* statesmen." Then he abandoned the project.[13]

A final study, done while he worked on the *History*, centered on the most important single European figure to influence the Jefferson administration. In 1884 the *Revue historique* carried Adams' interpretation of Napoleon and the Dominican. revolution of Toussaint L'Ouverture.[14]

This "type" approach to the larger work had advantages both aesthetically and historically. Aesthetically it intensified the dramatic clash of personality; historically it emphasized the equally dramatic clash of opinion. The historian with literary inclinations might have used these differences as the means to sharpen individuality. How would Adams depict the individuality of his

12. Unpublished letter, dated Apr. 9, 1881, in the estate of John T. Morse, Jr.

13. Oct. 8, 1882; Ford, *1*, 341. In defending Houghton against Adams' wrath Morse admitted that he, as editor, had decided against the inclusion of Burr in his series; Morse, *op. cit.*, pp. 385–388. J. T. Adams, *op. cit.*, p. 154, mentions the vanished manuscript. Part of a letter in the Morse estate, dated Sept. 26, 1883, indicates that Houghton Mifflin was apparently willing to publish the Burr outside the series, and further shows that Adams at least toyed for a while with the idea of publishing the Burr just previous to the appearance of the first two volumes of the *History* in order to whet the public appetite for the series. See also Ford, *1*, 345. ¶ "Many thanks for your kind interest in Burr. Perhaps it was you who put Osgood up to asking for it last winter. I told Osgood that I had made other arrangements. I say the same thing to Houghton now. ¶ The 'Burr' was written to help your series, if you wanted help. On the general principle of always backing one's friends, if one's friends need backing, I was glad to give you something which I knew would make a sensation. I did not write it for Houghton, and don't mean to give it to him, or to have any dealings with him at all. You can tell him so. If you want the volume for your series, with your name on it, I will not refuse it; but I don't propose to be dictated to by any damned publisher. ¶ I apprehend that this is a clear answer to his proposition; but, as it is barely possible that you may not care to deliver it verbatim, I will add that, for reasons connected with the appearance of my 'History,' I have decided in any case to withhold the 'Burr' another year from publication. If the 'History' cannot appear before 1886, the 'Burr' will not appear before 1885. As this delay makes the whole matter of no consequence for the moment, you can, if you prefer, say simply that I am not now ready to publish on any terms."

14. "Napoléon Ier et Saint-Domingue," *Le Revue historique, 24* (1884), 92–130, tr. and reprinted in *Historical Essays* (New York, Scribners, 1891), pp. 122–177.

leaders and yet suggest that they symbolized the "intellectual activity" and even the personal characteristics of the many thousands whom they represented? How, especially when to his other types Adams added Thomas Jefferson, whose personality as compared with those of all other major American statesmen has proved among the most complex? He stated his problem in the *History*.

> Historians and readers maintained Old-World standards. No historian cared to hasten the coming of an epoch when man should study his own history in the same spirit and by the same methods with which he studied the formation of a crystal. Yet history has its scientific as well as its human side, and in American history the scientific interest was greater than the human. Elsewhere the student could study under better conditions the evolution of the individual, but nowhere could he study so well the evolution of a race. The interest of such a subject exceeded that of any other branch of science, for it brought mankind within sight of its own end.[15]

From old-world sources, of course, Adams had obtained his ideas on scientific history. Hence his implicit contrast of old-world with new-world history typified his frequent tendency to exaggerate for effect. But insofar as some old-world historians had glorified the pageantry of the past or the genius and idiosyncracies of leadership, they had provided narrative almost popular in character; so had many of the new-world historians who wrote in the literary tradition. Although Parkman's volumes did not attain the success of those by Prescott, Motley and the two Bancrofts, the great literary historians were on the whole extravagantly rewarded for their efforts. On the other hand, whatever other virtues scientific history might possess, vast popularity seemed not among them. Adams' *History* sold approximately 3,000 sets in the first decade following its publication.[16] Compared to the sales of

15. *History*, 9, 224 f. Adams foreshadowed this point of view in his article (*NAR, 120* [1875], 180) on Von Holst's *Die Administration Andrew Jacksons in ihrer Bedeutung für die Entwicklung der Demokratie in den Vereinigten Staaten von Amerika*, which he hailed as an indication "that our country at last is considered . . . as offering material for scientific treatment. Whether American history . . . will, even at this early day, bear the test of careful scientific analysis, is the point to be ascertained."

16. Figures in the files of Charles Scribner's Sons. The size of the original printings of the *History* successively decreased as the volumes were published:

Vols. 1, 2: Oct., 1889 (3,550 copies), reprinted 1898, 1909.

his most popular predecessors, this was small indeed. Considering the nature of the *History*, the sale was not insignificant,[17] while its steadiness compensated for its lack of volume. Aside from professional historians and those who make a hobby of serious history, few have read the nine volumes. Adams' subject was intricate, and he did not tempt the amateur by dramatic simplification. On the contrary, the "severest process of stating" hardly permitted space for the sort of prose created by the great literary historians. "File and burnish," Adams once urged Parkman in commenting on the latter's style; "strike out every superfluous word," he admonished Lodge. With his brother Brooks, Henry stated even more firmly his "general rule of correction: to strike out remorselessly every superfluous word, syllable and letter. Every omission improves." [18] The remorselessness with which the elder brother followed his own advice appeared statistically when, for his publisher, he computed the brevity of his chapters in the first six volumes of the *History*. "My chapters have averaged $23\frac{1}{3}$ pages till now." [19] The chapters were short, the pages small; yet each summarized a vast amount of research. Few historians with literary pretensions can boast of greater precision.

If the austerity of his style precluded the dramatic effects of the literary historian, his subject matter also made such drama dubious. To render colorful the Jefferson and Madison administrations might well have taxed the descriptive powers of a Prescott. The *History* reviewed eight Congresses, with eighteen sessions full of speeches, many inconsequential, many absolutely foolish. From such prosy scenes as these Adams turned repeatedly to the White House, the Department of State, the British Foreign Office, or Napoleon's headquarters, where statesmen pondered some reply to a communication. What swaggering heroics would serve

---

Vols. 3, 4: Feb., 1890 (3,280 copies), reprinted 1898, 1909.

Vols. 5, 6: Sept., 1890 (2,850 copies), reprinted 1896, 1901, 1909, 1917.

Vols. 7, 8, 9: Jan., 1891 (2,800 copies), reprinted 1904, 1911.

The data on reprintings were gathered from a check of five major libraries. Subsequent reprintings: new edition, 697 sets (blue binding replacing the olive green of earlier editions) in 1921; four-volume edition, 1,000 sets (New York, Boni, 1930); chapters on the War of 1812 as *The War of 1812*, ed. H. A. DeWeerd (Washington, Infantry Journal, 1944); a two-volume condensation of all volumes as *The Formative Years*, ed. Herbert Agar (Boston, Houghton Mifflin, 1947).

17. Charles Scribner, in writing to an English publisher (Feb. 28, 1890; files of Charles Scribner's Sons), considered the sale of the *History* had been good.

18. Citations from letters dated Dec. 21, 1884, June 15, 1875, and June 5, 1895, respectively. Cater, p. 134; Ford, *1*, 269; *2*, 71.

19. Feb. 8, 1890; unpublished letter in the files of Charles Scribner's Sons.

as an enlivening contrast to the passive cogitation of the letter writer? The Dominican revolution of the Negro, Toussaint L'Ouverture? The western conspiracy of Aaron Burr? The intrepidity of a few military leaders who showed their valor in scattered fighting during the War of 1812? On Adams' stage these were the extras. To his publisher he revealed the reluctance with which he allotted space to the purely dramatic.

> In regard to the battle of New Orleans I have been profuse of maps. This course is not due to the importance of the battle, which was really of little importance, military or political; but for some reason, probably sectional, the Battle of New Orleans has always held an undue place in popular interest. I regard any concession as to popular illusions as a blemish; but just as I abandoned so large a space to Burr—a mere Jeremy Diddler—because the public felt an undue interest in him, so I think it best to give the public a full dose of General Jackson.[20]

Adams chose to resurrect a diplomatic exchange which the ramifications of Napoleonic foreign affairs dwarfed almost to inconsequence. The instances of military heroism and leadership in the War of 1812 almost disappeared beneath the absurdities of a comedy of errors; on the civilian front Madison's administration revealed a timorous president, a penny-pinching Congress, and a treasonable New England.

If he shunned the more obvious elements of such dramatic action as the War of 1812 provided, Adams also refused to treat the failure of Jefferson's idealism as the tragedy which other historians might have made it. The tragedy of failure has always afforded the historian a theme as susceptible to emotional treatment as the triumph of success. Behind Adams' restraint—so befitting the president who bore the mortifications that closed his tenure "with dignity and in silence" [21]—there may have lain a

20. May 3, 1890; quoted by Roger Burlingame, *Of Making Many Books* (New York, Scribners, 1946), pp. 158 f. The Burr episode resembled "the plot of a comic opera rather than the seriousness of a historical drama" (*History, 3,* 233); see also *History, 3,* 287, 328, 442, 454. Samuels, p. 303, points out that Adams treated Burr more as a symptom of society than as a melodramatic figure. Note, too, how perfunctorily Adams dismissed the celebrations following the battle of New Orleans; *History, 9,* 57. However, an early and anonymous reviewer (*Atlantic Monthly, 65* [1890], 277) did find the narrative on Santo Domingo among the most interesting parts of the first two volumes.

21. *History, 4,* 469.

sympathy the more sincerely portrayed for its lack of histrionics. But sympathy so muted possessed a character too private to embrace the *History* as a whole. Adams pictured Jefferson's disappointment almost as a personal affair. Where Parkman lashed his volume to the triumphs and the ultimate failure of La Salle, Adams merely ushered one president from the White House to bow another in.

This simple exchange of President Jefferson for President Madison was, narrowly speaking, "what actually happened" on March 4, 1809. Was Adams too matter-of-fact, too austere in his reliance on the document? He could be: as in his battle scenes where the general staff eclipsed the soldier; or in some of the congressional sessions where incompetence provided slight opportunity for interesting narrative.[22] Every historian who seeks the indisputable event through the deliberate emphasis of source materials risks sinking into factualism, just as the literary historian risks changing fact to fancy. Thus the modern reader detects something of the funeral orator in Parkman's eulogy of La Salle. Parkman's drama depended first on his stress of the overt action implicit in his subject matter, then on the intensification of this action by the equally overt eloquence of his style. Yet whoever dismisses Parkman's drama as a somewhat transparent means to artistry must ask how many have equaled his skill. After all, few nations can boast of themes with more dramatic possibilities than the American Revolution, the Civil War, or westward expansion. American history is rich in drama, but Parkmans are few. Even so, and regardless of personal preference between the two historians, who would deny that Adams sought a brand of drama subtler than Parkman's? Spurning both the surface drama of subject matter and the surface bravura of style, Adams could better concentrate upon a drama particularly appropriate to "mere commentary on the documents." Only by examining his use of documents does Adams' artistry appear.

Take, for example, the seven pages closing Adams' chapter on the failure of Jefferson's embargo.[23] Certainly not the most brilliant of his passages, these few pages nevertheless reveal his

22. Some of the early reviews expressed disappointment at the amount of tedious material which Adams discussed; *Atlantic Monthly, op. cit.*, p. 277; Doyle, *op. cit.*, pp. 805 f. Those copies of the privately printed edition of the *History* in the Massachusetts Historical Society read by Charles Francis Adams, Jr., are sprinkled with his comments on the dullness of certain sections or chapters.

23. The following excerpts appear in *History, 4*, 354–360.

method in an easily comprehended episode. For almost four volumes the historian had painstakingly traced the wavering course of the Republican commercial system. Designed to insulate America from European conflict, it had instead resulted in lawlessness, financial ruin, and worst of all, in that very centralization of national power against which the Sage of Monticello had marshaled his sagacity. The Republican party had already selected Madison as its standard bearer for the 1808 election. Jefferson longed only to escape the burdens of his office, to leave the problems of embargo for solution by the next administration.

> After the meeting of Congress, November 7, when doubt and confusion required control, Jefferson drew himself aside, repeating without a pause the formula that embargo was the alternative to war. "As yet the first seems most to prevail," he wrote . . . and no one doubted to which side he leaned, though as if it were a matter of course that he should quit the government before his successor was even elected, he added: "On this occasion I think it is fair to leave to those who are to act on them the decisions they prefer, being to be myself but a spectator . . ."

Within these two sentences Adams adroitly wove his commentary through the document defining Jefferson's position. At the same time he indicated a flaw in the Virginian's reasoning. The chronicler with a heavier hand might immediately have enlarged upon this weakness; Adams turned instead to the third president's principal subordinates. As though Madison and Gallatin sat beside him in his Harvard seminar, the historian impartially queried their opinion of Jefferson's decision.

> "Both Mr. Madison and myself," wrote Gallatin [to Jefferson], "concur in the opinion that considering the temper of the Legislature it would be eligible to point out to them some precise and distinct course . . . I feel myself nearly as undetermined between enforcing the embargo or war as I was at our last meeting. But I think that we must, or rather you must, decide the question absolutely, so that we may point a decisive course either way to our friends. . . ."

Adams mentally confronted Jefferson with the criticisms of his closest friends.

Jefferson's reply to this request was not recorded, but he persisted in considering himself as no longer responsible for the government. Although Madison could not become even President-elect before the first Wednesday in December, when the electors were to give their votes; and although the official declaration of this vote could not take place before the second Wednesday in February,—Jefferson insisted that his functions were merely formal from the moment when the name of his probable successor was known.

"I have thought it right," he wrote on December 27, "to take no part myself in proposing measures the execution of which will devolve on my successor. I am therefore chiefly an unmeddling listener to what others say . . . As the moment of my retirement approaches I become more anxious for its arrival, and to begin at length to pass what yet remains to me of life and health in the bosom of my family and neighbors, and in communication with my friends undisturbed by political concerns and passions."

In permitting Jefferson to elaborate his point of view Adams rent the tissue of the president's argument just enough to clarify his previous objection. Now—in the next paragraph—the historian could rip the fabric into shreds! As though still in his Harvard seminar, Adams pointed to the eager Josiah Quincy and asked whether this ardent Federalist cared to complete the task.

So freely did he express this longing for escape that his enemies exulted in it as fresh proof of their triumph. Josiah Quincy, his fear of the President vanishing into contempt,— "a dish of skim-milk curdling at the head of our nation,"— writing to the man whom eight years before Jefferson had driven from the White House, gave an account of the situation differing only in temper from Jefferson's description of himself:—

"Fear of responsibility and love of popularity are now master-passions, and regulate all the movements. The policy is to keep things as they are, and wait for European events. It is hoped the chapter of accidents may present something favorable within the remaining three months; and if it does not, no great convulsion can happen during that period. The Presidential term will have expired, and then—away to Monticello, and let the Devil take the hindmost. I do believe that not a whit deeper project than this fills the august mind of your successor."

"Differing only in temper from Jefferson's description of himself": how slyly Adams inserted his own conviction and yet seemed not to interpose his personality between the original document and its reproduction as part of his historical narrative.

The scrutiny of even a few paragraphs illustrates the enormous simplification of Adams' advice to Sarah Hewitt. "Only give a running commentary on the documents in order to explain their relation." Just as the consummate novelist plans every incident that each may define character and motivation more precisely, while each simultaneously advances the narrative, thus Adams utilized the document. So skillfully was research fused into narrative, so inexorably did the findings in one document anticipate the next that the reader is almost unaware of the historian's manipulation. Adams smoothed away the paste pot hitchings of lesser historians; he submerged their obvious argumentation, their intruding backgrounds, summaries, and conclusions. The lack of either explanatory or disputatious footnotes, even of prefaces, emphasized Adams' reliance on the unembellished document.[24]

Hence in the best pages of the *History* there is an almost mathematical sense of precision; an almost mechanistic sense of cause and effect and resultant motion; above all, an evolutionistic sense, not so much of progress (although this element is present) as of progression. This quality of linear progression is intensely evident in much of the best of nineteenth-century history because of the emphasis on a chronological narrative which cuts a narrow swath through the breadth of human experience. Here the histories of Parkman and Adams are similar, and the similarity relates their histories, however significantly they contrast in tone, in method, and in aim. Increasing the scope of his investigations, the historian of the twentieth century has obtained a broader view of society at the cost of the neat—certainly too neat—linearism of nineteenth-century narration. Even the chapter has lost its old unity, for history today tends to shorter than chapter lengths, kaleidoscopic

24. In an unpublished letter dated Nov. 26, 1888, in the files of Charles Scribner's Sons where Adams said, "My taste rather inclines towards simplifying the page," he added: "I want no marginal notes. They were never of use to me in any book (except Coleridge's Ancient Mariner)."

or cross-sectional rather than linear. The gain in breadth of treatment is positive; no one would recommend retreat. But lessons in narrative, whether literary or scientific, are still to be learned from nineteenth-century masters.

Perhaps his novel *Democracy*, published in 1880, had sharpened Adams' sense of narrative, a skill appearing only in scattered passages within his earlier articles. The extreme rapidity with which he seems to have composed a first draft of his *History* may also have helped to keep details subordinated to larger ends. Returning to Washington in 1880 from his search of European archives, Adams found himself settled and ready for writing only about the first of November. By the end of January, 1882, he could report that he was "getting to Chase's impeachment and the close of my first four years, the easiest quarter of my time." Although he kept "hammering ahead, day by day, without looking backwards," even so a first draft of almost two volumes in fifteen months represented a considerable accomplishment, the more so as he completed the "very dull book about Randolph" by the first of June, 1882, and led an active social life the while.[25]

The care with which Adams planned his narrative in the *History* received its explicit justification in his review for the *North American* of William Stubbs' *Constitutional History of England*, where Adams had found Stubbs "better adapted to the work of compilation than to the art of story-telling. The historian must be an artist. He must know how to keep the thread of his narrative always in hand, how to subordinate details, and how to accentuate principles." It was then that Adams branded Stubbs a "lexicographer," more interested in facts than in the development of an idea.[26] The few pages remaining to Adams' chapter on the failure of the embargo reveal how studiously he avoided lexicography and how unerringly he unrolled his recital to its ultimate climax.

Having condemned Jefferson's premature abandonment of office—first on the testimony of the Virginian's own colleagues, then on the evidence of his opponents—Adams opened a new attack. Bad as Jeffersonian logic had been, it was at least a policy. The president made the bad policy of noninterference worse when he failed to follow it.

25. Ford, *1*, 327, 334, 338, 341. A letter dated Mar. 2, 1882, in the estate of John T. Morse, Jr., gives the date of the completion of *Randolph*. Samuels, p. 303, suggests the possible effect of *Democracy* on Adams' style.
26. *NAR, 119* (1874), 235; see above, p. 7.

Had Jefferson strictly carried out his doctrine, and abstained
from interference of any kind in the decision of a future policy,
the confusion of Congress might have been less than it was, and
the chance of agreement might have been greater; but while
apparently refusing to interfere, in effect he exerted his influence to prevent change; and to prevent a change of measures
was to maintain the embargo.

Then followed vituperation from the Federalist pen of Joseph
Story, a still stronger condemnation from the hostile Timothy
Pickering, and finally Adams closed the chapter.

Canning's defiance and Napoleon's discipline reduced [Jeffer-
son] to silence and helplessness; but even when prostrate and
alone, he clung to the remnant of his system. Disaster upon
disaster, mortification upon mortification, crowded fast upon
the man whose triumphs had been so brilliant, but whose last
hope was to escape a public censure more humiliating than any
yet inflicted on a President of the United States. The interest
attached to the history of his administration—an interest at
all times singularly personal—centred at last upon the single
point of his personality, all eyes fixing themselves upon the
desperate malice with which his ancient enemies strove to drive
him from his cover, and the painful efforts with which he still
sought to escape their fangs.

With these words Adams established his central vantage point
for the handful of disasters yet to be borne by the third president
until, some pages later, he "quitted Washington forever." In concluding his chapter Adams did more than fix a vantage point for
succeeding action. He also softened the contempt which his reader
must feel toward the statesman who cannot confront his failure.
Not that Adams ostensibly demanded pity, but he abruptly
stripped away the public leader to reveal for one brief moment
the private man beneath. Momentarily he disclosed the idealist
crushed beneath reality, to tell his reader in effect that he had
finished his attack on Jefferson and now presented a fundamentally
honest idealist for our indulgence if we chose to give it. If we chose
to give it! Here is the important qualification. Had Adams demanded sympathy for a private individual, he would have deviated
from his scientific approach when he abandoned his strict commentary on just those documents needed to define a general de-

velopment in history. He would have ceased simply to appraise the motivation and effectiveness of the statesman insofar as the statesman merely participated in the most significant events of history. For it was the public aspect of the individual on which the scientific historian necessarily concentrated, since even the most ambitious among them could hardly pretend to discover a necessary pattern of causality in the private life of so much as a single statesman.[27] Adams, then, was a stern judge because he evaluated Jefferson's public career without reference to the private man.

If the greatest artists have always tempered justice with compassion, then Adams was perhaps too stern a judge to rank among the greatest of historians. And yet nothing in the *History* really refuted the remarks—not uncritical, to be sure, but essentially friendly—with which Adams introduced Jefferson in his fifth chapter.[28] Adams saw Jefferson as idealistic, public spirited, friendly, sanguine, intellectual, essentially honest and honorable. The list might be extended, except that the virtues which Adams saw in Jefferson are less important for present purposes than his vices. To Adams, Jefferson's major faults were four. There was his occasional deviousness in the means employed to reach generally honest ends. There was his frequent evasiveness, especially when confronted with unwanted responsibility. There was his desire for the esteem of mankind, which accounted in large part for both the deviousness and the evasiveness. And finally, overlaying all his other faults, there was Jefferson's idealism, at once his cardinal strength and weakness. Even the modern biographer would find it difficult to relieve Jefferson of these charges.

So radically has the philosophical reputation of Jefferson grown during the New Deal that it is difficult to imagine the almost purely political Jefferson known to the late nineteenth century. To be sure, Adams remarked at one point in the *History* that "not until the embargo and its memories faded from men's minds did the mighty shadow of Jefferson's Revolutionary name efface

27. See Hajo Holborn, "The Science of History," *The Interpretation of History,* ed. Joseph R. Strayer (Princeton, Princeton University Press, 1943), pp. 75 ff. Raymond Walters, at present preparing a new biography of Gallatin, estimates that Adams used only about a third of the bulky collection of Gallatin papers in the New York Historical Society in writing his biography. Walters believes that the modern biographer would use another third dealing with Gallatin's personal affairs. A final third, mostly on local Pennsylvania legal affairs, would be largely unused even today.

28. *History, 1,* 143–148.

the ruin of his Presidency." [29] But the capital *R* showed that even the revolutionary name depended on so narrow a segment of Jefferson's career as to be today all but incomprehensible. In fact, a sampling of the original reviews of the *History* shows that none attacked Adams as being particularly unfair to Jefferson, although some did comment on the occasional austerity of his judgments.

At least two charged him rather with being too fair! The first by J. A. Doyle in the *English Historical Review* stated that at least on "one point most impartial critics" would probably think Adams "biassed by party loyalty." [30] By this mention of party loyalty Doyle referred to Adams' Republican leanings throughout the *History*, strongly opposed as he was to New England Federalism. If John Adams had been a Federalist, he was after all a devoted correspondent of Jefferson in his old age. John Quincy Adams had of course aligned himself against the extreme Federalists beginning in 1803, definitely joined the Republican party in 1808, gone as Madison's minister to Russia in 1809, served on the peace commission ending the War of 1812, and eventually in 1817 become Monroe's secretary of state. Indeed, the early opposition of John Quincy Adams to the Federalist extremists in Massachusetts had marked the starting point of the *History* in the *Documents Relating to New England Federalism.*[31] Hence Doyle felt justified in maintaining that "The Jefferson tradition has affected [Adams], as the attractive personality of Jefferson affected contemporaries, and has strangely clouded his judgment on a most noteworthy and typical incident in Jefferson's career." Then Doyle summarized the Callender incident.

> In 1798 a disreputable hack writer, one James Thompson Callender, of Scotch extraction, published a pamphlet attacking the federalists. He was fined and imprisoned for libel. When the democrats came in he asked for his reward, a government office, and was refused. Thereupon he published a string of charges against Jefferson's private life . . . [Among these] Callender announced that Jefferson had paid him for writing the libellous pamphlet and had supplied him with material for it. Jefferson at once put forth a disclaimer. "No man," he

29. *Ibid., 4,* 464. Ford, *op. cit.,* p. 542, reviewing the *History,* regretted that Adams had not considered the early career of Jefferson. See also below, p. 61.

30. Doyle, *op. cit.,* p. 805, for this and the following citations.

31. See discussion, Samuels, pp. 272 ff.

wrote, "wished more to see his [Callender's] pen stopped."
Thereupon Callender produced a letter from Jefferson in
which he had said, "I thank you for the proof sheets you enclose
me; such papers cannot fail to produce the best effects." This,
according to Mr. Adams, was merely an instance of Jefferson's
"kindly prevarication."

The reviewer went on to cite Adams' sentence, "To tell Callender
that his book could not fail to produce the best effect was a way
of hinting that it might do harm." And Doyle concluded, "In
other words Jefferson wrote and spoke not English but Jeffer-
sonese . . . Surely Mr. Adams must see that to take this line of
defense is admitting that his hero is no longer to be judged as a
responsible being, amenable to the ordinary laws of human conduct."

Another, and particularly interesting, review of the first and
second volumes of the *History*, anonymously written for the *Atlantic Monthly*, went further in noting the lengths to which Adams
would go in Jefferson's defense.

> Mr. Adams admires Jeffersonianism, and so depicts it that his
> readers will admire it likewise, at least as an abstraction. But
> the observant ones among them will separate Jeffersonianism
> from Jefferson. The doctrine Mr. Adams sets forth attrac-
> tively, but his position as towards the man is curious. He con-
> stantly interrupts his narrative to attribute some fine quality
> to his hero, yet it is impossible not to remark how widely the
> Jefferson of his fancy differs from the Jefferson of his facts;
> for no sooner does he ascribe a trait than he seems to adduce
> evidence to disprove it. He utters repeatedly the undeniable
> assertion that Jefferson was a great man, but he wholly fails
> to set forth how or wherein he was great.[32]

The reviewer then stated that most scholars believe the earlier
Jefferson—again the Revolutionary name!—far greater than the

32. *Atlantic Monthly, 65* (1890), 275 f. For a very hostile but something of a
crank article attacking the *History* for its hostility to the Federalists see Housatonic (pseudonym), *A Case of Hereditary Bias; Henry Adams as an Historian*,
privately printed pamphlet of articles originally appearing in the *New York Tribune*, Sept. 10 and Dec. 15, 1890 (Washington, 1891). Housatonic is identified on a
copy of the pamphlet in the New York Public Library with the legend, "written by
William Henry Smith, who sent this copy to Paul Leicester Ford, on the appearance of Vol. 1 of the Writings of Jefferson." Adams' library in the Massachusetts
Historical Society contains a copy of Housatonic inscribed, "To Mr. Henry Adams
kindly, but firmly presented, by Theodore Roosevelt, April '93."

president and suggested that perhaps Adams could have justified his praise had he opened the *History* with an account of Jefferson's background. But Adams did not mention the Declaration of Independence,

> contenting himself with alleging the greatness at frequent intervals throughout a history in which he shows his hero abandoning every principle he has ever avowed, creating no new policy in place of that which he throws away, yielding to others, failing to carry his own points, drifting along the current of circumstances. Even if Mr. Adams were Jefferson's detractor instead of his admirer, this would be unfair; and as it is, the reader feels a little irritation at a display falling so far short of the advertisement, and is justly provoked that the showman will not make his monkey perform his boasted tricks.

The analysis continued with a page of specific illustration.

This last review is especially interesting in that it gives a clue to Adams' praise, however puzzled the reviewer apparently remained as to Adams' motive. For his ironical purpose in the *History* Adams had to establish the essential integrity of Jefferson, together with the intellectual acumen and the essential rightness of Jefferson's cause. (After all, John Quincy Adams had originally gone along with the embargo.) Had Jefferson been a mediocrity, and his cause the fabrication of a nonentity, then to what avail an elaborate analysis of its failure? Like Hamlet, Adams' Jefferson must appear a man of substantial worth who failed through some particular fault. But the documents continually deflated Adams' protagonist, and well before the end of the drama. To keep him buoyed throughout the four volumes Adams had repeatedly to puff Jefferson's better qualities. Since he puffed only to prepare for the next deflation, the over-all effect to the modern reader is rather to exaggerate the criticism of Jefferson. The fault lay more in history than in the historian. Unlike Shakespeare, Adams could not control his Hamlet by completely calculating his climax.

Present knowledge of Jefferson does permit a fairer view of the deficiencies in Adams' portrait. Knowledge of the private man enables a re-evaluation of the presidency in terms of the extraordinary scope of Jefferson's thought. So much is gain; but in taking a broader than exclusively political view of statesmanship, what has history lost? It has tended to lose precisely those aesthetic qualities which make Adams' volumes the literary master-piece they are. The rigorous progression of his narrative along a path of narrow scope permitted an intensity in Adams' penetration of character, temperament, and motive in public life rarely surpassed in history. One critic has compared the *History* to a novel by Henry James,[33] a valid comparison provided the analysis of mind in the one is not confused with the analysis of emotions in the other. Occasional comments in his letters make it seem that Adams at least partially agreed with his wife's emphatic pronouncement on James: it was "not that he 'bites off more than he can chaw' . . . but he chaws more than he bites off." Even so, the *Education* recorded the "pleasure of seeing the lights of [James'] burning-glass turned on alternate sides of the same figure." [34] In the first volume of the *History* Adams explained why only the historian with Jamesian insight into the subtleties of human motivation could ever do justice to Jefferson.

> The contradictions in Jefferson's character have always rendered it a fascinating study. Excepting his rival Alexander Hamilton, no American had been the object of estimates so widely differing and so difficult to reconcile. Almost every other American statesman might be described in a parenthesis. A few broad strokes of the brush would paint the portraits of all the early Presidents with this exception, and a few more strokes would answer for any member of their many cabinets; but Jefferson could be painted only touch by touch, with a fine pencil, and the perfection of the likeness depended upon the shifting and uncertain flicker of its semi-transparent shadows.[35]

The portrait needed careful touching precisely because of the sincerity of Jefferson's noble vision.

No American historian, and few, if any, European, has sur-

33. Yvor Winters, *The Anatomy of Nonsense* (Norfolk, Conn., New Directions, 1943), pp. 28 f.

34. Dec. 4, 1881; Thoron, p. 306; see also p. 320. *Education*, p. 163. For Adams' opinion of James see Ford, *1*, 333; *2*, 333, 413, 416. Actually Adams' only praise of James, aside from the remark in the *Education*, was for *William Wetmore Story and His Friends;* see below, pp. 283 f. Undoubtedly Richard Blackmur is far closer to the truth than Winters when he says of Adams and James that each appreciated the other's society far more than his work. Richard P. Blackmur, "Henry Adams: Three Late Moments," *Kenyon Review*, *2* (1940), 18. But Blackmur's argument does not affect the use made of Winters here.

35. *History, 1*, 277.

passed Adams' portrayal of the labyrinthian unfolding of human thought and the subtle interaction of one mind upon another. Insofar as the *History* boasted of drama it was obviously an inward drama, not one of outward circumstance. "The story of diplomatic adventure, which has so often an interest beyond what could be supposed possible from the contact of three or four quiet and elderly gentlemen meeting about a green table, or writing letters inordinately long, owes that interest in most cases to a hope or a despair, to a mystery or an elucidation . . ." [36] This was precisely the kind of interest which Adams' eight years in the legation would have stimulated. By choosing a period in history crowded with negotiation, he could use his training to best advantage. By excluding the surface drama of colorful incident except insofar as it filtered through the documents, he subordinated all elements in the *History* to his intellectualistic analysis. He matched the intricacy of the human intellect with the precision of the scientific approach to history. With a wider purview of the past, the contemporary historian can tell more about past economics, philosophy, popular emotions, everyday life—much, in short, about the whole vital panorama of the past; but he usually tells less about the sinuous ramifications of a sequence in human thought.

Using the sequence of human thought—as he later called it in the *Education*—for the thread of his narrative, Adams projected this thought both inward toward the human conscience and outward toward the social forces of which his statesmen sought control. For Adams' appraisal of statesmanship, then, the touchstones were two: first, the morality of the end; second, the efficiency of the means.

Behind the human intellect Adams disclosed man's struggle with the inner voice of conscience. Thus his interest in the Louisiana Purchase lay less in the grandeur of its acreage than in the method by which the Republicans would justify an acquisition which, in Jefferson's own words, made "blank paper" of the Constitution.[37] So he investigated the moral implications of Jefferson's inability to disown the embargo after its acknowledged failure. Instances might be multiplied indefinitely, since Adams probed not the personality of his statesmen but their character.

36. *Ibid., 2*, 292.
37. *Ibid.*, pp. 90 ff.

To be sure, a comparison of the *History* with the *Gallatin* shows in the later volumes a tremendous improvement in Adams' depiction of personality,[38] for he had become fascinated with the problem around 1880. He had previously brightened his early articles with occasional character sketches, sharp but short and usually satirical; in 1869 he had even considered a biography of "an ancient lady of our house," presumably Abigail Adams.[39] But until he worked on Gallatin there was little need in any of his writing to consider the role of personality in history. Even the sober, practical-minded, almost pedantic Gallatin—for so his biographer viewed him—permitted minimal attention to personality traits. The *Gallatin* completed, however, it seems almost as though Adams consciously strove to repair his deficiency. In preparation for the *History* he turned successively to Randolph, Burr, and Napoleon —three men whose careers were absolutely inexplicable without study of their personalities. In the early eighties he also wrote his two novels, *Democracy* and *Esther*. What accounted for this sudden interest in personality? Baym has noted the beginnings of Adams' reading in psychology while he taught at Harvard.[40] Certainly, too, the urbane life in Washington and the enthusiasm with which Adams greeted it after his period of "banishment" in Boston accounted substantially for his new interest. Finally, his wife must have been influential in making her husband conscious of personality, for her letters disclose the usual feminine absorption in personal idiosyncrasies, with unusual perceptivity in recording them.

However significant these influences in developing Adams' abilities as a historian, even in the *History* he continued to emphasize character above personality.[41] More precisely, he exploited the personality of his subjects in such a way as to emphasize their character; further than this he remained unconcerned with the role of personality in history. Hence his biographies of Randolph, Burr (as he appears in the *History*), and Napoleon represented not so much three contrasts in personality as three studies of public morality, all three in turn contrasting with the earlier *Gallatin*. This interest in public morality remained throughout life. Apparent in the young secretary's letters from London, obvious in

38. Samuels, p. 303.
39. *Ibid.*, pp. 183 f. Apr. 19, 1869; Ford, *1*, 157.
40. Baym, pp. 92 f.
41. See John B. Black, *The Art of History* (London, Methuen, 1926), pp. 170 ff., for a discussion of "character" as opposed to "personality" in history.

his reform articles and in the *History*, the theme eventually made a chapter in the *Education* and formed the basis for Adams' condemnation of the world in which he lived. Man wrestling with the devil which is himself, even amidst the practical exigencies of politics: the theme had come to Massachusetts with the *Mayflower*. Certainly no New England family had eyed the devil more persistently than the Adamses, or held themselves more strictly accountable for their transgressions. Reading intensified the morality of his family heritage. For his historical development, his reading of the moral historians of the eighteenth century and the extension of eighteenth-century morality into nineteenth-century history were particularly important.

Gibbon can stand for all, since of all moralists in history it was "my dear Gibbon," the "amiable Gibbon," whom Adams most frequently mentioned. He inevitably thought of Gibbon as he finished his own *History* in September, 1888.

> I have composed the last page of my history, and the weather is so wet that for a week I've been in vain trying to do Gibbon and walk up and down my garden. I wish Gibbon had been subjected to twelve inches of rain in six weeks, in which case he would not have waited to hear the bare-footed monks sing in the Temple of Jupiter, and would have avoided arbors as he would rheumatics. I am sodden with cold and damp . . .[42]

On brighter days, if the *Education* correctly recalled his student wanderings through Italy in 1860, the youth of twenty-two had mused on the steps of the church of Santa Maria di Ara Coeli,[43] where almost a hundred years before another youth of twenty-seven had supposedly glimpsed the theme that he immortalized. And in the *Education* Adams would include Gibbon along with Maine, Tylor, McLennan, Buckle, Comte, and a few philosophers as one responsible for stirring the "scandal" of literary history in giving history significance.[44] By 1907, of course, Adams could parallel the decline and fall of Roman morality with his curve of moral degradation for his own world of the nineteenth century, for by then he had applied on a much larger scale the moral yardstick which measured the actions of his statesmen in the *History*.

---

42. Citations from letters dated Feb. 17, 1908, July 5, 1909, and Sept. 23, 1888, respectively. Ford, *2*, 490, 521; *1*, 392.

43. *Education*, p. 91.

44. See above, p. 1.

The nine volumes remain the greatest moral history ever produced in America.

Moral standards tend toward absolutism, and notably so for all the Adamses. If some of Henry Adams' strictures against the leaders of the Jeffersonian era seem unduly harsh, their severity is due in part to the rigorous, even impossible, moral standards which he maintained.[45] He also tended toward absolutism in evaluating the role of leadership in respect to the external forces of society—another theme preoccupying him for life.

Although Adams rarely disputed the morality of Jefferson's ends, he repeatedly assailed the efficiency of his means, for Jefferson lacked what Adams once called the sense of "practical statesmanship." [46] His sympathy with Jefferson's miscalculations was limited by a conviction that the measures adopted resulted in the disaster which a more practical-minded statesman might have foreseen. Although Adams condemned the "Napoleonic kind of adventuredom" in the personality of Alexander Hamilton—"equally ready to support a system he utterly disbelieved in as one that he liked" [47]—he ranked Hamilton with Gallatin as a preeminent example of what he meant by practical statesmanship. To Adams the specific source of Hamilton's fame did not rest on mere departmental or party activity or even on his brilliant reports while secretary of the treasury. His stature depended rather on the "mass and variety" [48] of his activities. Hamilton did not let his aristocratic inclinations deter him from decisive action in his society. His sense of what was practical permitted him to channel social forces in accordance with a will admittedly obsessed with personal ambition, but an ambition linked to national benefit.

It was Gallatin, however, who inevitably offered Adams an excuse for his personal definition of statesmanship. This definition occurred in connection with the treasurer's report for 1808, designed by Gallatin to implement Jefferson's scheme for internal improvements, soon dispelled by war. And significantly, among subsequent leaders, John Quincy Adams was one of the few who

45. See Bibliography, Sec. D, for criticisms by subsequent historians of Adams' overly harsh judgments.

46. *Gallatin*, pp. 267 f. On Jefferson's morality see also above p. 59, below pp. 83 f.

47. May 15, 1876; Ford, *1*, 284. In writing his *History* Adams preferred "not to touch him if I can help it," and when Lodge's biography appeared Adams went so far as to admit that "much as I want to read your *Hamilton*, the subject repels me more than my regard for you attracts." *Ibid.*, pp. 335, 342.

48. *Gallatin*, p. 268.

embraced Gallatin's vision and during his presidency futilely
urged a policy of national improvements which the factionalism
of growing sectional rancor forbade. Of Gallatin's report Adams
wrote, "To make one comprehensive, permanent provision for the
moral and economical development of the people, to mark out
the path of progress with precision and to enter upon it at least
so far as to make subsequent advance easy and certain, this
was the highest statesmanship, the broadest practical philan-
thropy." [49] The same definition was implicit in his later statement
in the *Education* that "Unless education marches on both feet—
theory and practice—it risks going astray." [50] It was implicit,
too, in his earlier writing as a journalist, where article after article
had called for the kind of leadership which Gallatin epitomized.
The same ideal of practicality appeared in his course in medieval
institutions. The first page of Thwing's notebook revealed Adams'
attack on the "constitutional" approach to history for its too
theoretical character.[51] Again and again Thwing noted his teacher's impatience with the treatises of jurists. They had little to do
with the development of legal institutions. Law evolved from everyday practice and needs. Indeed, twice Thwing's notes show the
phrases "historically speaking" and "from the historical point of
view" in clear-cut opposition to the juridical interpretation of
law, while the contrast between legal theory and history appeared
repeatedly within the nine volumes. For example, Adams wrote
of the Essex decision,

> The lawyer is required to give facts the mould of a theory;
> the historian need only state facts in their sequence. In law
> Sir William Scott was considered as one of the greatest judges
> that ever sat on the English bench, a man of the highest per-
> sonal honor, sensitive to any imputation on his judicial in-
> pendence,—a lawyer in whom the whole profession took pride.
> In history he made himself and his court a secret instrument
> for carrying out an act of piracy.[52]

49. *Ibid.*, p. 355. *History, 1*, 163. Gallatin is implicitly contrasted with the other
principal members of the Jefferson administration as one who "understood the
practical forces of society." In the *Education*, p. 333, Adams invoked Gallatin's
name when discussing the practicability of Pennsylvania politics in the person of
Senator Don Cameron, although confessing the imperfection of the comparison. See
also the definition of "practical politics," *History, 8*, 20.

50. *Education*, p. 424.

51. See above, p. 34 f.

52. *History, 3*, 45 f.

And later—a veritable motto for Adams' course in medieval institutions—"History has nothing to do with law except to record
the development of legal principles." [53] There was nothing like
diplomacy—and especially the diplomacy of neutral rights—to
emphasize the gulf between law and history, while the differences
provided a major component in the irony of the Adams volumes.

If this attitude toward the law explained much about Adams'
inability to become a practicing lawyer, and much, too, about his
discomfiture under the yoke of "Sac" and "Soc," it also partially
explained his greater interest in Jefferson than in Madison. To
Adams Madison made neither "comprehensive" nor "permanent
provision" for the public welfare during his administration; nor
did he act with practical vigor on the program which he inherited
from Jefferson. Quite the contrary, the legalistic Madison "showed
the habit of avoiding the heart of every issue, in order to fret
its extremities." "Balancing every suggestion of energy by a corresponding limitation of scope, Madison showed only a wish to
remain within the limits defined by his predecessor." [54] In combination with Adams' growing disinterest in his *History* when he
worked on the last half, Madison's personality scarcely inspired
the same interest as Jefferson's.

The practical-minded man of vision stood as Adams' ideal
leader; but if the statesmanship of the great leader represented
the limits of free will in history, then Adams saw free will as
limited. To look again at the *Gallatin*, which often revealed the
framework of the *History* shorn of complications: the Republicans
argued that "government must be ruled by principles; to which
the [moderate] Federalists [like Rufus King] answered that government must be ruled by circumstances." Again Adams might
have mentioned his grandfather, who eventually abandoned the
Federalists because their principles ignored the circumstances in
which the country found itself during the first decade of the
nineteenth century. Or, as the grandson expressed the same idea
in the *Education*, "Everyone admits that the will is a free force,
habitually decided by motives. No one denies that motives exist
adaquate to decide the will; even though it may not always be
conscious of them." [55]

53. *Ibid., 4,* 265.
54. *Ibid., 3,* 74; *5,* 3. Ford, *op. cit.,* p. 698, reviewing the *History* in 1890, observed that Adams seemed more the "advocate" in the fifth and sixth volumes than
he had in the first four; see also below, p. 121.
55. *Gallatin,* pp. 278, 879. See *Education,* p. 487.

Hence his Jefferson and Madison appeared as mere "types of character, if not as sources of power." [56] Such puny heroes could readily serve as subjects for amusement. Indeed, in contrasting Adams' *History* with its great predecessors in both England and America, Winters astutely termed it the first historical classic consistently to evoke the comic muse.[57]

In a letter complaining of the necessity for taking the "lunatic monkey" Randolph *"au serieux,"* Adams confessed to the risible possibilities of the other members in his menagerie. "For that matter, however, I am under much the same difficulty with regard to T. Jefferson, who, between ourselves, is a character of comedy. John Adams is a droll figure, and good for Sheridan's school; but T. J. is a case for Beaumarchais; he needs the lightest of touches, and my hand is as heavy as his own sprightliness." [58] As Adams described them, the heroes of the nine volumes resembled bit-part character actors.

For eight years this tall, loosely built, somewhat stiff figure, in red waistcoat and yarn stockings, slippers down at the heel, and clothes that seemed too small for him, may be imagined as Senator Maclay described him, sitting on one hip, with one shoulder high above the other, talking almost without ceasing to his visitors at the White House. His skin was thin, peeling from his face on exposure to the sun, and giving it a tettered appearance. This sandy face, with hazel eyes and sunny aspect; this loose shackling person; this rambling and often brilliant conversation, belonged to the controlling influences of American history, more necessary to the story than three fourths of the official papers, which only hid the truth.[59]

As for Jefferson's successor,

Madison had a sense of humor, felt in his conversation, and detected in the demure cast of his flexile lips, but leaving no trace in his published writings. Small in stature, in deportment nodest to the point of sensitive reserve, in address simple

56. *History*, 9, 226.
57. Winters, *op. cit.,* pp. 77 f. George M. Trevelyan, *Clio, a Muse and Other Essays* (London, New York, Toronto, Longmans, Green, 1930), p. 146, says, "Carlyle uses constantly an historical method which Gibbon and Maitland use sometimes, and other historians scarcely at all—humour." These historians have used the humorous incident but not the humorous motif as did Adams.
58. Sept. 3, 1882; Ford, , 338, also p. 323.
59. *History, 1,* 187.

and pleasing, in feature rather thoughtful and benevolent than strong, he was such a man as Jefferson, who so much disliked contentious and self-asserting manners, loved to keep by his side.[60]

The drollery of these Republican leaders indicated how Adams scorned the hero. He prodded too deeply into their correspondence, he focused too incisively on their foibles, to allow of deification. They existed in the *History* as rather average mortals, exposed for good or ill by their own testimony. This dependence on the document gave, to the virtuous at least, the peculiar dignity of virtue wrought by its own course through the vicissitudes of political life, without apparent intervention from the historian. This very independence of Adams' statesmen from their historian insured against the degeneration of his comic point of view into travesty, while he disliked his *Randolph* precisely because he knew the extent of its satire. "If you like 'Randolph,' " he wrote the editor of the "American Statesmen Series," "I am pleased, for you are the only person I was bound to satisfy. To me it is an unpleasant book, which sins against all my art canons. The acidity is much too decided. The rule of a writer should be that of a salad-maker; let the vinegar be put in by a miser; the oil by a spend-thrift." Then he immediately justified himself, "In this case however the tone was really decided by the subject, and the excess of acid is his." [61] Hence Adams' comedy was that of Jovian detachment. From the Olympus of his study table he repeatedly asked of his statesmen: Are your intentions good? Are your actions practical? But he put the questions so slyly—"I have tried here rather to suggest than assert" the greatness of Gallatin [62] —that they appear not to come from the historian. Rather they seem to occur to the reader as he too peers down on the very process of the dead recording their own judgments.

Insofar as this Jovian perspective diminished the scale of his statesmen, it reinforced his conviction that only the very occasional individual could wrench from circumstances a policy sufficiently realistic, yet farsighted, to channel future development. Even Gallatin failed. As for Gallatin's colleagues, Adams admitted in

60. *Ibid.*, pp. 189 f.
61. Sept. 26, 1883; unpublished letter in the estate of John Torrey Morse, Jr. See also Ford, *1*, 338, 341. Compare with the statement in the *Education*, p. 278, that "Adams never cared to abandon the knife for the hatchet."
62. See above, p. 47.

1883 of Jefferson, Madison, and Monroe, "I am at times almost
sorry that I ever undertook to write their history, for they appear like mere grasshoppers kicking and gesticulating on the
middle of the Mississippi River . . . They were carried along on
a stream which floated them, after a fashion, without much regard
to themselves." [63]

The mood of melancholy regret grew beside the intellectual
conviction of man's helplessness before powers larger than himself until both mood and intellect merged on this point. The result
was psychological paralysis, failure to arrive at decisive conclusion, a sense of drift. Adams returned again and again to the
theme. There was Jefferson paralyzed amidst the ramifications of
Napoleonic diplomacy, and Madison after him; Madeleine in
Democracy, fleeing to Egypt to escape the blunders of her love,
as Jefferson had fled from the responsibilities of his embargo;
Esther in his second novel, loving a man she could not marry;
Marau Taaroa in his South Seas memoir, recalling a vanished
paradise; Bay Lodge in another memoir, dying before he could
finish his poetry and never quite realizing his aims in what he did
write. To be sure, the cathedral of Chartres was evidence of decision, while many of Marau's ancestors had acted conclusively.
But decisive action was long ago or far away. Who can fail to
see the reformer who so easily turned futilitarian? "The two
parties made their offers for us, and we dissolved like a summer
cloud. I am left smiling at the ruins." [64]

Finally he turned to himself. In his best-known book he declared that "education should try to lessen the obstacles, diminish
the friction, invigorate the energy, and should train minds to
react, not at haphazard, but by choice, on the lines of force that
attract their world." Or, some pages later, "Susceptibility to the
highest force is the highest genius; selection between them is the
highest science; their mass is the highest educator." [65]

What, then, was the failure of Jefferson but a version of the
failure which Adams later celebrated in his *Education*?

63. Jan. 24, 1883; Cater, pp. 125 f. He added: "My own conclusion is that
history is simply social development along the lines of weakest resistance, and that
in most cases the line of weakest resistance is found as unconsciously by society as
by water."

64. Sept. 8, 1876; Ford, *1*, 299.

65. *Education*, pp. 314, 475.

IV. THE HISTORY:

THEME AND BACKGROUND

"LEARN to appreciate and to use the German historical method, and your style can be elaborated at leisure." [1] Thus Adams advised Lodge. The aesthetic aspects of the *History* obviously accounted for only part of its significance, just as the aesthete—the art collector, the polished conversationist, the later author of *Chartres*—represented but a facet of Adams' personality. Although the *History* combined intellect and artistry, the intellect implicit in both his method and the development of his great idea came first.

The thoroughness with which he investigated the political, constitutional, diplomatic, and military aspects of the Jeffersonian period have broadly justified his confidence that the nine volumes would serve "the future historian as a fixed and documented starting-point." [2] To summarize the additions and alterations of subsequent scholarship is of less purpose here than the investigation of Adams' premises and generalizations. [3] His harsh strictures on the two Republican administrations were obviously caused by more than narrow differences of party between John Adams and Thomas Jefferson. Before their deaths these two were reconciled; the *History* was virulently anti-Federalist. To Charles W. Eliot in the spring of 1877, when Adams still planned to stay at Harvard, he even wrote, "I propose that Mr. Lodge should have a course in U.S. history coterminous with mine. His views being federalist and conservative, have as good a right to expression in the college as mine which tend to democracy and radicalism." [4]

1. June 2, 1872; Ford, *1*, 228.
2. See above, p. 16.
3. For some corrections of Adams' work by subsequent scholars see Bibliography, Sec. D.
4. Mar. 2, 1877; Cater, p. 81. Lindsay Swift, who took Adams' course on the "History of the United States from 1789 to 1840" in 1876–77, stated, "It was a legend in the college that Mr. Adams conducted the democratic side of American

Like Gallatin and John Quincy Adams, Henry Adams took his position beside the northern Democrats, in opposition to both Virginia Republicans and New England Federalists.[5] But if he marked the position finally adopted by his grandfather, Henry's filial piety depended on the great idea which had moved three generations of the family. From the federalism of John Adams to the moderate abolitionism of Charles Francis, through the shifting requirements of party and circumstance, the idea of nationality had given the family both its continuity and its integrity. Chiding Lodge for his excessive bias toward the Federalist position, Adams advised, "Unless you can find some basis of faith in general principles, some theory of the progress of civilization which is outside and above all temporary questions of policy, you must infallibly think and act under the control of the man or men whose thought, in the times you deal with, coincides most nearly with your prejudices." [6]

He proclaimed his own "theory of the progress of civilization" in reviewing Von Holst's *Constitutional and Political History of the United States* for the *North American* just before he left Harvard.

> the people of the United States, as they pass further and further from the vital struggles which characterize this first period of their national history, are quite right in believing that, above all the details of human weakness and corruption, there will appear in more and more symmetry the real majesty and force of the national movement. If the historian will only consent to shut his eyes for a moment to the microscopic analysis of personal motives and idiosyncrasies, he cannot but become conscious of a silent pulsation that commands his respect, a steady movement that resembles in its mode of operation the mechanical action of Nature herself.[7]

Writing to a friend in 1876 Adams termed this his "centennial oration." [8] He gave the oration its monumental utterance in his

history and Mr. Lodge the Federalist or 'aristocratic' side." Swift, however, found little in the rigorous impartiality of his teacher to confirm this rumor and, in fact, became pro-Federalist before he had completed Adams' course; "A Course in History at Harvard College in the Seventies," *Proceedings of the Massachusetts Historical Society, 52* (1918), 74.

5. See, for example, *History, 1,* 302; *2,* 76 f., 80, 117; *3,* 3, 17, 123, 137, 168, 350.
6. Feb. 1, 1878; Ford, *1,* 305.
7. *NAR, 123* (1876), 361.
8. Aug. 23, 1876; Ford, *1,* 296.

History and simultaneously eulogized the greatness of his family. "In 1815 for the first time Americans ceased to doubt the path they were to follow. Not only was the unity of their nation established, but its probable divergence from older societies was also well defined." [9] The silent pulsation of nationality overran whatever obstacles either the Republican administrations or the New England Federalists threw before it.

What better period could the historian have picked to investigate those energies distinguishing the American democracy from all other types of government than that moment when the democracy became a nation, when it finally flung aside both foreign domination and its own internal doubts to assert the power of that larger community of interest which posterity has simplified into the "era of good feeling"? What better era for an Adams at least? Even though internal disaffections reappeared, to culminate eventually in the Civil War, this son of New England saw southern disunion as but another of the futile attempts to reverse the inevitable course of nationalism. "What Calhoun really defended was, not State rights, but the slave power; and what the North really had to fear was, not State rights, for if Calhoun had become President he would in all probability have been as strong a centralizer as Jefferson, but the perversion of the Constitution to the interests of slavery instead of those of freedom." [10] To Adams, once the American people had committed themselves wholeheartedly to their nationalism, men like Jefferson, Pickering, and Calhoun could at most pervert but never destroy the Constitution so long as the nation itself existed.

"New England learned then [in 1815], once for all, not to trifle with the Constitution and with the Union." [11] In the course of time the South also learned this lesson.

As early as 1881 Adams was at work on the first chapters of his *History*. In this year he wrote the librarian of Harvard, from whom he had received some newspapers of the period around 1800, that he desired further shipments of periodicals and books to give him an insight into banking practices, educational methods, medical knowledge, and "a *good* sermon of that date, if such a thing existed . . ."

9. *History*, 9, 220.
10. *NAR, 123* (1876), 360.
11. *Ibid.*, p. 358.

Thus far my impression is that America in 1800 was not far
from the condition of England under Alfred the Great; that
the conservative spirit was intensely strong in the respectable
classes, and that there was not only indifference but actual
aggressive repression towards innovation . . . I should wish
to correct this impression. Did Harvard or Yale show anything
to the contrary *before* 1800? I can see that Philadelphia was
reasonably liberal and active-minded; was any other part of
the country equally so? Was there a steam-engine in the United
States? [12]

Not until two years after this request of Adams did John Bach
McMaster publish the initial volume of his *History of the People
of the United States* which was destined to awaken the majority
of American historians to the need for social history.[13]

Although McMaster and Adams were certainly unaware of
one another's research, each coincidentally derived inspiration
from Macaulay. McMaster certainly, for he admitted his debt; [14]
Adams less certainly, but in portraying the simplicity of American society in 1800 he must have recalled Macaulay's picture of
the even simpler state of England in 1685. Both historians rather
exaggerated the primitivism of the past. Macaulay had made a
study of population "one of the first objects of the inquirer" into
social history. With more directness than his mentor, Adams
opened his first volume, "According to the census of 1800, the
United States of America contained 5,308,483 persons. In the
same year the British Islands contained upwards of fifteen millions; the French Republic, more than twenty-seven millions."

12. Sept. 27, 1881; Ford, *1*, 329 f.
13. *A History of the People of the United States, from the Revolution to the
Civil War* (8 vols., New York, Appleton, 1883–1913); William R. Taylor, "Historical Bifocals on the Year 1800," *New England Quarterly, 23* (1950), 172–186,
contrasts the types of materials and methods used by Adams and McMaster in
their discussions of the United States in 1800.
14. Eric F. Goldman, *John Bach McMaster, American Historian* (Philadelphia,
University of Pennsylvania Press, 1943), pp. 13, 16, 45, 109, 119–127. McMaster
brought his first volume to completion with great secrecy lest he be anticipated in
his idea of a social history of the United States (p. 36). Contrast this provincial
attitude with Adams' realization that the idea of social history was well established. See *NAR, 121* (1875), 220, where he casually stated that "All ages have
agreed in considering the public acts of men and states as forming the ground-
work of history. Upon this foundation moderns have built two upper stories, so
to speak; they have made it almost essential that every history nowadays should
contain an account of the modes of life and another of the modes of thought, which
characterized the period described."

Both historians then discussed (and in roughly the same order) the wilderness condition of society, the state of its agriculture as compared to industry, and the rustic character of its inhabitants. Each then moved from city to city: Adams from Boston, southward, to Charleston, Macaulay from the commercial towns, through shire and recreational centers, to London. Each paid marked attention to economic life, civic improvements, transportation, and communication before turning to intellectual life. Macaulay closed with a brief notice of the "great body of the people," Adams with a chapter on "American Ideals." [15] Where Macaulay had noted that "the noblest of Protestant temples was slowly rising on the ruins of the old Cathedral of St. Paul," Adams remarked the "shapeless, unfinished Capitol" appearing above the swamps of the Potomac. When each came to measure what Adams called the "conservative habit of mind," each recounted the hostile reception accorded the first experiments with the steam engine. And each observed that, had the public accepted steam navigation, then "wind and tide" (both used the phrase) [16] would have seriously inconvenienced man no longer.

A letter written by Adams to his publisher in 1888 further suggested Macaulay's influence on the first two chapters of the *History*.

Ought these chapters to be set apart and headed *Introduction*, or ought they to run directly into the narrative? The question has greatly perplexed me. I do not fancy Introduc-

15. Minor differences do occur in the order in which the two historians treated their topics, as might be expected where the influence is of a general rather than a specific nature, notably in respect to transportation and everyday customs of the common people. Furthermore, after his discussion of population, Macaulay mentions the police, taxation, the inefficiency of the army and navy, and the wealth of a few nobles, topics either ignored by Adams or reserved for the main body of his *History*. See Sir Charles Firth, *A Commentary on Macaulay's History of England* (London, Macmillan, 1938), p. 116, for a brief account of the topical arrangement of Macaulay's third chapter. Among the books in Adams' library at the Massachusetts Historical Society there is a preliminary outline for all of Adams' introductory chapters, together with notations as to some of his sources. The outline appears in a stiff-covered notebook simply stamped "Records" on the spine. Adams himself identified another notebook—similar, although not identical with the first, and without any label on the spine—as "Note Book/ Manners and Customs/ Aug. 1877." Under Adams' heading "Notes on American Travellers" there follow 57 pages of comments by foreign observers who visited America. These pages are in turn followed by 29 more on opinions of the United States by Englishmen in England, headed "English Memoirs." Collected while Adams was in England in 1877, a number of these excerpts appear among the first few chapters of the *History*.

16. *History, 1,* 30, 65, 67.

tions. I see that most of the historians had the same feeling. Gibbon ran his introductory chapters into his narrative, and Macaulay actually broke off his narrative to insert his introductory chapter. On the other hand I admit that my first seven or eight chapters are wholly introductory, not only to my sixteen years but also to the century. They ought to stand by themselves.[17]

Surprising that a matter seemingly so trivial should have perplexed Adams. Such bewilderment disclosed a conflict, however slight, between his desire for an aesthetic unity and his demand for scholarly precision. It also hinted at the extent to which Adams and Macaulay parted company in their concepts of social history.

Macaulay employed his third chapter as mere descriptive background, lest "the subsequent narrative [be] unintelligible or uninstructive." Adams, on the other hand, conceived of his opening chapters as giving a cross section of American society at the year 1800, introducing therefore not merely his "sixteen years" but the "century" as well. Hence his title assumes special significance. After choosing his publisher Adams drew up a list of specifications, among them: "Every pair of volumes to make a separate work with titlepage and index." [18] At the publisher's request Adams reluctantly compromised to the extent of permitting the consecutive numbering of his volumes on the spine, provided that the volumes showed by dates the period covered in each pair. Thus the binding of the first edition shows the invariable title *History of the United States* followed by (*1800–1804*), Volumes 1, 2; (*1805–1809*), Volumes 3, 4; and so on. The title pages show Adams' original conception of a series of volumes in pairs with the invariable *History of the United States of America* modified four times in the course of the nine volumes to match each of the four administrations under consideration. *History of the United States of America during the First Administration of Thomas Jefferson*, Volume 1, Volume 2; *History . . . during the Second Administration of Thomas Jefferson*, Volume 1, Volume 2; *History . . . during the First Administration of James Madison*, again Volume 1, Volume 2; *History . . . during the Second Ad-*

17. Dec. 19, 1888; unpublished letter in the files of Charles Scribner's Sons. In an earlier letter dated Nov. 26, 1888, Adams unsuccessfully opposed the use of chapter headings for his *History* in the interest of simplifying the pages by noting that "Neither Macaulay nor Mahan used Chapter-headings."

18. July 12, 1888; same source.

ministration of James Madison, which Adams had planned for
two volumes, but which ran to three. So the awkward titles ran.

When pressed by Scribner's before publication for an explanation of this cumbersome bibliographical device Adams replied through Theodore Dwight, his research assistant at the
time, that he considered "each pair of volumns [*sic*] as a distinct
publication to stand by itself." If, Dwight's letter went on, the
volumes were all to appear at once, one might have numbered them
consecutively; then he added that when the volumes "come to be
issued as a complete work together, new title-pages will be provided
and a distinct, continuous numbering of [the] volumes." Finally
in 1890 Adams did give Scribner's permission in "rearranging
the nine volumes" to use a "consecutive title page (if you like)," [19]
by which time the publisher understandably preferred to use
plates already on hand.

Aside from indicating the difficulties which any publisher confronted in accepting a manuscript from Adams, this tortuous
correspondence indicated that Adams essentially saw his study of
the Jefferson and Madison administrations not as a self-contained
entity but as four increments to a much larger history of American nationality. He eventually compromised with his publisher's
demands, to be sure, but only reluctantly, and not completely
until 1890 when, with the prospect of a reprinting of the early
volumes, the awkwardness of the original idea must have struck
him forcibly.[20] As he wrote quite sincerely in 1899, his work "was
merely an Introduction to our history during the Nineteenth
Century," a "fixed and documented starting-point" on which the
"real History that one would like to write, was to be built." The
"merits or demerits" of his work would appear "only when the
structure, of which it was the foundation, was raised." Not, be it
noted, that subsequent investigation might prove the faultiness
of his work, for his *must* be the foundation of the structure. But
when other historians had completed the task which he had begun,
then the resulting *History of the United States of America—*

19. The information on the numbering of the volumes of the *History* is contained
in unpublished letters dated Jan. 30, 1889 (cited), Aug. 21, 1889, Dec. 27, 1889, and
Jan. 1, 1890 (cited); files of Charles Scribner's Sons. The first three letters were
written by Theodore Dwight, the fourth by Adams. The letters uncited contain
the information on the contrasting numbering of spines and title pages as summarized in the preceding paragraph.

20. Although they were apparently not immediately reprinted; see above, p.
50, n. 16.

far larger than his own nine volumes—would prove the validity both of his hopes and of his premises.

As he had opened the *History* with a cross section of the American society of 1800, so he closed his nine volumes with another cross section of 1817. This comparison recorded some progress during the sixteen years of the two Republican administrations; but Adams held out no guarantee of endlessly upward progress as Macaulay had done. On the contrary, the nine volumes terminated in the well-known series of questions.[21] If the queries disclosed Adams' skepticism, his tentative conclusions on national progress evinced his hope.

In short, Adams saw the history of American nationality as a graph, capable of cross-sectional measurement here and there in its progression, until the future appeared by mere extension of the line. Is this presupposing too much on slender evidence? After all, a series of letters to his publisher in the late eighties and another letter in 1899 hardly suffice to draw a parallel so strikingly similar to that of Adams' later speculation. Fortunately the *History* itself provides further testimony that when Adams wrote it he already thought in graphical metaphors; moreover, he already hinted that the extension of an established trend would automatically reveal future events. "Young as the nation was," he wrote in the third chapter of his first volume, "it had already produced an American literature bulky and varied enough to furnish some idea of its probable qualities in the future, and the intellectual condition of the literary class in the United States at the close of the eighteenth century could scarcely fail to suggest both the successes and the failures of the same class in the nineteenth." [22] Or another aside, this time his assertion in the sixth volume that the centralization of American government seemed to advance in a series of twelve-year cycles of "energy" so rhythmically that "a child could calculate the result of a few more such returns." If a child could predict the result on governmental centralization of a few more swings of the national pendulum, certainly the mature historian might reasonably expect to predict the result of the "mechanical evolution" of society in other spheres. "With almost the certainty of a mathematical formula, knowing the rate of increase of population and of wealth, [the American people] could read in advance their economical history for at least

21. See above, p. 16.
22. *History, 1,* 75.

a hundred years." Perhaps they could, although it might be doubted that the "movement of thought, more interesting than the movement of population or of wealth, was equally well defined." By 1814, Adams eventually generalized, "the character of people and government was formed; the lines of their activity were fixed." [23]

Dangling the prospect of large-scale prediction before his readers, Adams would disconcertingly snatch away the prize, as when he closed the *History* with the assertion that his final series of questions required for answer "another century of experience." So his recurrent suggestions as to the predictive possibilities of history remained asides. Suddenly proposed, then abruptly dropped as though the historian could see no further beyond the documents than Jefferson or Madison, these asides were the more significant of Adams' thinking for their casualness. It is just such asides, mere intimations as they are, which give even the perfunctory reader of the *History* that sense of deeper meanings than appear on its deceptively limpid surface. Repeatedly, but especially in the opening and closing sections, the *History* reveals the impatient tug of generalization at the tether of its evidence. Yet the generalizations never quite appear. Once again Adams "rather suggests than asserts" them. An essential part of his belief that in scientific history the documents disclosed their own conclusions, it was even more an essential part of his oracular personality. He loved to toy with ambiguities, suggesting but never quite asserting their meaning. Under the circumstances it is perhaps best not to be too explicit where he himself was not.

Perhaps, then, the explicitness of the neat parallel between the graph in the *History* and the graph which would come in later life needs modification. Say only that the theme of the *History* is American nationalism. It clearly suggests the notion of linear progress, or at least of progression. It indicates that this progression is measurable not only in the past but in the future as well. And finally, it contains, at least as asides, the notion of graphical metaphor. All these concepts were prophetic for Adams' subsequent writings.

23. *Ibid., 6,* 123; *9,* 224, 174, 175, 195; in *5,* 167, he suggested that society might drift toward "growth or decay"; see also below, p. 117. Interestingly enough, Adams closed his *Education* by wondering whether Hay, King, and he might return on the centenary of his birthday to find a better world than the one they left.

If the Jefferson and Madison administrations supplied examples of the inevitability of the national ideal, the period of their presidencies also promised to indicate the kind of nation which Americans would develop in contrast to Europeans. Interrupting work on his first chapters in May, 1881, to congratulate Lodge on his *Short History of the English Colonies in America*, Adams observed,

> If fault is to be found, I am inclined, in going over the same ground a little later, to put it on the extreme monotony of the subject, and I have pretty much made up my mind not to attempt giving interest to the society of America in itself, but to try for it by way of contrast with the artificial society of Europe, as one might contrast a stripped prize-fighter with a life-guardsman in helmet and breastplate, jack-boots and a big black horse. The contrast may be made dramatic, but not the thing. This is to be, however, the acid test of my own composition.[24]

Contrasts were a favorite device both in Adams' thought and in his artistry. Those in the *History* comprise a pallid, yet most significant, prelude to his dramatic juxtaposition of the twelfth and twentieth centuries in *Chartres* and the *Education*. He contrasted the moral character of the principal leaders during the Jeffersonian period. Through this opposition he suggested a contrast in sectional characteristics. Finally he meant to contrast the society of the United States with that of Europe. Much later, in 1908, he wrote to William James deprecating his *Education* in terms strikingly similar to those in his letter to Lodge some thirty-five years earlier. "It is the old story of an American drama. You can't get your contrasts and backgrounds." [25] Perhaps he was not thinking solely of the *Education* in this confession, for in the *History* too he had attempted contrasts only partially realized, and then only after some exaggeration.

While the opposition of American and European societies had its dramatic purpose, the juxtaposition of prize fighter and lifeguardsman indicated an underlying contrast in energy as well. Adams made this explicit in the *History:* "Stripped for the hardest work, every muscle firm and elastic, every ounce of brain ready for use, and not a trace of superfluous flesh on his nervous and

24. May 21, 1881; Ford, *1,* 328 f.
25. Feb. 11, 1908; *ibid., 2,* 490.

supple body, the American stood in the world a new order of man."

> Compared with this lithe young figure, Europe was actually in decrepitude. Mere class distinctions, the *patois* or dialect of the peasantry, the fixity of residence, the local costumes and habits marking a history that lost itself in the renewal of identical generations, raised from birth barriers which paralyzed half the population. Upon this mass of inert matter rested the Church and State, holding down activity of thought. Endless wars withdrew many hundred thousand men from production, and changed them into agents of waste; . . . behind this stood aristocracies, sucking their nourishment from industry . . . pressing on the energies and ambition of society with the weight of an incubus. Picturesque and entertaining as these social anomalies were, they were better fitted for the theatre or for a museum of historical costumes than for an active workshop preparing to compete with such machinery as America would soon command. From an economical point of view, they were as incongruous as would have been the appearance of a medieval knight in helmet and armor, with battle-axe and shield, to run the machinery of Arkwright's cotton-mill; but besides their bad economy they also tended to prevent the rest of society from gaining a knowledge of its own capabilities . . . Where Voltaire and Priestley failed, common men could not struggle; the weight of society stifled their thought. In America the balance between conservative and liberal forces was close; but in Europe conservatism held the physical power of government.[26]

Students of European history had necessarily concentrated on the whims of such arbitrary leaders as Napoleon. Not Jefferson, but Napoleon, was the real villain in the *History*. Ambitious, restless, selfish, energetic, ignorant in many spheres, with a "moral sense which regarded truth and falsehood as equally useful modes of expression,—an unprovoked war or secret assassination as equally natural forms of activity . . .": such was Adams' Napoleon.[27] Nothing nearly so damning appeared about either Jefferson or Madison. While Adams criticized their practical politics, he never denied their sincerity of purpose or the enlightened

26. *History, 1,* 159, 160 ff.
27. *Ibid.,* p. 334.

impulses whence this sincerity had sprung, with the single major exception of their Florida policy. In attacking the devious methods by which the two Republican presidents sought to defraud Spain of territory through what amounted to the bribery of France, Adams insisted that the Virginians lost their "moral leadership" in respect to this issue.[28] Of course the Florida intrigue could be dismissed as an episode, or even condoned insofar as the Republican presidents sought by seemingly the only means at their disposal to secure a peninsula for the American people which by the nature of its location would inevitably fall to the United States. The Florida policy was to Adams their only major lapse in moral leadership, a quality which Napoleon lacked in respect to every issue.

The necessity of concentrating on the kind of despotism represented by Napoleon deprived European history of most of its significance. Possessing all the "advantages of European movement and color," few historians had succeeded "in enlivening or dignifying the lack of motive, intelligence, and morality, the helplessness characteristic of many long periods in the face of crushing problems, and the futility of human efforts to escape from difficulties religious, political, and social." [29] Exaggerating, Adams found "even the history of England was chiefly the story of war." [30] Closely bound to a warring continent—and indeed almost as guilty of instigating conflict as any of her national neighbors—England necessarily had consumed much time in fighting.

> For a thousand years every step in the progress of England had been gained by sheer force of hand and will. . . . the English people . . . had grown into a new human type,— which might be brutal, but was not weak; which had little regard for theory, but an immense and just respect for facts. America considered herself to be a serious fact, and expected England to take her at her own estimate of her own value . . . England required America to prove by acts what virtue existed in her conduct or character which should exempt her from the common lot of humanity, or should entitle her to escape the tests of manhood . . . Jefferson had chosen his own methods of attack and defense; but he could not require

28. *Ibid.*, *4*, 339; also *3*, 115.
29. *Ibid.*, *9*, 223.
30. *Ibid.*

England or France to respect them before they had been tried.[31]

England might boast more democracy than all other states in Europe. Even so, Adams could not forget the somewhat exaggerated impression of English aristocracy which he had received at the legation. One day he would show through no less than five chapters in the *Education* how the British aristocracy and monied classes had opposed the pro-Union sentiments of workingmen, and how aristocratic prejudice had prevailed in British policy until altered by the force of Yankee arms.

Here, then, were the types: Europeans made brutal by the whims of arbitrary rule, since their "systems were permanent in nothing except the general law, that whatever other character they might possess they must always be chiefly military." [32] On the other hand, both republican traditions and the lucky accident of geography permitted Americans to develop naturally. In tracing this natural development of a people the scientific historian could sense "something ultimate" [33] in nationalism. Such at least was Adams' picture of European despotism, and such the measure of his affection for his native country.

His view of American nationalism was, of course, familiar. Since their establishment as a nation Americans had never tired of painting their good fortune in hues all the brighter for being laid against the somber background of European oppression. This conviction of the uniqueness of the American destiny had accounted for much of Jefferson's program. Thus far Jefferson and his historian agreed. Adams questioned only whether force did not require "equivalent energy" [34] in opposition. Jefferson and Madison "as types of character, if not as sources of power," stood as the primary representatives in our history of an expression of force, nonmilitary in character, to fit the essentially nonmilitary aspect of a democracy so isolated from the rest of the world that it believed it could rid itself of war. Ironically enough, Americans feared war because they might win almost as much as they feared to lose, for victory in battle might bind this country to the military despotism characteristic of Europe.[35]

31. *Ibid., 4,* 74.
32. *Ibid., 9,* 222.
33. *Ibid.,* p. 225.
34. *Ibid., 4,* 289.
35. *Ibid.,* p. 211.

Could geographical isolation have combined with the Republican commercial policy and Jefferson's plea to "palliate and endure" in such a way as to bring obsequiousness from both France and England? Adams answered in the negative. The nation realized its ideals only when it backed them with practical force. Enlightened as was Jefferson's theory of government, it "had the virtues and faults of a priori reasoning."

> Far in advance as it was, of any other political effort of its time, and representing, as it doubtless did, all that was most philanthropic and all that most boldly appealed to the best instincts of mankind, it made too little allowance for human passions and vices; it relied too absolutely on the power of interest and reason as opposed to prejudice and habit; it proclaimed too openly to the world that the sword was not one of its arguments, and that peace was essential to its existence.[36]

From his opening sentences in which he measured the populations of England, France, and the United States, Adams repeatedly appraised two types of power—the energy of the American people and that of individuals who seized control of European nations principally for their own ends and, by their actions, forced both their own people and even other peoples to pursue an existence highly military in character. This contrast gives a second broad reason for the drama of the *History* to those who will patiently follow Adams' microscopic examination of the documents. First, the complex unfolding of human thought, groping toward ends which are constantly redefined by some internal transformation, by collision with the thought of other men, or by outward circumstance; then, the larger conflict between the energies of two contrasting types of nationalism. Already, in the *History*, Adams hinted at his later preoccupation with the influence of varied types of energy in history.

To follow Adams' power analogy further: By what means might a nation wield energy? Had Adams answered this question with reference to his vague definition in the *Education* of historical "force" as anything that "does, or helps to do work," [37] his reply would certainly have included much that was commonplace. For example, politics, diplomacy, law, armies—these did work, as

36. *Gallatin*, p. 272.
37. P. 474. *Degradation: Letter*, p. 156.

even the most conventional historian would admit. So, for that matter, did personality, chance, delay, etiquette, and a thousand other causes, the extensiveness of the list measuring both the subtlety of the historian's mind and the range of his experience. If Adams' definition was too large to have much meaning, at least it can serve as a convenient starting point to consider three other forces evident in the *History*, none of them unique with Adams certainly, but of particular significance for his nine volumes. Adams was especially interested in finance, science, and finally, underlying all other forces, the energy of a people. One might more properly term the people as a pressure compelling those who wielded the instruments of power to do the work of history; but Adams considered the people in a more positive sense. He saw the people as at once the embodiment and the culmination of all national power. He saw them as he later viewed the Virgin, as a kind of mystical prime mover in history. As such, the people almost mechanically determined national destiny.

The power of finance makes a convenient starting point, and in this instance finance is more appropriate than economics, for although financial policy developed from economic considerations, Adams' interest in business conditions lay primarily in the effect of fluctuations in popular prosperity on governmental planning. Hence Gallatin's prominence in the *History* as the statesman most responsible for the practical force of Jefferson's theories.

This emphasis on the power of finance beneath governmental energy lay buried, like a vein of ore, within Adams' earliest writings. As the geologist could trace the mineral lode by sampling, so we might track this single concept back until it disappeared in the conglomerate of youth's half-formed notions: in 1880 the assertion in *Democracy* that "there are two officers, at least, whose service is real—the President and his Secretary of the Treasury"; [38] for 1879 the *Gallatin* of course; then back through articles for the *North American* like the "Session" essays, "American Finance, 1865–1869," "The New York Gold Conspiracy," and "The Legal-Tender Act"; back once more to the legation, where Adams wrote two essays on British finance; and finally

---

38. *Democracy*, p. 182. Later in the *History, 1*, 218, Adams stated that the president, the secretary of state and the secretary of the treasury were the "officers whose responsibility was greatest."

to the youth of twenty-three who left London one weekend for a trip to Manchester, where he studied the effect of the Confederate cotton boycott on British economy. Here the striation of one idea disappears—but disappears, it would seem, approximately at its point of origin. With the near success of a boycott designed to close England's textile mills until she joined the southern cause, Adams undoubtedly sensed the potency of economic power as a means of implementing national policy. In this juxtaposition of economics and military force during the Civil War the minister's private secretary observed at firsthand a variant of the conflict which he later analyzed in the *History*.

Having traced this theme backward, from historian to private secretary, we might now reverse the process, beginning in 1861. It was in December of this year that the *Boston Daily Courier* postponed Adams' journalistic career by carelessly dispelling the anonymity of "A Visit to Manchester." About two months earlier he had begun his essay on John Smith, over which he dawdled for a year, until he finally reported to Palfrey in November, 1862, that he had "dished out our friend Capt. John" to his "satisfaction." He had planned to publish in England but after an adverse criticism from an English scholar sent the manuscript to Palfrey who was to pass it on to Adams' brother John for safekeeping. An adverse opinion and the recollection of his recent humiliation in journalism must have made Adams cautious. Even after Palfrey's approval of the article, Adams confessed that he "should hesitate a long time before attacking so respected a gentleman, as a *coup d'essai* in print." But timidity about publication was joined to boredom with what he termed his "literary toy" even as he worked on it. The very month, March, 1863, in which Adams told Palfrey that he had laid aside "antiquarian researches" for new activities saw him elected to the St. James Club. In April he met Charles Milnes Gaskell, who became among his closest friends; thereafter he began an active social life with a liberal and literary coterie.[39]

Temporarily both the career in journalism and that in history stopped. Generally snubbed during the first two years of his London stay, Adams gladly moved into English society. Perhaps with equal joy he again postponed thought of a future vocation. Society and miscellaneous study must easily have filled whatever time he

39. The letters referred to are dated between Mar. 20, 1862, and Jan. 15, 1864; Cater, pp. 14–22. Samuels, p. 127.

could spare from his unofficial duties as private secretary during the diplomatic crisis centering in the episode of the Confederate rams. But as the months flew by and as Union victories dampened the ardor of British officialdom for the Confederate cause, the diplomatic crises diminished in both magnitude and frequency. Henry now had more leisure to write and study, and, equally important, more leisure to contemplate the awful possibility that with his father's recall he faced unemployment.

What to do? Publish, of course. Journalism was impossible. History was not. First, he reluctantly revived the essay on Smith. When he posted this essay, together with "British Finance in 1816," to Palfrey, he enclosed a letter to say, "I would be greatly obliged by your reading the second essay, (I care little about the Smith) . . ." [40] Literary toys interested Adams less than a vocation and prodded by the more practical-minded Charles, who had originally suggested the trip to Manchester,[41] Henry doubtless saw public finance as the means toward a career, whether in government or in journalism. Following "British Finance in 1816," he immediately wrote "The Bank of England Restriction" on the suspension of specie payments in 1797 and their resumption in 1821. Although these weighty essays may seem excessively historical, they doubtless had the ulterior purpose of preparing Adams for an active life in Washington on his return to America. The first article dealt with the problems of postwar finance, the second with the problem of specie payments, which was also among the major issues confronting the American government after the Civil War.[42] No wonder Adams deprecated his essay on John Smith by the time he dispatched it to the *North American*. Small wonder, too, that when he arrived once more in the United States he turned to journalism rather than history.

"As for finance," Adams wrote a friend in 1869 from his Washington post as journalist, "I carry buckets of it about with me, and duck it over the head of everyone I meet." [43] Everyone included those subscribers to the quarterlies who waded through the further articles on finance which he wrote in Washington. One of his essays—"The Legal-Tender Act," written in collabora-

40. Aug. 23, 1866; Cater, p. 31.
41. *Cycle, 1,* 33–37, 43 ff. See above, p. 28, n. 19. Samuels, pp. 112 f.
42. Although Adams' article acknowledged that English experience in respect to the resumption of specie payments was not comparable to the problems faced in the United States. *NAR, 105* (1867), especially 404 f., 434. Samuels, p. 159.
43. July 11, 1869; Ford, *1,* 164.

tion with Francis A. Walker, then in Washington supervising
the 1870 census—requires further notice. It was here that the
name "Gallatin" made its first conspicuous appearance in Adams'
writing; not Albert Gallatin, to be sure, but James, his second
son. Like his distinguished father, James Gallatin had become a
banker, and during the course of debate on the legal-tender issue,
he had appeared at the capital to suggest a plan for the immediate
resumption of specie payments. As the "only man who seems to
have had a clear and practical knowledge of what the occasion
required," [44] James Gallatin appeared as the hero of this essay,
just as Albert Gallatin later emerged as the most competent statesman in the *History*. James Gallatin had died before Adams obtained the family manuscripts from Albert Rolaz Gallatin, the
"only now surviving son and literary executor," as Adams noted
in the preface to the *Gallatin*. The second Albert Gallatin was
apparently in search of some scholar to work on his father's papers,
since he paid Adams' expenses.[45] When he gave Adams access to
the family papers Gallatin was not personally acquainted with
him, for having finally received a copy of the completed life of his
father, he wrote in appreciation, "You were personally unknown
to me, but your name of Adams was all sufficient for me to place the
most implicit confidence in your discretion, integrity and talents." [46] Despite the sufficiency of his family name, certainly
Adams' praise of one of the Gallatin brothers, his proficiency on
questions of finance, and of course his teaching at Harvard must
also have played a part in his selection as editor and biographer.[47]

44. *NAR, 110* (1870), 307, 309, 314.
45. James Gallatin died in 1876; the information that Albert R. Gallatin fi-
nanced the preparation of the three volumes of letters and the biography of his
father comes from two of Adams' letters recently discovered by Wayne Andrews
during the process of arranging the Gallatin papers, now deposited in the New
York Historical Society. In one of these, dated Oct. 14, 1877, Adams wrote Gallatin
in part, "I enclose a memorandum of money advanced by me. I hope this will be all
I shall have to spend, but I may need a little more copying at Washington. We will
try to make the publisher refund it all, but as yet I have not sounded publishers."
L. Lawrence Gallatin—mentioned by Samuels, p. 293, as a member of the family
from whom Adams received permission to use the Gallatin papers—was no son of
the famous secretary, nor apparently any very close relation, since he is unmentioned in William P. Bacon, *Ancestry of Albert Gallatin* (New York, Tobias A.
Wright, 1916); see following footnote.
46. This statement by Albert R. Gallatin occurs in a letter dated May 27, 1879,
which Ernest Samuels recently unearthed from among the books in Adams' library at the Massachusetts Historical Society and very kindly communicated to
me. This letter has, Samuels admits, forced him to modify his account.
47. Samuels also suggests that the mediation of George Bancroft may have

If finance appeared as a force in the *History*, so did science, as might have been expected of the grandson of John Quincy Adams and the eager pupil of both Louis Agassiz and Charles Lyell. The science learned by Adams was of a cosmological sort. He never assimilated the experimental point of view. Agassiz had stressed the need for observation, and many of his pupils had absorbed this lesson; but his religious convictions coupled with a dramatic flair for rhetoric led Agassiz into sweeping generalizations which opposed, with idealistic metaphysics, materialistic explanations for evolution and geology. Although Adams discounted the religious bias of his teacher, he was strongly attracted by Agassiz's flights into ultimate cause, far more than by any instruction at Harvard in the painstaking niceties of the experimental method.[48]

Even his contact with Sir Charles Lyell while he served at the London legation did little to further his appreciation of the scientific method. It was rather scientific syntheses which continued to catch his attention in England. "You may think all this nonsense," the London student wrote his soldier brother in 1862,

> but I tell you these are great times. Man has mounted science, and is now run away with. I firmly believe that before many centuries more, science will be the master of man. The engines he will have invented will be beyond his strength to control. Some day science may have the existence of mankind in its power, and the human race commit suicide by blowing up the world. Not only shall we be able to cruize in space, but I see no reason why some future generation shouldn't walk off like a beetle with the world on its back, or give it another rotary motion so that every zone should receive in turn its due portion of heat and light.[49]

Adams' statement that man might "commit suicide by blowing up the world" anticipated by more than four decades a similar de-

---

helped his protégé's cause, a likely hypothesis since Albert R. Gallatin might very possibly have consulted with Bancroft in his search for a suitable editor and biographer. In his preface Adams expressed his gratitude to "his friendly adviser, George Bancroft," the only individual mentioned who contributed to the *Gallatin* by giving general assistance rather than specific information. Bancroft later read and commented on the privately printed editions of the *History*.

48. Samuels, pp. 17–22, gives an excellent account of Adams' education in science while he was at Harvard, although I disagree somewhat with Samuels on the influence of Lyell on Adams. See below, pp. 178–81 and nn. 51, 52, p. 192 and n. 85.

49. Apr. 11, 1862; *Cycle, 1,* 135.

nouement for humanity in his *Rule*. But if science might also
provide the means to furnish every zone with its due portion of
heat and light, then the universe—and man's place in it—looked
decidedly more beneficent to the young student in London than it
later seemed to the valetudinarian in Washington.

As private secretary he eagerly welcomed the new scientific
ideas dominating progressive thought in midcentury England.
The prospect of social reform based on an optimistic view of
science challenged his imagination. In the *Education* Adams recalled that he "became a Comteist [*sic*], within the limits of evolution." [50] And with this philosophic bent he entered "professordom." In a letter written prior to his arrival in Cambridge the
new teacher snickered behind the back of Harvard's Board of
Overseers: "my predecessor was turned out because he was a
Comtist!!!" [51]

As a Comtist within the limits of evolution Adams embraced
Comte's tripartite division of history into a theological, a metaphysical, and a positive phase. The French philosopher had stated
that society progressed through successive periods, with each
period in history characterized by new methods of examining the
universe. Thus, for the largest part of human history, religion
or fetishism had colored man's observations about his universe.
Then, during the seventeenth and eighteenth centuries, metaphysical had replaced religious absolutes. Man increasingly explained his world no longer in terms of a divinity but in the
rationalistic vocabulary of the Enlightenment. Finally, by the
nineteenth century, Comte maintained, mankind had learned to
analyze phenomena so precisely and so incontrovertibly that real
knowledge of society was possible for the first time. To the bud-
ding Comtist in the American legation this slicing of history into
phases, which retained its powerful attraction for Adams throughout his life, undoubtedly appealed initially because of its positivistic climax. The idea that science might ultimately afford the
open sesame to history could hardly help but titillate. And the
excitement of the young secretary, who jokingly dramatized the
possibility of an equal apportionment of heat and light over all
the earth's surface, appeared in the *History*, subdued but evident

50. *Education,* p. 225; Adams rejected the Catholic leanings of Comte's later
thinking, as did Mill. See Samuels, pp. 128–135, for a discussion of the influence
of the "new science" on Adams.

51. Sept. 29, 1870; Ford, *1*, 194. John Fiske was the "predecessor."

in the numerous analogies from physics sprinkled through its pages. The idea that American democracy represented some sort of ultimate stage in nationalism owed much to the social-scientific optimism of Comtian positivism; Adams' teaching at Harvard on the development of democratic institutions only reinforced from another point of view a conviction implicit in his youthful faith in science.

His emphasis on the power of circumstance over that of individuals particularly suited his analogies from physics. So did the linearism of his progression, especially because of his awareness of the elements of compulsion in every situation. But he specifically indicated the extent to which the physical energies of science might determine national destiny in his contrast of the *Chesapeake* with the *Clermont*. Less than two months after the disabled *Chesapeake* had limped into Hampton Roads following the historic assault of the *Leopard*, Robert Fulton's *Clermont* puffed triumphantly up the Hudson River.

> That the destinies of America must be decided in America was a maxim of true Democrats, but one which they showed little energy in reducing to practice. A few whose names could be mentioned in one or two lines,—men like Chancellor Livingston, Dr. Mitchell, Joel Barlow,—hailed the 17th of August, 1807, as the beginning of a new era in America,—a date which separated the colonial from the independent stage of growth . . .

Again the neat cleavage of history into stages—this time, significantly, a division based on physical energy.

> for on that day, at one o'clock in the afternoon, the steamboat "Clermont," with Robert Fulton in command, started on her first voyage. A crowd of bystanders, partly skeptical, partly hostile, stood about and watched the clumsy craft slowly forge its way at the rate of four miles an hour up the river; but Fulton's success left room for little doubt or dispute, except in minds impervious to proof. The problem of steam navigation, so far as it applied to rivers and harbors was settled, and for the first time America could consider herself mistress of her vast resources. Compared with such a step in her progress, the mediæval barbarisms of Napoleon and Spencer Perceval signified little more to her than the doings of

Achilles and Agamemnon. Few moments in her history were more dramatic than the weeks of 1807 which saw the shattered "Chesapeake" creep back to her anchorage at Hampton Roads, and the "Clermont" push laboriously up the waters of the Hudson; but the intellectual effort of bringing these two events together, and of settling the political and economical problems of America at once, passed the genius of the people. Government took no notice of Fulton's achievement, and the public for some years continued, as a rule, to travel in sailing packets and on flat-boats. The reign of politics showed no sign of ending. Fulton's steamer went its way, waiting until men's time should become so valuable as to be worth saving.[52]

To move the engines of war with this new power of science proved beyond the Americans' imagination in 1807. The Tenth Congress voted for the sailing vessel. "Fulton's steamer, the 'Clermont,' with a single gun would have been more effective for harbor defence than all the gunboats in the service, and if supplemented by Fulton's torpedoes would have protected New York from any line-of-battle ship; but President Jefferson, lover of science and of paradox as he was, suggested no such experiment."[53]

To Adams, who was openly skeptical of Jefferson's commercial system, science promised the only real power available to Jefferson in his attempt to coerce England and France, except of course the force of arms; and even science would be used so as to increase military might. Admittedly, Adams left Fulton's demonstration as a minor incident in his treatment of the War of 1812, for after all, his *History* was limited by history. But certainly Adams exploited, and rather insistently recurred to, an incident which the average political, constitutional, diplomatic, or even military historian might have missed. Perhaps he overexploited the Fulton episode; perhaps he exaggerated the possible effect of the steam warship on the outcome of the War of 1812. Whatever his exaggeration, the fact remained that, to Adams, Jefferson might have solved his dilemma in foreign affairs by matching the military force of Europe with an equivalent energy of his own. This force

52. *History, 4,* 134 f.
53. *Ibid.,* p. 161. On Adams' use of science and technology in the *History* see above, pp. 50, 77, 80, 83, below, pp. 127 f.; *History, 1,* 65–74, 171, 178; *2,* 290; *3,* 213–217; *5,* 215 f.; *7,* 318–330; *8,* 194–211; *9,* 171 f., 221, 227–236. Aside from these direct mentions of science or technology, Adams sprinkled scientific metaphors and analogies throughout the *History.*

could have been military or perhaps it could have been the product of science, which might have so extended military power as to constitute practically a force in its own right.

Here Adams was not quite fair to Jefferson. The commercial system almost attained its purpose when in 1812 Britain bowed to Madison's demands by repealing her Orders in Council against American shipping just five days after the United States had declared war. Speaking of the embargo as force, Adams had earlier admitted that

> the embargo, as an engine of coercion, needed a long period of time to produce a decided effect. The law of physics could easily be applied to politics; force could be converted only into its equivalent force. If the embargo—an exertion of force less violent than war—was to do the work of war, it must extend over a longer time the development of an equivalent energy.[54]

Under the circumstances Adams should have mentioned that had transoceanic communication been a matter of hours, as it was when he worked on his *History*, the War of 1812 might have been avoided and Jefferson's policy of "palliation and endurance" had its ultimate vindication within the very framework of Adams' concept of equivalent energy.

Yet if Adams unfairly ignored the force implicit in Jefferson's policy, he might quite correctly have held that any historical defense of the commercial system for what it accomplished too late could not meet the objection that a show of physical force might have produced an earlier change in British policy. Nor would such a defense have altered the fact that American nationalism was fused at the cannon mouth, much as Adams had averred for all the countries of Europe. It was; and then again, it was not. Americans supported the War of 1812 with wholehearted fervor only after it had ended; and once hostilities had ceased such popular support did not extend to a military system for the very good reason that none was necessary.

If Adams' metaphor of power be granted, then, political, diplomatic, constitutional, financial, scientific, and military forces converged at last on the central energy in Adams' *History*. All but leaderless, the people redeemed the blunders of their statesmen and stumbled through the War of 1812.

54. *History*, *4*, 289.

The Federalists were greatly and naturally perplexed at discovering the silent under-current which tended to grow in strength precisely as it encountered most resistance from events . . . Not so much the glories as the disgraces of the war roused public sympathy; not so much the love of victory as the ignominy of defeat, and the grinding necessity of supporting government at any cost of private judgment . . . The slow conviction that come what would the nation must be preserved, brought one man after another into support of the war, until the Federalists found their feet in quicksand.[55]

In his analysis of the most incomprehensibly bungled war in American history Adams discovered that vessels built in the private shipyards of the young republic and manned without the centralized control of an efficient admiralty immediately forced British insurance rates to prohibitive levels, an achievement which French privateers had sought in vain for twenty years; that the artillery on land and gunnery on sea of a nation at peace for more than three decades wrought more destruction than the guns of a monarchy almost continuously at war; and, finally, that the fortifications erected by graduates of the newly established West Point proved impregnable to the engineers of an army which had brought Napoleon to his knees.[56]

If the War of 1812 demonstrated the resourcefulness of the American people, it also showed the eagerness with which they abandoned the products of resourcefulness once the need for military power had passed. The American, Adams decided, saved himself from the curse of extremity, whether in the military, in morals, in religion, or in theory of government, by insisting upon only sufficient energy in any field to achieve practical results. Bold generalizations (and perhaps bolder in 1890 than they are today), they already implied that conventional history had not "many years to live." Weight of populace and a geographical isolation which permitted population to increase naturally and inevitably made all other forces mere "kicking and gesticulating" on the surface of this vast undercurrent.

Finance, science—and the energy of a vast people; it was this last and most generalized source of energy which particularly

55. *Ibid.*, 7, 69, 70.
56. *Ibid.*, 9, 228–236.

accounted for what Adams called the "scientific" aspect of his *History*. American democracy had "its scientific as well as its human side" and, according to Adams, "in American history the scientific interest was greater than the human. Elsewhere the student could study under better conditions the evolution of the individual, but nowhere could he study so well the evolution of a race. The interest of such a subject exceeded that of any other branch of science, for it brought mankind within sight of its own end." [57]

If, as he maintained, the study of race was the essence of history, then he revealed his scientific bent among his first few chapters describing national character, not in terms of its leaders but as the end result of "popular characteristics," of sectional "intellect," and of "American ideals." National character sprang from the people, even though they "adorned with imaginary qualities scores of supposed leaders, whose only merit was their faculty of reflecting a popular trait." As such the United States presented the historian with a history which, compared to that of Europe, was relatively undisturbed by the vagaries of personality. Here was history examined, as Adams hoped, "in the same spirit and by the same methods with which [one] studied the formation of a crystal." [58]

Of course the concept of national character was general to the nineteenth century, a product of the rise of nationalism with the corresponding decline of eighteenth-century cosmopolitanism. Where the historian with literary inclinations attempted to define national character from what he considered as typical episodes and heroes or from a patriotic approach to the history of particular countries, the scientifically minded historian sought a comparable definition in the slow, impersonal development of either institutions or some broad idea, both presumably larger than their demonstration in the history of any specific nation. If Buckle chose England to illustrate the ultimate phase of Western civilization, while Guizot picked France and Adams the United States, personal sentiment might have seemed too much a part of their selection to meet the standards of the physical and natural sciences. Nevertheless the history produced by these three revealed their quest for universal laws and processes operating through history according to a necessary pattern suggestive, to some historians at

57. *Ibid.,* p. 225.
58. *Ibid.,* p. 224.

least, of the aims of natural science. As long as historians could believe that society moved through inevitable stages toward some ultimate state—whether it was the Comtian progression from a theological, through a metaphysical, to a positivistic state; or the more generalized nineteenth-century notion of a progression from barbarism to civilization; [59] or some other—just so long could the historian believe it possible to study mankind by examining a single segment of human society. He need only demonstrate that his particular case study represented some ultimate in a necessary process. And if, as Adams believed, the trend in Western civilization had been toward democracy, then his case was good for using the United States as a laboratory for the investigation of mankind—at least for that substantial part of mankind within the Western tradition.

Because Adams' scientific approach to history not only embraced the idea of necessary stages in society but also involved the metaphoric notion of force, he snarled himself in difficulties. As a composite abstraction inevitably moving toward some predetermined stage, his people comprised the energy behind the actions of his statesmen. Hence, although he focused on the statesman, Adams demonstrated that a mysterious force outside statesmanship counted as the irresistible energy in history. To Adams this latter force was mysterious precisely because he could not rationally explain it through his selection of documents. Thus his nine volumes necessarily ended in irresolution. In a lifetime of paradox Adams contrived none greater than that implicit in his *History*. It was sufficient to account for his later allegations in the *Education* as to the pointlessness of conventional political history, although, like most of his paradoxical remarks, this complaint had its element of irrationality. Since he had particularly investigated the events of the Jefferson and Madison administrations in order to demonstrate that the idea of centralized nationalism had triumphed over all obstacles flung in its path, his ultimate conviction that the political aspects of his *History* proved nothing was somewhat perverse. They proved precisely what he set out to prove. If Adams never really answered the question of *how* nationalism had triumphed, but left the reason for its realization a paradox, he might have come at least a little closer to an explanation had he made a wider selection of documents.

59. On the concept of civilization see Charles A. Beard, *The American Spirit* (New York, Macmillan, 1942), chaps. i, ii, iii.

In Adams' *History* no crowds cheered at Jefferson's inaugural; no weary private stumbled across his well-kept battle plans; no celebrations greeted Jackson's victory at New Orleans. The abstraction "people" merely served as the repository for those other abstractions—popular characteristics, sectional intellect, and national ideas. Even as an abstraction Adams' awareness of the people had come slowly. Aloof throughout his life from what he finally called the "crowd," he disclosed an instinctive dislike of mobs in his early letters on European events to the *Boston Daily Courier* in 1860.[60] Typical of this aloofness, too, was his "Great Secession Winter," where some magical power embodied in the Constitution accounted for the ability of the nation to "bear and forebear" in the face of internal disunion.[61] With time, however, a series of circumstances in Adams' life modified, even if it did not eliminate, his insularity.

There was, first of all, his experience in the legation, where he witnessed the support of the Union cause by the working class. Still, the fervor with which he recorded his approval of popular sentiments in letters to Charles did not appear in his longer articles written in England. Their subjects of course—John Smith, British finance, and geology [62]—hardly called for any treatment of popular opinion; but the choice of subjects perhaps signified Adams' disinclination to venture outside the library to mingle with the mob. So did his gentlemanly existence in London, penetrated as it was by only such middle-class reformers as Cobden and Bright, and punctuated, so far as is known, by his semi-official visit to a Manchester factory and his official attendance at a labor union meeting. In the article which resulted from his visit to Manchester Adams devoted only two sentences to the working class: "The operatives were dirty, very coarsely dressed, and very stupid in looks; altogether much inferior to the American standard. About a quarter of the spindles were silent, and, as they told me, a corresponding number of the operatives discharged, to starve as they best might." In the report of the labor union meeting, once more, a single sentence was devoted to the audience, whom he found "very respectable in appearance, but generally bearing the mark of labor in the workshop and of intellectual

60. Samuels, pp. 72 f.

61. See above, pp. 27 f.

62. He undoubtedly also made extensive notes for his later essay, "The Declaration of Paris, 1861," unpublished until 1891, in his *Historical Essays* (New York, Scribners, 1891), pp. 237–278. See Samuels, p. 142.

cultivation rather at the expense of physical strength." [63] Little wonder that in the *Education*, when he looked back on his first visit to England in 1858 immediately after his graduation from Harvard, he should have recalled his aversion to the "journey up to London through Birmingham and the Black District."

> The plunge into darkness lurid with flames; the sense of un- known horror in this weird gloom which then existed nowhere else, and never had existed before, except in volcanic craters; the violent contrast between this dense, smoky, impenetrable darkness, and the soft green charm that one glided into, as one emerged—the revelation of an unknown society of the pit —made a boy uncomfortable . . . The boy ran away from it, as he ran away from everything he disliked.[64]

Yet his subsequent experience in the legation undoubtedly did make him more aware of the people, not with any sense of them as individuals or with any inkling of the real problems they faced but as a force, an underlying entity, the ultimate, if indistinct, source for both the ideas and the idealism motivating society. This awareness of the people appeared in his subsequent career as a Washington correspondent and particularly in an article on the civil service.[65] Here Adams indicated what became his fixed point of view toward the role of the people in reform. Once more he wrote from a constitutional bias. The practice of senatorial courtesy in respect to political appointments had robbed the ex- ecutive department of its independence, thus weakening the tradi- tional division of powers embodied in the Constitution. Although the "first five Presidents had in fact formed a continuous govern- ment," the executive had steadily lost that continuity of per- sonnel which alone permitted efficient administration. Presidents had become the mere "representatives of so many violent revolu- tions." Hence the reformer would only waste his time on existing parties, since the overthrow of a reformed party automatically

63. Arthur W. Silver, ed., "Henry Adams' 'Diary of a Visit to Manchester,'" *American Historical Review, 51* (1945), 84; see also p. 80 where he commented on the city as "dull and gloomy, from want of handsome private houses." Charles I. Glicksberg, "Henry Adams Reports on a Trades-Union Meeting," *New England Quarterly, 15* (1942), 725.

64. *Education*, pp. 72 f.

65. "Civil Service Reform," *NAR, 109* (1869), pp. 443–476. Quotations below cited from pp. 451, 474 f., 475.

undid the good. Instead, the reformer should appeal directly to the people. Some three decades before the muckrakers advocated a similar program, Adams stated the "true policy of reformers" as that of attacking "corruption in all its holes, to drag it before the public eye, to dissect it and hold the diseased members up to popular disgust, to give the nation's conscience no rest nor peace until mere vehemence of passion overcomes the sluggish self-complacency of the public mind." Intellectuals like Adams would awaken the conscience of the sluggish multitude. For such intellectuals Adams set a noble objective: "To build by slow degrees this deep foundation of moral conviction, to erect upon it a comprehensive and solid structure of reform, and to bequeath the result to posterity as a work not inferior in quality to that of the Republic's founders, is an aim high enough to satisfy the ambition of one generation." Adams' ideal in reform was nothing less than that ideal which, in the *Gallatin*, he later pronounced as necessary for the "highest statesmanship." [66]

He never altered his opinion that enlightened leadership should dominate the public will. Child of eighteenth-century concepts of stewardship and of their extension into the nineteenth, he was child of such as Burke, Gibbon, Taine, Guizot, Mill and Tocqueville. These authors still adorn those substantial fragments of Adams' library deposited at Western Reserve University and the Massachusetts Historical Society; but his special admiration for Mill and Tocqueville, while serving as his father's secretary in the legation, can stand for the others.

In the same letter in which he told his brother Charles that the "great principle of democracy is still capable of rewarding a conscientious servant," Henry fervently mentioned his study of "De Tocqueville and John Stuart Mill, the two high priests of our faith." From both, of course, the young secretary could have learned the virtues of democracy; from both, the tyranny of majorities. Tocqueville became Adams' "model, and I study his life and work as the Gospel of my private religion." [67] Tocqueville's classic analysis of democracy became a bible of English liberalism. John Stuart Mill enthusiastically heralded each volume on its appearance, while Henry Reeve, a friend of the Adams family in London, made the original English translation. Ponder-

66. See above, p. 68.
67. May 1, 1863; *Cycle, 1,* 281 f.

ing his gospel, the disciple could have supplemented his firsthand observations in England of the differences between aristocracy and democracy with Tocqueville's extensive comparison. With Tocqueville Adams would have willingly granted that aristocracies were a thing of the past and the increase in equalitarianism an "irresistible revolution which has advanced for centuries in spite of every obstacle." With him Adams would single out the United States as the "one country in the world where the great social revolution . . . seems to have nearly reached its natural limits." If there was achievement in this revolution, both Adams and his mentor perceived dangers too. Like Tocqueville his pupil might wag a warning finger that "none but attentive and clearsighted men perceive the perils with which equality threatens us." [68] And in Tocqueville's life, which according to his letter to Charles he also studied, Adams must have glimpsed that happy combination of scholarship, reform, politics—and immortality— craved by himself.[69] To his older brother he confided that he saw "in the distance a vague and unsteady light in the direction towards which I needs must gravitate, so soon as the present disturbing influences are removed."

In such wise the lessons of his reading took their place beside his personal observations of liberal England and his articles on reform. All played a part in his awareness of the people. Even when cloistered at Harvard he kept the "great principle of democracy" firmly in view. Tracing democracy back to its remote Teutonic origins, as he eventually did in the *Essays in Anglo-Saxon Law*,[70] Adams necessarily dealt with a heroless history in which an anonymous people had somehow originated and transmitted a significant concept through their institutions; or, as the Teutonists would have it, the anonymity implied in "race." Adams employed this latter term occasionally in the *History* [71] to signify the cultural affinity of a people gradually becoming aware of their common destiny through geographical proximity, shared experiences, and, in the United States, the relatively undisturbed development of their country. Adams never used the word more

68. Alexis de Tocqueville, *Democracy in America* (New York, Knopf, 1945), *1*, 6, 13; *2*, 96.

69. Adams might have studied the same kind of accomplishment in the lives of John Stuart Mill and Henry Reeve, or, for that matter, others of the liberal-minded literary set with whom he identified himself in England.

70. See above, pp. 35 ff.

71. For example, Vol. *4*, 136, 289; *5*, 211; *6*, 287; *9*, 225.

positively than in the *Education*, where he pondered the "Russian inertia of race": "Race rules the conditions; conditions hardly affected race; and yet no one could tell the patient tourist what race was, or how it should be known. History offered a feeble and delusive smile at the sound of the word; evolutionists and ethnologists disputed its very existence; no one knew what to make of it; yet, without the clue, history was a nursery tale." [72]

To the institutionalist, races or peoples bore institutions much as ether carried the waves of nineteenth-century science. But the institutionalist's ether was neither a passive nor a universal medium. Various races accounted for divergent developments in institutions, as nineteenth-century theories of inheritance and historical development steadily defaced Locke's *tabula rasa*. Although it was true that, like Adams, most of the institutionalists emphasized historical and cultural differences as the cause of divergent institutions, it was tempting to be careless and either purposely or unwittingly to imply that inheritance also played a part. The Teutonic or Nordic race became "law-abiding," "liberty loving," and so on, with variations in degree from nation to nation; the Mediterranean race, by contrast, "volatile" and "extremist"—at least to Teutons and Nordics. A mélange of personality traits and value judgments matched the gamut of races and nationalities. Hence the ambiguity in remarks by institutionalists as to precisely what determined the characteristics of peoples. Like the literary historian the institutionalist usually left race and nationality too little defined. But whatever the vagueness of this racial concept, Adams' research in medieval institutions while at Harvard acquainted him with the work of three Oxford historians who together represented the culmination in England of a mild racist theory of history.[73] As used by Edward Freeman, William Stubbs, and John R. Green, race readily merged with national character. Of all Freeman's popular lectures none was more famous than his series before American audiences in 1881–82 on "The English People in Its Three Homes," Germany, England, and the United States, while his ardor for the English stock and the heroes of its early history led to exaggerations in two other books which elicited

72. *Education*, pp. 411 f. For Adams' concept of race see also Edward N. Saveth, *American Historians and European Immigrants, 1875–1925* (New York, Columbia University Press, 1948), p. 86.

73. I am particularly indebted to an unpublished paper written at Yale University by Joseph W. Keena for some of the ideas on race in relation to English historiography presented below.

Adams' most devastating reviews for the *North American*. Even Stubbs, the most cautious of the three historians, stated in his lecture on "The Elements of Nationality among European Nations" that England "is the country in which Teutonic genius had most freely developed" its peculiar bent "in physique, in language, in law and custom." Or, to turn to his notable *Constitutional History*, the development of English constitutionalism had depended on the interaction of "national character, the external history, and the institutions of the people." [74]

Yet of the Oxford trio neither Stubbs nor Freeman, but Green, was Adams' favorite. On a trip to Europe in the summer of 1879, when he probably met Green for the first time, Adams mentioned the English historian as a man who "bids fair to become my most intimate guardian and teacher." A few days later he described Green as "the brightest and pleasantest of the men in London." By the spring of 1880 the intimate guardian and teacher of the previous year had become one of Adams' "intimate friends." In a letter to Parkman one year after Green's death Adams gave final testimony to his affection for the consumptive Englishman: "My favorite John Green was the flower of my generation; and in losing him, I lost the only English writer of history whom I loved personally and historically." [75]

Inevitably Adams had given a favorable review in the *North American* to the *Short History of the English People* on its appearance in 1874. In contrast to the institutional approach of both Stubbs and Freeman, Green described national character broadly in terms of individuals. While Adams' portrayal of the people in the *History* recalled the institutionalist's interest in a composite psyche, his affection for Green betrayed a fascination

74. Edward Freeman, "The English People in Its Three Homes," *Lectures to American Audiences* (Philadelphia, Porter & Coates, 1882). Adams reviewed Freeman's *Historical Essays* (first series, London, Macmillan, 1871) and his *History of the Norman Conquest* for the *NAR, 114* (1872), 193–196, and *118* (1874), 176–181; for the aftermath see Thoron, pp. 331 f. Stubbs' lecture appeared in *Lectures on Early English History*, ed. A. Hassal (London and New York, Longmans, Green, 1906), p. 211; see p. 210 for his discussion of racial purity and blood versus historical and political factors as causative elements in institutional history. His remarks on national character are in the much reprinted *The Constitutional History of England* (Oxford, Clarendon Press), p. 1.

75. Citations from letters dated Aug. 2, 1879, Aug. 31, 1879, May 13, 1880, and Dec. 21, 1884, respectively. Ford, *1*, 312, 313, 323; Cater, pp. 133 f. Adams expressed a desire to meet Green as early as 1871; Ford, *1, 205*. Although a meeting could have taken place during Adams' visit to England in 1872–73, the two historians seem only to have met during Adams' next European trip in 1879–80.

with individuality in history even as he worked on medieval institutions. If Adams' eagerness to abandon "Sac" and "Soc" for the Gallatin papers reflected an innate interest in American history, did it also disclose his reluctance to work further in a field where anonymity was inevitable? In such a transition Green quite naturally would have attracted Adams.

In his preface to the *Short History* Green stated that he meant "to pass lightly and briefly over the details of foreign wars and diplomacies, the personal adventures of kings and nobles, the pomp of courts, or the intrigues of favourites, and to dwell at length on the incidents of that constitutional, intellectual, and social advance in which we read the history of the nation itself." Especially in the first two thirds of his book (up through the chapter on Puritan England) [76] Green introduced something of the life, customs, and arts of the populace into a history organized within the pattern habitual for political and military histories. He gave the popular cast to his *Short History* partly through general descriptions of conditions in England at various times and partly by mentioning popular leaders among the masses of the people, like the obscure figure, William the Long Beard, who defied corruption among the aldermen in medieval London at the price of his head, or William Grindecombbe during the Peasants' Revolt of the late fourteenth century. Then, too, Green extended the traditional list of heroes so as occasionally to include the "figures of the missionary, the poet, the printer, the merchant, and the philosopher." But even these innovations did not wholly explain his portrayal of the people, since any sample—say, his treatment of the Reformation, where only a third of the pages dealt with purely social and intellectual movements—indicates that he, like McMaster, passed over "drum and trumpet" history less lightly than he supposed. It is in the warm informality of Green's portraits of major figures that he also gave a sense of the people, insofar as he seemed to extend his all too brief discussions of the populace up into the ruling classes. Take, as typical, part of his characterization of Alfred the Great: "His work was of a simple

76. Green confessed to the reason for failing to carry out his original scheme for *A Short History of the English People* (London, Macmillan, New York, Harper) after the year 1660 in Leslie Stephen, ed., *Letters of John Richard Green* (New York and London, Macmillan, 1901), p. 408; but even in this letter he hardly intimates the extent to which the end of his volume, particularly for the nineteenth century, became almost exclusively political history. Quotations and references are from his preface; chap. iv, sec. 4; chap. v, sec. 4; chap. i, sec. 5.

and practical order. He was wanting in the imaginative qualities which mark the higher statesman, nor can we trace in his acts any sign of a creative faculty or any perception of new ideas. In politics as in war, or in his after-dealings with letters, he simply took what was closest at hand and made the best of it."

Such a portrait suggests Adams' unheroic heroes; but Green's warmth and obvious love of characterization carried him too far toward literary history to suit Adams' austere standards. Green all too readily became enmeshed in the colorful idiosyncrasies of his heroes, and where these extraneous, if delightful, details occurred, he abandoned the people to concentrate on their leaders. So although Green did tentatively extend the scope of political history to include social and intellectual events, his *Short History* was hardly a radical departure from Michelet's feeling for the populace in his *History of France*, also of some consequence for Adams' volumes.[77] Fond of individuality in history though he was, Adams retained enough of the institutionalist approach to scorn superfluous forays into the personalities of his statesmen if these merely enlivened the narrative without being essential to it. There is of course Adams' picture of Napoleon in his perfumed bath, coolly informing Lucien and Joseph Bonaparte that he had illegally disposed of Louisiana to the United States. There is as well the amusing account of Jefferson's institution of social democracy at the White House dinner table.[78] But such incidents are few. Moreover, Napoleon's bath never interrupted the continuity of his pronouncement to his indignant brothers, while Jefferson's accidental slight to the wife of the British ambassador proved an exacerbating factor in Anglo-American relations. By thus minimizing incidents of purely biographical significance Adams sought to hew his narrative to the theme of popular development more closely than did Green, whose focus in the *Short History* wavered between the people and the age-old hero whom he deplored.

Of course Adams' volumes were political history. He held that "the nation could be understood only by studying the individual[s]" responsible for political leadership;[79] but insofar as the leaders had risen from the people and reflected their constituents in their unheroic demeanor, they articulated the thought,

77. Baym, pp. 47–61, emphasizes Michelet in connection with Adams' Harvard teaching and his *Chartres*.

78. *History*, 2, 33–39, 367–377.

79. *Ibid.*, 9, 226.

emotions, the very behavior of the inarticulate population as a whole. Excessively intellectualistic in his conception of the people, Adams did not make his reader nearly so aware of them as did Green or any of a number of literary historians; for the people must be more than conceptualized if the historian means them to live in his pages. To the extent that the leader in American history did stand beside the people, not above them, to that extent Adams stood on the threshold of social, and even cultural, history.

If he never really crossed the threshold, it was because he largely formulated his goals for history within existing practice, without seeking essentially new means by which to realize his ideals. Reconsider the sources of Adams' views on the people. Almost all historians, and none more than the literary historians, realized that every leader reflected certain aspects of the society he led. Many historians, Gibbon and Macaulay for example, had given social history more attention by interrupting their narrative to insert cross-sectional studies of society designed to give some sense of setting for the events with which they were primarily concerned. A few historians like Green and McMaster, of whom Green only was important for the *History*, went a cautious step further in fusing the popular and intellectual aspects of society more continuously with political events; but even these last two conceived of social history as a mere accompaniment to the political past, for both organized their works in conformity with political events, while both devoted by far the majority of their pages to material indistinguishable from that of the political historian. Reflections of all these important, but nevertheless rather timid, approaches to social history appeared in Adams' thinking. He could have learned far bolder lessons in social history from certain institutionalists—another historical trend of major importance for his concept of the people—had he pondered the full implications of what would become, largely through the interposition of anthropology, the cultural approach to history. While teaching at Harvard he had thoroughly investigated such studies of the primitive family and its relation to the community as those by John McLennon, Edward Tylor, Lewis Henry Morgan, and Fustel de Coulange. In 1876 he had even addressed the Lowell Institute on primitive woman, holding that she possessed more power than her modern successor—a theme prophetic for his later study of the cult of the Virgin in *Chartres*.[80] "The Primitive

80. See an excellent discussion by Samuels, pp. 260-266.

Rights of Women," however, centered in their legal status, and, when Adams turned to his *History*, he wrote with the bias for legal, constitutional, and political institutions of such writers as Maine, Stubbs, and Freeman, or the German Rudolph Sohm. Hence the *History* was, first and foremost, political history. It was, moreover, political history through which Adams would show the people by utilizing certain aspects of all the conventional and decidedly tentative approaches to social history prevalent in his day.[81]

Such were not all the influences on Adams' approach to the American people. If the moral view of history pervaded his analysis of statesmanship, Adams also examined the people as both the source and the reflection of national morality. In a democratic nation the moral premises of statesmanship should reflect the moral state of society. Only in a nation where people enjoyed "conditions of undisturbed growth," [82] unburdened by European aristocracy and militarism, could Jefferson's policy of "palliation and endurance" have originated. Hence the policy reflected the universal tendency of a people to desire, above all, the peaceful pursuit of their individual happiness. But a federal policy designed to preserve peace could lead to dissension precisely because it blocked some individuals—New England shipowners and merchants, for example—from attaining the happiness they sought. Furthermore, if peace and individual freedom were the two moral goals most important to any people, then a nationalism dedicated to the protection of these aims also possessed moral significance. It was, however, questionable whether the virtue of peace could uphold the virtue of nationalism in a world where nations customarily survived by war.

Viewed as moral history, then, the nine volumes weighed the conflicts which could occur among the three components basic to a genuinely popular, and therefore moral, nationalism. The virtue of democratic nationalism seemed to the average American in 1800 less obvious, because more abstract and remote, than the immediate benefits of peace and individual freedom. The democratic statesman must seek measures to implement these popular ideals; but above all he was the steward of nationalism. His far-sightedness should compensate for the limited vistas of private

81. Adams himself realized that new types of history would require techniques which he did not possess; Cater, p. 134; Ford, *1*, 382 f.

82. *History, 9*, 222.

life. If the steward bungled his trust, then the people themselves would slowly come to realize the importance of their national unity, thereby proving that democratic nationalism was the overarching virtue sheltering all other popular virtues. Their action demonstrated that in a democracy nationalism was not imposed from above, but emanated from below. The fountainhead of virtue did not reside in an elite clustered by birth, brawn, or brains at the top of society, whence it trickled down to the masses below. Rather the stream flowed in the opposite direction. The function of leadership was that of appraisal rather than of bestowal.

This origin of statesmanship in popular morality both conditioned and justified such force as the statesman required for his measures. Adams believed with his forebears that a great nation somehow struck a balance between physical and moral force. Without the judicious use of physical force moral energy proved no energy at all. Spineless morality begot not what it intended but precisely what it shunned. "Jefferson's measures of peaceful coercion bore unexpected results, reacting upon foreign nations by stimulating every mean and sordid motive. No possible war could have so degraded England." [83] Although contempt for flaccid rectitude stirred the mean and sordid in every Englishman, its effect was far more blighting on the American. The economic cost of embargo, large as it loomed, proved smaller than the moral loss. "The strongest objection to war was not its waste of money or even of life; for money and life in political economy were worth no more than they could be made to produce." The scientist had spoken—and with Olympian offhandedness—about the value of life; the moralist continued,

A worse evil was the lasting harm caused by war to the morals of mankind, which no system of economy could calculate . . . Yet even on that ground the embargo had few advantages . . . The embargo opened the sluice-gates of social corruption. Every citizen was tempted to evade or defy the laws. At every point along the coast and frontier the civil, military, and naval services were brought in contact with corruption; while every man in private life was placed under strong motives to corrupt. Every article produced or consumed in the country became an object of speculation; every form of industry became a form of gambling. The rich could alone profit in the

83. *Ibid., 4,* 97.

end; while the poor must sacrifice at any loss the little they could produce.

If war made men brutal, at least it made them strong; it called out the qualities best fitted to survive in the struggle for existence. . . . War, with all its horrors, could purify as well as debase; it . . . taught courage, discipline, and stern sense of duty. Jefferson must have asked himself in vain what lessons of heroism or duty were taught by his system of peaceable coercion, which turned every citizen into an enemy of the laws,—preaching the fear of war and of self-sacrifice, making many smugglers and traitors, but not a single hero.[84]

No militarist, Adams nevertheless realized that good and evil were warring forces, powers as real as the New England preacher had warned. Confronting the power of evil, good emerged victorious only if its force in some way matched the energy unleashed against it. Where once diplomatic protest might serve to maintain the moral balance, occasionally the evil of arms became less immoral than any alternative. Jefferson's enlightened program for international peace ended in the blackest evil that a nation could confront—the threat of treason on the part of a considerable segment of its population. Had this evil swept the country as it had some New England Federalists, then the nation itself would have collapsed. The final call to arms hardly produced a spontaneous crusade, for the policy of "palliation and endurance" had wreaked too much moral havoc on the nation. But enough Americans answered. At the last moment the need for action produced activity, as the need for heroism called up the occasional hero. Strengthened at last by the "slow conviction that come what would the nation must be preserved," national morality did battle with the devil.

Viewed as allegory, the *History* might have stood among the grandest sermons to emerge from Massachusetts morality if only the nation had prosecuted the War of 1812 with a fervor steadily increasing as the war went on. Unfortunately, the facts made dubious any such progression in intensity. Even the British were astonished that the battle at Washington should have left Americans so grateful at the preservation of private property that they almost forgave the destruction of their public buildings.[85] The American government was so embarrassed for men and money,

84. *Ibid.*, pp. 276 f.
85. *Ibid.*, 9, 36.

the military campaigns so ineptly generaled on the whole, that only British bungling and her activity elsewhere may have saved the United States from defeat. Nevertheless, once the war was over Americans ironically celebrated its conclusion as a victory, although one wondered "why a government, which was discredited and falling to pieces at one moment, should appear as a successful and even a glorious national representative a moment afterward." [86] The grandeur of Adams' moral rather disappeared in the uninspiring conduct of most Americans during the War of 1812. What else could the scientific historian expect? He could hardly hope for extraordinary valor, especially in the situation into which Jefferson and Madison had led the United States. Rather it seemed as though Americans had simply followed the line of least resistance to their nationalism, putting forth a minimum of effort during the fighting and happily shucking European entanglements when such was possible. What would have happened to American nationalism had the British bungled less, or concentrated greater energy on their campaign, was uncertain. The *History* implied that more danger would have encouraged more resistance. In other words, the American would employ only so much energy as he needed for his purpose; his kind of society was not given to excess. It followed that his national morality was bound to be modest.

> That the individual [American] should rise to a higher order either of intelligence or morality than had existed in former ages was not to be expected, for the United States offered less field for the development of individuality than had been offered by older and smaller societies. The chief function of the American Union was to raise the average standard of popular intelligence and well being, and at the close of the War of 1812 the superior average intelligence of Americans was so far admitted that Yankee acuteness, or smartness, became a national reproach; but much doubt remained whether the intelligence belonged to a high order, or proved a high morality . . . American morality was such as suited a people so endowed, and was high when compared with the morality of many older societies; but, like American intelligence, it discouraged excess. Probably the political morality shown by the government and by public men during the first sixteen years of the century offered a fair gauge of social morality. Like the char-

86. *Ibid., 9,* 80.

acter of the popular inventions, the character of the morals corresponded to the wants of a growing democratic society; but time alone could decide whether it would result in a high or a low national ideal.[87]

Time alone would decide whether American nationality resulted in a high order of intellect and morality; again Adams declined to predict, while simultaneously hinting at its possibility. Were the people, as he remarked at one point in the *History*, the "iron energy" of democratic nationalism? Or were they, as he declared at another, mere "ants and bees," their power for good dissipated in routine? Adams spoke of the "weight" of population, of its "inertia," or its "drift";[88] but the chief reason for the inconclusiveness of the *History* was his hesitancy before the paradox which he had raised. On the one hand the people did grope toward their national destiny; they did develop the technology necessary to see them through the War of 1812; they did display a morality unknown to aristocratic and military societies. On the other hand they somewhat disappointed Adams. "Democracies in history always suffered from the necessity of uniting with much of the purest and best in human nature a mass of ignorance and brutality lying at the bottom of all societies."[89] If there was no mistaking the virtue implicit in the easygoing tolerance of the American people as Adams portrayed them in the *History*, there was also no disguising the danger of their mediocrity.

To Adams the fate of history depended on solving two riddles. The inertia of the undisturbed growth of a vast population might take history in one of two directions. History might follow the example of China and remain static for centuries,[90] an extreme example of the people as "ants and bees." Or it might follow the course of the United States, the opposite extreme of "iron energy." Adams pondered these alternatives when in later life he briefly visited Russia for his strangely prophetic, if only semiserious, inquiry into the weight of one vast population as opposed to another. "My chief resource," he wrote half in jest to a correspondent, "is to try to collect elements for calculating whether the

87. *Ibid.*, p. 237.
88. *Ibid.*, *3*, 58, 212. For the words "weight," "inertia," "drift," or their implication see, for example, *ibid.*, *1*, 73; *3*, 118, 196, 212, 367, 395; *5*, 289; *7*, 68, 69; *9*, 87, and chap. x.
89. *Ibid.*, *6*, 405.
90. *Ibid.*, *1*, 163; *9*, 222.

average American equals, in energy, three, four, five, or six Russians." Even if, as he eventually decided, the average American commanded an energy equivalent to that of four Russians,[91] his equation did not really answer the riddle of history unless the historian knew which of the two populations would ultimately triumph over the other. But a second riddle, and one closer to home, preoccupied Adams even more. Where would the energy of the American carry him and his civilization?

Quite obviously the *History* reflected the central problem of conservative liberalism of the middle of the nineteenth century, that is, the role of leadership in relation to the growing democratization of an industrial society. Adams' ideas on this relationship came from many sources,[92] but one source is particularly important. Indeed, Comte provides the master key to the meaning of the *History* and to its meaning in Adams' life as well. For Comte, as for Adams, the people comprised the intellectual and moral foundation of society. Both believed that only a class superior to the mass of the people in intellect and morality could guide society with a maximum of benefit and a minimum of friction toward its inevitable destiny. Both held that when leadership erred in its appraisal of social forces, then society would drift toward its inevitable destiny, albeit with considerable confusion because of the lack of enlightened guidance. Both discussed social development in terms of its movement and its rate of movement, while both found the increase of population among the major factors affecting the rate of social change.[93] But parallels in the thought of Comte and his pupil, who had eagerly devoured Harriet Martineau's translation of the *Cours de philosophie positive* while in the legation, are far more detailed.

Comte believed that society had for too long suffered guidance

91. Aug. 14, 1901; Ford, *2*, 338. See above, p. 103.
92. For example, see above, pp. 101 f.
93. * Auguste Comte, *The Positive Philosophy of Auguste Comte*, tr. and condensed by Harriet Martineau (London, Trübner, 1853). In the second volume in the Henry Adams library at the Massachusetts Historical Society all of the annotations occur between pages 157 and 279 in the sections dealing with Comte's law of phases and the period of fetishism. References herein are to the more accessible one-volume edition (New York, Blanchard, 1855, but reprinted in various editions from the same plates); pp. 519 ff. Comte's mention of the "ennui" of intellectuals as a cause of deceleration in social progress (pp. 517 f.) is significant in view of Adams' repeated use of the word in later life. Comte's repeated return to his favorite ideas makes documentation, other than for citations, impossible.

from the ordinary mentality of most politicians, or else from "men of letters" who let their fancies ramble among high-flown abstractions.[94] As a result the potentialities of social development were lost in anarchical improvisation. Such, according to Comte, was the curse of the Enlightenment, where appeals rooted in personal predilection rent intellectuals into factions, until the contributions which they should have made to their society vanished in skepticism. Not negative criticism but positive guidance was demanded of what Comte called the "speculative class," for he thought in terms of class rather than profession. Only by renouncing improvisation and turning to the study of society could this elite "impart a homogeneous and rational character" to "desultory politics"; only thus could the elite connect the present with the "whole past, so as to establish a general harmony in the entire system of social ideas." [95]

Coining the term "sociology" for the new science which would unify past and present in terms of social laws, Comte demanded that the speculative class should study the methods of the physical and natural sciences. As the scientist investigated the phenomena which his senses presented to him rather than such fancied entities as the "nature," the "essence," or the "virtues" resident in objects, so the student of society should exorcize metaphysical abstractions like the natural rights of man. Abstractions of this kind explained nothing about society. They were both imaginary and absolutist. To be valid, social principles could not be the products of rationalization but must originate from the study of actual conditions which varied among different societies and varied especially through time. Such study would provide impersonal data freed from the prejudices of the investigator. Like scientific research, the sociological findings of one man could be verified by other men. The speculative class as a whole could agree on the great principles which had governed society in the past. By their extension, laws operating in the past would guide future development. Indeed, in summarizing his method in his unwieldy prose Comte clearly pointed to the function of "prevision" as the end of positivistic inquiry.

Comprehending the three characteristics of political science which we have been examining, prevision of social phenomena

94. *Ibid.*, p. 430.
95. *Ibid.*, p. 431.

supposes first, that we have abandoned the region of meta-physical idealities, to assume the ground of observed realities by a systematic subordination of imagination to observation; secondly, that political conceptions have ceased to be absolute, and have become relative to the variable state of civilization, so that theories, following the natural course of facts, may admit of our foreseeing them; and, thirdly, that permanent political action is limited by determinate laws, since, if social events were always exposed to disturbance by the accidental intervention of the legislator, human or divine, no scientific prevision of them would be possible. Thus, we may concentrate the conditions of the spirit of positive social philosophy on this one great attribute of scientific prevision.[96]

Realistic, relativistic, and deterministic, positivism also demanded a further quality for its laws. They must be synthetic statements encompassing vast quantities of special instances; or, in Comte's words, the function of positivism was that of deriving from the "mass of unconnected . . . information" the "laws of social life" by "stripping off from [these data] whatever was peculiar or ir-relevant" to the larger problem at hand and thus transferring re-search "from the concrete to the abstract." [97]

If the natural and physical sciences thus suggested the goal of sociology more than its methods, the large generalization in science indicated the kind of unification which the sociologist must seek to give meaning to his miscellaneous data. Indeed, the gener-alization was absolutely necessary provided modern man was to avoid what Comte considered the greatest potential danger in the positivistic phase of society—the danger of overspecialization. The ever increasing complexity of human knowledge threatened to fragment the intellectual class of the modern world as tragically as metaphysical bickering had paralyzed the same class during the Enlightenment. Hence Comte pleaded for an integration of the "aimless labors" [98] of isolated scholarship. His science of sociology would fulfill "the famous suggestion of Pascal, by repre-senting the whole human race, past, present, and future, as con-stituting a vast and eternal social unit, whose different organs, individual and national, concur . . . in the evolution of hu-

96. *Ibid.,* p. 456.
97. *Ibid.,* p. 543. I have here and elsewhere in quoting from Comte altered the present to the past tense.
98. *Ibid.,* p. 476.

manity." [99] Thus the methodical and cumulative discovery of laws for society would insure an orderly and progressive development for the future.

As Plato's ideal society had demanded the highest intellects in the topmost stratum, so did Comte's. Both also required of their speculative class standards equally rigorous. For Comte the speculative class must be selfless in its quest for truths beneficial not so much to its own members as to the whole of society. The speculative class must also be selfless, Comte did not forget to add, because it would be very much underpaid for its services. To insure that its vision remain independent, dispassionate, and progressive, the positivist elite should be planners only, leaving the execution of their programs to active leaders. In an industrial milieu financiers and businessmen had superseded the military and theological leaders of past societies as the active leaders. It needed no positivist to remind Comte's readers—most of them candidates for highest honors under the new dispensation—that financiers and businessmen did not customarily share either the elevation or the unselfishness of the speculative class. Hence the potential good in an industrial society could be realized only by correcting the myopia of practical-minded men with the farsighted vision of the positivist. For this reason the speculative class was the best friend of the people. It protected them against the business leadership. It guided society in directions which the people had inarticulately selected for themselves, since only the "popular point of view" could offer the positivist "a survey sufficiently large and clear to connect the present with the whole of the past, and to give an organic direction to the general mind." [100] Such benefits for the people would certainly enlist popular support for positivism, while the speculative class would also favor a system which promised to accord them the topmost honors in their society. And employers? After all, they would retain their status as the active leaders. Their leadership would be the more secure because the speculative class could sense social trends and therefore plan in such a way for inevitable change as to minimize the continuous friction between the active leaders and the people. So Comte closed the positivistic circle of felicities.[101]

With two possible exceptions the *History* so obviously echoed

99. *Ibid.*, p. 473.
100. *Ibid.*, p. 782.
101. This summary appears in *ibid.*, p. 783.

the positivistic program that the similarity hardly requires elaboration. The first exception was of course the specific nature of the *History* as opposed to the synthetic generalizations recommended by Comte; but the documents from the Jeffersonian era pointed to the larger conclusion of the inevitability of nationalism. The second was the identification of the speculative and active classes in the same individuals; but this coincidence occurred by virtue of the peculiar nature of American democracy. Perhaps significantly, in precisely these two apparent exceptions are centered problems which preoccupied Adams throughout the remainder of his life: the relation of the facts of history to their generalization and the relation of the active to the passive life. With these two exceptions the parallels between teacher and pupil need no more than allusion: Jefferson as the metaphysical theorist; Gallatin as the positivist; the chaotic result of Jefferson's well-intentioned but unrealistic statesmanship; the opposition of the New England financial class to both the speculative class and the populace; the ideal derivation of statesmanship from the incoherent desires of the people; the insignificance of personality in history; the importance of intellect and morality, and their relation to popular intelligence and virtue; the inevitable triumph of popular ideals; and all within the context of a nationalism where the industrial—the positivistic—phase of society seemed most evident because of the complete overthrow of the antiquated ideals of militarism.

> The success of the American system was, from this point of view, a question of economy. If they could relieve themselves from debts, taxes, armies, and government interference with industry, they must succeed in outstripping Europe in economy of production; and Americans were even then partly aware that if their machine were not so weakened by these economies as to break down in the working, it must of necessity break down every rival. If their theory was sound, when the day of competition should arrive, Europe might choose between American and Chinese institutions, but there could be no middle path; she might become a confederated democracy, or a wreck.[102]

Consider, too, the role of the historian implicit in Adams' volumes. He should be impartial, basing all his judgments on unimpeach-

102. *History, 1,* 162 f.

able evidence. He should derive all principles from the actualities of society, not from personal predilection. He should, like the scientist, have in mind some generalization to justify his research before beginning it. He should select his area of inquiry with particular regard for its value as a case study illuminating his generalization. He should rigorously exclude any data extraneous to understanding the generalization under scrutiny. He should, while admitting the diversity of human society, nevertheless relate his generalization to the unity of human development. Because he examined principles underlying and guiding all social development he could make his work relevant for the future development of society as well as its past. Because of the inclusive nature of the principles which he investigated, as well as his dispassionate manner of investigating them, he could make a permanent contribution in the progressive and cooperative unfolding of historical knowledge.

If the *History* revealed its Comtian inspiration in both subject matter and conception, it also disclosed a Comtian bias in its method. Comte suggested four means by which his sociologist might attain the positivist ideal.[103] One of these—the use of history to relate the present, and by implication the future, to the past—needs no further comment. Nor perhaps does the so-called method of "observation"; for under this omnibus category Comte included, first, his admonition for dispassionate research, and then his requirement that the sociologist begin his research with some principle in mind lest he become lost in trivia. Under this same category he also included the reminder that the sociologist should study "apparently insignificant customs" as well as political events—a lesson exemplified in the opening and closing chapters of the *History*. As a third method Comte suggested that of "comparison," whether of different societies or different periods. Again the relevance to the *History* needs no belaboring. Perhaps the fourth and final method is, if no more significant than the others, most interesting for the *History*. This Comte called "experimentation," but experimentation in a special sense, for Comte realized that the sociologist, and particularly the historical sociologist, did not enjoy the privileges of the experimental scientist. Taking his cue from pathology, Comte wondered whether it would be possible to investigate a period when "the regular course of [a] phenomenon [like that of democratic nationalism] was interfered with" and to

103. Comte, *op. cit.*, pp. 475–485, 495 ff.

prove the inevitability of the phenomenon by demonstrating its triumph over conditions adverse to its development. Comte was uncertain as to the value of this method for, he said, it had never been tried. It is tempting, although doubtless a little overdramatic, to imagine the attention of the young student in the legation arrested by the paradoxical suggestion of his mentor and eventually making of this allegedly untried experiment the central theme of his *History*.

Of course the elements of the Comtian program, considered item by item, were not exclusive with Comte; nor did Adams embrace Comte without reservation. On the contrary, while at Harvard toiling over medieval institutions, he reviewed Maine's *Lectures on the Early History of Institutions* and complained at one point that certain theories advanced by the English historian required "two or three volumes" in substantiation. Then he went on,

> What is called Aryan or Indo-European law is likely, however, one day or another to become a tolerably complete science and one of no little value to mankind. As for still more ancient systems, however, the temptation to speculate becomes strong in proportion to the mystery of the subject. The mania for producing philosophical systems of social development, like that of Auguste Comte; the temptation to make such a system symmetrical and to pass every individual human being through every phase which has left a trace of its existence behind it; the fervor with which each new investigator presses his own historical novelty;—all this is merely the symptom of advancing knowledge, but has little intrinsic value.[104]

Astonishing confession for Adams! This statement undoubtedly represented his position in the seventies and early eighties. At that time he made painstaking research the prerequisite to generalization. Indeed, this was a major theme of his historical reviews for the *North American*. Nevertheless, even in attacking Comte's brashness, Adams disclosed the Comtian tinge to his thinking by his suggestion that a "tolerably complete science" of ancient law could be of "no little value to mankind."

Viewed as a whole, then, Comte, more than any other single influence provided, if not the catechism, at least the spirit of Adams' early ideas on history. Other influences, especially Mill

104. *NAR, 120* (1875), 437.

and Tocqueville, enriched and reinforced Comtian ideals. Like Comte's *Positive Philosophy*, the *History* also reflected that mixture of reform and history dominating Adams' life during youth and middle age. The reform journalist eventually turned historian; but essentially the two vocations blurred as Comte had blurred them. To regulate the future in the light of wisdom from the past—the *History* reflected the Adams heritage beneath its Comtian dress Like Henry Adams his forebears had also maintained their faith in the people when counseled by an intelligent and moral stewardship. Henry shared their ardor for American nationalism, together with their conviction that his country had a larger than nationalistic significance for the world. He likewise shared the family sin of vanity; but, like them, he almost redeemed his conceit in the idealism of his intention.

Those who know only the skeptical Adams of the *Education* or the nostalgic Adams of the *Chartres* should turn to his chapter, "American Ideals," in the first volume of the *History*. Read against the background of his later life, there is a poignancy about these pages, reflecting as they do his intense love of country. This fervor is the measure of frustration; frustration the key to failure. In the *Education* he designated the year in which he made final corrections in the *History* as the watershed of his life.[105] Well he might; the enigmatic irony of his historical masterpiece concealed a genuinely personal tragedy—the tragedy of one who sought fame in return for service, only to find his services unwanted. Until his wife died in 1885 he could stifle his disappointment in the hope that he would somehow find a suitable destiny. At its inception the *History* seemed in some vague way the dawn of a new day in life. In any event, at no other point in Adams' career does his critic need fewer apologies.

105. See above, p. 42, below, p. 126.

V. THE CURVE OF DEGRADATION

Y<small>OU</small> find my last two volumes more critical—deliberately fault finding?—than the earlier ones," he wrote a correspondent about his *History* in 1891.

They were written chiefly within the last five or six years, and in a very different frame of mind from that in which the work was begun. I found it hard to pretend either sympathy or interest in my subject. If you compare the tone of my first volume—even toned down, as it is, from the original—with that of the ninth when it appears, you will feel that the light has gone out. I am not to blame. As long as I could make life work, I stood by it, and swore by it as though it was my God, as indeed it was.[1]

How different the frame of mind with which he had started. Having left Harvard for Washington to begin his historical work, Adams loftily informed a friend,

As I belong to the class of people who have great faith in this country and who believe that in another century it will be saying in its turn the last word of civilisation, I enjoy the expectation of the coming day, and try to imagine that I am myself, with my fellow *gelehrte* here, the first faint rays of that great light which is to dazzle and set the world on fire hereafter. Our duties are perhaps only those of twinkling . . . But twinkle for twinkle, I prefer our kind to that of the small politician.[2]

A few months earlier he had declared himself "very contented under my cloak of historian. I am satisfied that literature offers higher prizes than politics, and I am willing to look on at my friends who differ from me on that point of theory." [3] Although

1. Jan. 2, 1891; Ford, *1*, 458.
2. Nov. 25, 1877; *ibid.*, p. 302.
3. Apr. 14, 1877; *ibid.*, pp. 300 f., also p. 333.

the psychiatrist might find an element of compensation in Adams' sudden preference for history over politics, once the politicians had ignored his counsel, the historian's enthusiasm for his new occupation was nevertheless genuine. And in 1884 the Washington *Gelehrt* again hinted to an English friend at a crusading intention for his *History*. "I admit to thinking the book readable, but to you it would be sadly dull reading. You see I am writing for a continent of a hundred million people fifty years hence; and I can't stop to think what England will read." [4] These high-flown expectations are incomprehensible unless the *History* is seen in the Comtian glow of its conception.

Once, in 1872, Adams had attempted to convince Lodge of the advantages of the "historico-literary line" by enumerating the goals possible to the historian. Through history Adams believed that Lodge might become a "species of literary lion with ease." He might even attain "social dignity, European reputation, and a foreign mission to close." [5] Thus had history served both John Motley and George Bancroft; so it would serve John Hay. Did Adams hope to duplicate their destinies? A bit of vocational advice given in 1872 to an ambitious student would not necessarily indicate Adams' own state of mind some five years later, especially since he had flirted with politics in the interim to his thorough disillusionment. Yet Adams' advice to Lodge did disclose ambitions far broader than those held by most scholars.

Never again, or so his published letters indicate, did he specify what might have been his ulterior purposes in scholarship. He usually discussed his future in unspecific terms; but the vista was not less grand for its lack of clarity. As a student in the legation he would serve the "great principle of democracy." As a journalist he would become a "power in the land." As a historian he included himself among an elite which would "dazzle and set the world on fire hereafter." He would write for no less than "a hundred million people fifty years hence." The grandiloquence of such visions indicated his ambition to shine as his ancestors had shone. Their vagueness reflected the sheltered condition of his early life, shielded as it was from the necessity of making specific decisions. Until he joined the Harvard faculty in his thirty-second year, he had made only three crucial attempts to maintain a degree of independence of family. Each was short-lived; each involved jour-

4. Feb. 3, 1884; *ibid.*, p. 357; also p. 403.
5. June 2, 1872; *ibid.*, p. 228.

nalistic ambitions. The first occurred in 1859 when he broke from his studies of civil law in Berlin to vacation in Europe and contribute occasional pieces to the *Boston Daily Advertiser*, while repeated admonitions from home warned of the necessity for settling on some serious purpose in life. Rescued from further waste of time after nineteen months as a tourist, he clung to the family for the next eight years, very briefly in Quincy and Washington, much longer in London. Although continuing his occasional journalism in Washington for a session of his father's term as congressman, Henry's second opportunity to sever family ties came at the end of 1861 when the revelation of his secret career as journalist permitted him, had he so desired, to leave the legation and frankly avow his hidden occupation. What specific pressures the family may have exerted in London to keep their son in the legation cannot be known; but his older brother at least wrote from an American battlefield urging Henry to break his semi-official connection and openly work as a correspondent for the *New York Times*. Henry did not accept the challenge, first, he said, because all his information came from his connection, second, because "there are few beings lower in the social scale in England than writers to newspapers." Doubtless this latter reason had much to do with keeping him at the legation; but so did his scholarly inclinations. Social and scholarly aspirations perhaps accounted for his remark in the *Education* that, on returning to the United States in 1868, he did not aspire "to become a regular reporter; he knew he should fail in trying a career so ambitious and energetic." [6] He assayed instead the more gentlemanly role of irregular contributor to quarterlies, the *Nation*, and the *New York Evening Post*. Barely established after two years of work in Washington, he again reluctantly bowed to family pressure and set out for Harvard. Small wonder that Adams' visions of greatness remained throughout his life ill-defined, with little sense of the

6. Sept. 7, 1861; *Cycle, 1,* 43; Charles' suggestion appears on p. 32. *Education,* p. 255. In this connection note the still puzzling failure of Adams to seek a job of the editor of the *New York Times* on his return to the United States (compare *Education,* p. 244, with Samuels, p. 172). Among the crises in Adams' pre-teaching life, Hume, pp. 16 f., would probably include Adams' short-lived desire in 1861 to obtain a commission in the army (*Cycle, 1,* 24), which actually elicited his brother's countersuggestion that Henry become a journalist in England. This desire for an army career does not appear to have been a crucial decision in Henry's life, for he was certainly very easily persuaded to remain where he was, although the opportunity to leave the legation did represent another neglected occasion to strike off on his own.

specific measures necessary for their complete attainment. The vagueness of his goals and his easy dissatisfaction with his progress toward their realization led him to substitute one for another equally vague, although always in some way related to the mixed goal of history and reform. Despite the thoroughness with which he plunged into each new career, these changes of aim gave an appearance of drift to his life. But who could doubt that, even in drifting, an Adams would happen on fame?

Had he stayed with journalism, or succeeded in establishing a liberal organ for a liberalized Republican party, his destiny might possibly have come to focus. Or had his wife not died as he worked on the *History* another focus might have been brought to view. This last tragedy proved the breaking point, the culmination of a series of personal frustrations. His desire to escape public notice extinguished whatever zeal he might once have had for public recognition. He became the passive observer, and his passivity proved fatal to whatever convictions potentially existed. Perhaps his later verdict was right; for even while trying for an active life he had been all too ready to acknowledge as inevitable the force of circumstance. Was it that the closer he came to the active life he sought the less appealing it seemed? Journalist? Reformer? Teacher? Historian? Certainly the pattern of discontent and indecision was well established before 1885. His sensitive awareness of the real forces in his society acted as a deterrent to his ambition for worldly success rather than the spur it might have proved to one with a tougher will. This sense of reality fed the innate skepticism of his nature.

If he had failed, his sense of superiority would not allow him to fail alone. The whole of human history must fail with him. Cosmic vanity, to be sure; and joined with vanity, an element of pose. To strip the sham that overlay the sincerity of his disillusionment is rarely easy; but Adams was obviously insincere when he complained in the *Education* that his *History* had brought no more "consideration" [7] than it netted revenue. Of course he could have headed the historians of his day had he wished. The American Historical Association elected him one of its vice-presidents for 1891, its president for 1894. He did not attend a meeting. Harvard offered him an honorary degree in 1892, but he would not accept the distinction. In the same year he did accept an honorary degree from Western Reserve University, doubtless because John

7. *Education*, pp. 326 f.

Hay warned his fellow trustees not to require his friend's attendance at commencement. His *History* won the coveted Loubat Prize in 1894; he tried, unsuccessfully this time, to refuse this honor. An active role in history was offered in 1896; he declined the invitation.[8] These honors came despite his withdrawal from society except for a rather large but select circle of friends. Adams chose to renounce the role of leader among scholars; and gradually, as he turned down invitations, the invitations ceased to come.

If there was an element of pose in what one of Adams' friends termed his "ostentatious retirement," [9] the element of sincerity went deeper, to depths he left unsounded except within himself. We can follow the surface of his life for the few years that marked the wane of his career as an orthodox historian. There was a brief escape to Japan; then back to Washington, where the partially completed manuscript awaited him. Doggedly the historian returned to his task. "I am trying to boil up my old interest in history enough to finish my book, but the fuel is getting scarce. I think the chances about even whether it will ever be published or not." Or a little later, ". . . I hope in two years to close up my life as far as literature and so-called usefulness go. I have got to the point where they bore me." As the conclusion of the ninth volume loomed in sight a spurt of enthusiasm gripped the historian. To John Hay he wrote, "the frenzy of finishing the big book has seized me, until, as the end comes nigh, I hurry off the chapters as though they were letters to you." [10] And finally with the proofreading of the final volumes in 1890 the labor was done. For a while thereafter he gathered more materials, with the idea of revising and correcting his *History*,[11] and in 1895 he favored the first issue of the *American Historical Review* with an article correcting and extending his remarks on a minor figure in the

8. On the American Historical Association: Cater, pp. 278; 328, n. 2; 329, n. 1; in each instance the election occurred in December of the preceding year; Ford, *2*, 59, n. 1. On the Harvard degree: *ibid.*, pp. 7 f.; 8, n. 1; 10 f., and n. 1. On the Western Reserve degree: *ibid.*, p. 12, n. 1; P. H. Bixler, "A Note on Henry Adams," *The Colophon*, Pt. 17 (1934), No. 2; Cater, p. 269. On the Loubat Prize: Ford, *2*, pp. 43 ff., and n. 1. The offer of 1896 came from John Franklin Jameson; in his reply, *ibid.*, pp. 118 f., Adams made his oft-quoted comparison of history to a "Chinese Play."

9. Margaret (Mrs. Winthrop) Chanler, *Roman Spring* (Boston, Little, Brown, 1934), p. 299.

10. Dec. 12, 1886; Oct. 30, 1887; July 8, 1888; Ford, *1*, 382, 386, 389.

11. Cater, pp. 255 and n. 1; 259. In the *Education*, p. 317, he speaks as though he would write on a new subject, but this seems never to have been his intention.

tangled diplomacy of the War of 1812.[12] But his career in the orthodox practice of history had really ended with the last of the nine volumes. The eventual epitaph to a period in his life appeared in the *Education:* ". . . life was complete in 1890; the rest mattered so little!" [13] When he wrote this Adams had already haloed those years that did matter with his allegory on Chartres, as a time when "one knew life . . . and has never so fully known it since." [14]

Externally, the twenty-seven years which remained to him seem, above all, a period of travel, to the South Seas, the Rocky Mountains, Cuba, Mexico, Europe, another trip to the Nile, but always returning to the Richardsonian "romanesque" structure on Lafayette Square. Had any of his select group of friends an inclination to travel, no matter where, he could be counted on as a possible companion. If no one was traveling, then the "professional wanderer" [15] set off alone, for, with some exaggeration, he found, "Three days in any place on earth is all it will bear." [16] He constantly complained of ennui, and travel kept him busy. His occupations, if occupations they were, appeared as desultory as his destinations. Occasionally he "geologized"; [17] he collected coins; [18] he read widely. From the South Seas trip he prepared a privately printed volume of local history. He closed his tenure as president of the American Historical Association with *The Tendency of History.* For Senator Don Cameron he drew up a congressional report of twenty-odd pages to advocate an independent Cuba. Something of his own experiences in Cuba with Clarence King appeared in a short memoir written after the geologist's death. Another memoir followed the sudden death in 1909 of the young poet George Cabot Lodge. Adams composed two poems himself. Then, of course, there were the letters—the letters recording his pilgrimages, perceptively, pessimistically, wittily, sardonically. Now they were lyric with description of scenery; again, pungent with personality, or sparkling with gos-

12. See below, pp. 129 ff.
13. *Education,* p. 316.
14. *Chartres,* pp. 3, 7.
15. Feb. 10, 1894; Ford, *2,* 36.
16. Jan. 8, 1895; *ibid.,* p. 63.
17. Especially when in the South Seas in 1890–91 and when in Cuba with Clarence King in 1894.
18. The collection, with a meticulous catalogue in Adams' handwriting, is now in the Massachusetts Historical Society.

sip, or snobbish about tourists, or narrow about Jews, or, again
and again, partly fatalistic, partly bemused, and frequently tedious about the vaguely approaching doom of western civilization,
in which he only half believed himself. Above all the letters reflected the loneliness, the aimlessness, and the mild discontent of
the pilgrim. When allowance is made for the contemplative years
required for most significant thinking, it yet seems as though this
period showed much waste of time and even greater waste of mind.
He might have avoided the waste had his pocketbook been smaller;
but had less money been available, posterity might not have had
the *History*, to say nothing of those books for which he is best
known.

Toward the middle of this last period, in the decade from
1900 to 1910, he wrote *Mont-Saint-Michel and Chartres, The
Education of Henry Adams, The Rule of Phase Applied to History*, and *A Letter to American Teachers of History*. Before
Adams' death the first of these had appeared in an edition for
the public, the second and fourth had a private printing, the third
lay in manuscript. These four volumes have won Adams a promi-
ment position in American literature, as well as a somewhat ambiguous place in American thought.

If the *History* revealed Adams' keen awareness of power beneath his commentary on the documents, his final investigation of
social energy represented but an enlargement of scope. He expanded his earlier analysis of power from those forces which
had fused a single nation into a unique entity to those acting
upon the multiple civilizations of the human past. In a final chapter of his *History* Adams had used a metaphor to stress the importance for the social scientist of research in American history.

> Travellers in Switzerland who stepped across the Rhine where
> it flowed from its glacier could follow its course among mediæval
> towns and feudal ruins, until it became a highway for modern
> industry, and at last arrived at a permanent equilibrium in
> the ocean. American history followed the same course. With
> prehistoric glaciers and mediæval feudalism the story had little
> to do; but from the moment it came within sight of the ocean
> it acquired interest almost painful. A child could find his way
> in a river-valley, and a boy could float on the waters of Hol-
> land; but science alone could sound the depths of the ocean
> . . . In a democratic ocean science could see something ulti-

mate. Man could go no further. The atom might move, but the general equilibrium could not change.[19]

In 1909 Adams reintroduced the identical metaphor in the *Rule*.

This solvent, then,—this ultimate motion which absorbs all other forms of motion is an ultimate equilibrium,—this ethereal current of Thought,—is conceived as existing, like ice on a mountain range, and trickling from every pore of rock, in innumerable rills, uniting always into larger channels, and always dissolving whatever it meets, until at last it reaches equilibrium in the ocean of ultimate solution.[20]

With the passage of time Adams' perspective on the metaphoric ocean had changed. From his optimistic belief that democracy afforded the ultimate theme for historical study, Adams shifted to the pessimistic assertion that annihilation provided the final goal for historical prophecy.

The earlier study had assumed that samples taken from the democratic mass might, upon analysis, reveal the components of that system of government which had "brought mankind within sight of its own end." As early as 1884 he had even admitted, "I am satisfied that the purely mechanical development of the human mind in society must appear in a great democracy so clearly, for want of disturbing elements, that in another generation psychology, physiology, and history will join in proving man to have as fixed and necessary [a] development as that of a tree; and almost as unconscious." [21] His preference for the physical sciences finally consigned the psychologist's "thought," "will," and "instinct" to the physicist's curve of degradation. Insofar as Adams turned away from man toward those sciences based upon physical matter, he confessed in effect that the ideal of democracy might prove so futile as to be unworthy of analysis. Little more than a year before his death Adams wrote a friend speculating as to "whether the revolution of 1790–1816 was as great as that between 1890–1916." [22] He himself had long ago concluded that the second revolution—a cataclysm of naked power—had overwhelmed the earlier idealism on which the Adamses had pinned their faith.

19. *History, 9,* 225; also Samuels, Epilogue, pp. 299–310.
20. *Degradation: Rule,* p. 281; also Ford, *2,* 522.
21. Dec. 21, 1884; Cater, p. 134.
22. July 10, 1916; Ford, *2,* 640.

About two years after the last of the nine volumes had come from the press Adams addressed *The Tendency of History* as a letter to the American Historical Association in lieu of the usual presidential address.[23] This letter expressed a hope that historians would undertake the exploration necessary to formulate a "science of history." Had such an exposition appeared immediately after the publication of Darwin's *Origin of Species* in 1859, Adams believed that it might have been couched in the "form of cheerful optimism"; but in view of subsequent scientific thought in Europe he considered that any attempt must "take its tone from the pessimism of Paris, Berlin, London, and St. Petersburg, unless it brought into sight some new and hitherto unsuspected path for civilization to pursue." [24] As it happened, the *Tendency* posed the problem which intermittently engrossed Adams for almost two decades.

Only after a considerable interval did he mail to a select group of libraries and intellectuals a privately printed report of his progress toward a science of history in the futile hope that his cause might gain adherents. Before jumping the seventeen years between his presidential address to the American Historical Association in 1893 and the publication of *A Letter to American Teachers of History* in 1910 it might be best to pause a moment at 1895 when Adams wrote the last bit of orthodox history in his career. This was the essay entitled "Count Edward de Crillon" for the first volume of the *American Historical Review*.[25] His contribution was almost certainly solicited in order to get the newly established *Review* off to an illustrious start, since Adams kept company with William M. Sloane, Moses Coit Tyler, Henry C. Lea, and Frederick Jackson Turner. For his part in the issue Adams submitted a minor correction to his *History* in respect to the insignificant but colorful Count de Crillon. The correction made, Adams continued on the basis of documents newly discovered at the French Foreign Office to tell something of the count's career as a "curious chapter of the social history of the world at the beginning of the century." The substance of the article is perhaps less interesting than its introduction, for the necessity of correcting his "fixed and documented starting point," as he

23. Cater, pp. 328, n. 2; 329, n. 1, gives the amusing details of Adams' dodge to avoid a personal appearance before the American Historical Association.

24. *Degradation: Tendency*, p. 130.

25. Pp. 51–69. The citations below are from pp. 51, 53. On the infinite relations of every historical fact see also *Education*, p. 410.

would describe his nine volumes a few years later, led Adams to
speculate on the question of historical accuracy. At no other time
in his career did Adams so cogently attack the absolutism implicit in his documentation within the *History*.

The article opened by appraising the increment of error in
the observation of historical facts.

> According to mathematicians, every man carries with him a
> personal error in his observation of facts, for which a certain
> allowance must be made before attaining perfect accuracy.
> In a subject like history, the personal error must be serious,
> since it tends to distort the whole subject, and to disturb the
> relations of every detail. Further, the same allowance must be
> made for every authority cited by the historian. Each has his
> personal error, varying in value, and often unknown to the
> writer quoting him. Finally, the facts themselves carry with
> them an error of their own; they may be correctly stated, and
> still lead to wrong conclusions. Of the reader's personal error
> nothing need be said. The sum of such inevitable errors must
> be considerable.

His inclination for pseudoscientific allusions irrepressible even in
this context, Adams went on to estimate the errors in Macaulay's
History of England where "at least thirty thousand of [his] so-
called facts must be more or less inexact."

Although the article amplified what Adams termed the "rule"
of historical error for a page and a half, the first paragraph contained the truths from which relativistic theories of history grow:
the error occurring in the individual fact, its accumulation in
the relationship of fact to fact, the historian's bias, the fallibility
of witnesses and evidence. Not that Adams was a relativist in this
article, for relativism demands a positive statement as to the nature
of history owing to the impossibility of the historian's ever attaining the Rankean ideal of *wie es eigentlich gewesen ist*. Adams
merely cited cautions found in every elementary treatise on historical evidence or, for that matter, discovered by most historians
in the course of their labors. Even in the *History*, where he had
approached the Rankean ideal, Adams had confessed his difficulty
in comprehending the subtleties of Jefferson's mind; [26] but he
assayed no foolproof philosophy of history. He did not mind—
indeed he relished—some contradictions in his thinking. So the

26. See above, pp. 58, 63, 70.

contradiction is of less significance than the occasion of its pronouncement. That a mere correction should encourage a rather too elaborate introduction on the opportunities for error in history was characteristic of Adams, particularly since his introduction mildly jibed at the seriousness of history shortly after the publication of the nine volumes, when he had begun to disparage their significance. Moreover, this lapse from his customary scientism appeared about two years after his presidential address when, with Brooks Adams' *The Law of Civilization and Decay* particularly in mind,[27] he had called for a science of history which would view the past in terms sufficiently broad to transcend the petty confusion of detailed treatment. As such the introductory paragraphs to his "Count Edward de Crillon" forecast Adams' later assertion in the *Education* that historical facts all but obliterate historical truths; "if history ever meant to correct the errors she made in detail, she must agree on a scale for the whole." [28]

For more than a decade and a half after the appearance of his modest article on Crillon Adams' erstwhile colleagues heard almost nothing of his quest. What little they heard came as rumor from those few who had read the privately printed *Chartres* and *Education*. But for most historians Adams must have gradually attained the remote status of an old master as the period of silence grew. Then in the spring of 1910 the distribution of the privately printed *Letter* broke the silence. This essay consisted of two chapters: "The Problem" and "The Solutions." Adams opened his first chapter by noting that the physical and natural sciences had promulgated three major hypotheses for force. The earliest in point of time was the law of the conservation of energy; the other

27. Charles A. Beard, Introduction to Brooks Adams, *The Law of Civilization and Decay* (New York, Knopf, 1943), p. 13. Beard, pp. 15–24, correctly minimizes Henry's direct influence on his brother's volume; but Beard, especially p. 28, is inaccurate in stating that Henry's later ideas on history derived from Brooks' volume. No doubt Brooks' volume did stimulate his older brother. By adopting the traditional picture of Henry Adams' historical career—the first part concerned with the "conventional" treatment of history, the second part with a theory of history—Beard fails to realize that the real intellectual relation existing between the brothers was probably of a much more reciprocal nature. Henry initially influenced Brooks; then Brooks intensified Henry's lifelong interest in a large theory for history when in 1893 Henry returned from his trip to the South Seas. Brooks' work doubtless did give Henry some notion of the scale on which such a theory should be built. But certainly Brooks' work was influenced by the Comtian thought of his brother; compare, for example, *History, 1,* 162 f. (cited above, p. 117), and the letter in which Adams summarized what he conceived to be the theme of the *Law;* Ford, *2,* 163, also 153, 197.

28. *Education*, pp. 434, 457.

two were the second law of thermodynamics and biological evolution. Unless man as a force somehow stood outside the energies he studied, Adams argued, both he and society must fit into one of these vast energetic systems.

It seems almost unnecessary to recall that, according to the law of the conservation of energy, the quantity of matter in the universe remains constant—no energy is created, none destroyed. The second law of thermodynamics extends the earlier law by asserting that, even if the total amount of energy remains constant, the potentiality of this energy to do useful mechanical work in closed systems constantly diminishes by a universal tendency toward the dissipation of energy as heat. Coining the term "entropy" as the opposite of available or useful energy, Clausius expressed the first and second laws in 1865 in the famous generalizations which Josiah Willard Gibbs later used as a motto for *On the Equilibrium of Heterogeneous Substances.* "The energy of the world remains constant. The entropy of the world tends toward a maximum." Quite obviously, Adams' third suggestion as an analogy for historical development, that of biological evolution, did not necessarily contradict the two laws of thermodynamics, for if, as Adams suggested, evolution fell under thermodynamics, then all elevation in evolution occurred at the expense of energy.

Now the neatness of Adams' presentation hid embarrassing complications; but in justice to his case, he meant to attack the overeasy manner in which other nineteenth-century historians had employed optimistic interpretations of Darwinian evolution to justify the doctrine of continuously upward progress in history. His lack of caution has a certain amount of justification in theirs. So it will be best momentarily to ignore such distortions in science as Adams' theory involved in order that he may have his say. The metaphor should come first, the criticism later.

Assume, for example, that the passage of historical time be represented as a straight line. Although Adams chose curved lines for his graphs, his theory is perhaps best visualized by starting with a simpler figure. What teacher of history has not chalked a "time line" across his blackboard? On such time lines, then, the three hypotheses for energy offered three possible paths for historical development in terms of the total energy potential remaining to society at successive points in time. It is worth noting at the outset that Adams viewed history in terms of its future

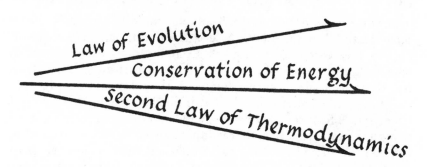

rather than its past. Where most historians had applauded the
constant increase in energy available to man, Adams worried over
the diminishing residue for future use. Like the physical scientist,
in contradistinction to the natural scientist, Adams tended to look
toward the termination of a process. It seemed to him far less important to ask how far history had come than to wonder how much
further it could go. His interest in both predictions and limitations,
evident in the *History*, had flowered at last.

From the start, then, Adams made three tacit assumptions.
He assumed, first, that of all the factors accounting for historical
development the discovery and utilization of energy have been
the most significant; second, that a choice was possible from among
the three hypotheses relating to energy; third, that knowledge
of the future of history was more important than of its past, because the former permitted the historian to distinguish the insignificant events of the past from the important. With these
presuppositions Adams considered the initial decision of the scientific historian. This was his choice of path.

A mere glance at the mounting statistics on coal production
during the nineteenth century alone conclusively demonstrated
to Adams that, however valid the first law of thermodynamics for
science, it was useless as a synthesizing device for history—an
admission sufficiently damning in itself for his hope for a science
of history.[29] Certainly progress of some sort had occurred, and
the average historian had instinctively grasped at Darwin. As for
the degradationist position, sentiment proved a stronger refutation than all the statistics in any atlas. Incredulity, if not outright
scorn, would greet the teacher of history who dared to preface
his course with a statement that he would "treat the history of
modern Europe and America as a typical example of energies

29. *Ibid.*, p. 490. *Degradation: Letter,* p. 209.

indicating degradation 'with headlong rapidity' towards 'inevitable death.' " [30] So, Adams asserted, Darwin had prevailed, but largely for reasons of sentiment. Contemptuous of sentiment in scholarship, despite his own aberrations in this direction, Adams felt that the truly scientific historian should ascertain which of the three paths charted by the natural sciences was trod by most scientists. Then the historian should follow that course, even though it required a drastic readaptation of historical "force" to the realities of natural energy. Adams pursued various fields of study and decided that the weight of opinion leaned toward the degradationist position.

To attack historians for accepting a prevailing faith by citing the prevailing faith of scientists certainly had an element of unconscious humor, which Adams would have relished had Jefferson written the *Letter*. Nothing was more typical of the positivistic tendency to place scientific truths in a consummate category of their own. Characteristic, too, was the layman's search of science, less for specific data than for trends with cosmic implications. Yet, in fairness, if historians were to select any one of the three hypotheses as a metaphoric guide, they were obliged to examine the other two, and especially the postulate that seemed most antithetical to the results for which many historians hoped.

Adams summarized the cumulative evidence on degradation most extensively in the first chapter of his *Letter*. Although not completely logical in his progression from one field to another, he moved generally from physics and geology through paleobotany and paleozoology to anthropology, sociology and, finally, psychology—a sequence which suggests, if it does not precisely duplicate, Comte's hierarchy of science ranging from the physical toward the social sciences. Throughout this gamut of science Adams found two tendencies which, taken together, gave what he conceived as the "drift" of scientific thought. In all the organic sciences it seemed that the ancient beliefs in vital force were giving way to physical-chemical substitutes. In every science, inorganic as well as organic, research indicated that the total availability of physical-chemical energies must steadily decline in intensity. Since scientists had already hinted at the electrical properties of a brain wave, and since history was thought, Adams dared to suggest that history itself might prove to be but one long chronicle of degradation.

30. *Degradation: Letter*, p. 243.

It is worth glancing at some of his specific evidence to determine the major ingredients in his research, although, again, detailed criticism can come later. Having accepted the degradationist trend in physics, he turned to paleobotany and paleozoology,[31] especially to the work of Oswald Heer and Louis Saporta on the arctic flora. According to Adams both scientists thought that the poles had cooled until they could no longer support their original luxuriance. Saporta further suggested that the energy of vegetable growth might have reached its climax "as early as the carboniferous." It was but a step for the French botanist to assert that man had " 'come late, when a beginning of physical decadence had struck the globe, his domain.' " The geologist Albert de Lapparent not only agreed with Saporta but added that the " 'organic world has enriched itself with no new species' " since the glacial epoch. Indeed, " 'several forms have disappeared.' " These gloomy views of a shrinking, cooling earth no longer capable of its prehistoric fecundity inevitably affected Adams' view of Charles Lyell's law of uniformity. Change in the physical world was not primarily the slow, steady affair that Lyell had emphasized and Darwin loosely accepted. On the contrary, change could occur, and generally did, with catastrophic suddenness. The paleontologist Louis Dollo, for one, altered the law of uniformity which Adams had learned while at the legation. Adams paralleled Dollo's own aphoristic summary of his findings: "1. Development has proceeded by leaps.—2. It is irreversible.—3. It is limited." This three-part formula practically corresponded to Adams' concept of phase in history; but since history implied man, paleontology promised to be less significant than anthropology. Adams consulted the physical anthropologist.[32]

Frankly admitting that the drift seemed somewhat less decisive in physical anthropology than in the sciences previously examined, Adams nevertheless assembled statements from many sources which, when ordered to his liking, seemed to indicate that man was a decidedly degraded animal reflecting the degraded energies of his earthly habitat. Specifically, the intellectual specialization of the human being had occurred at the expense of his physical well-being. If—and here Adams adjusted the cheerful faith of his old teacher Louis Agassiz toward a gloomy view of science—man stood as the " 'last term of a series beyond which . . . no

31. *Ibid.*, pp. 160–170.
32. *Ibid.*, pp. 171–179.

further progress [was] materially possible,' " then man's very high degree of intellectual specialization forecast his extinction. To be sure, where both the geologist and the paleontologist had gone over to Kelvin wholeheartedly the anthropologist appeared to be "somewhat painfully hesitating, obedient to the physicists, but trying to remain true to humanity, though acutely conscious that the two directions [could not] be reconciled." Caught between "science and sentiment," all physical anthropologists seemed driven to the conclusions of Paul Topinard, one of their more pessimistic colleagues: " 'our earth will cease to be habitable; it will grow cold; will lose its atmosphere and its moisture, and will resemble our actual moon.' " But long before the earth had cooled, " 'evolution, from progressive [would] become stationary, then regressive.' " Back to the prehistoric lichens, to the Diatomaceae, to the *Protococcus*, and finally " 'nothing!' " If this prophecy seemed black, it was hardly dismal enough for Adams, since "according to [Topinard's] own paleontologist authorities, the evolution of life on the earth had ceased to be progressive some millions of years ago, and had passed through its stationary period into regression before man ever appeared."

After some melancholy predictions of a future ice age by Jacques de Morgan and Camille Flammarion,[33] Adams turned immediately to a mixed group of sociologists, philosophers, and psychologists.[34] All that had gone before pointed toward this latter group of specialists, most akin to historians. If the physical anthropologist hesitated to embrace the second law of thermodynamics out of deference to humanity, the psychologist and the sociologist shut their eyes even tighter against what they did not wish to see. Nothing daunted, Adams still found means to fit psychology and sociology to his larger trend.

He entered on his discussion of these fields in an impressionistic, not a scientific, manner with the assertion that,

> every reader of the French or German paper knows that not
> a day passes without producing some uneasy discussion of
> supposed social decrepitude;—falling off of the birthrate;—
> decline of rural population;—lowering of army standards;—
> multiplication of suicides;—increase of insanity or idiocy,—
> of cancer,—of tuberculosis;—signs of nervous exhaustion,

33. *Ibid.*, pp. 181–184.
34. *Ibid.*, pp. 186–200.

—of enfeebled vitality,—"habits" of alcoholism and drugs,—
failure of eye-sight in the young;—and so on, without end,
coupled with suggestions for correcting these evils such as remind a historian of the Lex Poppaea and the Roman Empire
rather than they prove that careless confidence in itself which
ought to stamp the rapid rise of social energy which everyone
asserts and admits . . . Rarely does the press dwell on proofs
of social evolution except as shown negatively in decline of
death-rate, or of illiteracy, or in relief from pain, and never
does the statistician or sociologist help the historian to any
clear understanding of the progress expected as his literary
goal.

Here was the bridge between Adams' personal experience in his
society as recorded in the *Education*, and the science which he
affected for his *Letter*. Impressions gleaned from headlines could
hardly be considered scientific. When coupled with his views on
social legislation, Adams' choice of headlines savored even more
of personal bias. "The legislators pass half their time, in Germany, France, and England, framing social legislation, of which
a large part rests on the right and duty of society to protect itself
against itself, not under the fiction of elevating itself from lower
to higher, but—as in the case of alcohol and drugs—to protect
itself from deterioration by the exercise of powers analogous to
the power of war." Having thus condemned as deterioration the
tendency in Europe toward social legislation, Adams noted the
"extension of philosophical schools founded on the supposed failure of society" as the "most serious symptom of all." Émile Durkheim, in his study of suicide, had elaborated on the " 'collective
melancholy' " pervasive at the turn of the century. This supposed
aura of melancholy introduced what was actually the climax of
Adams' essay, that is, the connection between instinct and reason.

"Nothing in the history of philosophy is more distinctly
marked," Adams acutely observed, "than the effort of physics
and metaphysics, since 1890, to approach each other." The two
fields met, as Adams saw it, in will or instinct. Philosophers like
Giacomo Ciamician and Eduard von Hartmann had followed
Schopenhauer in his attempt to equate vital energy with will,
while a psychologist like Wilhelm Wundt and a biologist like
Jacques Loeb offered considerable encouragement from the laboratory. Loeb's theory of tropism particularly interested Adams,

since Loeb had already demonstrated that, among the lower organisms at least, instinct was mere physical-chemical response to outside attraction. If instinct was a physical force, what was thought? William Hanna Thomson, in his study on the brain, declared that the brain itself had developed by will-stimulus which " 'not only [organized] brain-centres to perform new functions, but [projected] new connecting,—or, as they are technically called, association-fibres, which [made] nerve-centres work together as they could not, without being thus associated.' " In short, thought was the creature of will. Man had shown his highest energy potential precisely at the moment when he became man —at a time when the earth itself already showed signs of senescence. Thought or reason only reflected man's helplessness, his overspecialization preparatory to his final extinction.

To Adams history as a "Science of Vital Energy in relation with time" [35] must bring its notion of vital energy into accord with the realities of science. And yet the historian might well despair of pushing his science to Adams' extreme.

> Very unwillingly can he admit Reason to be an energy at all; at the utmost, he can hardly allow it to be more than a passive instrument of a physico-chemical energy called Will;—an ingenious economy in the application of power; a catalytic medium; a dynamo, mysteriously converting one form of energy into a lower;—but if persuaded to concede the intrinsic force of Reason, he must still reject its independence. As a force it must obey the laws of force; as an energy it must content itself with such freedom as the laws of energy allow; and in any case it must submit to the final and fundamental necessity of Degradation.

The inevitable degradation of reason, already the degraded product of will, applied "by still stronger reasoning" to the will itself.[36]

Here was the dilemma of the scientific historian; and to Adams all other historians were, as their name implied, but storytellers.[37] History recounted the growth of reason; therefore history was a chronicle of degradation. Behind this view of history lay Adams' fourth and most important assumption. It was in reality the pur-

35. *Ibid.*, p. 207.
36. *Ibid.*, p. 208.
37. *Education*, p. 382.

pose of all the research that had gone before. Reason was the degradation of instinct.

Although Adams promised solutions in his second chapter, he never realized this enticing prospect. Quite the contrary, his solutions left the problem as knotty as before. First of all the evolutionist historian might compromise with degradationist theories. Adams suggested several compromises, each of which proved vain.[38] At the opposite extreme the historian might completely disagree with the physicist.[39] But Adams had already suggested the futility of such a disagreement in his first chapter. There the possible solutions ended. Adams could hope only that the "department of history" would cooperate with "the departments of biology, sociology, and psychology" to furnish "some common formula or figure." Historians, social scientists, psychologists, and biologists, he believed, should link their subjects to the physical sciences by means of a "working model" for handling "vital energies," a model "brought into accord with the figures or formulas used by the department of physics and mechanics to serve their students as models for the working of physico-chemical and mechanical energies." Such a solution seemed "not impossible; but at the present,—for the moment,—as the stream runs,—it also seems, to an impartial bystander, to call for the aid of another Newton." [40]

Thus Adams both stated his problem and eliminated certain solutions in the *Letter*. This essay presented the most balanced and most extended statement of his research. Prior to the publication of the *Letter* he had fixed on a figure of his own, presented only sketchily in the *Education* and elaborated in *The Rule of Phase Applied to History*: that of the curve resulting from a graphic representation of the increased molecular motion occurring during a physical-chemical transformation. A more arbitrary essay than the *Letter*,[41] the *Rule* is less illuminating as to both the

38. *Degradation: Letter*, pp. 210–232.

39. *Ibid.*, pp. 232–237. Thereupon Adams exhorted the historian to learn science and then he returned to the idea of compromise. He reached "the extreme limit of the physicist's concessions" on pp. 256 f. (see below, p. 204), which hardly diminished the dilemma posed.

40. *Degradation: Letter*, pp. 262 ff.

41. Having criticized an early draft of the *Rule* for Adams, Henry A. Bumstead, a mathematical physicist at Yale, was sent the *Letter*. Of this latter essay he wrote that it "impresses me very much more than the essay on the Phase Rule applied to History. With the latter I could not altogether avoid the feeling that

method and the conclusiveness of Adams' research. Yet the *Rule* summarized his theory in a dramatic figure of the sort which he had repeatedly demanded of history departments. The historical positivist consummates his quest only when he has achieved a simplification at once so comprehensive as to constrain an infinite disparity of events to some vast continuity and so dramatic as to challenge the imagination even where the facts refuse to fit the theory. This reason alone justified Brooks Adams, as editor of the essays for the posthumous *Degradation of the Democratic Dogma*, in placing the prolix *Letter* as a prelude to the incisive but at the same time much more capricious *Rule*. But the *Rule* was substantially written in 1909, one year prior to the *Letter*.[42] However much his critics may prefer the *Rule*, they should not—as they almost universally have—confound the two essays.[43]

If the *Rule* was less judicious than the *Letter* and to that extent less scientific, the vivid symbol of the curve of degradation showed the amateur scientist for what at heart he was, a literary man, at once aesthete and rationalist. Catching at the lucid tag ends of scientific research, Adams sought some figure to unify his mosaic of scholarship much as Viollet-le-Duc had combined the sensitivity of the aesthete with the rationalism of the engineer to interpret the Gothic cathedral as a completely logical structure designed to carry the eye along a line from floor through pier to vault. It was no accident that the overly rationalistic ideas of Viollet-le-Duc on Gothic architecture prevailing around the turn of the century should have enticed Adams.[44] If the medieval cathedral reinforced the lesson of line, scientific writing taught the same values to Adams.

there was something arbitrary and artificial in the analogies you drew." Unpublished letter in the estate of Henry Adams; for Bumstead's criticism of a draft of the *Rule* see below, pp. 152, 225, and 239 f.

42. Observe the qualification "substantially"; see below, p. 152.

43. The general tendency to regard the *Letter* as the preparation for the *Rule* unconsciously led Robert E. Spiller to call the *Rule* "later" than the *Letter;* "Henry Adams," *Literary History of the United States*, ed. R. Spiller, W. Thorp, T. Johnson, H. Canby (New York, Macmillan, 1948), *2*, 1098.

44. Pol, Abraham, *Viollet-le-Duc et le rationalisme* (Paris, Vincent Fréal, 1934). Viollet-le-Duc's discussion on construction in his *Dictionnaire de l'architecture française du XI au XVI siècle* has been translated under the significant title, *Rational Building*, tr. George M. Huss (New York and London, Macmillan, 1895). On the rationalistic theory of Gothic architecture, see also James S. Ackerman, "Gothic Theory of Architecture at the Cathedral of Milan," *Art Bulletin, 31* (1949), 84–111; George Kubler, "A Late Gothic Computation of Rib Vault Thrust," *Gazette des Beaux-Arts, 26* (1944), 135–148.

I seem to fancy that it teaches line, and follows the laws of architecture and sculpture; while narratives teach color, and follow the laws of music and painting. That is to say that the complexities of art are infinitely greater in color-composition.

That must be the reason why we care so little what is thought of our artistic work. We are quite drowned in the ocean of doubt [as to] what we think of it ourselves. "Why the devil was I such a fool as to put that high light there! it ought to have been over there!" [45]

History must ideally search for line; excessive color confused. Line as opposed to color: this was both the aesthetic and the didactic lesson of the *History*. But only by eliminating the complexities of his linear treatment of the Jeffersonian period could Adams join Chartres and the Columbian Exposition.

Having accepted the second law of thermodynamics in preference to either the law of the conservation of energy or that of evolution, Adams obtained a downward direction for history measured in terms of the energy potential remaining to history at successive points in time. Again a straight line may help to explain the curve which Adams finally used.

Granted this long descent in power potential as the graph of man's ultimate decay, the historian had to account for change in society, since, after all, change caused direction in the first place. Comte had substituted the word "phase" for "period," "age," "era," or other vocabulary common to history, doubtless because "phase" suggested a developmental rather than a temporal division. Faithful to the mentor of his youth, Adams adopted the Comtian term but altered its meaning to fit his own concept of history as energy. He maintained that he used phase as Willard Gibbs had used it— an assertion which clamors for correction, but remember Adams still holds the floor. Even without correction, it is apparent that he used Gibbs' phase rule in the simplest of metaphors. A given

45. Mar. 8, 1909; Cater, pp. 642 f.

volume of ice, under conditions of pressure and temperature which energized the sluggish molecules, became water; water in turn disappeared as steam. Thus Adams conceived of historical phases. Each phase of society gathered speed in terms of the particular power basic to it, until it reached a critical point. The molecules energizing one phase whirled history into the next. Man had no choice, since human energy comprised but a fraction of total energy. To be sure, the thought energy of a few scientists produced the means to release new types of physical power in the first place; but the insatiable desire for ever greater power urged the scientists on.[46] If scientists lacked freedom of will, then how much less the average man possessed. Energies outside man dragged him willy-nilly where they would.

Man and the energies he could tap (which served as the ingredients basic to Adams' historical theory) represented a volume acted upon by—what? Certainly not pressure and temperature. Adams altered the physicist's terms to "attraction" and "accelera-ton," explaining his vocabulary as follows:

> The processes of History being irreversible, the action of Pressure can be exerted only in one direction, and therefore the variable called Pressure in physics has its equivalent in the Attraction, which, in the historical rule of phase, gives to human society its forward movement.

> In history . . . the Temperature is a result of acceleration, or its equivalent, and in the Rule of historical phase Acceleration takes its place.[47]

Behind his logic lay acute observation, although the observation is perhaps more easily understood without the logic. The "child of the eighteenth century" watched the speed of the steam engine increase year by year in the nineteenth, as it hurtled across the continent toward manifest destiny. Then, before the new century dawned he stood in the Hall of Machines at the Chicago Columbian Exposition. He listened to the silent hum in the dy-

46. It is only by some such rationalization as this that one can account for a confusion throughout Adams' essay. At times he used a gravitational metaphor in that outside forces dragged man into a new phase by the magnitude of their attraction; more frequently he used a physical-chemical or electromagnetic analogy, where forces at work within a given phase accounted for succession of phase; see immediately below, n. 52.

47. *Degradation: Rule*, p. 280.

namo. He foresaw this energy hitched to the drive wheel of history. With new power came new power potential; with new power potential the electrical phase superseded the mechanical. Hence a certain quantitative increase in energy so altered the quality of human culture that society changed its state as decisively as did ice in becoming water. The change was the more decisive since energy whirled mind with matter. Although Pulitzer and Hearst had only hinted in Adams' lifetime at the mass production possible to the press, and although he saw the motion picture (if at all) in its infancy, while radio and television were yet to be born, still Adams sensed the intellectual as well as the material centralization increasingly evident with every passing year.

Adams bemoaned the tendency; but not with the fondness of a conservative for the bric-a-brac of the past. As early as 1892, four years before Langley hopped the Potomac in his "aerodrome," Adams had eagerly talked with the inventor. As early as 1904 he had owned an automobile.[48] To Adams the curse of centralization was not the gain in convenience but the loss of individualism: "men become every year more and more creatures of force, massed about central power-houses."[49] The powerhouse attracted all men and all thought, as the toy magnets on Adams' desk drew steel filings,[50] until one day the humming dynamo would in its turn spin so fast that it reached the limit of its possibilities. The search for energies capable of still greater speeds, still larger tasks, would hurl history, and mankind with it, into a new phase faster than any that had gone before.

The year 1900 roughly marked for Adams the division between steam and electricity. Adams asked himself what had preceded mechanical power as a force in society. With Comte he declared that religion—whether as fetish or God[51]—had energized mankind, as it had energized his thought. The religious phase in history had ended with the Renaissance simultaneously with the beginning of the mechanical phase in the discoveries of Bacon, Galileo, and Descartes. Historians, said Adams, had variously lifted the curtain on the Renaissance at about 1500, 1600, or

48. Ford, 2, 11, 437; also *Education,* p. 469.
49. *Education,* pp. 421, 466.
50. *Ibid.,* p. 396.
51. *Degradation: Rule,* pp. 293 f. Where Comte had divided the religious phase into three parts—fetishism, polytheism, and monotheism—Adams thought that no "change of Direction" was implied in these stages, only a "concentration" within the religious phase.

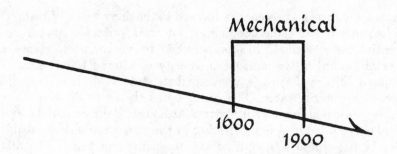

Mechanical

1600

1900

1700. For his theory he arbitrarily selected the middle dating. The mechanical phase, therefore, spanned 300 years.

How long had the religious phase lasted? The question had always puzzled ethnologists, who found the savage bowed before his fetish, until the image disappeared in the furthest reaches of time. Another question fascinated Adams even more. How long would the electrical phase last? The historian who solved this riddle would also have discovered a genuine science of history. Adams believed that if history were ever to become a true science the historian must predict the future as precisely as the physical chemist foretold the moment when a given chunk of ice under a specified set of conditions became a certain volume of water.

The second law of thermodynamics had furnished the downward direction; a primitive sequence of phases had provided the formula for change. Adams now required a timetable for change, if he were to ascertain the length of the religious and electrical phases which flanked the 300 years of mechanical power. Scooping the grab bag of science for one last essential, he brought up what he called the "law of electrical squares." This law stated that "the average motion of one phase is the square of that which precedes it." [52] The more quickly the molecules moved, the more

52. *Ibid.*, p. 305. Adams referred this "law of inverse squares" specifically to gravitation in the *Education*, p. 492; but formulas answering his less specific statement in the *Rule* appear for various phenomena in magnetism and electricity as well as gravitation. In the private edition of the *Education* (1907) Adams, invoking the comet analogy (see below, pp. 146 ff.), would "use the formula of terrestrial gravitation to serve for the law of the mind," although he added that almost any other formula would serve as well. In the posthumous edition of the *Education* (1918, precise date of revision unknown), he would "use the formula of squares," the vagueness indicating his retreat from the purely gravitational image to a more general image including magnetism and electricity. In the *Rule* (1909) he spoke of the "electric law of squares." The precise formula used was of little import in any event, because he never really determined the precise degree of

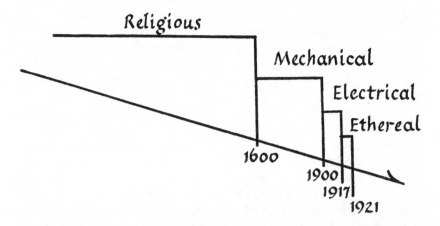

energy they released; hence the sooner one phase became the next, according to an inverse geometric progression, until the sequence had been completed and energy dissipated to impotence. Adams easily transformed the phases of physical science into his parallel for social science. Mechanical forces surpassed the energy of religion, while the power of electricity eclipsed that of mechanics. Successive types of energy chopped history into increasingly narrow segments of time. Each phase ran its course faster than the last. For Adams' theory the rest was simplest arithmetic. If 300 represented the middle term of an inverse geometric series, then the electrical law of squares gave the segment preceding the mechanical phase a value of the square of 300; the segment following, its square root. The time table therefore showed a religious phase of 90,000, a mechanical phase of 300, and an electrical phase of about 17½ years. What then? The future itself dangled by a square root!

Adams predicted that the dynamo would whirl civilization into what, with his background in nineteenth-century science, he called the "Ethereal Phase" for a mere four years. Thus his *Rule* would "bring Thought to the limit of its possibilities in the year 1921." [53]

He not only attempted to formulate his theory of history in terms of laws as devised by natural scientists but also sought to

acceleration in history. In the *Education* (1907) Adams wrote, "it [the human meteoroid] may be supposed to have doubled its speed and energy every five and twenty years." In the posthumous edition (1918) he altered the statement to "the attraction of one century squared itself to give the measure of attraction in the next." In the *Rule* (1909) the squaring was by phase.

53. *Degradation: Rule*, p. 308.

make it vivid by suggesting a series of linear analogies for history: ice on a mountain top melting and flowing downhill to the ocean, the movements of nebulae, the paths of comets, the phase rule, the curve of water vapor. Of this hodgepodge of imagery Adams barely mentioned the ocean and nebula analogies; hence they can be omitted for discussion of those graphs to which he gave most attention.[54] The straightedge has thus far furnished the time line of history for this presentation of Adams' theory. Although Adams used the line, it was never straight. Before selecting the curve of water vapor as the most promising illustration for his *Rule*, he experimented with the path of a typical comet like that of 1843 streaking in a parabola toward the sun and constantly gaining speed as it approached this massive powerhouse. Since outside forces attracted both the comet and man's thought, the analogy seemed to promise a possible path for history, although this first graph reflected Newtonian gravitation, not the phase rule. The comet realized the peak of its speed as it rounded the sun. Adams believed that man was at perihelion, that he had almost reached his maximum speed, his maximum power, and hence his maximum capacity for thought.

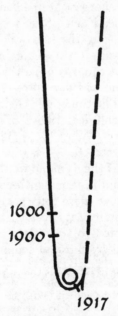

54. *Ibid.*, pp. 299 f., for the graphs to which Adams merely alluded; pp. 300–303 for the comet analogy.

To transpose a simple time line into the more complex curve of thought as visualized by Adams the successive time units comprising the longest phases in history obviously receive the shortest segments on the graph. In other words, Adams' graph represented not time but the totality of thought possible to history. As he asserted in the *Education*, "If [the human mind] behaved like an explosive, it must rapidly recover equilibrium [at a lower level of energy potential]; if it behaved like a vegetable, it must reach its limits of growth; and even if it acted like the earlier creations of energy—the saurians and sharks—it must have nearly reached the limits of its expansion." [55] History was not chronology but thought. Like the useful work available from a particular source of power in a closed thermodynamic system, thought had limits. Hence the space on Adams' graph allotted to the four years of the ethereal phase might be equivalent to several thousand years of the religious. [56]

Now Adams could not have pondered the implications of his comet analogy very intensively, for his graph is hardly a valid depiction of his historical theory. To reach perihelion, history (or thought) would have had to travel a tremendous distance. On such a graph the long religious phase would account for a large part of the total movement of thought toward historical entropy, while whatever the phase of instinct which preceded the religious it would necessarily account for more. The ethereal phase would be a mere fillip at the end. But this was not at all Adams' conception. Nor can criticism of his comet analogy stop here. Moving away from the sun to complete the opposite arm of the parabola, the comet lost gravitational pull; hence its speed constantly slowed. Had Adams followed the comet analogy far enough, the cave man at one end of this celestial parabola must have ultimately returned to the habitat of the cave bear at the other extremity. Such an analogy would bring about not man's end but merely a progressive and relatively comfortable debasement toward imbecility. Indeed, the long-range future for a comet-like development to history was even brighter than its mere promise of a return to Adams' happy age of instinct, for comets move in long elliptical paths around the sun, to sweep through perihelion at regular intervals, some as frequently as every three or four

55. *Education*, p. 496.
56. The graph in this volume represents both a simplification and a slight adjustment of Adams' graph; *Degradation: Rule*, p. 302.

years, some with periods vastly more extensive. To be sure, a few
comets have disintegrated, but not before making many turns
around the sun. Nor does their disintegration necessarily occur at
perihelion as Adams' metaphor would seem to demand. The comet
therefore offered a better analogy for a cyclical than a degradationist scheme for history. While no evolutionist historian would
have found the prospect of future progress along the path of a
comet particularly cheerful, certainly no convinced degradationist
could have tolerated its optimism. If Adams thought of these
flaws in his comet analogy he never mentioned them; but he did
caution his readers that he intended the analogy "only to introduce the problem." [57] Far safer to abandon the metaphor than to
examine it too deeply, especially when science offered such a wide
selection of graphs from which to choose.[58]

Whereas the comet analogy simply exhibited Adams' fatal
fondness for the vivid scientific image, the curve to which he now
turned might well interest the historian because of its striking
resemblance to modern graphical representations of the increase
in speed, power potential, and military might available to society
during the nineteenth and twentieth centuries. The ice–water–
vapor analogy on which Adams finally settled promised a far
more dismal future than had the comet image; more dismal and
more appropriate, too, according to Adams, who believed that
society had moved much faster than the comet. Furthermore, a
comet as material mass followed the material path of Newtonian
gravitation. Scientists had at least postulated the electrical nature
of the brain wave. Thought could therefore be better likened to
the graph of a molecular substance like ice, reaching the phase
of vapor through the increased energy of its atomic structure.
Adams' new curve was hyperbolic, its infinite extensions tending
toward right angles with one another.

	Religious	Mechanical	Electrical
Time required for each phase	t^2	t	$\sqrt{t}$
Movement of thought toward its limit	$\sqrt{m}$	m	m^2

57. *Ibid.*, p. 303.
58. *Education*, p. 489: "Images are not arguments, rarely lead to proof, but
the mind craves them, and, of late more than ever, the keenest experimenters find
twenty images better than one, especially if contradictory; since the human mind has
already learned to deal in contradictions."

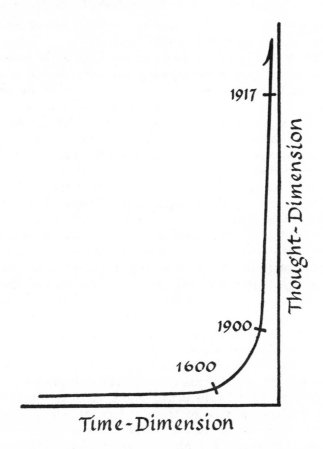

1917

Thought-Dimension

1900

1600

Time-Dimension

One arm of the curve stretched into the past as an almost inter-
minable progression of time units moving toward the present at
a relatively slow velocity; the other rose sharply toward the future,
time almost annihilated in speed as man approached the limit of
his possibilities.

Not that this final graph was perfect. Far from it. For example, the physicist would immediately discard as worthless any
graph without coordinates, a defect here remedied by labels suitable enough for Adams' historical analogy but woefully unmathe-
matical. Moreover, the physicist would certainly note the discrepancy between Adams' calculations and his graph. The calculations would not give an equilateral hyperbola. Indeed, since
Adams conjured an imaginary physicist in his *Letter*,[59] it may

59. *Degradation: Letter*, pp. 201 f., 221–230.

not be inappropriate to call up another here and let him continue the criticism. Such a physicist might begin,

"I would object to Adams' frequent reference to the phase rule throughout his essay, since he replaces the phase rule by the curve of water vapor as soon as he attempts to visualize his theory graphically. Vapor is, of course, only one phase of the ice–water–vapor sequence. The curve of vaporization—which, incidentally, is not an equilateral hyperbola—represents only a fragment of a much more complex curve. Moreover, while I can very well understand how distance affects force in gravitation, or how temperature affects pressure and vice versa in thermodynamics, I cannot see how time, merely by its passage, affects thought. It is thought which affects thought.

"Time is at least a measurable dimension. But 'movement of thought'? This phrase may mean many things. Adams may refer to the increasing sum of the total power potential available to society through time and measured by such statistics as those indicating the mounting production of coal or electric power. Or he may refer to the optimum performance of a succession of new inventions and improvements on old, like the increasing speeds of trains, automobiles, and airplanes. Or he may refer to something as yet unmeasurable, for he implies that the movement of thought itself, the very essence of thought, must somehow quicken its pace in order to keep up with the contrivances which it brings forth. If such a mechanistic view of thought has any meaning at all, perhaps the physiologist may someday measure its movements; but I doubt this possibility and, anyway, mechanistically speaking, it is almost certain that men in the past have expended as much energy in their thinking as we do today. No, Adams can hardly have meant us to interpret his phrase from such a narrowly physiological point of view, although he undoubtedly did intend us to understand him in a psychological and historical sense. In other words, he implied that thought moves faster and faster in terms of its necessary adjustment to social and emotional problems created by increased speed and power. This may be true, but again the physicist cannot measure such an entity, nor apparently can either the psychologist or the historian, since otherwise they would not have come to us physicists. Actually, Adams seems to desire an omnibus meaning for his 'thought-movement' coordinate. As a physicist, I must criticize his coordinate because, supposing we know what 'thought-movement' means, it is impossible to measure as a whole, and he doesn't give us permission to measure any particular part.

"Up to now I have criticized Adams as though his coordinates were 'time' and 'thought-movement'; but he actually mentioned 'attraction' and 'acceleration.' With these latter coordinates, no coordinate for chronology is possible on his graph, however curious the omission in any theory of history. Chronology cannot be fitted to the coordinate for acceleration unless centuries are shrinking. They may somehow seem to be shrinking with our increased speeds, but Adams' theory takes no account of any such psychological illusion. With even less reason can chronology conceivably be fitted to the coordinate for attraction. Rather Adams indicates that the accumulating thought attracts itself with an acceleration which increases by virtue of its own accumulation. Please don't ask me to unravel this puzzle. In fact, the puzzle is even more puzzling because if the volume of thought constantly increases, very much like books in a library, Adams' graph allows for no increase whatsoever.

"Finally," the physicist may conclude, "after such a tangle it will be anticlimactic to comment on deficiencies of detail in vocabulary and mathematics. Adams used 'velocity,' 'acceleration,' and 'motion' as though they were synonymous. Without knowing precisely how he meant to use these noninterchangeable terms it is impossible to assign values to his successive phases of thought. Moreover, the physicist would deplore the squaring of units of religious energy (whatever these might be) to get units of mechanical energy. He would likewise condemn the dependence of all the time sequences on the arbitrary figure 300 for the mechanical phase. From this figure Adams derived 900,000 years for the religious phase and 17½ years for the electrical. Substitute three centuries for 300 years for the mechanical phase, and the religious phase is a mere nine centuries, while the electrical is all of 1⅓. The physicist can never permit a formula which depends on unique circumstance—in this instance a particular set of figures—for its operation. Perhaps Adams' work has some value for historians, and certainly his attempt to relate history to energy will interest some physicists. But I'm afraid that his errors vitiate his theory."

So much for the imaginary physicist. As a matter of fact, a real physicist raised some of these criticisms, for Adams submitted a first draft of the *Rule* to his friend John Franklin Jameson in an effort to obtain professional comment. As director of the historical department of the Carnegie Institution and holding other important posts in the historical bureaucracy, Jameson was familiar with American universities and their faculties. Adams reasoned that he would know of some likely critics for the essay. Jameson sounded four candidates, who either refused or made prefunctory reply, before writing Henry Bumstead, mathematical physicist at Yale and a pupil of Gibbs. Bumstead went through the manuscript carefully, making typewritten comments now deposited in the Massachusetts Historical Society.[60] Among the comments were those criticizing the confusion of the terms velocity, acceleration, and motion,[61] together with the warning that a change in the mechanical phase from 300 years to three centuries would completely alter the time scale. Bumstead's remarks did not reach Adams until some time in January, 1910, but Adams had not waited for the critique before continuing his efforts toward a science of history. He was at work on the *Letter* as early as September of the preceding year and distributed the privately printed volume to a roster of college presidents, professors, and libraries, drawn up for the most part by Jameson, in the spring of 1910. Only after this distribution must Adams have returned to the *Rule*, rewriting it without substantially altering its meaning in accordance with most but not all of Bumstead's suggestions. Moreover, Adams enlarged the *Letter* with handwritten addenda, as a copy of the private edition in the Massachusetts Historical Society shows. Hence he may have begun the original version of the *Rule* in 1908, dated it 1909, and rewrote it after receiving Bumstead's comments sometime following the distribution of the *Letter*. As for the *Letter*, he wrote most (probably all) of this in 1909, dated it 1910, and subsequently altered it only by adding further evidence. It is the rewritten *Rule* and the revised *Letter* which appear in *The Degradation of the Democratic Dogma*. Adams certainly completed all this work on the two essays prior to a stroke on April 24, 1912. The revisions indicate that until his illness ended any further "serious study" he continued to

60. On Bumstead's critique see Cater, pp. 646 f., 650, n. 1.

61. Confusion among these terms had permitted the first draft of the *Rule* to be interpreted in any of three ways. Bumstead suggested that Adams eliminate all mention of "acceleration" and speak only of the total "motion" in each phase. Adams accepted Bumstead's criticism for the final version, *Degradation: Rule*, p. 305; but elsewhere in the essay he retained the terms "acceleration," "attraction," and "volume" with which he had earlier introduced his theory of history; see above, p. 142.

think about his scheme for a science of history and sought to improve it.[62] Since he grafted all his improvements on the original essays, however, there is no evidence that further revision would have substantially altered his scheme.

On learning that so much is wrong with a single graph in this scheme, the historian may well choose to pursue the theory no further. Still Adams' theory was not necessarily wrong merely because he became muddled over units and graphs. Momentarily let the criticism of physicists stand as an aside to the analogic suggestiveness of Adams' graph. Unlike the comet analogy, the new graph disclosed man's fate as no longer that of increasing imbecility, followed by a later return to the perihelion of civilization. Instead his future was one of increasing motion, but of such decreasing productivity that man's existence (or at least his effectiveness) seemed as dubious as that of a cubic centimeter of steam evenly distributed within a cubic mile of atmosphere. Here once more the septuagenarian leaped from the human band wagon, by virtue of his seniority, and left it plunging faster and faster toward the ultimate void. For unlike water vapor which could condense and fall as rain, or within the very restricted limits of a closed mechanical system could be cajoled (by either increased pressure, decreased temperature, or their combination) first into water, then back into ice, history was irreversible. Man could only accelerate his headlong rush to oblivion.

62. July 15, 1912; Ford, *2*, 597. The complex documentation for this paragraph follows. Adams dated a projected preface for the *Rule* Jan. 1, 1909 (Cater, p. 781); he wrote Bumstead for comment, Mar. 17, 1909 (Cater, p. 646); Adams' note of gratitude, Feb. 1, 1910 (Cater, p. 676), dates Bumstead's critique; the vague statement by Brooks Adams in his Introduction to the *Degradation* (p. 7) that he printed the *Rule* as his brother "left it eight years ago" would indicate that Brooks received the rewritten version sometime in 1911. Assisting Brooks Adams in the editing of the *Degradation*, Worthington Ford discovered Bumstead's criticisms but found that the line references in the critique did not jibe with the manuscript in Brooks Adams' possession; Ford later discovered the earlier version as he announced in a letter dated Apr. 21, 1919 (Henry Adams Collection, Massachusetts Historical Society).

The first mention of work on the *Letter* occurs Sept. 9, 1909 (Ford, *2*, 524); Adams completed it before 1910 since a printing order for the volume, in the files of J. H. Furst Co., Baltimore, Md., shows that printing began in 1909; he mentioned final corrections in a letter of Feb. 9, 1910 (Ford, *2*, 534), and dated the Introduction Feb. 16, 1910; the bulk of the distribution was completed by Mar. 14, 1910 (Ford, *2*, 537). This last letter stated that approximately 250 copies were distributed; figures in the files of J. H. Furst Co. show a printing of 500 copies. For further proof that Adams added data to the *Letter* up to the time of his stroke see below, pp. 211 f.

The year 1921 has come and gone. The oblivion promised by Adams is still wanting.

Like his Delphic predecessors Adams left a fuzziness in his prediction by adding that "even if the life of the [mechanical] phase, 1600–1900, were extended another hundred years [to meet the specifications of those historians who dated the beginning of the Renaissance at 1500], the difference to the last term of the series would be negligible. In that case, the Ethereal Phase would last till about 2025." [63] In the broad sweep of historical time the lack of coincidence between 1921 and 2025 would be little more important than the frequent lack of coincidence between color and line in the Sunday comic section—especially since nothing in the formulation prevented thought from abrupt termination during some intermediate year. Hence the fuzziness as to date was less serious than the ambiguity in respect to the character of the ultimate debacle.

What precisely did Adams mean by bringing "Thought to the limit of its possibilities"? With the advent of the atomic bomb the American Nostradamus has attained new stature not only for his *Rule* but quite as much for his letters with their amazing perception of future events.[64] Despite a record more impressive than that of most prophets, Adams scarcely predicted the atomic bomb as such.[65] Yet he did foretell the moral of atomic energy: that nonhuman energies increasingly imprisoned man. Once he conjured force man had to live with his creation; there was no turning back. Could man reassert his individuality? For Jeffersons, for Madisons, for Adamses, for all others of the eighteenth century, thought was indeed finished. To this extent the growth in impersonal power was a personal tragedy for those who lived in the shadow of eighteenth-century greatness. In reality the tragedy had universal scope. The child of the eighteenth century could perceive disaster more clearly than his nineteenth-century successor who hugged the machine too closely to realize the fatal consequences of his love.

Adams came no closer to a prediction of the atomic bomb. Cer-

63. *Degradation: Rule*, p. 308.
64. See below, pp. 160 f.
65. Adams suggested as one of his "solutions" (*Degradation: Letter*, p. 211) that the bitter pill of degradation might be sweetened by a mere alteration in vocabulary. "In strictness, no doubt, water which falls and dynamite which expands are equally degraded energies, but the mind is repelled by the idea of degradation while it is pleased by the figure of expansion." Were he writing today could Adams possibly have used the "expansion" of dynamite as a phenomenon for pleasurable contemplation?

tainly he came close enough; but there were more specific meanings
to his warning that thought (or history) would reach the "limit
of its possibilities." Reconsider the first chapter of his *Letter*.
Various scientists might fix the limit of thought for various reasons
—and all were grist for Adams' mill. Thus Adams implied that the
cosmologist might say that thought will end when the energy of
the universe is dissipated to nothingness; the historical geologist,
when the earth shrinks and cools so as to become uninhabitable;
the physical anthropologist, when man's physical structure becomes
so overspecialized that he is superseded by a more adaptable species;
the conservationist, when man dissipates all resources which are
practically convertible into useful energy; the sociologist and social
psychologist, when man's society degenerates into an unthinking
mob. Other psychologists, philosophers, and especially mathematical physicists might make the most daring suggestion of all:
thought will reach the limit of its possibilities when it finally centers in abstractions so far removed from experience that man can
no longer relate them to reality.

From the ultimate cul-de-sac of reason, how easy—and at the
same time how perverse—to postulate that reason is the degradation of instinct. Not that Adams was alone. He cited Henri Bergson,
who sought to dispel the gloom of mechanistic and intellectualistic
philosophies with the white light of man's creativity but admitted
that " 'intuition is almost completely sacrificed to intelligence . . .
a lamp, almost extinguished . . . it casts a feeble and flickering
light, but a light which pierces, none the less, the darkness of the
night in which our intelligence leaves us.' " [66] The phase of intuition, of pure instinct, of will, preceded the religious phase on the
degradationist curve of history.[67] Adams put his society at the opposite extreme of the hyperbola of history, about to enter the
ethereal phase of absolute reason, of pure intellect. If the

> function of man is, to the historian, the production of Thought;
> but if all the other sciences affirm that not Thought but Instinct
> is the potential of Vital Energy, and if the beauties of Thought
> —shown in the intuitions of artistic genius,—are to be taken

[66] *Degradation: Letter*, pp. 204 f.

[67] To one correspondent Adams asserted that he would have chosen as a case
study of the intuitional stage of history a period earlier than the Middle Ages
had he been able to obtain sufficient evidence; Ford, *2*, 546. Somewhat spurious as
apology, the apology nevertheless validated the consistency of his dialectic—if this
is important. See also *ibid., 2*, 574, n. 1, on Adams' interest in Cromagnon man.

Reason - Intelligence

Instinct - Will - Intuition

for the last traces of an instinct now wholly dead or dying, nothing remains for the historian to describe or develop except the history of a more or less mechanical dissolution.[68]

To a friend Adams noted that his *Letter* was a "connecting link between the *Chartres* and the *Education*." [69] For all its supposed objectivity, then, his historical theory possessed an undertone of autobiography. A quotation from André Lalande in the *Letter* might well have served as an inscription to the *Education*. " 'Thought comes as the result of helplessness. Thought . . . is the refraining from speech or action . . . action comes first . . .' " [70] Deprived of an active role in life, Adams had been driven to thought. Here in the *Letter* and the *Rule* was the end of all his thinking.

Could perversity be carried further? All Adams' scientific

68. *Degradation: Letter*, pp. 205 f.
69. Feb. 28, 1910; Ford, *2, 536*.
70. *Degradation: Letter*, p. 203.

evidence merely proved the superiority of art. Holding that science was the degradation of art, he still insisted on a science of history. Once achieved, such a science apparently proved that the proper teaching of history eliminated the study taught.

VI. THE DECREASE OF ENERGY

ADAMS loved a paradox, and the paradoxical stimulates critical dissension. Where one critic attacks the logic another lauds the paradox itself. What one calls irrational another finds suggestive. To chart a middle course is difficult, and yet necessary for any understanding of Adams' contradictory nature. He said the ridiculous and yet appeared profound; or just the reverse, he spoke wisely and yet seemed nonsensical. How serious, for instance, was his proposal for teaching history? In the first of his speculative essays, *The Tendency of History*, Adams had frankly offered his remarks in the "paradoxical spirit of private conversation." [1] Even after he had mulled for more than a decade and a half over the problems which he initiated in his *Tendency*, he apparently still proffered his conclusions in the same spirit. To one correspondent he wrote of his *Letter*, "I'm amusing myself by printing a little volume to make fun of my fellow historians. The fun of it is that not one of them will understand the fun. The *pince-sans-rire* is not an American form of humor. I don't know that I should see the joke myself if I were not its author." [2]

Paradox was, after all, merely a means of emphasizing the puzzling elements in any situation. Throughout his life Adams stopped short of final solutions. In his Harvard seminar in American history he had stressed problems more than answers. [3] So his *History* seemed to leave its readers to draw their own conclusions about the Jefferson and Madison administrations. Or again in 1889, when Henry Holt asked whether he might reveal the author of *Democracy*, Adams replied that "the riddle is more amusing . . . than the solution would be"; [4] while with his second novel, *Esther*, he again toyed with anonymity. [5] When in Cuba with Clar-

1. *Degradation: Tendency*, p. 133; also *Education*, p. 339.
2. Jan. 24, 1910; Ford, *2*, 531.
3. Lindsay Swift, "A Course in History at Harvard College in the Seventies," *Proceedings of the Massachusetts Historical Society*, *52* (1918), 73 f.
4. Aug. 8, 1889; Cater, p. 187.
5. Cater, p. 130, and the subsequent series of letters to Henry Holt.

ence King he purposely disputed the major conclusions of geology merely to hear King's response.[6] On another occasion, after some amateur geologizing on an island in the south Pacific, he wrote on the formation of coral islands, "just for fun I like to make theories of my own, and have manufactured six or eight that delighted me." [7] For fun he listened to the baffled comments of tourists who visited the hooded figure which St. Gaudens had designed as a monument to his wife. "Most took it for a portrait-statue, and the remnant were vacant-minded in the absence of a personal guide. None felt what would have been a nursery-instinct to a Hindu baby or a Japanese jinricksha-runner." [8] If none felt, Adams did not intend to help them feel, any more than he meant to explain to the duller readers of his *Education* why a reasonably successful man had failed. There was method in his ambiguity, for a work of art needs no literary explanation; [9] but there was also an exclusiveness of intellect and sensitivity which assumed a discerning audience. His was the kind of ambiguity suitable to the coterie. Only boors, with no sense of the deft touch suitable to cultivated conversation, would quibble over his logic. Only simpletons would swallow it whole. Was his historical speculation absurd? Or astute? Those who refuse to enter into the paradoxical spirit of the occasion had best seek another author.

The spirit in which Adams approached his science of history might well arouse the suspicions of the scientist. Certainly the scientist would suspect a "scientific" theory of history which substantially owed its tonality to the pessimism of the *Education*. Since his encyclopedic observations on his world formed the foundation of his speculation, their quality is significant. A sampling from those on foreign affairs shows Adams at his best.

That the Liberal Republican of 1876 should have commented extensively on the Sherman Anti-Trust Act, on the Populist party, on Henry George, and on the tribulations of a burgeoning labor movement might have been expected, but these and other important aspects of American liberalism during the last two decades of the nineteenth century went almost unmentioned in both his letters and

6. "King," *Clarence King Memoirs* (published for the Century Association, New York, Putnam, 1904), p. 171.

7. Dec. 4, 1890; Ford, *1*, 448.

8. *Education*, p. 329.

9. Although Adams did imply that art should have a symbolic or literary meaning, he never suggested it might have a formal significance, without literary overtones; see below, p. 279, n. 70.

the *Education*, unless (as in the case of the labor movement and the silver campaign of 1896) he generalized the specific into vast impersonal forces.[10] Ever fascinated by his quest of a formula for history expressed in terms of the nonhuman energies of natural science, Adams became impatient with the trivialities of domestic affairs. Of what significance were national politics when compared to the slightest shift in the energy equation implicit in an international balance of power.[11] In the nineties not only Adams but many other Americans viewed the international scene with a growing interest which marked the emergence of the United States as a power in world affairs. Yet few matched Adams' sensitivity to diplomacy; few could boast of his opportunities to acquire such sensitivity, first at the legation, then as historian of the tangled diplomacy of the War of 1812, finally as both friend of Hay and global tourist. His scattered predictions on the relationship between the United States and Europe, from a decade of correspondence centering in 1900, seem amazingly foresighted.

He recorded the beginnings of England's decline by noting the overextension of her empire as revealed in Boer victories and the flight of her capital from London to New York.[12] He predicted trouble from an expanding Germany and forecast that in alliance with Russia she might dominate the globe.[13] The United States, he believed, must therefore aid England and France in order to perfect an "Atlantic system" against central and eastern Europe.[14] He foresaw that ultimately the United States and Russia must face one another as the two great world powers.[15] All these predictions between 1895 and 1905! Finally, from the *Education*, "The last and highest triumph of history would, to his mind, be the bringing of Russia into the Atlantic combine, and the just and fair allotment of the whole world among the regulated activities of the universe." [16] If, as he maintained, the historian ought "to triangulate from the widest possible base to the furthest point he thinks he can see," [17] then Adams certainly fulfilled this duty.

10. See below, p. 272.
11. *Education*, p. 421.
12. For example, Ford, *2*, 269, 276, 303, 381, 383 f.; Cater, pp. 482, 501. On Adams' predictions see also Herbert Edwards, "The Prophetic Mind of Henry Adams," *College English, 3* (1942), 708–721.
13. For example, Ford, *2*, 130, 276, 394; Cater, p. 484.
14. For example, Ford, *2*, 195, 212, 297, 352, 447 f., 461.
15. For example, *ibid., 2*, 200 f., 269; Cater, p. 354.
16. *Education*, p. 439.
17. *Ibid.*, p. 395.

Unfortunately praise needs tempering. An aura of vaguely impending catastrophe all but obliterated his most cogent observations.

> Such a chaos! Wall Street goes wild, while Lombard Street is dead broke, and living on French charity. London and Berlin are standing in perfectly abject terror, watching Pierpont Morgan's nose flaming over the ocean waves, and approaching hourly nearer their bank-vaults. England, if figures have value, is walking straight into bankruptcy . . . Russia is in convulsions . . . I have been shivering in a ghastly panic.[18]

Exaggeration can be entertaining in a letter; and if repetition surfeits, the fault lies in reading at a sitting what originally appeared as notes, widely spaced in time. When the exaggeration became pose, even an obsession, then no New England Calvinist ever fitted all experience more relentlessly to his formula.[19] Critics can today arrange scattered remarks from Adams' writings and thus prove that he analyzed the course of foreign affairs for three decades beyond his death. He did not analyze; he merely sensed. He never ordered his perceptions on international events into a consistent development.[20] Nor did he evaluate his data so as to indicate which factors would be expected to contribute most to the ultimate debacle and which seemed less potent harbingers of disaster. Nor, finally, did he discuss the means toward such a goal as the "Atlantic combine" beyond the absurdly inadequate suggestion of lowered tariffs. However perceptive his remarks on foreign affairs, then, they remained no more than scattered observations tinged by a theory of catastrophe, which too often meant that they were simply tinged by a state of mind. This state of mind became more important to his historical speculation than the work of Kelvin and Gibbs. It gave to his later thinking, even when most perceptive, an element of irresponsibility.

18. Apr. 8, 1901; Ford, *2*, 324.

19. Yvor Winters, *The Anatomy of Nonsense* (Norfolk, Conn., New Directions, 1943), pp. 23–87, ingeniously maintains that Adams' "nonsense" comes from a Calvinistic view of the world. He saw the real world at one remove in terms of a symbolism arbitrarily fitted into a theory suggestive of Puritan predestination. Winters takes no notice of the positivistic influences on Adams which account more rationally for his theory and, in conjunction with his life, for its pessimistic cast as well.

20. He may have occasionally approached such a synthesis in conversation, if a page from John Bigelow's diary, reproduced by Cater, p. lxxxvi, is more than an isolated instance.

He enjoyed the paradox "for fun." Here lay the danger. Although the paradox introduced serious questions, Adams had such fun with the riddle that he rarely looked for answers. Like many good conversationalists he loved to startle. At most he furnished solutions only to the point where they maintained the puzzle or where they made it more insoluble. He did not need to look for answers, as did the more penurious teachers to whom he addressed his *Letter*. If his fun inevitably led to failure, he could afford the luxury of indecision. He could withdraw from participation in the central energies of his world until he read his daily paper with much the same aloofness as he had once leafed the documents on the Jefferson administration. "I am seriously speculating whether I shall have a better view of the *fin-de-siècle* circus in England, Germany, France or India, and whether I should engage seats to view the débacle in London, Paris, Berlin or Calcutta." [21] Wealth alone finally permitted such a show of cosmopolitan indifference; but his apparent indifference covered bitterness. To laugh and wonder why he laughed, such was Adams' fate.[22] Hence the ambiguity in his historical speculation between the serious and the ironical.

If some have emphasized the distortions, the contradictions, the irrational in his historical theory they have repaid Adams in his own coin. Although he might theorize for the sake of amusement, he could not fairly boast with Whitman: "Do I contradict myself? Very well then I contradict myself." Where Whitman strove for a cumulative emotional image, Adams pretended an intellectual argument and deserved chastisement where his logic faltered.[23] Other critics protest that to concentrate on the logic is to lose the image, where the image is all important. Where rationalistic criticism tends to assail Adams' means, impressionistic criticism tends to applaud his purpose. Although both are valid approaches to the *Rule* and the *Letter*, the more sympathetic may have greater validity in that it promises larger rewards.[24] Yet the

21. Sept. 21, 1893; *ibid.*, p. 290.
22. See below, p. 273.
23. See especially Robert A. Hume, "Henry Adams' Quest for Certainty," *Stanford Studies in Language and Literature* (Stanford, Stanford University Press, 1941), pp. 361–373, which is an excellent study of some of the inconsistencies in Adams' thinking, insofar as a purely rationalistic approach to Adams' later writing is profitable. For a hostile account of Adams' irrationality see Winters, *op. cit.*, pp. 23–87, although Winters does use Adams' irrationality as a means to examine his personality.
24. Robert E. Spiller takes this point of view, asking why the critic should

sympathetic critic has usually erred in the assumption that all inquiry into Adams' use of scientific data must focus on the mere
matter of accuracy. Whether or not Adams correctly interpreted
his scientific evidence is in itself unimportant, since on the score
of exactitude the literary man has always enjoyed considerable
leeway. But where scientific data comprise the stuff out of which
the image appears, and without which no image would exist, it is
certainly mandatory to examine the choices made, the basis of
choice, and the effect of this choice on the intended imagery. In
Adams' instance his pattern of selection has particular importance,
for he sought a tension between the scientific fact, the emotional
image, and the personal reference. So must his critic.

As the *History* showed the impatient quest for generalization
underlying Adams' rigorous dependence on the documents, so the
generalizations of his later speculation on scientific history ostensibly resulted from the accumulation of data merely arranged
by Adams for the reader's analysis. Unfortunately the closer the
examination of the evidence, the larger the gap between Adams'
proof and his conclusions. No matter how extensive the historical
data originally suggesting the generalization, every scientific
theory of history at some point requires the priority of generalization over evidence. The evidence is thenceforth hand-picked to
prove a foregone conclusion. It could not be otherwise. Even when
most suggestive, so-called scientific formulas for history demand
an enormous simplification of an infinitely complex past—let alone
the infinitely complex future which Adams dared to predict.

They also demand a simplification of science as drastic as that
of history. Adams consulted science for historical certainty. Where
scientists groped he must find solutions. Where they disagreed
he must choose. Unless he settled the unsettled, history was the
worse confounded. He could pretend judiciousness by admitting
in the *Education* that the "details of science meant nothing: he
wanted to know its mass" [25]—as though the mass were not vexed
by controversy. Moreover, even the seemingly immutable parts
of science occasionally undergo striking revision, as the Einstein

concern himself with the validity of Adams' science any more than the modern
critic concerns himself with the validity of Milton's science. "Henry Adams: Man
of Letters," *Saturday Review of Literature, 30* (Feb. 22, 1947), 12; "Henry Adams," *Literary History of the United States* (New York, Macmillan, 1948), *2*, 1099.
Hume, *op. cit.,* p. 37, apparently reversing his earlier position, agrees with Spiller.
    25. *Education,* p. 377.

theory of gravitation has altered the once all but universally accepted theory of Newton. Adams' preference for a single faction in matters of scientific dispute recalls the impatience with which in 1876, long before he had ever thought of his speculative essays, he had closed a letter to Lewis Henry Morgan discussing an uncertainty about Indian societies. "I care little which theory is adopted. One is for scientific hypotheses as good as the other. But I wish it might be settled which of the two shall be used as *the* scientific hypothesis." [26] This was precisely Adams' dilemma in both the *Rule* and the *Letter*—and unfortunately it is to no small extent the dilemma of his critic. Yet it should be possible, despite unavoidable simplification, to suggest the relation of Adams' facts to the science of his day within each of five areas of investigation: from physics, the second law of thermodynamics; from astronomy and historical geology, the shrinking sun and cooling earth; from paleontology and physical anthropology, the degradationist course of evolution; from sociology and history, the trend toward socialism; and finally, returning to physics, the universal ether.

As a starting point none is better than the pre-eminence which Adams accorded to the second law of thermodynamics in his historical speculation. Ultimately every closed system doing work "settles down more or less asymptotically into a dead level of quiet and uniformity from which it can be aroused only by some sort of action from the outside—that is, only by breaking the condition that the system be isolated." [27] To take the specific example of a steam engine: in adding fuel to the furnace the fireman opens the system; in shutting the door he closes it. If the system remains closed entropy increases until the engine eventually stops. What has happened of course is that the energy potential of the coal has been dissipated, as promised by the second law, to a level insufficient to drive the machine. But in accordance with the first law, energy was not itself destroyed in the destruction of the coal, as the mechanical engineer can testify by allotting so much to the work of driving the wheels, so much to loss by friction, so much to conduction through the boiler, and so on—until an accurate tally would add up to the potential energy available to the coal before combustion. Moreover, long after the engine has stopped, the

26. Apr. 29, 1876; Cater, p. 78.
27. Percy W. Bridgman, *The Nature of Thermodynamics* (Cambridge, Harvard University Press, 1941), pp. 161 f. For general bibliography on the second law see Bibliography, Sec. K.

energy would remain undestroyed because the particles which once comprised the energy potential of the coal continue to exist. They exist but, in Willard Gibbs' famous phrase, in a state of "mixed-up-ness" as compared to the pattern of their existence in the coal. It is almost unimaginable that trillions and trillions of particles should of their own random movements ever precisely fall into such an arrangement as to reconstitute the coal originally introduced into the system. Hence the first and second laws of thermodynamics. Energy can be neither created nor destroyed; or in Clausius' phraseology, the energy of the world is constant. In closed systems doing work entropy tends toward a maximum; or Clausius again, the entropy of the world tends toward a maximum.

The condition of closure for the system is all important in the second law, for on this condition depends its universality. Is law for the steam engine also law for the universe? No one knows; but what applies to the level of our everyday experience need not be true for the universe. Although enunciated in the nineteenth century, and especially toward its close, this precaution has become axiomatic only within the present century. As long as scientists posited a mechanistic universe they habitually extended mechanical laws beyond the bounds of observation. The modern scientist realizes that the mechanics accounting for the commonplace experience of human beings certainly do not explain the microcosm of atomic phenomena, or probably the macrocosm of the universe. In the example of the unreplenished steam engine man closed the system. No one as yet knows whether or not the universe is likewise closed. If an isolated system, how did the isolation occur? Might the system again be opened? Even if closed in the conventional sense of mechanical systems, the universe may contain some means, as yet undiscovered, for creating energy. Confronting such problems, scientists would today incline toward a less sweeping view of the second law than that which the vagueness of Clausius' use of Welt permitted, and which Adams vaguely accepted.[28] Whatever the final verdict on the universal applica-

28. The concept of the "expanding universe," popularized by Eddington somewhat later than the publication of the Adams essays, would have nicely fitted into Adams' scheme for the universal dissipation of energy. Holding that the universe was once densely packed, Eddington and other astronomers believe that the galaxies are rapidly separating, as the molecules of a gas separate in doing work. But there have been growing doubts about the validity of the concept of the expanding universe, with most astronomical opinion dubious of the concept at the present time, although it has not been disproved.

bility of the second law, Adams could have avoided the criticism by decisively limiting his problem. The sun contains a finite degree of energy and will presumably die in accordance with the second law long before the demise of the entire universe. Solar death would of course end history—at least on this earth. While Adams did focus his degradationist argument on an energy decline of solar rather than universal proportions, he nevertheless preserved the suggestion of universality about the second law. The appeal to grandeur of operation as justification for historical laws is a familiar fallacy, although few have exploited the error more assiduously than Adams.

If the astrophysicist could question the universality of the second law, so might the molecular physicist; perhaps not quite so decisively as his colleague, but even more significantly in relation to Adams' theory. It happened that Adams was initially attracted to Gibbs' phase rule because the word "phase" must have seemed an echo of his youthful fervor for Comte. It also appealed to Adams because it dealt with aggregates, for the scientific historian must inevitably consider people en masse or change en bloc. If thermodynamics had traditionally dealt with the physical states of chemical aggregates in terms of phases like "ice," "water," and "vapor"—rather than with the atomic valences of "hydrogen" and "oxygen"—it is also possible to think of a thermodynamic system in terms of the trillions of particles underlying any of these states. Not of course that the scientist can explore what happens to any specific particle; but he can tell much about the statistical behavior of individuals in a population. Whatever Adams may have known of Gibbs as the virtual founder of physical chemistry with *On the Equilibrium of Heterogeneous Substances*, the amateur apparently knew nothing of Gibbs' subsequent work on the statistical aspects of thermodynamics. Very significant for present atomic research, Gibbs' later work was also of a pioneer nature, although here he shared honors with two other investigators. Maxwell and Boltzmann had earlier determined that the individual particles in a gas moved at varying speeds, where most approximated a medium rate, while extreme rates tapered off on either side of this median in accordance with a curve of normal probability.[29] Ironically enough, Adams does not

29. In attempting to imagine some means other than the virtually unimaginable probability that chance could substantially reverse the operation of the second law, Maxwell conjured a demon capable of distinguishing the fast- from the slow-moving

seem to have known of Gibbs' suggestion that the universality of the second law is doubtful after all if thermodynamics be considered in a statistical sense. To the work of Maxwell and Boltzmann on the varying speeds of particles in a gas Gibbs added his mathematical hypothesis of their unequal distribution. In other words, entropy does not in all instances continue to a maximum, but only approximates this extreme. Patches of fast-moving particles remain, even when the gas seems to be at maximum entropy. A uniform distribution is only apparent, according to Gibbs, because the tiny concentrations of fast-moving particles average out to ostensible uniformity. Or in Gibbs' own sentence: "The impossibility of an uncompensated decrease in entropy seems to be reduced to a probability." Shorn of its New England angularity, this statement means that the tendency for entropy to reach a maximum in closed systems is, when viewed statistically, not a certainty but only a very high probability. All further advances in the subject have borne Gibbs out.[30]

To be sure, Gibbs' qualification of the second law hardly invalidated Adams' belief that the total energy available to man must

---

particles. If such a demon could divide a closed system into two parts connected only by a frictionless sliding panel, then it might separate the fast-moving from the more sluggish particles of a gas at maximum entropy. It could thus recreate a difference of potential so that more work was possible in the system without the introduction of more energy from the outside. Adams was naturally interested in Maxwell's whimsy; see *Degradation: Rule*, p. 279; Adams marked *Karl Pearson's mention of the demon (*The Grammar of Science* [2d ed., London, Black, 1900], p. 84), asking how the demon could open and close his panel without doing work; in the index to Pearson, Adams added a reference to Maxwell's demon; he made a like addition to the index of Lucien Poincaré, *The New Physics and Its Evolution* (London, Paul, Trench, Trübner, 1907) [*La Physique moderne, son évolution* (Paris, Flammarion, 1906)]. For a good exposition of the demon see Lord Kelvin, "The Sorting Demon of Maxwell," *Popular Lectures and Addresses* (London and New York, Macmillan, 1889–1894), *1*, 137–141; Roderick Seidenberg, *Posthistoric Man* (Chapel Hill, University of North Carolina Press, 1950), pp. 164–169, although Seidenberg seems unaware that quantum mechanics makes the demon impossible. If it estimates the speed of a particle correctly, the demon cannot tell the position of the particle in order to gauge the proper moment for opening the panel, and vice versa.

30. See *The Collected Works of Willard Gibbs* (New Haven, Yale University Press, 1948), *1*, 167, for Gibbs' statement. A technical discussion appears in Paul S. Epstein, "Application of Gibbs' Methods to Modern Problems of Thermodynamics," *A Commentary on the Scientific Writings of Willard Gibbs*, ed. Arthur Haas (New Haven, Yale University Press, 1936), *2*, 105–112; a popular discussion in Seidenberg, *op. cit.*, pp. 142 f. L. Poincaré, *op. cit.*, pp. 85 f. [*pp. 84 f.], discussed Gibbs' famous qualification of the second law; and somewhat later, p. 145 [p. 139], referred to this qualification as the "paradox of Gibbs," a term sometimes accorded to it. Opposite this latter phrase Adams placed a "?".

eventually decline to a level too low for the continuance of history. Microscopic islands of fast-moving particles in an entropic sea could do no work from the historian's point of view. But mention of Gibbs' qualification of the second law is more than mere digression for two reasons. Experimental proof of the failure of entropy to attain a maximum in some instances gives scientists further reason to question the universality of the second law. More important for present purposes, it raises the problem of the extent of Adams' knowledge of Gibbs. Adams never pretended to use more of Gibbs than the single momentous chapter of but four pages on the phase rule, and this he doubtless knew at second hand. Yet a myth links Adams' name to Gibbs', giving rather too much credit to the scientific acuity of the amateur for his use of the allegedly neglected phase rule.[31] This myth is worth investigating.

Adams must first have heard of the phase rule sometime around the midnineties from his friend Samuel P. Langley, then director of the Smithsonian Institution, who had consulted Gibbs in preparing one of his early papers on aerodynamics.[32] Langley's acquaintance with Gibbs' work doubtless meant that Adams learned of the phase rule during the very decade when the equations of the Yale physicist were finding widespread use in the burgeoning field of physical chemistry. In 1906 the first collection of Gibbs' works was gathered into a posthumous edition which occasioned considerable comment. Moreover, several volumes had appeared devoted exclusively to the phase rule and its applications before Adams attempted to relate the rule to history. One of the most important of these by the British chemist Alexander Findlay exists with Adams' marginal comments in his library at the Massachusetts Historical Society.[33]

Had he used Gibbs in any profound sense in the *Rule*, the reverence for Adams' depth of insight in this instance would be wholly justified, for even as late as 1909 only the unusually perceptive layman would have appreciated Gibbs' stature. But Adams

31. Especially Muriel Rukeyser, *Willard Gibbs* (New York, Doubleday, Doran, 1942), pp. 404–415. Lynde P. Wheeler, *Josiah Willard Gibbs, the History of a Great Mind* (New Haven, Yale University Press, 1951), chap. vi, reassesses the notion of Gibbs' neglect and self-effacement.

32. On Langley's letter to Gibbs see Edwin B. Wilson, "Willard Gibbs on Soaring Flight," *Proceedings of the National Academy of Sciences, 31* (1945), pp. 233 ff.

33. *Alexander Findlay, *The Phase Rule and Its Application* (London, Longmans, Green, 1906). The first edition appeared in 1904; subsequent revisions still make this work a basic technical text on the phase rule. On other early commentaries on the phase rule see Rukeyser, *op. cit.*, pp. 372 f.

did not use the phase rule profoundly, as even the most superficial criticism of his graphical representation has already made clear. In this connection, an error in the final version of the *Rule* is of more than pedantic interest. Where Gibbs had entitled his chapter "On *Co*existent Phases of Matter," the published version of the *Rule* shows the omission of the significant prefix. Since Adams had correctly cited the title in an earlier draft,[34] the error resulted rather from carelessness than ignorance, while it is just possible that not Adams but some copyist was at fault. Hence not the error itself but rather its appropriateness warrants criticism. Gibbs was concerned with the *co*existence of phases in equilibrium, Adams with their succession as a result of disequilibrium. Indeed, it would be difficult to imagine how Adams could possibly have distorted Gibbs' phase rule more completely had this been his purpose.

Specifically, Gibbs' phase rule gives for any chemical mixture the relation which must hold between the number of components, the number of coexistent phases, and the number of possible variations of phase that can take place. The basic formula in phase rule mathematics—so simple that even the historian need not wince—is $F = C + 2 - P$, where F represents the number of possible degrees of freedom, C the number of components, and P the number of phases in a chemical system. A specific example will best clarify these terms. Taking the elementary analogy used by Adams, assume that the problem is the number of degrees of freedom which will exist when the three homogeneous, physically distinct, and mechanically separate phases of ice, water, and vapor coexist. The number of components is one, since the "component" in the phase rule is not identical with the two "constituents" (hydrogen and oxygen) which go to make up water but only with those constituents, or that combination of constituents, which can undergo independent variation under changes of temperature, pressure, and volume. Hence $1 + 2 - 3$ gives no degrees of freedom for the coexistence of ice, water, and vapor. In other words, these three phases exist simultaneously in equilibrium at only a single point in pressure, temperature, and volume—the so-called "triple point." To alter any one of these conditions is to destroy the equilibrium of three clearly bounded phases. Thus the experimenter desiring the coexistence of these three phases has no free-

34. Italics in Gibbs' title mine. In the draft of the *Rule* which Henry A. Bumstead criticized, now in the Henry Adams Library at the Massachusetts Historical Society.

dom whatsoever to determine any factors involved in the equilibrium. Now change the problem for the coexistence merely of ice and water. Again: $1 + 2 - 2$. In this instance one degree of freedom is possible. Given a volume of ice, the experimenter can, within certain limits, arbitrarily select a value for either temperature or pressure, which is the one degree of freedom promised by the phase rule; the other variable is automatically specified by the equilibrium sought.

No more than this simple formula in this simplest of variations is needed to comprehend Adams' use of the phase rule. Is even this much necessary? Apply the formula to history. Of how many components does history consist? Wisely, Adams does not say. Phases? To be sure, he offers seven; but is he interested in the conditions of acceleration and attraction (his replacements for temperature and pressure) under which, say, the religious, electrical, and ethereal stages would coexist? To ask the question is to reveal the absurdity. Adams' theory has no relation, even analogically, to Gibbs' equation. The *Rule* might have confused Adams' scientifically illiterate colleagues less had he used the obvious example of a cube of ice over a Bunsen burner. His mention of Gibbs, then, merely indicated the abracadabra of authoritarianism so essential to his theory.

So little did Adams know about Gibbs, in fact, that the private edition of the *Education*, printed in 1907, shows that he mistook the Yale physicist for a Harvard chemist. Thus it was "Wolcott Gibbs" whom Adams praised as among the "three or four greatest minds of his century" in the 1907 version, and only subsequent correction in what became the posthumous edition published for the general public gave Willard Gibbs his due.[35] Should the historian wish further proof of how unessential was Gibbs' work for Adams' theory, he need only look at the *Letter* which followed the

35. A corrected version of the *Education* with the notations in Adams' handwriting exists in the Massachusetts Historical Society, showing on p. 377 (trade edition) two mentions of Wolcott Gibbs; the second, ". . . schools, much as Wolcott Gibbs himself was treated, with . . ." The correction "Willard" seems to have been noted in the margin, then erased, and the words between commas deleted. On p. 449 Adams intended to confess his error since the 1907 edition shows Wolcott Gibbs in the text, with Adams' admission, ". . . century,—the more so because in his ignorance he confounded him with another great mind, his rival Willard Gibbs, —and the idea . . ." This phrase was the only suggested change omitted in the trade edition, where "Willard" precedes all mentions of Gibbs, perhaps because of the confusion in which Adams had left his revision. Wilhelm Ostwald, *Lebenslinien eine Selbtsbiographie* (Berlin, Klasing, 1927), *2*, p. 63, observed that Willard Gibbs was so little known that his scientific contemporaries often confused him with the better known Wolcott Gibbs.

first version of the *Rule*. There Adams presented the same theory of history with but two mentions of Gibbs' name, both incidental, and with no very intricate discussion of the phase rule.

In the *Letter*, too, Adams significantly omitted the neat time scale of the *Rule* which has occasioned so much subsequent comment as to his prophetic version. Unlike the *Rule*, the *Letter* does not bring thought to the limit of its possibilities at any particular date. In the latter essay Adams satisfied himself by establishing a trend and omitting all dates, while even in the *Rule* he admitted that society might exist after 1921 for "an indefinitely long stationary period," presumably living routinely, incapable of further development.[36]

This inability to fix upon a precise date for the vaguely defined terminus of history is perhaps unimportant. Very important is the question of the imminence of catastrophe. Significantly enough, the second law could not help Adams here. This law gives direction but says nothing about time.[37] To obtain a time scale for the *Rule* Adams had to abandon science for history, although among the supposed advantages of scientific history that of historical prediction from science loomed large. According to the *Rule*, history might end somewhere between 1921 and 2025, while the sun continued to shine for billions of years. If history was blithely oblivious of the timetable for the universe, then the help that science could offer history was limited to the mere suggestion of direction. The rest of historical law must come from history—hardly the way to make history truly scientific according to Adams' original premise! Moreover, Adams' theory for scientific history was singularly unaesthetic if the annihilation occurred by stages. To be sure, the mention of an indefinitely long stationary period might have permitted a degraded history to mark time through the eons required for the sun to catch up; but this kind of improvisation was clearly intended rather to patch up weaknesses in the theory than to be taken seriously. How much neater, how much more dramatic, to have both solar and historical energy degrade in such a fashion that both went out together.

The *Letter* repaired a major deficiency of the *Rule* by deriving not only the sense of direction from scientific data but also the sense of time. Hence the *Letter* concentrated on the evolutionary

36. *Degradation: Rule*, p. 309.
37. L. Brillouin, "Life, Thermodynamics, and Cybernetics," *American Scientist*, 37 (1949), pp. 558 f.

sciences: historical geology, paleontology, and physical anthropology. Obviously these sciences would no more bring thought to
the limit of its possibilities at any particular date in the future
than would the second law of thermodynamics. Adams could at
best suggest, first, that evolutionary processes operated according to the second law and, second, that the total energy available
for their operation was degrading rapidly. If the energy available
for geological and paleontological evolution had degraded rapidly,
then the immensity of change on the earth from the dawn of geology to the present could be explained only through a series of
sizable jumps relatively closely spaced rather than through an
incredible number of tiny alterations during an almost unimagi-
nably long period of time. Of course a rapid depletion of energy in
the past implied a depletion equally rapid in the future. If he had
to eliminate the specific time scale of the *Rule,* Adams hoped at
least to suggest in the *Letter* that scientific and historical evidence
were in agreement as to the imminence of the limit of thought.
Moreover, in the process of enlarging the sphere of the *Rule* to
that of the *Letter* Adams made his demonstration the more encyclopedic. This was an aim of no mean significance to one interested, above all, "in connecting the phenomena." [38] The more connections, the more inclusive and, at the same time, the more inevitable the theory.

The premises of the *Letter* were, except for Adams' pessimism
about the future of evolution, those of the nineteenth-century catastrophists in opposition to uniformitarians.[39] Gradualism in
natural history was, and is, the position pre-eminently associated
in the nineteenth century with the names of the great British
naturalists Lyell and Darwin. Despite Lyell's constant revision
of his *Principles of Geology* from 1830 when the first edition appeared until 1875 which marked the twelfth and posthumous version, the theme of uniformitarianism underlay his famous survey.
Specifically, the Lyellian position depended on his demonstration
that changes throughout the whole of the geological past had occurred incredibly slowly by means of precisely the same processes
observable at the present time. Lyell believed that without this
basic premise historical geology could "never rise to the rank of

38. Feb. 16, 1912; Ford, *2,* 581.
39. For bibliography on this controversy see Bibliography, Sec. L.

an exact science," [40] since the alternative to uniformitarianism necessitated that major changes in geology depend on a series of unusual and hence highly conjectural catastrophes. Darwin underscored the lesson of his close friend by basing his *Origin of Species* on the uniformitarian conception of past environments. Like Lyell he denied the existence of exceptional agencies for change, to develop his theory of natural selection in large part by observing the breeding methods of the barnyard.

If Lyell and Darwin were patron saints for uniformitarians, certainly Cuvier, whose death approximately coincided with the appearance of the first edition of Lyell's *Principles*, occupied a comparable niche for catastrophists. To the French naturalist morphological change had followed cataclysmic alterations in environment in a series of special creations, presumably arranged by the Divine Creator. Catastrophic theories, variously modified from Cuvier's hypothesis, were much more prevalent among French than English naturalists throughout the nineteenth century. Significantly, Adams relied almost wholly on French authorities for his evidence on catastrophism in the *Letter*. More significantly, he was the devoted pupil of Agassiz in Harvard, who was, in turn, the devoted pupil of Cuvier.

So Adams' sympathy for the catastrophic point of view was not surprising; but, while in England during the Civil War, he became acquainted with Lyell who was warmly welcomed at the ministry as a friend of the Union cause. Immediately on his return to the United States after his father's recall Adams had even published a review in the *North American* on the tenth edition of Lyell's *Principles*.[41] The review emphasized two problems, both of particular interest to the disciple of Agassiz. First Adams discussed the problem of geological climates, and especially of glaciation which even the nongeologist associates with Agassiz's name. Then he compared Lyell's acceptance of Darwinian gradualism with Agassiz's belief in a series of special creations. On both scores the

40. Charles Lyell, *Principles of Geology* (12th ed., London, Murray, 1875), *1*, 318. Unless otherwise noted all citations from Lyell refer to this edition. As it happens, practically all references here made can be located on different pages in the tenth edition which Adams reviewed for the *North American* (see immediately below) and most of them on the same pages in the eleventh. I have preferred to use the last edition because Adams *could* have used it. American editions vary in their numbering from the English, that of 1877 (New York, Appleton) being the eleventh.

41. *NAR, 107* (1868), 465–501.

amateur found some fault with Lyell's reasoning, despite a letter in which he warned his editors while he worked on the manuscript that if they were "afraid of Sir Charles and Darwin, and prefer to adhere frankly to Mr. Agassiz, you have but to say so, and I am dumb. My own leaning, though not strong, is still toward them, and"—doubtless imagining that New England would favor special creation over so-called materialistic change in evolution—"therefore I should be excluded from even the most modest summing up in the *Atlantic*, I suppose. It is not likely that I should handle the controversy vigorously—the essay would rather be an historical one—but I should have to touch it." [42] However much Adams may have leaned toward uniformitarianism when thirty, he indubitably opposed this position when, some forty years later, he returned in the *Letter* to precisely the same themes which he had discussed in the *North American*, that is, the nature of geological climates and of biological evolution. It would seem as though Adams must test all the ideas and experiences of his youth in the acid of old age.

In this instance Adams' intimate friendship with Clarence King certainly reinforced his devotion to Agassiz and altered his alleged "leaning" toward Lyell. King was a confirmed catastrophist in geology. In 1877 he had attacked uniformitarianism in an address delivered before the Sheffield Scientific School of Yale College.[43] He spoke not of geological climates but of the spectacular geological formations of the American West with which he was so familiar. While admitting that the present geological period was uniformitarian in character, King denied that slow changes in environment had always characterized the past. He reached his climax in three assertions well worth extensive quotation, partly because King's virile expressiveness indicated something of his conversational fascination for the Adamses and the Hays when they met at teatime in the early eighties as the "Five of Hearts," but more because King's words epitomized Adams' protest against uniformitarianism in the *Letter*.

> I believe I am fully prepared to sustain the assertions: first, that the RATE of physical change progressing today in all departments of terrestrial action is inadequate to produce the grander features of American geological history; secondly,

42. Mar. 10, 1868; Cater, p. 42.
43. Clarence King, *Catastrophism and the Evolution of Environment* (no place, but presumably New Haven, 1877); passage cited below occurs on pp. 23 f.

that in the past, at intervals, the dynamic rate has been so sharply accelerated as to bring about exceptional results; thirdly, that these results have been catastrophic in their effect upon the life of America and the bounding oceans.

Uniformitarians could accept even the grandest features of the Rocky Mountains

with unruffled calmness; they would read the record exactly as a Catastrophist might, only they would assume unlimited time and their inch-by-inch process. The analogy of the present, they say, is against any acceleration of rate in the past, and besides, the geological record is a very imperfect document which does not disprove our view.

In plain language, they start with a *gratuitous assumption* (vast time), fortify it by an *analogy of unknown relevancy* (the present rate), and serenely appeal to the *absence of evidence* against them, as proof in their favor. The courage of opinion has rarely exceeded this specimen of logic. If such a piece of reasoning were uttered from a pulpit against evolution, biology would at once take to her favorite sport of knuckle-rapping the clergy in the manner we are all of us accustomed to witness. In forbidding us to look for past rates of change differing from the present, the British Uniformitarians have tied the hands of science. By preaching so eternally from the text of "imperfection of the geological record," they have put blinders on the profession . . . Geology, if not strangled in its own house, will . . . translate the strata into a precise language of energy and time.

Doubtless King had often spoken with Adams of geology in terms of energy and time, the very theme which Adams would later take for his historical investigation. Moreover, during the last decade of his life King had published an important essay estimating the age of the sun.[44] This latter subject was the logical starting point for Adams' investigation into catastrophism. If solar material burned very slowly, then uniformitarians could justify their assumption of gradualism, since in this event the sun would have permitted an environment suitable for organic development during the eons required for the "inch-by-inch" transformation defended

44. "The Age of the Earth," *American Journal of Science*, 3d ser., *45* (1893), 1–20.

by both Lyell and Darwin. On the other hand, if the sun had consumed solar stuff at a prodigious rate, then catastrophists might
challenge uniformitarianism in two ways. A much larger sun than
now exists must have made past environments quite unlike those of
the present, while a rapidly shrinking sun must have meant that
time did not exist for gradual change in either geology or evolution. If the sun should prove to be so far along in its dotage that a
relatively early demise might be expected, then so much the better
for the dramatic possibilities in Adams' dismal prophecy for history.

He based his reasoning on a prevalent nineteenth-century
comparison of the climate of the Carboniferous period with that
of recent geological time, vividly contrasting the picture of lush
Carboniferous forests stretching from pole to pole with that of
Pleistocene glaciation amidst which man made his appearance.
According to Adams' authorities, the Carboniferous forests, ultimately buried as coal, depended for their growth on a sun with a diameter as large as the orbit of Mercury, since the solar stuff to make
this smallest of planets had not, at that time, been whirled from its
furnace. The earth was still warm at its surface from the intense
internal temperatures of its molten creation.[45] Adams would doubtless have admitted, along with his authorities, that there was no
steady decline in terrestrial temperature during the geological past
but rather a broad trend with climatic fluctuations, now warmer,
now cooler. Yet circumstances of a temporary nature could not
alter the absolute thermal decline underlying all deviation. Where
the sun was once warm, it had cooled. Conditions existed in the
past which could never again exist.

In short, Adams dared to instruct teachers of history on the
"drift" of science in respect to no less than three interrelated
problems: the cause of polar forests in the geological past, the explanation for Pleistocene glaciation, and the thermodynamics of
the sun. When he wrote he fully realized the division of scientific
opinion on these matters and, in fact, on almost all other data in

45. For his views on the relationship between solar energy and terrestrial climates Adams particularly referred to Heer (whose work he mentioned in his
review of Lyell), Saporta, and Lapparent. Oswald Heer, *The Primaeval World of
Switzerland,* ed. and tr. James Heywood (authorized English ed., London, Longmans, Green, 1876), *2,* 262–274, especially pp. 267–270. Louis Saporta, *Le Monde
des plantes avant l'apparition de l'homme* (Paris, Masson, 1879), chap. iii, especially
pp. 139–150. Albert de Lapparent, *Traité de géologie* (5th ed., Paris, Masson, 1906),
3, especially 1951–1961. For bibliography on geological climates see Bibliography,
Sec. M.

his *Letter*. Hence his first sin was that of arbitrary choice, although the degree of the sin depended on the capriciousness with which he chose.

Present-day theories on geological climates are by no means inconsistent with the uniformitarian position; but it is only fair to add that, even in the final edition of his famous *Principles* (1875), Lyell did not deny an over-all trend toward cooler climates throughout geological time.[46] Quite obviously this trend provided ammunition for the catastrophist and indeed furnished Adams with the guiding concept for all his research in the *Letter*. But Lyell seemed to imply that this decline was something of an accident in uniformitarian development rather than evidence for catastrophism, while emphasizing the irregular fluctuations in past climates. In any event, he preserved his uniformitarianism by two major arguments as to the cause of climatic fluctuations, both of which Adams had disputed in his review of the *Principles* for the *North American*.[47]

Lyell's basic argument depended on slow alterations in geography and topography, causing continents to disappear beneath the surface of the ocean or to rise above it. Even the nongeologist knows that extreme climates are characteristic of vast land areas, while water moderates the extremes. Basing his theory on this meteorological commonplace, Lyell assumed that excessive land areas around the poles would cause arctic climates conducive to the formation of large-scale ice sheets which cooled climates throughout the globe—the reason for the relative coolness of present temperatures. Likewise, land concentrated in the torrid zone with water at the poles would create the warm climates requisite for the polar forests of the Carboniferous and Miocene. In Adams' words, "Land at the poles is a storehouse for ice and snow, while land within the tropics is a furnace for the distribution of heat." [48]

As a subordinate cause of climatic change, Lyell also included a modified version of an astronomical theory for glaciation developed by the English astronomer James Croll. Croll's hypothesis stemmed from observations on the shifting of the earth's axis and its irregular orbit around the sun. At certain rare intervals a particular conjunction of these two factors could so lengthen the winter in either the northern or the southern hemisphere as to

46. Lyell, *op. cit., 1*, 231.
47. *Ibid.*, chaps. xii, xiii.
48. *NAR, 107* (1868), 476.

cause widespread glaciation. Because the astronomical circumstances supposedly responsible for glaciation had occurred several times, Croll argued that glaciation must have appeared at irregular intervals throughout the entire geological past. Now, very few of Croll's contemporaries supported his notion that widespread continental glaciation had ever occurred at any time previous to the most recent, or Pleistocene, which is the only glacial period familiar to most historians. Lyell was among this majority of skeptics, despite the fact that the existence of ice ages prior to the Pleistocene would have nicely confirmed the uniformitarian hypothesis by providing the most intense climatic fluctuations, now glacial cold, now temperate and subtropical warmth, throughout the whole of geological time. To be sure, scattered pockets of glacial drift existed in pre-Pleistocene strata; but Lyell believed them the result of local ice sheets from nearby mountain peaks or of boulders frozen in icebergs and floated to their present places of deposit.[49] Hence only by subordinating Croll's astronomical theory to his favorite hypothesis of geographical change could Lyell discount the idea of ice ages prior to the Pleistocene. A particular relationship between the earth and the sun resulted in glaciation only if an excess of polar land existed to cool terrestrial climates. According to Lyell's theory this unusual conjunction of circumstances had presumably occurred at only one period in the geological past. But the uniqueness of Pleistocene glaciation in no way compromised his uniformitarian position. Continents would presumably rise and fall in the future as in the past; a particular relationship of earth to sun would likewise reappear.[50] These factors could again coincide so as to produce another ice age. In short, causes operating in the present accounted for all geological phenomena in the past.

In reviewing the tenth edition of the *Principles* Adams did not adopt the catastrophist position of his old age. Nothing in his review contradicted his assertion to the editors of the *North American* that he rather favored Lyell and Darwin over Agassiz,[51]

49. For Lyell's opposition to theories of pre-Pleistocene glaciation see *op. cit.*, *1*, 232, 359–362, 376–383. For his theory that glacial boulders in pre-Pleistocene strata were largely due to boulders frozen in drifting ice see *ibid.*, pp. 279, 287 f.

50. Lyell would also account for the rarity of large-scale glaciation by the relatively infrequent emergence of polar lands as compared to the much more frequent condition of polar water; *ibid.*, pp. 269 ff.

51. Samuels, pp. 163–167, discusses this review of Lyell's *Principles*, maintaining that Adams disclosed beneath his assumed impartiality a predilection for Agassiz and catastrophism rather than for Lyell and uniformitarianism. Certainly

although Adams did point out some decided inadequacies in Lyell's chapters on climate. He asked in effect how Lyell would explain the extensive arctic continent on which Heer had found his botanical fossils of the Miocene forests. The Miocene coming much later than the Carboniferous was, according to Adams, the very last of the warm epochs before the general decline in terrestrial temperatures which heralded, first, Pleistocene glaciation, then the cool climates of the present. Fossil sites proved the existence of parts of Greenland, Mackenzie, and Spitsbergen during the Miocene, while similar fossils on the continent of Europe indicated that the present insular sites of these ancient botanical species must once have belonged to the mainland. Thus land, not water as the geographical hypothesis demanded, must have been excessive in arctic regions during a period when forests reached to the North Pole. Adams further attacked the geographical explanation by calling attention to extensive submergence in northern latitudes during the Pleistocene, when the theory demanded extensive elevation. In other words, there was excessive land in the arctic zone when there should have been water, excessive water when there should have been land.

Lyell had arguments to answer Adams' criticisms. He believed that a considerable area of land (as much as one-fourth of the total area of the arctic zone) might have existed around the pole during the warm periods of the geological past without this amount's being "excessive"; moreover, the sites on which Heer had discovered his fossils might not all have been above water at any one time. As for extensive submergence during the Pleistocene, Lyell denied not the submergence but only its extent.

---

the letter cited above, p. 174, and also cited by Samuels makes his interpretation impossible. (Hume, p. 61, also disagrees with Samuels' interpretation but on rather vague grounds.) Why should Adams have pretended to favor Lyell and Darwin in writing to editors who he believed were hostile to the opinions of these two naturalists, when he really favored Agassiz all the while? At one place in particular (NAR, 107 [1868], 470) Adams definitely seems to indicate his uniformitarian preferences. Nothing cited by Samuels contradicts either Adams' assertion that he meant to avoid favoring one side over the other or the natural tendency of a man striving for impartiality to go a bit out of his way to prop up a position with which he somewhat disagreed, especially when the opposite opinion was that of a man whom he admired. Moreover, at this time in his life Adams was acutely conscious of historical continuity; it would therefore seem that Samuels is guilty of reading the review of Lyell with Adams' later opinions too much in mind. This is not to deny Samuels' major thesis, that Adams enjoyed the vivid generalizations of science far more than its methodical investigation (see, for example, NAR, 107 (1868), pp. 467 ff. and 475 for excellent examples); but uniformitarianism is as susceptible of dramatic treatment as catastrophism (again, ibid., p. 470).

Having dismissed pre-Pleistocene glaciation as local phenomena, Lyell interpreted Pleistocene submergence in like manner.[52] Since this argument was speculative rather than decisive, Adams could justifiably point to these elements of supposition as weaknesses in the theory, while cautiously and somewhat awkwardly concluding that he would "not say that the geographical theory in regard to climatic variations may not be the best solution yet offered of a very difficult problem, but [he] should be glad to know how it can be made to harmonize with the facts." [53]

Having disposed of the topographical-geographical thesis in the critical but noncontroversial manner which he had promised his editors, Adams turned to Croll's hypothesis. This is of particular interest in connection with his return to the problem of geological climates in the *Letter*. Again facts seemed to refute Lyell's neat demonstration. Since the "present eccentricity of the earth's orbit is very slight," Adams felt that Croll's hypothesis required present terrestrial temperatures to compare with the very warm climates antecedent to the Pleistocene. Nevertheless, despite his stricture, he thought the astronomical theory for glaciation preferable to the topographical-geographical. Although he did "not understand how [his] objection [could] be met," he added that if it were "satisfactorily overcome" then "the glacial theory may be considered as almost complete. Only the recurrence and the effects of these revolutions in the earth's economy would then remain to be studied, and we venture to think that not a long time could elapse before every geologist would find the basis for a new science in the history of climatic variations." [54] There was no more significant statement in the review. In effect, Adams suggested that if Croll's theory could overcome grave difficulties, then glaciation would occur at intervals throughout time. A series of revolutions in climate would have occurred within a uniformi-

---

52. *Ibid.*, pp. 477–480. Samuels implies but does not quite assert that Lyell radically recast his chapter on climate as a result of Adams' review. This is not the case. Adams' first argument—that Heer's discovery of plant fossils over a wide area in the arctic region indicated a large amount of polar land during the warm Miocene—resulted in the addition of three sentences in the eleventh edition (Lyell, *op. cit.*, p. 266); although Adams' argument had been at least partially anticipated by Lyell in the tenth edition (pp. 264 f.), the paragraph containing this partial anticipation was eliminated from the eleventh and the more explicit sentences added. The other major additions in the eleventh edition (occurring on pp. 237 f., 241, 245 f., 247, 250) discussed trade winds and ocean currents, both topics unmentioned by Adams.

53. *NAR, 107* (1868), 479.

54. *Ibid.*, p. 480.

tarian framework; Agassiz would be brought to Lyell in a new synthesis. Faithful to his old teacher, then, Adams nevertheless fully justified his assertion to his editors that he "leaned, but not strongly" toward Lyell and Darwin.

Returning in old age to the problem of glaciation Adams quite naturally looked into modifications of Croll's hypothesis to learn whether the "basis for a new science" existed in this theory. The principal exponent of Croll's theory at the end of the nineteenth century was the British astronomer Sir Robert Ball. He popularized his theory as *The Cause of an Ice Age*, first published in 1891 and republished as late as 1918. True to his profession, Ball reversed Lyell's verdict on the relative efficacy of the geographical and the astronomical causes for glaciation. His modification of Croll's conclusions required not only pre-Pleistocene glaciation but periodic glaciation as well. At one point in his copy of *The Cause of an Ice Age* Adams recorded a vigorous marginal protest, "The evidence of periodic Ice *Ages* is very doubtful and more than doubtful." A few pages later, "The *last* ice age; but of any previous ice age, either tertiary, mesozoic or azoic, the evidence is most doubtful, and of periodic changes, no evidence exists." [55] Of periodic ice ages prior to the Pleistocene there was indeed no evidence; but by the end of the century some evidence did exist of glaciation at irregular intervals, which James Dana (also in Adams' library) summarized without comment in his standard American textbook. Since Adams penciled the margin opposite this summary, he did know of scattered finds made mostly in southern Asia, Australia, and New Zealand (areas unfamiliar to Lyell) indicating extensive glaciation during the very Carboniferous-Permian which Adams believed so warm, and during the much earlier Cambrian when, according to Adams' logic, terrestrial temperatures should have exceeded those of the Carboniferous.[56] As these finds awaited comprehensive

55. *Robert Ball, *The Cause of an Ice Age* (New York, Appleton, 1891), pp. 34, 38. On p. 34 Adams underscored "Ages"; on p. 38 there seems to have been no specific reference, although "Ice Age," line 1, was underscored.

56. *James D. Dana, *Manual of Geology* (4th ed., New York, American Book Co.; London, Trübner, 1895), pp. 698 f. Dana had most of the data supporting the assertion of Permian glaciation set in smaller type than that used for most of his text to indicate the tentative nature of this hypothesis. On p. 737 he seemed to indicate that Permian glaciation might have occurred only on mountain tops owing to a refrigeration somewhat milder than that required for large-scale continental glaciation. For a summary of opinion toward the end of the nineteenth century on pre-Pleistocene glaciation see James Croll, *Climate and Time* (New York, Appleton, 1885), chaps. xvii, xviii.

investigation, Adams could justifiably maintain that majority opinion inclined away from the hypothesis of pre-Pleistocene glaciation. Geologists today, however, generally agree that glaciation has occurred at irregular intervals throughout the whole of the geological past; most of them believe that for as far back as they can trace the surface of the earth possessed temperatures not so excessively different from those now existing that any past climate could not recur.[57]

Of the two climatic extremes discussed in the *Letter*—Pleistocene chill and Carboniferous warmth—it was evidence centering in the latter phenomenon which provided Adams with his most decisive arguments for geological catastrophism. "The long epochs known as the [Carboniferous-] Permian, Triassic, Jurassic, Cretaceous and Eocene allowed ample time for [solar] shrinkage before the Miocene first proved by its temperate vegetation, that the sun had approached its present diameter, and could no longer equably warm the world." [58] For his data on this steady decline in temperature Adams depended primarily on the paleobotanists Oswald Heer and Louis Saporta, together with the geologist Albert de Lapparent.[59] From his studies of paleobotany Heer saw no indication of any major diminution of temperature from the Carboniferous through the Cretaceous periods. A slight decline did occur during the Miocene epoch. Cooler climates continued through the following epoch, that of the Pliocene, and of course became even colder during the succeeding Pleistocene. A careless reading of Heer's analysis of geological climates might seem to make it accord with Adams' view in the *Letter;* but Heer specifically emphasized the lack of any apparent decline in temperature during the immense span of time from the Carboniferous through the Cretaceous which certainly must have occurred if the sun had steadily shrunk while the earth had steadily cooled. Moreover, he

57. Arthur P. Coleman, *Ice Ages, Recent and Ancient* (New York, Macmillan, 1926), especially chart on p. 78.

58. *Degradation: Letter,* p. 162. Actually only the Permian and the Eocene are "epochs"; the other terms, referring to the next larger unit in geological periodization, are known as "periods" or "systems." Since the Permian is the last epoch of the Carboniferous period, it seemed clearer to use the hyphenated form here. American geologists refer to the period following the Cretaceous as the Tertiary. (There is some difference of terminology between European and American geologists.) The Tertiary period consists of four epochs—Eocene, Oligocene, Miocene, and Pliocene; the Quaternary period follows with the Pleistocene (or Glacial) and the Recent epochs, bringing historical geology to the present.

59. See immediately above, n. 45.

tentatively, and very safely, concluded that all variations in climate had perhaps resulted from geographical changes and the varying relationship of the earth to the sun, together with the unequal heating of stellar space.[60] Every one of these explanations for climatic change was uniformitarian: factors operating in the past could also operate in the future. So far from supporting Adams' catastrophism, then, Heer actually controverted it. Of the three authorities cited in the *Letter*—Heer, Saporta, and Lapparent—Adams had mentioned only the first in his early review of Lyell's *Principles*. Perhaps he never troubled to reinvestigate the work of the Swiss paleobotanist when writing the *Letter*, using Heer only for his picture of arctic forests.

Saporta disagreed with Heer's analysis in a manner more congenial to Adams' argument. According to Saporta, Heer's hypothesis demanded climatic fluctuations, whereas paleobotanical evidence did show a broad decline in temperature. After reviewing all existing hypotheses Saporta finally decided on the theory of a steadily shrinking sun, while the French geologist Lapparent concurred with Saporta's verdict, asserting among the final pages of his three-volume treatise that " 'contrary to the doctrines of the uniformitarian school' " the " 'ancient history of our planet has unrolled itself in the midst of external conditions very different from those which now surround us.' " [61] This was Adams' authorization for lurid catastrophism, and he made the most of it.

Since astronomers of the nineteenth century knew little about the chemistry of the sun, rapid shrinkage seemed the only means by which this body could retain its immense radiation—a shrinkage so rapid, it must be remembered, that Adams cited Saporta's authorities for a sun with a diameter approximating the orbit of Mercury as late as the Carboniferous. Relatively speaking, maximum entropy for the sun could not be far off if radiation consumed solar substance at such a prodigious rate. It was the uniformitarian's turn to blanch at such a spectacle. Confronting this thermodynamic debacle, Lyell rescued his point of view only by asking

60. Heer, *op. cit.*, pp. 264 f., 267-274; on p. 272 Heer agreed with Lyell that evidence appeared for a glacial period only during the Quaternary period. Poisson's theory of the unequal heating of space assumed that heat from the stars must vary at different points in space due to the unequal distribution of the stars. Moving through space along with the solar system, the earth would pass now through a warm area, now through a cold.

61. *Degradation: Letter*, p. 165. Lapparent, *op. cit.*, *3*, 1955. *Degradation: Letter*, p. 162. Saporta, *op. cit.*, pp. 148 f. Lapparent, *op. cit.*, *3*, 1954 f.; n. 1 gives the Blandet reference on the size of the sun during the Carboniferous.

"why should we despair of detecting proofs of [some sort of] regenerating and self-sustaining power in the works of a Divine Artificer?" [62] When such a respected uniformitarian clung so desperately to such an argument, he should not have wondered why some despaired, and none more devoutly than Adams who used as justification for his gloom Kelvin's famous estimate for the life of the earth in terms of the probable rate of the earth's refrigeration from the molten state of its origin. As early as 1861 Kelvin estimated that the earth had provided a suitable environment for life during a period of about 100 million years.[63] Some geologists and paleontologists, whose strata and fossils seemed to indicate a nonmolten earth during a much longer period, protested Kelvin's estimate; for example, Lyell, in the tenth edition of his *Principles*, believéd that 240 million years should suffice for his uniformitarian development. Adams noted this latter estimate in his review for the *North American*, in mentioning a problem prophetic for the *Letter*,

> Sir Charles does not, however, mean his estimate to be taken strictly. He would probably be fully as willing to assume a thousand million of years for the development of organic life as a quarter of that time. Nevertheless we may hope that scientific data for a closer calculation may possibly be discovered, and, were this once effected, that another step would enable science to fix the limits within which species have flourished, and the race of man among the rest may expect to carry on its development.[64]

62. Lyell, *op. cit.* (10th ed.), *2*, 213. In the eleventh edition, *2*, 214, Lyell somewhat enlarged this section but in no decisive manner. Hence the theological query remained.

63. Lord Kelvin (then William Thomson), "Physical Considerations Regarding the Possible Age of the Sun's Heat," *Report of the British Association for the Advancement of Science* (Manchester meeting, 1861), Pt. 2, pp. 27 f. See also "The Doctrine of Uniformity in Geology Briefly Refuted" (1865), "On Geological Time" (1868), and "Geological Climate" (1877), all reprinted in Lord Kelvin, *op. cit.*, *2*, 6–9, 10–64, 273–298. In the last-named essay Kelvin examined Lyell's topographical theory and Croll's astronomical theory for climatic change.

Since Adams accepted Lapparent as his "standard authority" (*Degradation: Letter*, p. 163) where is was convenient to do so, it is interesting to note that Lapparent mentioned three estimates for the age of the earth but favored between 75 and 80 million years, roughly three times Kelvin's minimum figure; Lapparent, *op. cit.*, *3*, 1955–1958.

64. *NAR, 107* (1868), 481. For Lyell's estimate see *op. cit.* (10th ed.), *1*, 300 f., an estimate so speculative that Lyell eliminated it from the eleventh edition. For the tremendous range of nineteenth-century estimates on the age of the earth—from 10 million to 6 billion years—see Dana, *op. cit.*, pp. 1024 ff.

Adams' casual willingness in 1868 to grant Lyell a billion years for what allegedly required 240 million contrasted strongly with the catastrophic limitation demanded by the *Letter*—and with some reason. Clarence King had reinvestigated Kelvin's original research on the refrigeration of the earth on the basis of new geological discoveries and in 1893 pronounced the nonmolten age of the earth approximately 24 million years. King's paper in turn led Kelvin to re-examine his earlier work and write the very famous and controversial paper in 1897, "The Age of the Earth as an Abode Fitted for Life," wherein he substantially confirmed King's estimate.[65] These thermodynamic investigations encountered vigorous opposition from all uniformitarians. If Kelvin's calculation was correct, they simply had to abandon their basic premise of gradualism.[66] On the other hand, catastrophists welcomed an estimate which quite literally threatened to squeeze uniformitarianism out of existence.

Needless to add, Adams took no cognizance of an impasse which required for its decisive solution the better part of the first quarter of the twentieth century.[67] Once again research subsequent to Kelvin's—this time on radioactive substances—has proved the folly of Adams' incaution. The slow disintegration of uranium and thorium into lead (the one at a rate which reduces a given quantity to half its size in 4½ billion years, the other in a period approximately three times as long) provides the modern geologist with the means to measure time back to the very formation of the earth's crust. These natural clocks indicate that the surface of the earth hardened about three billion years ago [68]— as compared to the mere 240 million which Lyell once thought

65. For King's article see immediately above, n. 44. Lord Kelvin's address, first delivered in 1897, was reprinted in the *Annual Report of the Smithsonian Institution*, *53* (1898), where Adams may have read it; for other printings see Silvanus P. Thomson, *Life of Lord Kelvin* (London, Macmillan, 1910), *2*, 1270. In 1912 the *DNB* (2d suppl.), *3*, 514, could say that Kelvin's work on the age of the earth was "never really shaken," although new discoveries of the radioactive matter in rocks might "somewhat increase" his figure. See immediately below, n. 68.

66. See, as typical, Thomas C. Chamberlin, "On Lord Kelvin's Address on the Age of the Earth as an Abode Fitted for Life," *Annual Report of the Smithsonian Institution*, *54* (1899), 223–246.

67. Although of course he knew of its existence; *Degradation: Letter*, p. 166.

68. Adolph A. Knopf, "Time in Earth History," *Genetics, Paleontology, and Evolution*, ed. Glenn L. Jepsen, Ernst Mayr, George G. Simpson (Princeton, Princeton University Press, 1949), pp. 1–9, provides a summary of recent opinion on the age of the earth. He gives 1931 as the date when serious opposition began to disappear to belief in the tremendously long history of the earth as revealed by investigations into radioactivity.

sufficient for his uniformitarianism! Meanwhile the study of atomic disintegration in radioactive substances has suggested that the sun derives its energy from the nuclear transformation, under tremendous heat and pressure, of elements ordinarily stable under the much less extreme conditions prevailing on our earth. A cyclical process transforms hydrogen into helium at an incredibly slow rate, yet with the intense radiation characteristic of the disintegration of radioactive substances.[69] Granted, the sun must have shrunk slightly from its original size; but scientists are unable to observe the effects of any diminution in radiation during the whole of geological time. Thus the problem of the shrinking sun has rather receded from the polemical proportions which it enjoyed at the turn of the century.

Adams himself knew of research on radioactivity by historical geologists. His library still contains John Joly's *Radioactivity and Geology* which fully reported early investigations. To be sure, results in what was when Adams wrote a new area of research were far from conclusive; but even the preliminary work revealed the age of the earth as many times Kelvin's figure. In fact, even the earliest estimates far exceeded what most uniformitarians among geologists and paleontologists had supposed.[70] Nothing but perversity, therefore, accounted for the dismissal of Joly's volume in the *Letter* with the offhand assertion that "the general reader gathers from it mainly the conclusion that physical science is more or less chaotic." [71] Adams scored two arguments for his catastrophic theory of history where a fair-minded reader might hesitate to see one. Kelvin was arbitrarily right; if Joly together with a great many geologists and paleontologists disagreed, their disagreement only proved that scientific knowledge was rapidly headed toward a meaningless mixed-up-ness analogous to the total entropy which Kelvin promised would soon befall all available solar energy.

In summary, then, the geologist has steadily gathered evi-

69. George Gamow, *The Birth and Death of the Sun* (New York, Viking, 1940), chap. v, gives a simplified account.

70. *John Joly, *Radioactivity and Geology* (London, Constable; New York, Van Nostrand, 1909), p. 227, states that "when we examine into the claims of the radioactive method . . . we postulate a degree of uniformity between present and past conditions which might give pause to the most advanced uniformitarian geologist." See also estimates on pp. 220, 229 f.

71. *Degradation: Letter*, p. 239.

dence for a uniformitarian earth during the presumed two to three billion years of geological time, while the astronomer has cooperated by positing a sun not too different from the orb we see. Even the "catastrophe" of continental glaciation seems explicable in terms of relatively slight shifts in temperature, shifts so much within the realm of possibility that glacial geologists question whether or not we now live in the very midst of an ice age.[72] Pleistocene glaciation was not a single advance of ice but a series of advances. At least four times the ice spread, four times receded. Do we therefore live in an interim period of glacial withdrawal prior to the fifth "wave" of ice? Or is the present withdrawal of a more permanent character? Do we stand on the threshold of a vast period of slowly increasing temperatures, rising until the earth regains its thermal "norm"? [73] Almost certainly ours must be a time of more than average topographical variation. Excessive land elevations make present climates rather cooler than they have been during most of the geological past or presumably will be during much of the geological future. As erosive processes gradually plane the mountains, oceans will encroach on the land and temperatures become more equable. If certain astronomical conditions are also favorable,[74] perhaps a period approaching the Carboniferous may again cause forests to move poleward. Then, if past experience is any guide, mountains will rise, temperatures drop. According to present interpretation such is roughly—very roughly—the cycle of past (and presumably of future) climates and topography throughout geological time. Clearly a qualified uniformitarianism has prevailed over the geological catastro-

72. See, for example, Charles E. P. Brooks, *Climate through the Ages* (New Haven, Yale University Press, 1928), p. 6.

73. See *ibid.*, Introduction, for the contrast between the temperatures in which we live and the much warmer "normal" temperatures of the earth. Lyell, *op. cit., 2,* 250 ff., called present polar climates "abnormal," a verdict on which nineteenth-century geologists, of whatever persuasion, were in agreement. Adams was definitely aware of the possibility of another glacial descent; *Degradation: Letter,* pp. 181 ff. Of course he used this future ice wave as further indication of man's doom; but evidence for the viability of animal species through preceding glacial descents (see below, p. 189) would seem to refute the dismal predictions of Jacques de Morgan as cited in the *Letter.*

74. Richard F. Flint, *Glacial Geology and the Pleistocene Epoch* (New York, Wiley; London, Chapman & Hall, 1947), chap. xxii, provides a compact and authoritative summary of hypotheses, possible as well as impossible, on the cause of climatic fluctuations. In addition to combinations of the major theories of the nineteenth century, that of fluctuations in solar radiation, first proposed in 1891, is important today.

phism [75] which Adams adopted as the starting point for his sweep of human knowledge in the *Letter*.

To be sure, Adams' opinions on geology were quite valid for the time at which he wrote, provided he arbitrarily settled all controversy in favor of the catastrophic point of view, no matter how serious the controversy.

> Men are born either Catastrophists or Uniformitarians. You may divide the race into imaginative people who believe in all sorts of impending crises—physical, social, political—and others who anchor their very souls *in statuo quo*. There are men who build arks straight through their natural lives, ready for the first sprinkle, and there are others who do not watch Old Probabilities or even own an umbrella.[76]

Thus Clarence King categorized the human race for his Yale audience, and there is little doubt as to how he would have characterized his close friend.

The catastrophic nature of geology established to his satisfaction, Adams turned to the effect of geological catastrophism on paleontology. Three conclusions emerge from the purposeful obscurities of the *Letter*. In the first place, if geological climates showed an over-all decline due to a cooling earth and a shrinking sun, then this refrigeration must have affected plant and animal life. Second, if Kelvin's estimate of geological time set the limits for the whole of paleontological evolution, then the catastrophism of Cuvier and Agassiz prevailed over Darwinian uniformitarianism. Finally, if all closed systems tended toward entropy, then perhaps the energies available to evolution (whatever these might be) were also waning. To prove his conclusions Adams successively alluded to, first, the demise of Pleistocene animals, second, the phenomenon of evolutionary "leaps," third, the limited and irreversible nature of evolutionary change within particular species. These proofs and the conclusions which they seemed to justify

75. See, for example, Gamow, *Biography of the Earth* (New York, Viking, 1941), chaps. vi, vii, although it should be added that his statements on the cause of mountain uplift are disputed. The cause of mountain building is still among the most hotly debated subjects in historical geology. Adams accepted the prevalent hypothesis that terrestrial shrinkage caused mountain uplift, for this fitted his view of a cooling and shrinking earth.

76. King, *Catastrophism and the Evolution of Environment*, p. 7.

led him to his attack on the physical frailties of man with their implications for human society.[77]

Having taken leave of the Carboniferous on the slightly wistful note of Saporta's " 'période de luxe, s'il en fut jamais' " [78]— a wistfulness just barely reminiscent of the *période de luxe* of *Mont-Saint-Michel and Chartres*, however ludicrous when applied to prehistoric flora—Adams turned to the extinction of certain animals which, very neatly for his theory, seemed to have occurred just as the earth cooled to its present degraded temperature. That many species of mammals have died out during recent geological time is true. Paleontologists now know that the defunct ground sloths, mammoths, mastodons, musk oxen, American camels, certain species of beaver, bears, cats, armadillos, and other ill-fated mammals actually lived through all or most of the four cold periods of the Pleistocene. They became extinct toward the end of the Pleistocene or during the present period of glacial withdrawal. Although reasons for this vast faunal decimation remain uncertain, it now seems impossible that cold climates were alone sufficient. But proofs that most of the disappearances postdated the bulk of glaciation appeared only after Adams had published his *Letter;* so his temptation to attribute the "zoologically impoverished world" [79] of the present time to glaciation was understandable.

If the energy of the sun had dwindled as rapidly as Kelvin maintained, then the whole of paleontological history must be squeezed within such narrow limits as to make floral and faunal evolution a series of gigantic leaps rather than of gradual change. Adams turned from Kelvin's thermodynamic data to the core of his paleontological argument, namely, three assertions by Louis Dollo. Evolution has occurred by leaps; it is irreversible; it is limited.[80] The first of Dollo's aphorisms suggested that Cuvier

77. For the basic paleontological argument of the *Letter* see pp. 167–170.
78. *Ibid.,* p. 167.
79. *Alfred R. Wallace, *The Geographical Distribution of Animals* (London, Macmillan, 1876), *1,* 150; on this and the succeeding two pages Wallace attributes the mammalian extinctions to glaciation. On the other hand, Lyell, *op. cit.,* *1,* 306, mentioned that Pleistocene glaciation did not significantly affect the bulk of species. For general bibliography on this subject see Bibliography, Sec. R.
80. *Degradation: Letter,* p. 170. The original source is Louis Dollo, "Les Lois de l'évolution," *Bulletin de la Société Belge de Géologie, 7* (1893), 164 ff.: "L'évolution est discontinue,—irréversible,—limitée." Adams doubtless found Dollo's assertions in Charles Depéret, *The Transformations of the Animal World,* tr. F. Legge

and Agassiz might be right in their catastrophism, while the irreversible and limited nature of the evolutionary process for any given species seemed to imply a striking parallel to the second law of thermodynamics.

The nature of evolutionary leaps is even today among the more controversial areas of paleontology. Since each individual in any species is distinct from all others, the slightest morphological change involves an element of discontinuity. Hence even Darwinians acknowledged small leaps, but leaps so small that a complete series of fossils for any particular species would reveal a step-by-step transformation. Unfortunately for neat demonstration of the Darwinian position, complete fossil records exist for very few species. Rather the record of gradualism seems punctuated here and there by abrupt transformations of an extensive character without any evidence of transitional forms. Darwinians generally explained these gaps in the paleontological record by the patent argument that the transitional forms merely awaited discovery by some fortunate paleontologist.[81] But as time went on and the gaps remained unfilled, many paleontologists concluded that the elusive specimens did not exist. Toward the end of the nineteenth century catastrophic theories of paleontology centered on this phenomenon of evolutionary leaps.

Quite obviously the simplest approach to the problem was that of environmentalism, which was King's approach in his Yale address. Briefly venturing outside his specialty to comment on the development of the horse, King suggested that major morphological changes had in every instance coincided with radical alterations in environment. But this explanation hardly answered the problem, for if one type of horse had disappeared, just how had a new type emerged? The catastrophist seemed driven back to the special creations of Cuvier and Agassiz.[82]

It was this very problem on which Adams also touched in concluding his review of Lyell's *Principles*, but in a somewhat

(New York, Appleton, 1909), p. 237 [*Les Transformations du monde animal* (Paris, Flammarion, 1907), p. 243]. Depéret coupled Dollo and Rosa in precisely the same manner as did Adams.

81. See, for example, Charles Darwin, *The Origin of Species*, chap. x; also the well-known section in Lyell, *op. cit.*, concluding chap. xiv.

82. King, *Catastrophism and the Evolution of Environment*, pp. 36 f. King ended his address on a theological note. Cuvier's hypothesis did not wholly depend on the creation of new species since he also believed that new forms, already extant but relatively insignificant numerically, might by migration and proliferation fill in areas occupied by their extinct predecessors.

more circuitous manner than had King.[83] Adams pondered the
paradox of the mutable, yet immutable, aspect of every species.
On the one hand, as Darwinians maintained, modifications obviously did occur in every species. Barnyard breeding proved the
point. On the other hand, limitations obviously existed for each
species beyond which change could not be effected. Horses bred
for fleetness could not attain an indefinite degree of speed; a
quality evident in the animal therefore defied limitless improvement. If evident qualities defied endless betterment, how could the
Darwinian possibly explain the emergence in a particular species
of some new quality previously nonexistent—a hoofed horse, to
use a classic example, out of the mating of however many three-
toed prototypes? The Darwinian response was that a sport had
appeared with superior adaptability and thence preserved itself
by natural selection. But, anti-Darwinians protested, certainly a
step-by-step uniformitarianism precluded the validity of any such
answer since the accident of a very slight fusion of the toes in a
particular animal would hardly give it any great survival advantage over other horses. If the element of the superior adaptability of the hoofed over the toed type only appeared after the
hoof was practically realized, then the process of natural selection must somehow possess an element of foresight. There was no
doubt that these arguments embarrassed Darwinians, while the
phenomenon of evolutionary leaps proved most embarrassing of
all. These among other deficiencies in Darwinism encouraged opponents to attack materialistic explanations of evolution as either
unfounded or blasphemous, the choice of adjective depending on
the vehemence of the conviction. The anti-Darwinian position demanded some comprehensive plan for the universe. In its most
extreme form this position required the periodic unveiling of new
forms. More frequently the anti-Darwinian saw each animal striving—through a vital force, a will, an *élan vital*, or whatever—
toward some ideal form predetermined by the Divine Creator.
Hence both sides ultimately used the same data for their divergent
opinions. Where the step-by-step transformation of animal forms
was evidence of adjustment for survival to the Darwinian, his
opponent saw the same phenomenon as evidence of the working
of some inner force toward its planned destiny. Where evolutionary leaps resulted from imperfections in the geological and paleontological record to the one, to the other they represented some

83. *NAR, 107* (1868), 482–499, especially p. 498.

drastic special creation. No wonder that many questioned with Adams whether "special creation and natural or artificial selection [were not] practically the same thing, and the whole dispute a mere question of words." [84]

Happily there is no need to dwell longer on Adams' discussion of this stalemate in his review for the *North American*. Suffice it to say that, while Adams leaned toward the Darwinian position,[85] he did indicate the arguments raised by the opposition. These arguments substantially remained when, some forty years later, he wrote his *Letter*. In this Adams made no attempt to appraise the impasse. It was enough to record Dollo's statement: evolution occurs by leaps. The very abruptness of the aphorism, unencumbered by discussion, implied a phenomenon unfathomably catastrophic in its operation. On the one hand, Adams implied that science was powerless to probe the origin of any new species, so cataclysmic was the event. On the other, he omitted any notion of a special plan for the universe beyond the power of scientific investigation, since the theological aspect of Agassiz's teaching was one with which the pupil never sympathized. Hope for the solution of the problem of evolutionary leaps therefore existed in neither science nor theology nor philosophy. Evolution occurred by leaps: Adams left the problem just so, a barrier impossible to circumvent.

In truth, when in 1892 Dollo made his statement, he himself attempted no explanation of the mystery—but of course without Adams' theatrical intentions. Dollo merely recorded his observations and thus decisively summarized the growing conviction of many paleontologists that the missing transitional forms simply did not exist. But by the time Adams published his *Letter* in 1910 beginnings had already been made in a new area of research which would revolutionize thinking on the vexatious leaps. Indeed, the twentieth-century science of genetics would basically alter thinking on all aspects of the evolutionary process. Today Mendel ranks beside Darwin in what Julian Huxley has called the "modern synthesis" in evolutionary thought.[86]

84. *Ibid.*, p. 498.

85. Again Samuels disagrees (see immediately above, n. 51). The paleontological section of the review does not reveal the specific evidence of uniformitarian bias which seems apparent in the geological section; but certainly Adams developed the uniformitarian argument at great length, and in *NAR*, 107 (1868), 495, particularly appeared to favor the Darwinian side.

86. Julian S. Huxley, *Evolution, the Modern Synthesis* (London, Allen & Unwin, 1942). For general bibliography on genetics see Bibliography, Sec. S.

Evolutionists now know that genetic mutations are important in the creation of new forms, while these mutations apparently account for the paleontological leaps which Adams found so catastrophic. There is no need to retell here the story of how Mendel in 1866 buried in the local *Naturforschenden Verein in Brünn* his findings on the statistical results of crossing varieties of peas, and how his paper remained unnoticed until it furnished the basis for genetics when three scientists almost simultaneously and independently discovered it in 1900. Mendel's work centered in traits which he knew to exist in the lineage; in other words, the problem of inheritance. On the other hand, much investigation in the present century has focused on a different problem, that of the appearance of characteristics not previously evident in the stock, the problem of evolution. Where Mendel was interested in the recombination of what the modern geneticist calls "genes," work stemming from De Vries' research on the sudden appearance of new characteristics centers in the problem of genetic "mutations." [87] Gene is the name given to the locus for an inheritable characteristic or a group of related characteristics, the precise role of each gene being a matter of intensive investigation at the present time. According to most geneticists a mutation involves some internal alteration within the gene (or some recombination of the gene in relation to others) which can actually or potentially affect a specific aspect of the offspring for which the gene is particularate. Since most (not all) mutations are recessive, they usually lurk unknown within a particular line for generation after generation until, by chance, the mutated recessive is identically paired. Then the hidden abnormality appears in the offspring. It may be some abnormality of bodily structure or of physiological function; it may be so small as to be unnoticeable or so gross as to be automatically lethal. Whatever the nature of the mutation —and for present purposes this is the significant point—if it is effective at all, it is totally effective. For example, if effective at all, the mutation for albinism does not reveal itself in gradual stages, by successive generations becoming lighter of skin and hair

87. Actually Hugo de Vries was one among several investigators working on this problem shortly after 1900; but he is the best known. The work of William Bateson, who began his work in the nineties, is generally conceded by geneticists today to be more distinguished than that of De Vries. The experimental controls of the latter were so shoddy as to increase the controversial nature of his work. Present-day geneticists know that De Vries was not actually investigating what is now known as a "mutation," but this technicality need not disturb the student of Adams.

until the extreme appears. Rather the albino comes without warning—"all at once," so to speak—as a sizable discontinuity with the past. Genetics, then, seems to make the mystery of evolutionary leaps less mysterious, even though evolutionary leaps apparently involve changes much larger than the mutation of a single gene.

Could Adams have penetrated beyond the element of mystery inherent in his simple statement of Dollo's aphorism? It is certainly too much to expect the layman to keep even generally abreast of scientific research. Genetics really begins with the discovery of Mendel's paper in 1900; only the most alert layman would have known much about the first decade of genetic research. Yet had Adams cared in the least to go beyond Dollo's statement he would certainly have discovered the work of De Vries on so-called "explosive" changes in plants. In fact, Adams learned of Dollo from Charles Depéret's popular history of paleontological theory.[88] Not fifty pages later Depéret mentioned De Vries' work and remarked that "the *explosions* or sudden creations" of species studied by De Vries in existing plants could doubtless give some idea as to the cause of the more rapid aspects of evolution.[89] De Vries had published his *Species and Varieties, Their Origin by Mutation* in 1904. An extremely controversial book, it went through two editions before 1910.[90] Certainly the interested amateur should have known of the volume and the almost boastful sequence of quotations with which De Vries prefaced it.

The origin of species is a natural phenomenon.

—LAMARCK.

The origin of species is an object of inquiry.

—DARWIN.

The origin of species is an object of experimental investigation.   —DE VRIES.

Although De Vries' confident assertion needed much bolstering by other investigators before gaining general acceptance, there was sufficient merit in his challenge to win many professional adherents and to induce much experimentation directed at the problem which he had set. Hence the catastrophic implication of the

88. See immediately above, n. 80.

89. Depéret, *op. cit.*, pp. 274 ff. [*pp. 281 ff.], where Depéret specifically mentioned De Vries in connection with Dollo, and p. 279 [*p. 286].

90. Hugo de Vries, *Species and Varieties, Their Origin by Mutation* (Chicago, Open Court, 1904). A third edition appeared in 1912.

unqualified statement in the *Letter* that evolution occurred by
leaps was either uninformed, reckless, or perhaps consciously
somewhat insincere. Even had he wanted, Adams could not have
been completely sincere without watering down his catastrophism;
for the catastrophic point of view is one of helplessness. So much
as hint that a catastrophe is "an object of experimental investigation," and the catastrophe begins to fade. To make the phenomenon of evolutionary leaps subject to the experimental method
is to bring it within the purview of uniformitarianism: forces operating in the present account for all past phenomena.

In fairness to Adams, the idea of discontinuity seems a little
less catastrophic today than it appeared when he wrote. Although
Planck had discovered the quantum reaction of the atom as early
as 1901, in this instance the amateur could be excused for missing
implications which around 1910 were none too clear even to professionals. No mechanist, Adams was nevertheless nurtured on
mechanistic physics, where every action had its corresponding
reaction. But discontinuities in the atomic realm underlie the
continuities of mechanics. To know that the perceptual world exists on a substratum of discontinuity rather vitiates the notion
that abrupt transformation is frighteningly unusual. In atomic
physics a gradually increasing action produces no apparent reaction whatsoever until a certain threshold is reached, whereupon
there occurs a very definite reaction—a "jump"—which is precisely the whole of the quantum involved. Here genetics and physics converge in a particularly significant fashion.

The paleontologist George Gaylord Simpson has recently bor-
rowed from the physicist's vocabulary to speak of a "quantum"
evolution rather than of evolutionary "explosions" or "leaps." [91]
He refers not to a quantum in the atomic sense but to a quantum
of adaptation. Some drastic change in climate, some alteration
in food supply, some pestilence or other misfortune may kill off
most of a particular species. With dwindling numbers, increased
inbreeding occurs; hence the greater likelihood that recessive
mutations will pair with like recessives to become manifest—the
genetic reason for not marrying close relatives. The process of
natural selection temporarily becomes less important than that
of mutation. A proliferation of odd and unusual forms appears,
in effect providing the species with new models among which there

91. George G. Simpson, *Tempo and Mode in Evolution* (New York, Columbia
University Press, 1944), especially pp. 206–217.

may exist the possibility of adjustment sufficient to avoid the threatened extinction. Most of these mutations will be lethal, since the accident of mutation is usually no improvement over the well-tested mean produced by generation after generation of natural selection. By chance, however, some individuals will mutate in a direction which promises survival; yet even these will perish unless their transformation is sufficiently large to "preadapt" them to a changing environment, with the size of each increment of preadaptation dependent on the rapidity of environmental change. In other words, a particular animal either makes the whole of a necessary adjustment or it perishes. This is Simpson's quantum of adaptation. Through a long series of such quantum steps a fortunate few continue to preadapt to environmental change, eventually achieving a situation where they can flourish. Then natural selection gradually reassumes its normal role of stabilization and perfection.

Nothing in this view of evolutionary leaps contradicts uniformitarianism; each quantum of adaptation depends on the process of mutation in the accepted sense of classical genetic theory, although again it is probable that the mutations involve more than a single gene at each of the quantum steps. A condition merely occurs in the species where mutations become more readily available for morphological change than is customary during periods of more stable development. Simpson and most paleontologists believe that such words as "leaps," "explosions," and "quanta" conceal enormous spans of time. The transitions occurring between periods of stability may occupy tens of thousands of years—leaps to paleontologists perhaps, but these leaps would often seem to require somewhat more than the whole of recorded history for their consummation. To account for gaps in the fossil record obscuring such vast transitional periods, Simpson would point to the relative paucity of the individuals involved and their rapid migration (presumably part of most adjustments), which would tend to scatter what few fossils the paleontologist might expect to find.

Despite the hypothetical nature of this theory, most paleontologists and geneticists tend to favor something like it. But Simpson's explanation for evolutionary leaps is not immune from the dissension which, unhappily for quests like Adams', bedevils science quite as much as history. If we ask for the modern geneticist whose position is most congenial to the requirements of Adams' theory, he would certainly be Richard Goldschmidt.[92] Although Goldschmidt is virtually alone in his heterodoxy, he would doubtless be the authority to whom Adams would turn were he rewriting the *Letter* today. Goldschmidt has attacked certain assumptions basic to the entire classical theory of genetics. He maintains that the mutations observed in *Drosophila*—the fruit flies which have served as the geneticist's favorite guinea pigs—are not identical with those responsible for evolutionary leaps. The latter, Goldschmidt believes, are of a much larger order. Two types of mutations exist to account for two kinds of evolution. The smaller and more usual variety, as observed in experiments with *Drosophila*, accounts for "microevolution," or diversification within the species. This type is comparable to the alteration of a single gene, just as classical neo-Darwinian genetics teaches. But Goldschmidt believes that there is also a larger, more extraordinary variety which accounts for "macroevolution," or the transition from species to species. This latter type occurs by some "systemic" alteration affecting the pattern of the entire chromosome containing all the many genetic loci for inheritable characteristics.[93] To Goldschmidt chromosomal alteration is the most significant factor in evolution.

This theory of evolutionary leaps would seem to place Goldschmidt's theory somewhere between the extremes of uniformitarianism and catastrophism as these positions were understood in the nineteenth century.[94] It requires leaps of a size not quite so large perhaps as the special creations of Cuvier and Agassiz but of that order, at least as compared to classical genetic theory. Of course Goldschmidt's catastrophism has neither the theological nor the environmental characteristics of the pregenetic theories of Cuvier and Agassiz. It is rather a variant of theories quite as materialistic as those of the majority of geneticists.[95] A catastrophist among modern geneticists, then, Goldschmidt is decidedly

92. Richard Goldschmidt, *The Material Basis of Evolution* (New .Haven, Yale University Press, 1940). The German paleontologist O. H. Schindewolf has made perhaps the most significant contributions among paleontologists to a theory similar to that of Goldschmidt. George G. Simpson has attacked Schindewolf in a review, *Evolution, 3* (1949), 178 ff.

93. Actually Goldschmidt does not believe in the existence of the loci called "genes." He holds that so-called changes in the gene are really very small changes of pattern within the entire chromosome, while "mutations" represent substantial alterations in the chromosomal pattern; *op. cit.*, pp. 203–210.

94. As Goldschmidt himself seems to admit; *ibid.*, p. 212.

95. Witness the title of Goldschmidt's work.

not a catastrophist in the sense of Cuvier and Agassiz. There is a significant difference between the flat statement "evolution occurs by leaps" in the *Letter*—which is Cuvier and Agassiz secularized and given pessimistic implications [96]—and the revision which would have to be made were Adams rewriting the *Letter* today. The new version might begin like the old, but it would be necessary to add, "Modern genetics [meaning that of Goldschmidt] teaches that these leaps are caused by changes in the chromosomal pattern, although the cause of such changes remains mysterious." Catastrophism again—provided that the imaginary revision of the *Letter* suggested that the mystery of these chromosomal changes must forever defy experimental analysis, an assertion which Goldschmidt of course does not make.[97] Even if the revised *Letter* were to mimic the original in this assumption of immutable mystery for further research on evolutionary leaps, the element of mystery has been so substantially narrowed that the vigor of the original metaphor almost entirely disappears. Further assume that time and experiment have won the majority of geneticists to Goldschmidt's point of view, while more time and more experiment have accounted for the unexplained element in the revised *Letter*. Carrying the revision one step further, then, another rewriting of the *Letter* at some future date might record solutions to past problems only to collide again with some unexplained element. Faith in the ability of the scientist eventually to eliminate the immediate difficulties in his theories accounts for the uniformitarian conviction of steady increase in scientific knowledge, while faith appears as much in the tone as in the statement. Hence it was one thing for Dollo to assert that evolution had occurred by leaps, with the implication that subsequent research must abandon the Darwinian explanation of deficiencies in the paleontological record. It was quite another thing for Adams to appropriate Dollo's aphorism, with the implication that further research was impossible. In attacking catastrophism Lyell characterized Adams' attitude completely.

> Never was there a dogma more calculated to foster indolence, and to blunt the keen edge of curiosity, than this assumption of the discordance between the ancient and existing causes of change . . . The student, instead of being encouraged with

96. See above, pp. 91 and 190.
97. He does of course point out that the methods used by most geneticists at present will not reveal the cause of macroevolution.

the hope of interpreting the enigmas presented to him in the earth's structure—instead of being prompted to undertake laborious enquiries into the natural history of the organic world, and the complicated effects of the igneous and aquaeous causes now in operation—was taught to despond from the first. Geology, it was affirmed, could never rise to the rank of an exact science; the greater number of phenomena must for ever remain inexplicable, or only be partially elucidated by ingenious conjectures. Even the mystery which invested the subject was said to constitute one of its principal charms, affording, as it did, full scope to the fancy to indulge in a boundless field of speculation.[98]

Certainly Adams made the mystery of scientific ignorance one of the principal charms of the *Letter*.

In part he suffered from his impatient necessity to know *the* truth about science, but in part he affected an elaborate pose. The elements of mutability and immutability in evolution seem the two halves of a balanced process. In determining what individuals will live to propagate, natural selection provides the ·element of continuity, without which no forms could be perfected. In creating new forms, mutation—whatever its mode of operation —provides the element of flexibility, without which extant species could not adjust to major environmental crises, while novel forms could not originate to enter upon new zones of life. Taken together, both natural selection and mutation are conserving forces, both creative forces. Hence the example of evolutionary leaps would seem a poor choice for the historical catastrophist. It might conceivably happen that man will one day confront a cataclysm in his environment with which his present anatomy cannot cope. If so, mutation is the only hope for history.

Probably no modern theories—certainly not Goldschmidt's— would substantially disagree with this picture of evolution. Of course modern genetics has done much to strengthen what was essentially the Darwinian view of evolution as the resultant of factors operating for stability and factors operating for change. Even if Adams is forgiven his ignorance of genetic research by De Vries and others immediately after 1900, his use of Dollo's first principle was still capricious, for common sense has always comprised a substantial part of the faith of scientists, and common

98. Lyell, *op. cit.*, *1*, 318.

sense required that evolutionary leaps be weighed against the evidence for evolutionary stability. The chaos implied in the *Letter* could not imaginably account for the existence of species over long periods of time, or for the oriented change characteristic of most evolutionary leaps, or for the over-all development of progressively higher forms of life measured by both complexity of anatomical structure and range of adaptability. Against such truths as these Adams' flippancy is all too apparent. On the whole, time has justified the uniformitarian faith of Lyell and Darwin, however greatly it has modified and extended their conclusions.

Of course what is uniformitarian from a narrowly scientific point of view could just possibly be catastrophic to the human race. In evolution the great catastrophe would obviously be human extinction as the result of some cataclysm which *Homo sapiens* could neither survive nor leap. In Dollo's terms there is a limit to the evolution of any species. Evolution has occurred by leaps; it is irreversible; it is limited.

The development of any particular species is, first of all, limited in that variation beyond a certain point so alters the species that it becomes a new organism. Some so-called extinctions are doubtless excessive transformations. In these instances a particular morphology is extinct; but it would be exaggerating to say that the species also perished. On the contrary, it adjusted so prodigiously that it survived. Thus man might metamorphose into a substantially new animal, although the trouble with this happy assumption is the difficulty of imagining it. Certainly the historical theorist must be prepared for the worst.[99]

Whether true or not, assume that man has reached a biological limit to his possibilities.[100] Most species do become extinct; eventually perhaps all. Adams cited Dollo's statement about limitation in conjunction with Rosa's law of the progressive reduction of variability.[101] In combination, as Adams used them, the two au-

99. See discussion in George G. Simpson, *The Meaning of Evolution* (New Haven, Yale University Press, 1949), chap. xx, who does not envision a foreseeable end to evolution.

100. Among contemporary, or near contemporary, paleontologists who see an end to evolution, Robert Broome, William E. Swinton, Teilhard de Chardin, Friedrich von Huene, and Henry F. Osborn might be mentioned, although the last named denied that he was a finalist. Not all these finalists, however, are pessimistic. Julian Huxley sees all evolution at an end except in man. Finalists among those writing of evolution in a more or less philosophical or theological manner are legion.

101. *Degradation: Letter*, p. 170. The original presentation of Rosa's views

thorities stated that the biological evolution of every species took place within certain limits, while increased perfection merely narrowed the bounds so as to decrease flexibility in meeting environmental changes. Extinction followed. Since every species adapts to a particular environment in certain ways, each inevitably limits the range of its adaptation. Yet specialization is the very basis of competition. On the other hand, *over*specialization does cause extinction. When does an animal become overspecialized, if specialization is also the basis for existence? Hence the vexatiousness of the problem of extinction.[102] A few species have changed but little in either structure or mode of life for what, even to paleontologists, is a considerable period of time. Oysters, as one familiar example, have remained substantially unchanged for over two hundred million years, as compared to about one million for man. Even if the human form has reached its biological ultimate, nothing in Dollo's rule prohibits a future of so many eons for the human race as to permit the historian to leave the remote catastrophe of its demise for some far-distant successor.

In any event, the extreme mental development of man does not necessarily portend his imminent end as Adams suggested. The factors to which extinction is attributable are rarely owing to the straight-line development of any particular specialization, however tempting it is on looking back at the evolutionary past to trace lines through an essentially complex process.[103] Extinction usually depends on a complex interaction of environment and organism by no means identical for all animals. The enormous plasticity of human behavior would seem to give man excellent odds for surviving future environmental changes. To be sure, the alarmist has sufficient cause for his warnings. Although man need not in the foreseeable future anticipate that any other animal can challenge his dominance, the very plasticity of human behavior

(which Adams doubtless never saw, see immediately above, n. 80) appeared as *La Riduzione progressiva della variabilita a i suoi rapporti coll'estinzione e coll origine delle specie* (Turin, Clausen, 1899). Simpson, *Tempo and Mode in Evolution,* pp. 36 f., has observed that variability can be retained without sacrificing adaptability; see also his discussion of nonadaptive trends, *The Meaning of Evolution,* pp. 145–154, 203.

102. Simpson, *The Meaning of Evolution,* pp. 192–196.

103. *Ibid.,* chap. xi, especially pp. 146–154. Rosa has been criticized for exaggerating the development of a single nonadaptive characteristic as the cause of extinction; but paleontology of the nineteenth century was generally conceived in terms of linear developments far simpler than most paleontologists would hold today. See, for example, Depéret's chapter on Jean Albert Gaudry who greatly influenced Adams. See also immediately below, n. 118.

enables him to contrive environments of such artificiality that his inventiveness may overreach his adaptive capabilities. His insatiable plunder of natural wealth may strip him of his sustenance. His ingenuity may be turned to the creation of means of physical destruction too terrible for human tolerance. Or at the opposite extreme, his solicitude for the unfit may lead him so to mitigate the rigors of natural selection that, as some eugenists fear, he may fatally debase his inheritance. But it is man's resourcefulness which promises to be his salvation as well as his undoing. Where prophecy can take either extreme, it is risky in any "science" of history to venture into personal preference, and especially to prophesy on the basis of evolutionary data. Man raises so many new problems in evolution that paleontology can offer no prototype for precise comparison. In this instance the answer would seem to lie more within history than paleontology.[104] Again Adams used scientific data as proof for future historical occurrences on the basis that science possessed a validity superior to that of all other fields of knowledge.

Dollo's assertion of the irreversibility of evolution provided Adams with yet another opportunity to tear scientific generalization from its context. Of the three statements in Dollo's triad— evolution has occurred by leaps; it is irreversible; it is limited— perhaps the second was the most significant for the *Letter*. For Adams' purposes, irreversibility linked evolution to history, and both to thermodynamics. This important paleontological concept, often known as Dollo's rule, touches on the significant fact that evolution does not double back on itself to recreate forms abandoned in the past. Statistical theory explains this continuous trend toward novelty by citing the improbability that any sizable change could, after a long process of selection, ever precisely be reversed so as to duplicate an antecedent form.[105] Dollo himself casually alluded in one of his articles, published two years after the appearance of the *Letter*, to this statistical explanation for irreversibility with the assertion that "in the last analysis, it

104. A glance at the apparent criteria for paleontological longevity enumerated by Simpson, *The Meaning of Evolution,* pp. 194 f., would seem to provide excellent odds for the continued existence of *Homo sapiens.* Man meets all the criteria, except perhaps the first.

105. Small mutations are often reversible; Hermann J. Muller, "Reversibility in Evolution Considered from the Standpoint of Genetics," *Biological Reviews of the Cambridge Philosophical Society, 14* (1939), 276. For general bibliography on thermodynamic interpretations of evolution and life see Bibliography, Sec. Q, and especially Seidenberg, *op. cit.,* pp. 144–172.

is, like other natural laws, a question of probability." [106] But for the most part Dollo's generalization simply summarized a series of specific paleontological observations. He paid no heed to the cosmic implications of irreversibility, whereas Adams heeded nothing else. Had Adams troubled to look into the particularities of Dollo's research, he would again have found much to embarrass the glibness of the *Letter*.

One problem especially attracting Dollo's attention was the reversion of certain animals to an environment abandoned by their ancestral prototypes. The most usual transitions of this sort involved changes from a land to a water habitat, followed by a later return to land; or the converse. Each transition involved major structural adaptations; but if evolution were reversible it might happen that the third stage in the series duplicated the first. The principle of irreversibility denied that such duplication could occur. A specific example may make this clear. The mammalian characteristics of the whale indicate this species' earlier existence on land. Should some future whale trundle back to the land, it will likewise presumably disclose in its structure some evidence of its ocean existence. In short, Dollo's primary interest in irreversibility lay not in the analysis of the quality of irreversibility but rather in the fact that because of this quality every species must disclose in its anatomical structure some vestige of its past evolution. As Dollo himself warned, anatomical structure only, not function, is irreversible.[107] Had Adams therefore meant to use the concept of irreversibility as Dollo used it, he must first have distinguished historical structure from historical function. Ignorance of Dollo's work spared Adams this impossible dissection.

Limited to anatomical structure, then, Dollo's rule specifically stated that all species could gain structures during the course of evolution; but once lost, structures never reappeared. A species might return in a later stage of development to an adaptation demanding functions similar to those once performed by the van-

106. As cited by Joseph Needham, "Evolution and Thermodynamics," *Time: The Refreshing River* (London, Allen & Unwin, New York, Macmillan, 1943), p. 222.

107. Edwin H. Colbert, "Some Paleontological Principles Significant in Human Evolution," *Studies in Physical Anthropology No. 1; Early Man in the Far East,* symposium of the American Association of Physical Anthropologists (Philadelphia, Press of the Wistar Institute, 1949), pp. 117–130, who mentions examples of functional reversibility; William K. Gregory, "On the Meaning and Limits of Irreversibility of Evolution," *American Naturalist, 70* (1936), 517–528.

ished structure. If so, not the original structure but a substitute would appear. Likewise, structures reduced during the course of evolution would never return to their former importance. Although a cultural historian might have made analogous use of Dollo's conclusions on structure, again Adams made no specific use of Dollo's work. It was the word "irreversible," like "leaps" and "limited," which caught his attention. He used Dollo's assertion as to the irreversible nature of evolution only in the general sense that the past development of every species conditions its future development.

To go beyond Dollo's own specialized interests: just how is the irreversibility of evolution related to that of the second law of thermodynamics? Here Adams touched on a problem significant to both science and philosophy, and doubly significant at the present time when biology and physical chemistry have become inextricably interrelated. Adams suggested that evolution occurred only by depleting in some way the total amount of energy available for future evolution. For example, he cited from Bernhard Brunhes' *Degradation* a position which is still valid in thermodynamic speculation.

". . . the principle of Degradation of energy [proves] nothing against the fact of Evolution. The progressive transformation of species, the realization of more perfect organisms, contain nothing contrary to the idea of the constant loss of useful energy. Only the vast and grandiose conceptions of imaginative philosophers who erect into an absolute principle the law of "universal progress," could no longer hold against one of the most fundamental ideas that physics reveals to us. On one side, therefore, the world wears out; on another side the appearance on earth of living beings more and more elevated, and,—in a slightly different order of ideas,—the development of civilization in human society, undoubtedly give the impression of a progress and a gain." [108]

Occurring toward the end of the *Letter*, Brunhes' position represented "the extreme limit of the physicist's concessions" to the evolutionist. With this concession Adams virtually closed his harangue to fellow historians, leaving the pessimistic implications of

108. *Degradation: Letter*, pp. 255 f.; Bernhard Brunhes, *La Dégradation de l'énergie* (Paris, Flammarion, 1908), p. 193. Citations immediately below, *Degradation: Letter*, p. 258.

the second law as the "logical foundation" for whatever optimism they might squeeze from biological evolution.

Assuming that evolution operates as a closed system, with only so much energy potential available for genetic mutation, then evolution does fall under the second law. Of course this is no mean assumption! Thermodynamically speaking, the mystery of life in both its biological and its paleontological senses depends upon the avoidance of the ultimate consequences of the second law by maintaining an open system where closure is death. This is no place to discuss thermodynamic theories of life, since, for the purposes of his theory, Adams could skirt the problem by making the thermodynamics of life depend on the thermodynamics of the sun.[109] Most scientists do believe that the energy of the sun is finite, while all life depends on the continuance of solar radiation. Measured against the vast dissipation of solar energy into space, or even against that small portion which lights and warms the earth, biological and paleontological evolution certainly has occurred at an overwhelming expenditure of energy. The exceptions are, so to speak, drowned in the rule. Moreover, it is far from clear that the exceptions really are what they superficially seem. Recalling Gibbs' label of mixed-up-ness for entropy, the English biochemist Joseph Needham has recently suggested that the process toward entropy can take place in one of two ways: by a trend toward either "chaotic mixed-up-ness" or "patterned mixed-up-ness." [110] Consider the analogy of painting in watercolor. The artist may spread his color haphazardly over the paper or he may apply it so as to form a pattern. In both instances the painter irrevocably depletes the block of color. Similarly, Needham imagines two kinds of dissipation for energy according to the second law: toward chaotic mixed-up-ness in the instance of dissipating solar energy, toward patterned mixed-up-ness in the

109. Needham, *op. cit.*, pp. 224–230; Erwin Schrödinger, *Science and the Human Temperament* (London, Allen & Unwin; New York, Macmillan, 1935), p. 39, cited by Needham, *op. cit.*, pp. 220 f.; Harold F. Blum, "A Consideration of Evolution from a Thermodynamic View-Point," *American Naturalist, 69* (1935), 354–369. For a classic discussion of the problem of life as related to thermodynamics see Erwin Schrödinger, *What Is Life?* (Cambridge, University of Cambridge Press, New York, Macmillan, 1946). An expansion of Blum's article appears in *Time's Arrow and Evolution* (Princeton, Princeton University Press, 1951).

110. Needham, *op. cit.*, pp. 224–230; I have substituted for the analogy suggested by Needham, p. 227, the water-color analogy suggested by Seidenberg, *op. cit.*, p. 160, in his discussion of Needham's viewpoint, roughly pp. 153–163.

instance of life and evolution. Despite divergent paths, their destination would seem the same.

So much is theory—but responsible theory. It justifies the pre-eminence which Adams gave to the second law; but life presents thermodynamic problems of tremendous difficulty. It demands an open system; it also presents mathematical problems in which science has made least progress. Briefly, life is organized complexity.[111] Hence it falls outside two broad categories of scientific problems: those of simplicity and those of disorganized complexity. Nineteenth-century science dealt largely with problems of simplicity containing few, usually two, variables. Toward the end of the century some scientists—Gibbs, Maxwell, and Boltzmann among the pioneers—went to the opposite extreme to inquire into phenomena involving billions of variables. Extensive investigation into problems of stupendous complexity has occurred only during the twentieth century with the emergence of quantum mechanics.[112] Between the extremes typical for mechanics and quantum mechanics there lies an area as yet resistant to similarly large analytical laws. Systems of organized complexity, like those of life, involve many more variables than those of simplicity, many less than those of disorganized complexity. And if organic systems have resisted the comprehensive mathematical treatment typical of the inorganic world, what of history? History is complex, but it is comparable neither to the disorganization of billions of molecular particles nor to the organization of an organic system.[113] Indeed no scientific definition for a system applies to history. Except as the rudest sort of metaphor, Adams' quest was bound to fail.

Whatever the role of the second law in life and evolution, scientific justification is hardly historical justification. After all, the historian is concerned with the path to entropy rather than the destination of entropy itself. Not the truth of Adams' statement on the trend toward entropy in evolution (and by implica-

111. Warren Weaver, "Science and Complexity," *American Scientist, 36* (1948), 536–544.

112. The second law, for example, furnishes problems of both simplicity and disorganized complexity.

113. Roy F. Nichols, "The Dynamic Interpretation of History," *New England Quarterly, 8* (1935), 163–178, closes his analysis of Adams' historical speculation with the suggestion that Adams might have found biology a more profitable field for historical speculation.

tion in history) is at issue, but its relevance. To make his statement relevant for history Adams had of necessity to adopt an
absurd position, actually the central fallacy of the *Letter:* the
steady decline in the amount of energy available for the future
use of both biological evolution and history automatically implied
a steady decline in the end products created by the depletion of
the energy reservoir. As though each barrel drawn from an ebb-
ing oil well were necessarily inferior as fuel to those which had
preceded it! Carried to its ultimate extreme, such nonsense demanded that everything was best before anything had happened.

Up to this point the reasoning of the *Letter* was, if faulty,
at least plausible; and, in fairness, was more plausible when Adams
wrote than it now seems. To prove the wretched biological status
of man, however, Adams arbitrarily looked for anatomical advantages in the earliest paleontological specimens and for anatomical deficiencies in the most recent.[114] A before-and-after comparison then sufficed to show degeneration, while Dollo's axioms
in conjunction with Rosa's concept of progressive inadaptability
indicated the eventual consequences of such deterioration. Why refute Adams in detail where he is so obviously absurd? For example,
the statement that because the young anthropoid looks more like
a human being than his parent, the "anthropoid might be a degraded man, but man could not be a developed anthropoid."
Nonsense! Adams must have known full well that the younger
the embryo the more it resembles the embryos of other animals.
Differentiation occurs with development; this observation lay at
the root of the exaggerated aphorism that ontogeny follows phylogeny, so pervasive toward the end of the nineteenth century
that the barest smattering of evolutionary thought would have
contained it.[115] Then he turned to Edward Cope's assertion that
man had descended from the Eocene lemur without passing
through any known species of anthropoids. Why, on such a controversial problem, Adams should have preferred Cope's geneal-

114. For a general bibliography on Adams' use of physical anthropology see
Bibliography, Sec. T.

115. In fact, Adams himself refuted his nonsense on the young anthropoid's
resembling man more than its parent in his review of Lyell's *Principles,* in *NAR,*
107 (1868), 496 f. Originally formulated by Geoffrey St. Hilaire, the concept that
ontogeny follows phylogeny was extended and promoted by Ernst Haeckel as his
"fundamental biogenetic law" during the latter half of the nineteenth century. A
French translation of Haeckel's *The Riddle of the Universe* mentioning the biogenetic law is in the Henry Adams library at the Massachusetts Historical Society
[*Les Énigmes de l'univers* (Paris, Schleicher, 1905)].

ogy for man rather than that of other authorities is somewhat mysterious, except that it permitted immoderate commentary. Adams maintained that such an ancestry "in a type far lower than that of the despised apes" was particularly damaging to any assertion of human superiority. More nonsense—and, this time, contradictory within Adams' own particular framework of absurdity. If degradation was directly proportional to the size of the cerebrum, then the feebler the brain in man's evolutionary past the better for man. Pity only that our descent should come from such a relatively intelligent animal as the lemur! Or reversing the logic, even if man had descended from the lemur rather than the anthropoid, would such descent signify degradation or rather an elevation the more prodigious for its humbler origin? [116]

"Hoping for the best," [117] Adams turned to the physical anthropologist and found, of course, the worst. The human being had fewer and smaller teeth than his animal ancestors; his sense of smell had all but vanished; his hair had thinned; his females were becoming unable to suckle their young. Even the evidence of man's superior mentality seemed inconclusive, largely because Adams either slighted or misrepresented whatever was conclusive. Like all other species, *Homo sapiens* is specialized and has no need for the fangs, the sense of smell, or the hair of some other animals. As Depéret wrote, "an organ is perfect when it fulfils its object perfectly." So obvious an observation scarcely warrants notice, except that Adams penciled it.[118] As for the inability of women to suckle their children, the fact that many choose not to nurse their offspring is no proof that they cannot. In many parts of the world, where a choice is less available, population has swollen so distressingly as to make doubtful this biological inability of women. And the brain: according to Adams the human brain dif-

116. The precise descent of man is still subject to considerable disagreement; see, for example, Earnest R. Hooton, *Up from the Ape* (rev. ed., New York, Macmillan, 1946), pp. 390–393.

117. *Degradation: Letter*, p. 174.

118. Depéret, *op. cit.*, p. 95 [*p. 98]. On the question of human teeth, it is amusing that Adams particularly noted in *Dana, *op. cit.*, p. 402, the following caution on the use of paleontological data in dating rock formations: "Moreover, where direct paleontological observation had ascertained in particular cases the steps of progress in the development of organs, as, for example, those of the teeth in Mammals, the facts become a basis for further use in the same direction. But decisions . . . have to be made with great reserve; since there were often . . . retrograde steps [in organs] . . . Man stands at the head of Mammals, and yet, as regards his teeth, he is below the Monkeys, and related to the earliest Tertiary Mammals." Adams marked the last sentence.

fered from those of the anthropoids in both weight and the number of ganglion cells. Weight? Well, lunatics often had heavier brains than so-called normal men. Typical of Adams' tendency to treat a complex interrelationship as though determined by a single factor, his statement that both lunatic and normal brains might weigh the same proved no more about their functioning than would the similar weights of two engines one of which was out of order. Number of ganglion cells? No refutation appeared; Adams quietly skirted whatever embarrassed his case. It may just possibly happen, as Adams paraphrased Branca, that "the progressive enlargement of the human brain can [not] go on indefinitely without enfeebling the body till it dies out"; [119] although if this extreme should prove true, its realization would falsify his assertion, a few paragraphs later, that society showed progressive enfeeblement because of the socialistic coddling of morons. But can the human head actually become so large that, for example, the embryo dies in the womb, unable—even with modern operative techniques—to force its way into the world? Here Dollo's concept of evolutionary limitation might work against Adams' argument. The extraordinarily big-headed human being may never appear. The brain that might have been may be selected out and future generations remain as modest in their intellectual capacity as we.

There are, to be sure, physical anthropologists and especially eugenists who have emphasized the frailties of the human species. Possibly *Homo sapiens* may ultimately owe his demise to some Achilles' heel smugly ignored by most of us. But even those eugenists who would sterilize criminals and feeble-minded, while bribing the intellectual class to reproduce, would do so in order to retain or promote a stock of which they basically approved. No eugenist would seriously depict man as the degraded animal of Adams' portrait.

Now of course the thought must long ago have occurred that Adams was not himself wholly serious. He purposely contrived a blighted humanity to fit the blighted society in which he lived. Or, if it momentarily served his argument better, he could deny that man showed maximum degeneration among the animals and agree with the orthodox position of Brunhes that evolution seemed to progress in a direction opposite to that posited by the second law.

119. *Degradation: Letter,* p. 176. See also below, p. 212, for evidence in Adams' possession that the brain of the Neanderthal man was somewhat larger than that of modern man.

In other words, Adams knew his follies for what they were. His *Letter*, then, was irony. Is it not feeble as irony? How much greater the ironic possibilities had Adams shown man as he is: a mysterious union of greatness and triviality within the vast impersonality of the universe. Whatever his weaknesses, man is not mere rubbish. To praise the tonality of the *Letter* regardless of its content would appear to require some justification, in aesthetics if not in science, for Adams' conception of man. Even the everyday aesthetics of housekeeping demands the disposal of trash. Adams' desire for consistency and his love of paradox drove him to deprecate what he most valued, to lose in sterile exaggeration a poignancy he might have gained.

The same exaggeration negated the value of much of his insight into the deficiencies of his society. This was especially tragic, for here he was very serious. The toothless, hairless, brainless product of evolution already dismayed social statisticians. As though he had never cited Branca's fear that the human brain would grow steadily larger, Adams mentioned Dr. Forbes Winslow's dire prediction on the increase of insanity in the world: "in three hundred years one half the population should be insane or idiotic." He quoted Durkheim on the increase of suicides and the growth of "philosophical schools founded on the supposed failure of society." He consulted statistics from the County Council of London demonstrating the deterioration of man in the swollen metropolises of western Europe. The individual was dying or dead, not only in a physical sense, but spiritually and intellectually as well. Society had reached the phase of crowd. " 'That which formed a people,' " Adams translated from Gustave Le Bon's *Physiologie des foules*,

> ends by becoming an agglomeration of individuals without cohesion, still held together for a time by its traditions and institutions. This is the phase when men, divided by their interests and aspirations, but no longer knowing how to govern themselves, ask to be directed in their smallest acts; and when the State exercises its absorbing influence. With the definitive loss of the old ideal, the race ends by entirely losing its soul; it becomes nothing more than a dust of isolated individuals, and returns to what it was at the start,—a crowd.[120]

120. *Degradation: Letter*, pp. 254, 188, 252, respectively.

Recalling perhaps the German tribes which had once served him as the source of energy for the evolution of democratic institutions, Adams added that the "end of social evolution" was "not at all the same 'crowd' that [had] made its beginning." The twentieth-century crowd was "wholly incapable of doing useful work." The difference between tribe and crowd suggested the difference between the mass of separated particles at the origin of the solar system and that at its end. In the beginning, according to the Laplacian hypothesis which Adams used,[121] the separate particles within a diffuse nebula had consisted of free energy, capable of contracting into the sun and all its planets, with some infinitesimal portion of its total energy expended in accomplishing the gigantic work of geology, organic evolution, and finally history, until it reached an end state resembling the initial nebula in the mass of separated particles. But the end was thermodynamic heat-death. Where all had once been free energy, all eventually would be bound, incapable of further work, and forever fated to move as isolated particles in the ocean of ultimate entropy. The ocean of democracy which Adams had tentatively but feelingly celebrated in his *History* became the ocean of socialism, of the mob, the crowd. Had Adams developed this theme to investigate the effects of industrialism and urbanization, he might so have redeemed his epithets against humanity as to make his essay, however conservative, among the most profoundly prophetic in the whole of American literature. He did not. If prophetic, the *Letter* is not profound. It is disappointing to find the climax of the *Letter* dissipated in the sensationalism of the daily press.

The evidence for Adams' shallow use of headlines may already suffice; but at the risk of overemphasizing a particularly unattractive aspect of the *Letter*, it is nevertheless instructive to catch Adams in the very act, as it were, of gathering his data from newspapers. Few of these clippings are dated. Those which are show that at least as early as August 1, 1906, or four years before the printing of the private edition of the *Letter*, Adams had begun his collection of clippings illustrative of his theory. The last dated item, February 19, 1912, indicates that he made occasional addi-

---

121. Adams believed in the Laplacian theory of the nebular creation of the universe, although when he wrote the Chamberlin-Moulton theory was definitely favored over the Laplacian; at the present time yet a third hypothesis is favored over both of these (see Gamow, *Biography of the Earth*, chap. ii, for a convenient summary). Compare Adams' statement with Needham, *op. cit.*, p. 225.

tions up to within about two months of his stroke on April 24. He tucked this lamentable accumulation (or part of it) into the same copy of the private printing in which he pasted addenda to the text.[122] A clipping from Paris, for example, stated that the yearly birth rate in France had dropped from 827,297 in 1900 to less than 800,000 in 1907–08; another showed comparable declines in England and Wales. Those unfortunate enough to be born faced the ravages of disease. Thus a letter to the editor of the *New York Herald* commented on the increase of tooth decay among children. Under the headline LITTLE HEIRESSES TO PULLMAN MILLIONS ILL Adams red-penciled the fact that an epidemic of infantile paralysis was "raging in many parts of America." Every day, according to an editorial from an unnoted newspaper, we see "hopeless, emaciated, obese, unnerved, paralyzed, demented, prematurely aged and half-dead specimens of humanity." Increase of mental illness was even more alarming for man than his physical shortcomings. A certain Dr. Lester L. Roos, addressing the Pharmaceutical Society of Registered Drug Clerks in New York, asserted that morphine caused insanity and estimated that half of all Americans might "use or have used injurious narcotics." WORLD GOING MAD the *New York Times* headed an item from London in which the same Dr. Forbes Winslow whom Adams cited in the *Letter* warned that the insane would soon outnumber the sane. Indeed, all would be insane within 250 years according to Dr. J. H. Kellogg, director of a sanitarium in Battle Creek, Michigan. Adams sent a request to Dr. Kellogg for further information, receiving in return a pamphlet which is still beside the clipping. The fate that doctors feared physical anthropologists confirmed. The Reverend E. H. Mullins, digging in his Derbyshire parish, discovered what he presumed to be a prehistoric skull indicating that both "contracted palate and misplaced teeth are modern conditions," while a skull reconstructed by Herman Klaatsch (another authority cited in the *Letter*) showed "However unexpected [that] . . . the Neanderthal race . . . had a brain which was larger than that of an European to-day." [123]

122. Now in the Massachusetts Historical Society. Only a minority of the clippings are dated, usually by Adams.
123. Physical anthropologists generally concur in this judgment today; but see, for example, the caution by A. Kroeber, *Anthropology* (New York, Harcourt, Brace, 1948), p. 123; difference in physiological structure may be more important than Kroeber's reason. His general discussion on brain weight and size (pp. 73–76) is also illuminating in respect to Adams' nonsense. The large head size is particu-

Like so many of his cultivated contemporaries at the close of the nineteenth century, Adams confronted social change with the standards of an earlier age. He shared in a pessimism widespread among intellectuals, partly genuine and by the nineties partly the self-conscious pose implicit in the phrase *fin de siècle*. Whether sincere or artificial—and in Adams' case it was something of both —this pessimism appeared more as a tonality of thought than as specific condemnation. The lack of specificity stemmed from the uselessness of outmoded standards to appraise an elusive but momentous transformation in society. To many it seemed as though the old institutions had merely altered their size without particularly changing character. Companies had become corporations; cities, metropolises; nations, world powers. To be sure, the problems of labor organizations and socialism were very evident; but to men like Adams such problems seemed the rumblings of some dim cataclysm of the future, essentially as remote and ill-defined as the cosmic catastrophes in the *Letter*. Adams simply failed to realize how completely a change in quantity had altered the quality of society, a failure the more ironical since his concept of change of social phase through a mere quantitative change in the utilization of energy is for historians today the most challenging aspect of his speculation.

Thus he cited from Le Bon's *La Psychologie politique* passages which might, in essence, have come from the diaries of John and John Quincy Adams.[124] " 'The surest symptom of the decadence threatening us is the general enfeeblement of characters.' " Character: Adams' ideal of reform stemmed from this quality. " 'Numerous to-day are the men whose energy weakens, especially among the choicest . . .' " Especially among the choicest! This was the most shocking aspect of a general moral collapse during the late nineteenth century; the natural leaders of society had forgotten eighteenth-century ideals of stewardship and openly joined hands with such as Grant, Blaine, and Conkling. " 'It was always by this enfeeblement of character, and not by that of intelligence that the great peoples disappeared from history.' " The natural leaders merely displayed the lack of character in the people whom they led and simultaneously reflected. " 'It would even seem as though to-day the dead alone gave us energy.' "

larly apparent in Cro-Magnon man, a prehistoric type of such interest to Adams that he helped to finance Henri Hubert in unsuccessful excavations for new specimens; Ford, *2*, 574, n. 1.

124. *Degradation: Letter*, p. 253.

Holding such ideas, however noble their intent, Adams inevitably missed the nature of the transition through which his society had passed. He could not even think in terms of transition but only of degradation. Nor could he relate his degradationist evidence to any consistent view of society. In effect, he linked cosmic to historical catastrophe not by investigating history but by the a priori assumption that a harmony existed in all spheres of the universe. No medieval scholastic more relentlessly fitted authorities to a harmonious universe. The *Letter* is to the *Education* what the chapter on St. Thomas Aquinas is to *Chartres*.[125] Adams was something of a latter-day St. Thomas, turning upside down the spiritual universe of God and man. Material power and something less than man marked the twentieth-century universe, where all had degraded in ironic harmony with the universal application of the second law.

William James can make the obvious reply, already mentioned, for the historians to whom Adams addressed the *Letter*. James stated his conviction with a witty decisiveness which warrants extensive quotation, the more so as Adams frankly avowed the telling effect of the criticism.[126]

> To tell the truth, it doesn't impress me at all, save by its wit and erudition; and I ask you whether an old man soon about to meet his Maker can hope to save himself from the consequences of his life by pointing to the wit and learning he has shown in treating a tragic subject. No, sir, you can't do it, can't impress God in that way.

James went on to discuss the question of the universality of the second law of thermodynamics.

> So far as our scientific conceptions go, it may be admitted that your Creator (and mine) started the universe with a certain amount of "energy" latent in it, and decreed that everything that should happen thereafter should be a result of parts of that energy falling to lower levels; raising other parts higher, to be sure, in so doing, but never in equivalent amount, owing to the constant radiation of unrecoverable warmth incidental to the process. It is customary for gentlemen to pretend to believe one another, and until some one hits upon a

125. See below, pp. 253 f. and 255.

126. Henry James, ed., *Letters of William James* (Boston, Atlantic Monthly Press, 1920), *2*, 344 ff.

newer revolutionary concept (which may be tomorrow) all physicists must play the game by holding religiously to the above doctrine. It involves of course the ultimate cessation of all perceptible happening, and the end of human history. With this general conception as *surrounding* everything you say in your "letter," no one can find any fault—in the present stage of scientific conventions and fashions . . .

Then James turned to the principal argument of the historian.

. . . the *amount* of cosmic energy it costs to buy a certain distribution of fact which humanly we regard as precious, seems to me to be an altogether secondary matter as regards the question of history and progress. Certain arrangements of matter *on the same energy-level* are, from the point of view of man's appreciation, superior, while others are inferior. Physically a dinosaur's brain may show as much intensity of energy-exchange as a man's but it can do infinitely fewer things, because as a force of detent it can only unlock the dinosaur's muscles, while the man's brain, by unlocking far feebler muscles, indirectly can by their means issue proclamations, write books, describe Chartres Cathedral, etc., and guide the energies of the shrinking sun into channels which never would have been entered otherwise—in short, *make* history. Therefore the man's brain and muscles are, from the point of view of the historian, the more important place of energy-exchange, small as this may be when measured in absolute physical units.

The "second law" is wholly irrelevant to "history"—save that it sets a terminus—for history is the course of things before that terminus, and all that the second law says is that, whatever the history, it must invest itself between that initial maximum and that terminal minimum of difference in energy level.

Following some further discussion on the possibility that history might rise while energy fell, James concluded his critique with the suggestion that even a millennium was not impossible to history immediately preceding the extinction of the universe. Energies might be so "skillfully *canalisés* that a maximum of happy and virtuous consciousness would be the only result . . . You don't believe this and I don't say I do. But I can find nothing in 'Energetik' to conflict with its possibility. You seem to me not to discriminate, but to treat quantity and distribution of energy as if they formed one question." [127]

There was but one answer which Adams could have made to James. It appeared in the *Letter;* not because of Adams' specific reasoning thus far, rather because this reasoning came to so little. The answer can wait, for it takes us away from the facts of the *Letter* toward the baffling personality of its author. Yet the facts themselves compel a return to the original question: where the emotional image depended so completely on the intellect, did lack of logic not vitiate the full power of the image? By now the answer is clear: it depends on the reader—more specifically on how he chooses to read. Skimmed, both the *Letter* and the *Rule* may seem a little farfetched to be wholly credible; yet they are impressive, by virtue both of Adams' sweep of knowledge and of the ideas with which his roving intellect collided. The audacious juxtapositions startle; the ambiguities in his meaning help to heighten his mood of catastrophic uncertainty. By forgoing detailed analysis of what he says, impressionistic criticism jauntily credits him with all sorts of intuition. He foresaw the evils in a world-wide trend toward socialism. He sensed the growing anti-intellectualism in the thought of his day. He felt the impact of science on our world. He comprehended the ignorance which must result from specialization in all branches of knowledge. He perceived human impotence in the face of powers too vast for its coping.

It may seem pedantic to probe beneath the surface of what he sensed to inquire as to what he said. Rationalism is in some ways an unproductive approach to Adams; emotions tell more, despite

---

127. Interestingly enough, Henry A. Bumstead suggested substantially the same sort of millennium in part of a letter dated June 16, 1910 (now in the estate of Henry Adams), which acknowledged receipt of the *Letter:* "When we come to the sociological analogy, I am not so sure—or rather I don't feel compelled to pessimism, short of the final catastrophy (*sic*). In the case of a gas whose temperature is equalized we call it degradation on account of our point of view. We are thinking of exploiting that gas to 'do useful mechanical work.' But perhaps the individual molecules might have a different point of view if they were possessed of intelligence and will. They are still individually active, going to and fro about their business. 'Progress' has stopped but only because it has reached its goal. Whether or not the molecules could be happy depends upon the answer to the old question of the debating societies: Whether the pleasures of pursuit or of possession are the greater." Bumstead went on to discuss the unequal velocities of the individual particles according to the Maxwell-Boltzmann curve (see above, p. 166) and some paragraphs later remarked, "This would provide for physicists and historians."

the deceptive (even obsessive) gloss of learning which coats the speculative essays. Only by temporarily dismissing the oracle will the man appear—temporarily, because the oracle must be recalled. The tension which Adams sought among the scientific fact, the emotional image, and the personal reference demands that balanced criticism should seek the same. Inevitably Adams' largest failure was that of reconciling a nexus of scientific fact to the larger purposes of imagery and autobiography. Considering the colossal boldness of his scheme, perhaps rationalistic criticism does seem ungrateful in pointing out the failure. But heroic failure depends on artistry and integrity. On both scores the rationalist has legitimate complaints of Adams.

Admit his amateur status in scientific matters, as he himself frankly admitted it, and still the haphazard quality of his research astonishes. His knowledge seems excessively bookish, remote from the realities of scientific investigation, and this despite a personal acquaintance with scientists rather larger than most literary men could boast. It was indicative of the bookish vacuum in which he worked that he should have called on Jameson to find a physicist to criticize a draft of the *Rule*. Not only bookish and haphazard, his research was also painfully biased. He lifted scraps from his authorities which often misrepresented their full positions; he pasted scraps together in such a way that a string of authorities might prove what no one of them meant to prove. He combined the findings of one decade with those of another. He placed the most sensational writings of men like Gustave Le Bon and Camille Flammarion, or the irresponsibilities of the headline writer, beside such names as those of Gibbs and Lord Kelvin. But why go on? Surely nothing would delight Adams more than the knowledge that some heavy-handed logician had come across the *Letter*.

What he missed in his research brands him a thoroughly nineteenth-century man. Even after allowance has been made for his status as an amateur in scientific and philosophical thought, he can hardly be said to have grasped the most progressive thinking of his day. He failed to interest himself in certain vital trends like pragmatism, atomic research in physics, organicism in biology and its tremendous influence in all other knowledge, the growing awareness of industrial and urban problems, the sense of relativism slowly seeping through fields as varied as history and the sciences, cultural anthropology and philosophy. The pessimism and delight in paradox which grew in Adams with age warped the

Comtian optimism of youth. His desire for a sweeping theory of
history remained; but the intensification, the dramatization, of
his desire resulted in his abandoning social analysis for that of
science, thereby disregarding the Comtian pyramid of knowledge,
where each step to its pinnacle in sociology involved the use of
progressively new techniques to analyze data steadily increasing
in complexity. By exaggerating the superlative inclusiveness and
determinateness of scientific knowledge above all other, Adams replaced the relativism of Comte with an absolutism which embraced
even the smallest increment of evidence in both the *Rule* and the
Letter. " 'These are facts!' " he echoed an authority who had made
the improbable prediction of insanity for one half the population
of England and Wales by 2209; " 'they cannot in any way be
challenged.' " [128] But unlike the facts of the *History*, those of the
essays reinforced, without complicating, their overarching generalization. In contrast to the complexity of social data which, in
truth, accounted for the elevated position of sociology in the
Comtian hierarchy of knowledge, Adams sought to bring history
within what to the Comtian at least were the relative simplicities
of science.

So the desire for an inclusive, determinate, absolutist, and
simple scheme for history drove Adams from the Comtian stand
of the *History* to the absurdities of his later historical speculation.
A second glance at the list of easy generalizations derived from a
wholly impressionistic approach to Adams' essays reveals how he
cheated himself of his richest conclusions. If this is repetition, it
also summarizes the position of the rationalist in his attack on
Adams. Thus Adams did sense the trend toward socialism, although
in many respects as remotely as the least creative armchair conservative. True, he had no selfish reasons for railing against the
mob, and of course not all conservatives would have joined in his
sensitive concern for leadership, morals, learning, and aesthetics
under the socialist dispensation. On the other hand, few would
have accumulated a "fact" here, another there, on epidemics,
feeble-mindedness, suicides, and similar woes, to see in such miscellaneous evidence a relation of thermodynamics to socialism. His
research in anthropology likewise found him preoccupied with the
precise measurements. Selecting items on head size, brain weight,
and anatomical deficiencies from physical anthropology, he completely missed the field of cultural anthropology. And this despite

128. *Degradation: Letter*, p. 254.

his early interest in institutions, his work on Gallatin's investigations of Indian societies, and his later study of Tahiti. He sensed the growing interest during the last decades of the nineteenth century in the importance of anti-intellectual elements in human behavior. Again he made no more use of these data than to sigh over the phase of crowd and perhaps to attribute want of reason to smaller brain weight, despite his alarm elsewhere in the *Letter* lest the head become too large. He sensed the impact of the physical sciences on modern society; but his haphazard investigations invariably terminated in straight-line developments for astronomy, geology, and physics, a linearism exaggerated by his metaphors— the path of the comet, the vortex of the nebulae, magnetic lines of force, and the succession of phases. Moreover, he used scientific data with the absolutist faith that science proved things once for all, and wherever he found disagreement or uncertainty there he also discovered either utter chaos or an absolute barrier to further progress. He sensed the increased specialization among all branches of knowledge. Nevertheless, he was primarily concerned because this departmentalization made it difficult to ascertain the precise status of the drift within each field and to fit the drift in each to the graph for all. Finally, he sensed the impersonal powers increasingly dominating man; but most of the straight lines running to his equivocal limit of thought have less to do with twentieth-century problems than his most ardent admirers like to believe.

This is the position at which rationalistic criticism finally arrives: Whatever the refutation, and however impossible that Adams' quest should have succeeded, the blunt truth remains that he was far less persuasive than he could have been had he been more logical. Thought-provoking, his historical speculation was not genuinely thoughtful. Insofar as it wanted profundity, of course it also lacked imaginative intensity. Little wonder that James despaired of his friend's salvation.

NOUGH perhaps of the essays; yet one further aspect of
Adams' historical speculation demands attention, precisely
because it does lead away from the facts of the essays toward
the baffling personality of its author. It also discloses better than
all his other evidence the difficulties of the amateur in confronting
the complexities of modern science. Finally, it places the essays at
a particular moment in scientific development. This is Adams' use
of the physical ether. In addition to his varied evidence for the
ways in which the depletion of physical energy would define the
limits of thought, Adams also held that man might reach his
mental terminus by thinking in abstractions increasingly removed
from empirical experiment. In his search for the reality of things
man would abandon reality by piling abstraction upon abstraction
until further abstraction was unimaginable. For Adams the ether
represented the final challenge to human intelligence; the ethereal
phase, that stage in history when intelligence confessed its ultimate
failure.

This new meaning for the limit of thought somewhat com-
plicates the already complicated implications of the catastrophe
following in the wake of cosmic, solar, terrestrial, biological, or
social degradation of energy. Whereas physical energy was close
to maximum entropy, while average mortals mimicked the dis-
parate molecules—mere items in an unthinking mob—the scientific
intelligentsia simultaneously reached an impasse before complexities in nature impossible to penetrate. Physical, popular, and
intellectual energy, each in its peculiar manner, simultaneously
reached the goal of maximum entropy. Perhaps the simultaneity
was contrived; certainly the relationship of the elements lacks
specificity. But oracles are entitled to ambiguities where their
import is clear.

The modern history of the concept of ether [1] opens with
Newton's dissatisfaction that his theory of gravitation implied

1. For general bibliography on the physical ether see Bibliography, Sec. W.

action at a distance, for the notion that one body could exert a force on another across perfectly empty space seemed at variance with the larger idea of a mechanical universe of pushes and pulls. To avoid this discrepancy Newton filled space with a hypothetical medium which he christened the ether, a name given by some of the ancient Greek philosophers as a possible addition to the usual four elements. This material continuum thus conducted gravitational pushes and pulls throughout the universe, transmitting as well Newton's corpuscles of light. Hence the continuity of ether joined the discontinuity of matter. But only with the supersession of the Newtonian corpuscular theory [2] of light by the classical wave theory during the first half of the nineteenth century did the ether concept become thoroughly established in theoretical physics. Light moving as particles through empty space was more easily visualized in mechanical terms than light moving as waves, for without some medium in which to move waves were completely inconceivable. Whether the luminiferous ether, as it came to be called, was identical with the gravitational ether remained in doubt; some physicists hypothesized several ethers. In any event, no sooner had physicists firmly established the idea of a luminiferous ether than they began to attribute to it a series of properties which, as the century went on, became increasingly difficult to visualize in mechanical terms.

In the first decades of the century Augustin Fresnel demonstrated that light waves were transverse to the line of their propagation, and since neither fluids nor gases could conduct transverse waves, the space-filling ether must have the properties of some sort of "elastic solid." [3] But Fresnel's elastic solid was not like any known in everyday experience. Since it conducted light without any loss in intensity (despite dilution by spreading), the ether must be absolutely transparent. Moreover, since light traveled at a constant speed unaffected by friction, the ether must be absolutely devoid of viscosity. Finally, the ether must be a stationary medium, permitting the waves of light to pass yet incapable of any locomotion in itself; otherwise the physicist was bound to posit

2. As is generally known, Newton himself did not deny the possibility that light might be a wave phenomenon, although he definitely favored the corpuscular theory which his followers accepted without reservation. In the twentieth century experiments have shown that light acts both like waves and like corpuscles; or, more precisely, light defies the mechanical explanation of either alternative.

3. Thomas Young was also important in establishing the wave theory; but Fresnel gave the theory its mathematical expression.

for it some source of internal energy. During the first half of the century, then, scientists generally conceived of the ether (or ethers) as a completely passive, imponderable, nonviscous, transparent, continuous, elastic solid, propagating wave (and perhaps gravitational) phenomena.

In 1845 Sir George Stokes propounded one of the most nearly complete of a number of these elastic solid or "perfect jelly" theories of ether; but there were a number of difficulties with Stokes' theory, the most important of which was the requirement for a slight but disturbing amount of viscosity in the ethereal medium. Therefore, as the century advanced, the idea of an elastic solid tended to give way to that of a perfect fluid in turbulent motion. The concept of a vortex movement of the ether stemmed in great part from investigations by Lord Kelvin in the eighties.[4] According to Kelvin each prime atom of ether was a perfect fluid spinning like a top. A fluid undergoing rapid rotational motion is stiffened, just as a spinning top is highly resistant to any pressure seeking to overturn it or as the vortex movement of a smoke ring stiffens the ring so that on collision with another ring it retains its identity. Imagine, then, a continuous fluid every part of which was comprised of tiny vortex movements. The absolute limpidity of the medium would insure the transmission of light with undiminished intensity, while the stiffness of the medium permitted the conveyance of transverse light waves. Like the spinning top, each prime atom of ether would bow before an outside force, only to right itself a moment later without changing position. Such an ether was as stationary as any posited by elastic solid theories. In fact, physicists described the ether as in "stationary motion," while popularizers referred to "motion gone to sleep" but continuing forever because of the frictionless character of the medium. Further imagine that each of these frictionless vortexes rotated at precisely the speed of light, and Kelvin's concept has explained a baffling constant. Before the turn of the century Kelvin's hypothesis had been proved erroneous; but the idea of some sort of spinning movement in a perfect fluid lingered on as a favored theory. Mathematical physicists like Joseph Larmor had devised elaborate constructions for what was frequently called the "gyrostatic" ether.

Empirical experimentation furthered, and indeed suggested,

4. *Karl Pearson, *The Grammar of Science* (2d ed., London, Black, 1900), pp. 258–276, is particularly illuminating in his contrast of the Stokes "jelly" theory of the ether with Lord Kelvin's "vortex" theory.

the conception of the ether held by most physicists around 1900. Quite as important as work on the nature of elasticity and vortex motions was the synthesis of wave phenomena which began with the work of Michael Faraday on the induction of electric currents by means of a magnet, researches basic for the invention of the dynamo. Faraday visualized the electromagnetic field mechanically by conceiving the field in terms of those "lines of force" which so powerfully attracted Adams' imagination. Clerk Maxwell gave Faraday's empirical work its mathematical formulation, and in an epoch-making paper completed in 1864 he computed the velocity of electromagnetic waves as identical with those of light. The late eighties saw Heinrich Hertz confirm the results of Maxwell's paper by a series of experiments showing that electromagnetic waves shared many properties of light other than its velocity. This trio of scientists—Faraday, Maxwell, and Hertz—were among those prominently mentioned by Adams as heralds of the ethereal phase in history, before Madame Curie in 1898 tossed "the metaphysical bomb she called radium." [5] It appeared certain that a single ether would unify electricity and magnetism with light. Indeed, the phenomenon of electrolysis promised an even larger role for ether. Electrolysis suggested the intimate relation between electricity and matter long before J. J. Thomson opened a new era in physics by his discovery in 1897 of the electron. If matter was related to electricity, and electricity was in turn related to light, then was matter simply some condensed form of ether? [6] Was matter the crystallization of a mother liquid? Was it an apparent hardness related in some way to a rotational motion of the ether? The challenge of such a synthesis redoubled efforts to achieve decisive results—but in vain.

What made ether concepts particularly confounding to the layman was the absence of any experimental evidence for the presence of the ether itself, while of course the want of such evidence made physicists a little uncomfortable too. Attempts had been made to come to grips with the ether, although by the nature of the problem it was as difficult for the physicist to grapple with the ether continuum as it would be for a deep-sea fish to characterize the medium in which it swam. Only two experimental means of detecting the physical presence of ether seemed open. The less

5. *Degradation: Letter,* pp. 272, 273, 277, 279, 291. *Education,* pp. 397, 426, 452.
6. Even in the earliest theories the ether was also related to matter through its property of inertia; see especially Sir Oliver Lodge, *Ether and Reality* (London, Hodder & Stoughton, 1925), chap. iii.

likely, which was of little significance by the end of the century, depended upon the hypothesis of private ethers for each of the heavenly bodies, with every ether envelope nudging its neighbor. If each body towed its own ether as the earth towed its atmosphere, then certain aberrations should occur in the light from a distant star due to its tortuous path through a series of ether envelopes. The results of all experiments conducted on this basis were negative. The second and more likely possibility depended on a single universal ether. In moving through this continuum did the earth create an ether drag? If so, was this drag measurable? The German-born American physicist A. A. Michelson conceived an ingenious and important experiment intended to measure the ether drag. His purpose was wider than that of ascertaining the existence of an ether; he especially hoped to determine the absolute motion of the earth by measuring its movement through a stationary medium. Such an absolute would provide a fixed standard to which investigators on the earth might relate all other movements. With E. W. Morley, Michelson designed an apparatus to split a beam of light into two rays so that they traveled at right angles to one another, the one projected in the plane of the earth's rotation and hence in the direction of the presumed ether flow, the other projected across this current. Both traveled equal distances to mirrors, which reflected the rays back to their point of origin. The difference in interval between the return of the two beams of light would measure the presumed ether drag. First conducted in a definitive manner in 1887, and frequently repeated during the first three decades of the twentieth century by other experimenters, at various locations, and on different apparatus, these notable experiments also produced a negative result. There seemed to be no ether; or if an ether existed, it seemed beyond detection. In the early nineties both George Fitzgerald and Hendrik Lorentz explained that the negative result was inevitable. In accordance with the electrical composition of every possible measuring device (whether material, optical, or electrical), all would shrink by precisely the amount of the motion measured.[7]

7. The original and subsequent experiments to determine the ether drag are conveniently summarized in the *Encyclopaedia Britannica* (14th ed., 1929), *15*, 417 f. James Jeans, *The Mysterious Universe* (rev. ed., Cambridge, University of Cambridge Press; New York, Macmillan, 1937), pp. 113 ff., doubts whether the Fitzgerald-Lorentz contraction actually takes place; see the remainder of the chapter for a simplified account of developments since 1905 making the ether theory no longer particularly useful as an explanation.

It was the results of the Michelson-Morley experiment and the papers by Fitzgerald and Lorentz which led Einstein to his generalization of relativity in 1905. But the Michelson-Morley experiment and its aftermath go beyond the point needed in order to appreciate Adams' perplexity respecting the ether.

As a layman Adams knew only that a completely hypothetical medium seemed encumbered by unimaginable complications. Yet the serious physicist remained undismayed. In criticizing a draft of the *Rule* Bumstead repeatedly chided Adams for his verdict of irreconcilable confusion in respect to the properties of ether.[8] When Adams stated that scientists "had vehemently resisted" the "inconceivable and self-contradictory" ether, Bumstead protested against the notion of the ether forcing itself upon a reluctant body of physicists who, after all, had themselves called the ether into being. He added that he saw nothing inconceivable or self-contradictory in its properties. "There are always difficulties outstanding; but the most puzzling difficulties of one decade are solved in the next." When Adams dramatized the progressive " 'dematerialization' of matter" as "a daily pursuit in every physical laboratory," Bumstead cautioned "but only by the 'materialization' of the ether." Or again, when Adams repeated his accusation of "self-contradictory" for speculation in the realm of "Hyper-thought," Bumstead asked, "Do mathematicians ever deal with 'self-contradictory concepts,' at least in the same train of reasoning?" If Bumstead's strictures revealed the difference between antiscientific sensationalism and the plodding search for scientific truth, Adams' assertions emphatically reflected the note of disquiet felt by laymen confronted with the ether concept, for Adams' criticisms of contradictoriness alluded not only to the inadequacy of all ether concepts to account for certain phenomena but also to the very complexity of even the most adequate.

Other things being equal, scientists have always adopted a simpler explanation over the more complex, ever since Pythagoras sought to explain the universe in terms of simple numerical relationships. Whether nature actually operates in accordance with simple modes, or whether scientific aversion to overelaborate explanations merely represents a psychological need of human beings, this preference for simplicity has resulted in steady advance for science. By making the sun the center of the universe Coper-

8. Bumstead critique of Adams' draft of the *Rule*, deposited in the Massachusetts Historical Society.

nicus exorcized the unaesthetic clutter of cycles and epicycles which the accretion of fourteen centuries of observation had forced on Ptolemaic astronomy; by replacing the cumbersome necessity for a caloric fluid with the far simpler explanation for heat as a function of work, the law of the conservation of energy made possible the extremely rapid development during the nineteenth century of that branch of physics known as thermodynamics. Not that simplicity is in itself a sine qua non of scientific hypotheses. The elliptical paths of Kepler's solar system were actually more complicated than the circular paths of the Copernican. Kepler merely adopted the simplest hypothesis consistent with the empirical observations which had accumulated up to his time. His dismay at having to abandon the nicety of Copernican circles is among the best known episodes in the history of science. It is therefore safer to speak of the desirability of economy in scientific explanation rather than of the simplicity of natural processes. As any explanation accumulates apparent exceptions it becomes suspect, and especially if the exceptions prove the rule only by elaborate rationalization which departs further and further from experimental confirmation. This is precisely what had happened to the ether by 1900. There was growing concern at the mathematical excrescences which had steadily diminished both the neatness of Fresnel's luminiferous ether and the unity promised in Maxwell's famous identification of electromagnetic waves with light. Nevertheless—to repeat—during the first decade of the twentieth century very few physicists disavowed the ether, whatever their concern over its complicated structure. The concept had acquired a prestige resulting from over a century of intensive investigation, a prestige all the greater because decisive synthesis seemed imminent. Besides, if ether went, what would take its place? True, the medium did seem to imply an extraordinarily complicated universe; but, after all, why should simplicity necessarily exist in the ultimate entity of nature? [9]

9. To be sure, most physicists tended to hope that the ultimate ether was simple; but its manifestations were exceedingly complex. See, for example, Lucien Poincaré, *The New Physics and Its Evolution* (London, Paul, Trench, Trübner, 1907), pp. 316 f., a passage marked by Adams [*La Physique moderne, son évolution* (Paris, Flammarion, 1906), p. 299]. "The present tendency of physicists . . . [is to] consider matter as a very complex object, regarding which we wrongly imagine ourselves to be well informed because we are so much accustomed to it, and its singular properties end by seeming natural to us. But in all probability the ether is, in its objective reality, much more simple, and has a better right to be considered as fundamental." Since no ether theory ever approached the ultimate

Thus it happened that Adams tried to enforce the simplicity of scientific formulas on history just when the problems of the ether made scientists more than usually ready to admit the complexity of natural processes. Necessity more than enthusiasm led scientists to the admission; at least so Adams interpreted their mood, and perhaps with justification, save for his use of the mood for exaggerated pessimism. In his well-marked copy of Henri Poincaré's *La Science et l'hypothèse* Adams particularly noted the repeated assertion of the French geometrician that science had abandoned much of its old faith in the simplicity of nature. Science, said Poincaré, was "led to act as though a simple law, when other things were equal, must be more probable than a complicated law. Half a century ago one frankly confessed it, and proclaimed that nature loves simplicity. She has since given us too often the lie. To-day this tendency is no longer avowed, and only as much of it is preserved as is indispensable so that science shall not become impossible." [10] Thus Adams translated his source, including this excerpt in the *Education* as the keynote for his assertion that scientists were rapidly reaching the cul-de-sac of their own reasoning.

Although he was no mechanist, Adams nevertheless envisioned nothing but chaos for science with the renunciation of its past certainties. What made this verdict of chaos easy for Adams was popular descriptions of the ether in quasi-mechanical terms, which simultaneously admitted that in all probability the ether defied purely mechanical explanation. Looking back, physicists now see that the replacement of the corpuscular by the wave theory of light marked the first major break with Newtonian concepts; but a mechanical ether filled the breach. The identification of electromagnetic waves with light had definitely destroyed the mechanistic dichotomy between inert mass and external energy; but Maxwell continued to depict the electromagnetic field by means of a semimechanical model, while simultaneously warning his read-

medium except through its manifestations, it is for all practical purposes not unfair to refer to the complexity of the ether despite the expectation that the medium itself must somehow be simple in order to enter into so many complicated and diverse relationships.

10. *Education*, p. 454. Henri Poincaré, *Science and Hypothesis* (London, Walter Scott Publishing Co., 1905), p. 206 [*La Science et l'hypothèse* (Paris, Flammarion, 1902), p. 239]. Poincaré's classic, of which chaps. ix and x are among the most important sources for Adams' ideas on the complexity of science, also appears in a collection of his translated writings, *The Foundations of Science* (New York, Science Press, 1913).

ers that he intended his "tubes of force" merely as an explanatory device without suggesting their replica in actuality. So deeply was mechanics rooted in physics that as late as the middle of the second decade of the present century Ernest Rutherford and Niels Bohr completed their model of the atom as a solar nucleus circled by planetary electrons, while not until well into the thirties did physicists wholly abandon this essentially Newtonian concept as inadequate.

While professionals clung to familiar modes of thought, no one could blame the amateur for his bewilderment. In his copy of Lucien Poincaré's *La Physique moderne, son évolution* Adams had penciled the margin opposite Lord Kelvin's often reprinted credo expressing the faith of the physicist about the middle of the nineteenth century in mechanical explanations: "It seems to me that the true sense of the question, Do we or do we not understand a particular subject in physics? is—Can we make a mechanical model of it? I am never satisfied so long as I have been unable to make a mechanical model of the object. If I am able to do so, I understand it. If I cannot make such a model, I do not understand it." [11] Fond of visualizing science in terms of graphs, and of moving magnets about his desk to watch iron filings fall into Faraday's "lines of force," Adams must have found in Kelvin a kindred spirit; but like so many kindred spirits in Adams' life, this one reflected ideas already challenged. Yet no more than Kelvin would Adams abandon without a struggle his attempt to comprehend the ether in mechanical terms. At the close of an explanation of Kelvin's vortex model in Pearson's *The Grammar of Science* Adams assayed his own summary of a mechanical ether, the complexities of the picture indicating something of the complexity of the subject. "Supposing ether to be occupied by corkscrew lines of force rotating with the necessary velocity," he asked himself, "would the conception meet the requirements? For vibrations, the lines might be elastic; for gravitation, etc. it might be continuous rotation, and appear incompressible. The lines need not interfere and would extend as far as the ether extends. There would be no transference of matter, and, as far as I conceive it, no loss of energy. Is this Faraday's idea?" [12] Finally, after a more complex presentation of the ether in Poincaré's *La Physique moderne*—in the course of which Adams had noted the uncer-

11. L. Poincaré, *op. cit.,* pp. 11 f. [*p. 15].
12. *Pearson, *op. cit.,* p. 277, at the conclusion of chap vii.

tainty of physicists as to whether the ether was mechanical in nature or only quasi-mechanical, or completely unmechanical—he gave up in despair and irritation. "Is it possible," he asked, "that this chapter conveys a clear idea to anyone?" [13]

He went on to pencil the concluding chapter entitled "The Future of Physics." His annotations emphasized the fact that physicists had not abandoned the idea "of one day conquering the supreme principle which must command the whole of physics." Not all physicists were optimistic. Some—again a penciled emphasis from Adams—"think such a synthesis to be impossible of realization, and that Nature is infinitely complex." Lucien Poincaré went on to say that the discovery of the electron enabled scientists to penetrate further into natural phenomena than their predecessors had ever done, "but we must not be satisfied with words, and the mystery is not solved when, by a legitimate artifice, the difficulty has simply been thrust further back . . . The indivisible is thus rendered, in a way, smaller and smaller, but we are still unacquainted with what its substance may be." [14] Pencilings in the margin beside this latter passage showed that Adams took a jaundiced view of the future of physics.

13. L. Poincaré, *op. cit.*, p. 321 [*p. 302], at the conclusion of the chapter entitled "The Ether and Matter." This chapter affords an excellent measure of Adams' confusion, induced partly by his impatience at problems remaining unsolved and partly by the uncertain state of physical theory in respect to mechanics. Poincaré opened his chapter with a discussion of luminescence which brought physics to the threshold between ether and matter. But the problem of luminescence was complicated by incandescence; hence "the problem becomes very complex"; p. 296 [p. 281]. Adams noted the complexity with a vertical line in the margin, and subsequent quotations will indicate some of his other markings. Gases seemed by their simple atomic structure to furnish a means by which to study the interaction between ether and matter; but "the simplicity of the medium vanishes through the complication of the circumstances" inherent in experimentation; *ibid.* Toward the end of the chapter Adams noted the mysteries surrounding gravitation; p. 320 [p. 302].

If these areas of ignorance caught Adams' eye, so did confusions as to the mechanical nature of the ether. In connection with an aspect of luminiferous and elastic vibrations Poincaré asserted, "Once again we find that the ether does not behave like matter, which obeys the ordinary laws of mechanics"; p. 298 [p. 283]. But a little later (p. 300 [p. 285]) he mentioned a "kind of friction" between ether and matter, which seemed to indicate that ether possessed a property akin to, but perhaps not quite identical with, that of mechanical friction. Purely mechanical explanations have "therefore failed"; the "electromagnetic theory" comes to a "standstill" before the problem; p. 302 [p. 286]. Larmor's model of the gyrostatic ether was a "most ingenious image, but one which is manifestly insufficient" (p. 316 [p 299]), and Adams went on to pencil the rest of the paragraph. See above, n. 9.

14. L. Poincaré, *op. cit.*, pp. 323, 325 [*pp. 304, 306].

The ether concept led Adams to an impasse; but this impasse was only part of a larger. If the traditional mechanistic foundation of science was crumbling, then what certainties existed in human knowledge? The growing problems of the ether therefore served Adams as a specific example from which to examine far-ranging problems in philosophy. What was the nature of physical reality? How did the scientist know this reality? And on the basis of these two questions, what validated scientific generalizations? Or to use the term popularized by Karl Pearson, were scientific "constructs" like the ether equivalents to reality?

As long as mechanism had gone virtually unchallenged in nineteenth-century physics, except by some philosophers and a few of the most philosophic among physicists, the workaday investigator was tempted to equate mechanistic interpretations of phenomena with reality itself. Although phenomenalistic views had always characterized epistemological theories of science, growing doubts as to the validity of mechanistic explanations for the entire universe led during the last decades of the nineteenth century to a significant strengthening of the phenomenalistic position. Developments within science itself gave particular urgency to the age-old philosophical dispute between realists and nominalists. Did such universals as those embodied in the laws of mechanics indicate some underlying reality or did they merely refer to human experience in the world of phenomena but without necessarily reflecting an ultimate reality beneath? Phenomenalists like Ernst Mach, Henri Poincaré, and Karl Pearson asserted that science had nothing to do with philosophical ultimates. Mechanical laws were not equivalents to reality; they were rather conceptual schemes derived either directly or indirectly from experimental evidence, each generalizing many specific observations, each related to all in such a manner as to create a generally coherent picture of the universe, and each productive of further research.[15] Ultimate reality was forever unknowable. Ernst Mach particularly emphasized the role and limitations of perception in scientific investigation. Approaching the problem of reality as a geometrician, Henri Poincaré demonstrated at one point that Euclid's geometry for a universe of plane surfaces had no more validity as geometry than Riemann's geometry for a universe where only

15. For general bibliography on the nature of physical reality and phenomenalism see Bibliography, Sec. W.

curved surfaces existed. But it was Karl Pearson's enormously successful *Grammar of Science*, first appearing in 1892, which undoubtedly had more impact than any other volume of the period in introducing phenomenalistic ideas to the intelligent lay public. Like Mach, Pearson emphasized the psychological basis for phenomenalism, then went on to relate his epistemological background to the whole gamut of science from physics to biological evolution with a vividness which could not fail to attract a large audience. It was these three—Mach, Poincaré, and Pearson—whom Adams emphasized in an important chapter of the *Education* entitled after Pearson "The Grammar of Science." Not that this trio was in complete accord, but its disagreements were of little import in Adams' thought. Nor did he terminate his investigation into the nature of science with them. For example, in the same chapter he also mentioned that Langley had recommended John Stallo's *The Concepts and Theories of Modern Physics*, while he "could see in such parts of the 'Grammar' as he could understand, little more than an enlargement of Stallo's book already twenty years old." [16] Papers by Crookes, Roentgen, and Curie in the annual reports of the Smithsonian Institution; books by Ostwald, Haeckel, and Helmholtz; an address by Arthur Balfour before the British Association for the Advancement of Science [17]—these, together with a sprinkling of philosophers, also contributed to what Adams

16. *Education*, p. 449. John B. Stallo, *The Concepts and Theories of Modern Physics* (2d ed., New York, Appleton, 1881) [*La Matière et la physique moderne*, preface by C. Friedel (Paris, Alcan, 1889)].

17. For example, the following issues of the *Annual Report of the Smithsonian Institution* for the first decade of the twentieth century contain articles relevant to Adams' quest: 1901, Lord Kelvin on the ether, J. J. Thomson on subatomic phenomena, A. Dastre on Roentgen rays; 1903, two articles on radium by E. Curie and J. J. Thomson, respectively, two on the nature of matter by O. Lodge and W. Crookes, respectively, two on the atom by F. W. Clarke and G. Le Bon, respectively; 1906, E. Curie on electricity and matter; 1908, J. J. Thomson on the ether and matter; 1909, J. J. Thomson on recent progress in physics. Adams' library contains *Wilhelm Ostwald, *Vorlesungen über Naturphilosophie gehalten im Sommer 1901 an der Universität Leipzig* (Leipzig, Veit, 1902); *Ernst Haeckel, *Les Énigmes de l'univers* (Paris, Schleicher, 1905). The address of Arthur Balfour to which Adams refers is his presidential address, "Reflections Suggested by the New Theory of Matter," *Report of the British Association for the Advancement of Science* (Cambridge meeting, 1904), pp. 3–14. Adams mentions Ostwald's *L'Énergie*, tr. E. Philippi (Paris, Alcan, 1910), rather extensively in *Degradation: Letter*. By his mention of Hermann von Helmholtz, Adams probably referred to *Popular Lectures on Scientific Subjects*, tr. E. Atkinson, 1st ser. (London, Longmans, Green, 1873), and particularly to the opening and concluding essays of the volume, together with two essays on thermodynamics.

called in the *Education* his grammar of science, although of course this list by no means exhausted his extensive, if desultory, forays into science.

The phenomenalist's view of science inevitably altered the role of the scientist as envisioned by the extreme mechanist. As long as scientists retained their faith that mechanistic theories coincided with ultimate reality, their function, at least to the philosopher of science, was somewhat passive. They devised means sufficient to bring them ever closer to a reality already prefigured in the hypotheses which the ultimate reality of the universe had inflicted on the scientists. They merely discovered what was temporarily hidden from view. Science was a kind of Easter hunt. Once all the eggs were gathered the game was over. Just so every discovery in science brought scientists closer to the revelation of ultimate reality. From about the seventies up to as late as 1895 not even the complexities of such quasi-mechanical explanations as those of Maxwell could dim a pervasive confidence in an imminent end to basic discoveries. The day would come—and soon, so many believed—when the scientist's job would be limited to the refinement of principles roughly established. Mechanics had accounted for such tremendous advances during the nineteenth century that the virtual end of science loomed in sight, with perhaps the mysteries of ether and life the only major barriers to its substantial completion.[18]

Should mechanics, however, prove only a mode of thinking about a vast, if limited, number of phenomena, then the scientist played a much more active role in conceptualization. This was the essence of the phenomenalist's position toward the end of the nineteenth century; no example makes it clearer than that of Riemann's geometry. Reconstructing geometry without Euclid's axiom of parallel lines, Riemann produced a peculiar geometry of curved space which Einstein could use many years later in his relativity theory of gravitation. If both Euclidean and Riemannian geometry possessed equal validity, but in different spheres, then the history of science was not that of the progressive discovery by ingenious investigators of aspects of an ultimate reality. This process of continuing discovery made the very goal of ultimate reality unreal to the scientist, since no absolute criteria existed for designating any one of the many manifestations exhibited

18. See, for example, Robert A. Millikan, *Evolution in Science and Religion* (New Haven, Yale University Press, 1927), pp. 7–11.

by each phenomenon as *the* reality. Yet Adams would flounder in his attempt to reach just such an absolute; or better, he floundered in his pretense that he sought scientific certainty, for the confusion of scientists served his aesthetic purposes.

To trace Adams' tortuous quest of contemporary views of ultimate reality as disclosed especially in annotations defacing his copies of Stallo, Henri Poincaré, and Pearson [19] would, for present purposes, be unprofitable. A few marginalia from Pearson will indicate the route Adams traveled, the more so as his dissatisfaction with the *Grammar* resulted in particularly revealing comment.

Pearson so delighted in contrasting the solid contributions of science with the unreliability of other kinds of knowledge, particularly metaphysics, that his complacency as to the superiority of his chosen field tinged his phenomenalistic point of view with an absolutism amusingly at variance with his major premise. For example, his statement in the introductory chapter of the *Grammar* that the scientific "frame of mind" instilled the impartial spirit essential to "good citizenship" more than merited Adams' rejoinder: "Assuming—does it not—that science aims at, and results in, unity; but how if science points to chaos? What right have we to assume the end?" A few pages later Pearson asserted that sublimely as poetry might depict the universe, "in the end it will not satisfy our aesthetic judgment, our idea of harmony and beauty, like the few facts which the scientist may venture to tell us in the same field." And Adams admonished, "The man of science must not meddle with poetry or art. He shows his feeble side." [20] Thus even before finishing the introduction to the *Grammar* Adams had become sufficiently irritated with Pearson's exaggerated statements on the value of science so that some of the annoyance doubtless spilled over into subsequent annotations. Despite his strictures, however, Adams could resist Pearson's penchant for lively metaphor no more than most.

To emphasize the relationship existing between the human consciousness and the world of external phenomena, Pearson contrived his still famous image of the brain as a telephone exchange. But the mind was a unique kind of exchange in which the operator was forever locked so that he never got closer to his subscribers

19. None of Mach's volumes remains in the Adams library at the Massachusetts Historical Society.

20. *Pearson, *op. cit.*, pp. 7, 17.

than the network of wires intervening between his switchboard
and their instruments. All man could ever know about the physical
reality of the universe ultimately originated as perceptions from
"the chaos beyond sensation," [21] while the isolated operator, which
was the scientist's mind, arranged diffuse sensations into "constructs," composed in part of immediately given experience or
experiment, in part of memory, and in part of the extension of
perceptions to such ideal abstractions as "points," "lines," and
"infinity." [22]

Not the image of the telephone operator itself so much as the
psychology implicit in Pearson's metaphor challenged Adams'
imagination. In the chapter of the *Education* for which he ap-
propriated Pearson's title, Adams created his own oft-quoted
metaphor of science as a "sensual raft in the midst of a super-
sensual chaos." [23] The contrast in metaphors is in itself significant.
If the analogy of the switchboard implied the process of making
intelligent connections, that of the raft implied rudderless drifting. Moreover, this contrast indicated something of Adams' fundamental disagreement with Pearson, to which the *Education* merely
alluded.

Adams reached the crux of his disagreement with Pearson's
argument as early as page 39, where he underscored all the "we's"
and sharply noted in the bottom margin, "The old science saw
at least that one must start by defining the 'ego.' Who are 'we'?"
He emphasized his Cartesian censure on the following page by
underlining all "I's": "All without knowing what I am! Thus
far I am a mere sense-impression, not even a sense." A few pages
later, when Pearson spoke of the "immediate sense-impression"
as "the spark which kindles thought, and brings into play the
still remaining impresses of past sense-impressions," Adams again
chided, "But what is the mind? a group of sense impressions.
[as Pearson had stated on page 66] how can the group pass
through itself?" [24] In short, one of Adams' major criticisms of

21. *Ibid.*, pp. 108, 137; Adams marked the phrase on both pages and reproduced
at some length a passage on the former page; *Education*, p. 451. Pearson's analogy
of the telephone exchange occurs in *Pearson, op. cit.*, chap. ii.
22. *Pearson, op. cit.*, pp. 41, 52.
23. *Education*, p. 452.
24. *Pearson, op. cit.*, p. 46. The reference to p. 66 (also mentioned by Adams in
the immediately preceding note beginning "All without knowing what I am!")
indicates a passage, which Adams lined in the margin, starting, "The group of
sense-impressions forming what I term *myself* is only a small subdivision of the
vast world of sense-impressions." Adams also revealed his persistent quest for a

Pearson centered in the ancient question as to who or what does the perceiving.

Having belabored metaphysicians so violently, Pearson invited metaphysical retort. He held that perceptions and the conceptualization of perceptions as constructs were the only absolutely certain elements in human knowledge, as though the certainty were not qualified by the metaphysics of "I" and "we" and "mind." [25] To Adams, Pearson's phenomenalism ultimately implied a physiological relativism to the universe, somehow built into the brain during the course of human evolution.

> If the universe to us exists only as sense-impressions, surely this merely turns the universe into us, as a part or the whole of us, and does not alter the problem except to extend the *ego*. What do we gain by abolishing the universe in order to enlarge *ourself?* The "thing-in-itself" is then me alone. It is the same complex. The metaphysics remain—"I rain"; "I snow"; "I am nature." "I am God." [26]

specific definition of the ego in his comments on "consciousness" in William James' *Psychology* (New York, Holt); see Max I. Baym, "William James and Henry Adams," *New England Quarterly, 10* (1937), 717–742.

25. For criticism of Pearson's absolutism in respect to scientific knowledge, despite his phenomenalist position, see James B. Conant, *Science and Common Sense* (New Haven, Yale University Press, 1951), pp. 7 f., 48 f.; A. Cornelius Benjamin, *An Introduction to the Philosophy of Science* (New York, Macmillan, 1937), pp. 8, 148, 151–154; Henry Margenau, *The Nature of Physical Reality* (New York, McGraw-Hill, 1950), p. 71.

26. *Pearson, *op. cit.*, p. 76, at the end of chap. ii. Following his comment Adams added the references, pp. 157, 185, 147. On p. 157 Adams marked the margin beside the sentence, "We express the problem and the mystery wrongly when we ask 'why space seems the same to you and me'; we ought more precisely to ask 'why your space and my space are alike.'" On p. 185, "[Moments spent in pondering the immensities of space and time] are like moments employed in examining the frame of a picture and not its contents . . . frame and canvas are only modes by which the artist brings home his idea to us . . . So it is with time and space . . ." Adams marked through the remainder of the paragraph and queried, "What does this mean? Is it a denial of objective realities or not? The proposition is that we know nothing about it, but here we reach positive denial of its existence." No markings appear on p. 147; but Adams doubtless referred to another statement by Pearson to the effect that space and time are "not inherent in an outside world, but are modes of discriminating groups of sense impressions."

Adams actually carried his argument of physiological relativism one step further by ridiculously attacking Pearson's statement that all men possess essentially the same science because all are similarly constructed; if a particular person possessed a unique kind of universe in his mind, this uniqueness would be evidence of madness (p. 101). To this Adams retorted, "Seeing that the utmost disagreement exists in the result of our reflections as these chapters show, madness seems to be the law of nature. 114–244–248." These last page numbers refer to examples of scientific disagreement.

In other words Adams studied Pearson not to learn the process of scientific conceptualization so much as to fix upon specific loci for both the inner consciousness and the outer universe. For all its progress, science had not progressed at all toward determining philosophical ultimates; indeed the tenor of science was frankly skeptical of their attainment. Hence scientific constructs were rootless. "Philosophy has never got beyond this point," Adams complained to a correspondent. "There are but two schools; one turns the world onto me; the other turns me onto the world; and the result is the same." [27] The end was relativism, as he sighed in the marginalia of his copy of Stallo: "Singular that the result of eliminating metaphysics should always be to become more metaphysical. Force becomes merely a mode of thought; mass is another; matter vanishes altogether; relation remains but only as a mathematical concept." [28]

So the quest for certainty ended in the mathematical relativism of the ethereal phase. The rootlessness of scientific constructs joined with what was to Adams the unimaginable confusion resulting from any nonmechanistic view of the universe, and together these elements accounted for his famous metaphor. Man drifted on a makeshift raft of constructs in an ocean uncharted by a science which had lost its old certainties. The experimental aspect of physics showed the chaos of the ether; its philosophical aspect showed the chaos of phenomenalism. To Adams, Pearson only underscored this chaos when he concluded the *Grammar* with one last jab at the much abused metaphysician. By contrast with the philosopher, Pearson warned, the scientist must be modest in his quest for truth: "We must dare to be ignorant. *Ignoramus laborandum est.*" To which Adams appended, "and the last word of science is 'Ignoramus!' what is the odds between optimism and pessimism?" [29]

27. May 13, 1905; Ford, *2*, 451.
28. Stallo, *op. cit.*, p. 170 [*p. 130], at the end of chap. x. In *Pearson, *op. cit.*, especially from p. 209 on, Adams also makes a series of inquiries on the relativism of science. For example, Pearson (p. 209) mentions the relativity of motion, "Why relativity of motion only? Why not relativity of time, space, continuity, force and thought? Science then becomes the study of relativities." On p. 241, in respect to Pearson's assertion that motion in the universe is actually a mere change in sense impressions: "Change is then a sense-impression. All change is relative. Then relativity is the perpetual reality?" On p. 257, commenting on Pearson's "form of motion moving," "Is not the word *moving* superfluous? What is motion *not* moving? P. 276. Matter then is motion! So is probably mind? Is motion absolute or relative? Surely relative! Then relativity is the last analysis."
29. In his closing sentence Pearson probably recalled the "Ignorabimus" with

Now to be sure, in their desire to attack mechanistic fallacies the phenomenalists tended perhaps to overstress the freedom with which the scientist manipulated constructs, and hence encouraged Adams in his metaphor of drift. Poincaré in particular spoke in his classic *La Science et l'hypothèse* of scientific concepts as mere conventions, or as mere conveniences for economy of thought. In the *Education* it was Poincaré whom Adams cited most tellingly on the floating quality of constructs, while the same source accounted for repeated suggestions in both the *Rule* and the *Letter* that the historian should test the theory "not for its truth, but for its convenience." [30] The creative thinker would rather have asked just what criteria did validate scientific constructs. This is not to deny that science has become more mathematical and less related to everyday experience. It was to Adams' credit that he pondered the trend at a time when most physicists clung to their mechanical models. The abstract character of modern science might well account for the despair of the amateur. Some professionals and some philosophers (more or less professional) today echo Adams' pessimism. But thus far men have appeared capable of comprehending whatever degree of abstractness has been required for the continuing exploration of physical phenomena. Whether an end will occur to the process is for the future to know. Most professionals retain, with Bumstead, a faith in themselves coupled with a just regard for the immensity of tasks unsolved. This mixture of self-confidence and humility has customarily accompanied the great advances in the history of science.

Little more need be said about the nature of physical reality, except perhaps to emphasize the absurdity of Adams' attempt to parcel reality, so much to the ego, so much to the external world. Since Adams was not philosophically naive, his insistence on a specific location for reality doubtless possessed an element of sham. In any event, Pearson himself demonstrated the meaninglessness of such a boundary by the ancient example of the amputated arm. Before the operation the arm is part of "me"; afterward it belongs to the world of external objects. Just so with the example of a needle penetrating the skin.[31] That portion of reality

---

which Emil Du Bois-Reymond concluded his well-known and much reprinted *Über die Grenzen des Naturerkennens*.

30. *Education*, pp. 455 f. See also, for example, *Degradation: Letter*, pp. 190, 237 f., 241, 243, 260 f.; *Degradation: Rule*, pp. 304, 309. Cater, pp. 782 f.

31. *Pearson, *op. cit.*, pp. 63–66. There are many marginal remarks bearing on Adams' concern to compartmentalize reality into "inside" and "outside"; a sampling

which man unthinkingly asserts to be "outside" himself merges imperceptibly with what is "inside," as Henry Margenau has explained by a series of five more examples roughly illustrative of increasing degrees of conceptualization.[32] First, the spontaneous rhapsodic reality of the immediately given object, say the apple tree outside the window, more readily available to artists than to scientists. The scientist attributes "mass" to an apple on this tree, and he moves considerably beyond the realm of the immediately given, although the elements "apple" and "mass" are quite directly intuitable from the nature of immediate sensation. He measures the wave length of the "red" in the apple on a spectroscope, and this new item of reality depends on sensation in addition to the variety of instruments designed to extend the range of our perception. Abandoning the example of the apple now, he designates the electric "field strength" for any point in a space within the neighborhood of two oppositely charged bodies, and reality depends on instrumental manipulation as well as on mathematical processes. Finally, he desires to know the position of an electron fired from a gun, and reality depends on the property of indeterminacy which is not only instrumental and mathematical in character but also involves a concept completely alien to our notion of position in ordinary experience. The properties derived from everyday experience, then, together with those of mass, wave length, field strength, and indeterminacy, are all portions of a reality which knows no clear-cut boundary between

(other than those already discussed above, pp. 234 f.) makes clear the negative aspects of much of Adams' inquiry—even when he occasionally scores on Pearson —which the arresting quality of the comments tends to obscure. "Is the law of gravitation the same thing as gravitation? is a law of Congress the same thing as Congress?" (*Pearson, *op. cit.*, p. 121, n. 1.) On p. 123 Pearson discussed the old philosophical example of the thrown stone; we may "will" the throwing, but the continued motion after the stone has left our hand involves a "mystery" which philosophies of will like that of Schopenhauer cannot profitably explain. "Is not this a demonstration of the objective world? P. 68. We demonstrate a mystery beyond sense-impressions. p. 74, 72, 73." Of Pearson's assertion (p. 159) that "space" could not be inferred where "psychical machinery similar to our own" did not exist, Adams queried, "Why not? Is not the earth one of our measuring instruments, —a part of ourselves—and does it not record space measurements? p. 169." Of instruments as magnifiers of sense impressions (p. 169) Adams asked, "Is not all nature, in this sense, a magnifier of our sense-impressions? Is not geological time an extension of our own time?" And a little later, on p. 184, "Geological time is then a human concept? or an objective fact independent of man? or is the earth a part of us? or are we a part of the earth?"

32. Margenau, *op. cit.*, pp. 64–68, see also p. 289; in this connection chaps. iii and iv are particularly valuable.

spectator and spectacle. To spacialize reality in terms of inside
and outside is merely metaphorical. Reality cannot be so allotted.
It evolves as an integral part of man's unfolding experience.

The universe did not therefore inflict man with the complexity
of the ether, for the ether was a man-made construct—as it turned
out, entirely too man made!—based upon a vast number of observations. The universe did not even inflict the observations on
the scientist. They depended on the scientist's conceiving of their
necessity, of his apprehending their import, and of his relating
their disparateness. They depended on elaborate mathematical
calculations and on complicated equipment. Whatever the fate of
the ether concept, the observations remained. The concept had
served to stimulate investigations into phenomena—for example,
those of elasticity and vortex motions—which have proved of
immense value in the development of physics. The very theory
itself enriched human thought by compelling scientists to think
in ways contributing to the subtlety and refinement of physical
theory. Finally, negative results in science are creative insofar as
they eliminate certain possibilities and thereby direct attention to
new problems; for the failure of the ether concept in no way
precluded other explanations for the phenomena which the ether
was meant to elucidate. The ether, then, was not some complex
absolute "out there" forever barring scientific advance by its complexity. The puzzle of ether, like Dollo's statement on evolutionary
leaps, represented a stage in a continuing process, a process which
did not occur because the cornucopia of the universe spilled just
so many secrets to man and then suddenly turned niggardly and
spilled no more. Rather man plied the secrets he got, using solutions in hand as leverage for future progress.

For this reason Bumstead could maintain his optimism even
though, in a long note at the end of Adams' manuscript, he recorded the belief of a few of his contemporaries that the ether
did not exist.

It is interesting to note that within the past few years, certain
German mathematicians have developed a way of describing
electromagnetic, optical and mechanical phenomena which does
not necessitate explicit mention of ether. It is based upon what
is called the "Principle of Relativity" and is descriptive in
Kirchhoff's sense that a fundamental differential equation is
the most complete and concise description of physical phenom-

ena and represents more truly than models and "explanations" all that we really know about phenomena. The new doctrine is perfectly satisfactory from a mathematical point of view; in fact it does not differ essentially from the ordinary theory except in its metaphysics. It does not appeal to me as an improvement on the old way;—and most *physicists* whether experimental or mathematical appear to be of this mind. But the pure mathematician is enthusiastic about it and many papers are being written on the subject.

This speculation is in line with Mr. Adams' prediction of the progress of physical theories toward pure mathematics or thought itself. But it suggests the introduction of a final step (or phase) beyond the etherial one. The latter still has a distinctly "material" basis, in that the ether possesses the most fundamental qualities of matter (substance, mass etc.). The "theory of relativity" has (at least formally) refined this out of existence.

I do not myself believe that it will supplant the ether; but that may be because I am becoming an old-fashioned molecule which will stick to the old phase as long as possible.[33]

Happy conjunction! The amateur, pessimistically confronting the complexities of the ether; the conservative physicist, able representative of his profession, admitting the complexity but confident of an eventual solution along old lines; finally, mathematicians pioneering in a theory that would shortly remove the impasse which Adams bemoaned as the limit of thought. In the whole of his celebration of how he had just missed out in life, Adams never contrived a misfortune more ironic than this one.

Bumstead did suggest that Adams might be even more nearly right about the final mathematical phase of thought by being wrong about the ether. To this extent it may superficially seem that Adams' error of fact did not really affect the substance of his argument. Such is not the case. Quite obviously the "mathematical phase" of thought has not involved such complexity as to terminate progress in physics. Ironically again—to stay with Adams' terms —the physicist has progressed because he embraced complexity; at least he embraced complexity if unity depended on a mechanical ether.[34] In all areas of intellectual endeavor times occur when

33. Bumstead critique of a draft of the *Rule* deposited in the Massachusetts Historical Society.

34. See Margenau, *op. cit.*, pp. 296, 459 f., on the fallacy of "convergence" in science.

bloated unities need surgery. At such times to accept complexity is to simplify the dilemma and perhaps to prepare the way for some new and greater unification. Dread of complexity yet repeated involvement with the very complexity he feared are among the major themes in both Adams' writing and his life. His passion for unity seduced him to his quest for a science of history, while no single element of the quest demonstrated better than this example of the physical ether the irrationality which his passion hid.

Reconsider, by way of summary, the implications of Adams' view of science. Science was a kind of picture puzzle of finite dimensions. Each piece fitted to the puzzle brought the scientist closer to the realization of the completed picture.[35] Essentially passive, the role of the scientist was that of discovering relationships inflicted on him by the nature of the picture. Of course there were pieces so difficult as to seem not quite part of the same picture; but there appeared no reason why a little ingenuity should not at last reconcile the difficulties to the total ensemble. To conclude the metaphor, suppose the pieces a little imperfectly made, then some final sanding would obtain a perfect fit.

The parallels are striking between this attitude of some scientists in the nineteenth century and that of Adams in approaching his *History;* as the nineteenth-century scientist concentrated on a mechanistic conception of the universe, so the nineteenth-century historian tended, in Freeman's phrase, to view "past politics" in the broad sense of political, military, and diplomatic events as the core of history. As mechanics became the first aspect of the physical world to undergo extensive investigation because of the availability of mechanical phenomena and their utility, so politics for comparable reasons predominated in the nationalistic orientation of most nineteenth-century history. Moreover, there was a peculiarly tangible quality common to both mechanical models and political documents, while the latter even partook something of the impersonality of science if, as in the *History*, the public servant suppressed the private man. Since the documents existed as hard cores of certainty, history existed "out there" like the mechanical universe. It inflicted itself on the historian whose function was that of mere discoverer and arranger. When the documents were ordered in such a manner as seemed "rigorously consequent," a "fixed and documented starting point" resulted, comparable to the ultimate reality promised by mechanists. Future historians, like

35. I owe this analogy in part to *ibid.*, p. 19.

future scientists, could refine what nevertheless must always remain an absolute point of departure. There were difficulties of course; for Adams, for example, the problem of fitting the people into a political history. Still the peculiar nature of American history permitted him to write of the American people by concentrating on such representative figures as Jefferson and Madison—all without disturbing the basic premises of Freeman's motto! The scientist had likewise unified diverse data from light, magnetism, and electricity within an ether which left his mechanistic modes of thinking perhaps not quite secure but essentially unscathed.

If the historian today seems hostile to the idea of scientific history, it is because both science and history seem more complex to him than they did when Adams wrote. The phenomenalists demonstrated the role of the scientist in formulating constructs at a time, around the turn of the century, when many historians—in the United States the so-called "new" historians [36]—had begun to emphasize the role of the historian in making history. During the first decades of the present century most of these rising historians professed no full-blown historical philosophy, although Croce would come to many with time and maturity. Not so much a philosophy of history as an active program for carrying on research interested the young historians. Hence they talked at that time less of the "relativism" of history than of its possible "interpretations." They found the sources for their interpretations in the burgeoning social sciences—political science, economics, geography, psychology, sociology, and anthropology—which had only begun to appear in American graduate schools during the last decades of the nineteenth century. The new historians hoped that by applying generalizations from the social sciences to history they might find principles in the past usable for the present. In their *Development of Modern Europe*—published in 1907-08—Robinson and Beard confessed that they had "consistently subordinated the past to the present." They hoped "to enable the reader to catch up with his own times; to read intelligently the foreign news in the morning paper; to know what was the attitude of Leo XII toward the Social Democrats even if he has forgotten that of Innocent III toward the Albigenses." Even the study of events and

36. The "new" historians take their name from James Harvey Robinson, *The New History* (New York, Macmillan, 1912); or it would perhaps be more accurate to say that Robinson took for the title of his volume a current phrase, which his essay did much to formalize. For general bibliography on the new history see Bibliography, Sec. I.

attitudes far more remote from present circumstances than the opposition of Innocent III to heresy could serve the present, Robinson advised in a later book, provided the historian subordinated the trivia of kings, dates, and battles to "the ways in which the people have thought and acted in the past, their tastes and achievements in many fields besides the political." [37] Since the new historians tended toward liberal and humane views, they further implied the importance of history for social betterment. However unconsciously, they were the true heirs of Comte through the nineteenth-century institutionalists.

Heirs of Comte, the new historians were not quite Comtians. For most of them there was no "positivistic" phase in social development, when the scientific study of society would attain such precision that a speculative elite could inevitably guide the future of society toward beneficent goals. The relativism in Comtian theory lay not so much in the general principles established by the sociologist as in the minor variations of these principles occurring in particular societies or in the peculiar conditions requiring the sociologist's attention before he could apply such principles to a particular society. The overwhelming Comtian goal was, to use a phrase of Adams, the establishment of "permanent principles." For Robinson, Beard, Becker, and the other new historians, their role in society was, if vital, neither as grandiose nor as absolutist as Comte and Adams envisioned it. [38]

To be sure, the opposition between new historians and Comtists was not quite so neat as the poles absolutism-relativism would imply. After all, the new historians obtained their interpretations from social "scientists." If they opposed the absolutism of the pseudo-Rankean position that history could be written once and for all as it had actually happened, the new historians occasionally came perilously close to the absolutism of extremists among social scientists. But in essence the new historians were relativists in history. [39] They opposed the certainties of the self-styled Rankeans in the American Historical Association, while they attacked the

37. *The Development of Modern Europe* (New York, Ginn, 1907–08), *1*, iii; *The New History*, p. 15. Cited by Morton G. White, *Social Thought in America; the Revolt against Formalism* (New York, Viking, 1949), chap. iv.

38. For comparison see above, pp. 113–119, and below, pp. 254 f. William R. Taylor, "Historical Bifocals on the Year 1800," *New England Quarterly, 23* (1950), 172–186, obliquely refers to similarities between Adams' *History* and new history.

39. Beard, of course, moved away from the relativist position in his last books to condemn Roosevelt "on the record."

excessive concern of many in the association with the past for itself
alone. More specifically, they rebelled against the tenor of such
remarks as those of George Burton Adams in his presidential
address of 1908, "History and the Philosophy of History." [40]
Fearing that historians were becoming infatuated with generalizations from the social sciences, the Yale historian asked, "Are we
passing from an age of investigation to an age of speculation?"
Although he extended a tepid welcome to speculation, G. B. Adams
clearly aimed to warn his colleagues that all speculation depended
on "sure facts" for its validity.

> None of the new battle-cries should sound for us above the call
> of our first leader, proclaiming the chief duty of the historian
> to establish *wie es eigentlich gewesen*. We have been told that
> to this should be added *wie es eigentlich geworden;* but let us
> not be deceived. To the true historian the being of a fact has
> always included all that portion of its becoming which belongs
> to the definite understanding of it. What is more than that
> we can safely leave to others. The field of the historian is, and
> must long remain, the discovery and recording of what actually
> happened.

Then, he added, "God has conceded two sights to a man. One,
of time's completed plan. That is our philosophy of history, under
the stimulus of which we work." But the other, he reminded in
concluding his speech, was "of the minute's work, man's first step
to the plan's completeness. That is our daily labor in building up
by long and right investigation the science of history."

This, then, was the essence of the controversy in the American
Historical Association between new and (by implication) old historians when Adams mailed his *Letter*. How curiously irrelevant
Adams' essay must have seemed to both groups. The *Letter* clearly
did not sympathize with G. B. Adams and the "science" of the
old guard. Even in the *History* Adams had intended much more
than "a fixed and documented starting point"; he would have welcomed an age of historical speculation. But would he have thought
the speculators too timid? With their interest in the "social
sciences," they would certainly have thought him a relic out of
the dim past, harking back to nineteenth-century notions of a
marriage between history and the physical and natural sciences.

40. *American Historical Review, 14* (1909), 221–236; quotations below from pp.
229, 235, 236.

It is tempting to imagine Adams attending the 1910 convention of the American Historical Association (sheer fantasy, of course, for he would never have attended such a gathering [41]). Had he appeared, to sit through the presidential address of Frederick Jackson Turner, Adams must have writhed in discomfort at what was undoubtedly a thinly veiled allusion to the *Letter* which the most illustrious portion of the audience had received some nine months earlier.

> It has become a precedent, fairly well established by the distinguished scholars who have filled the office which I am about to lay down, to state a position with reference to the relations of history and its sister-studies, and even to raise the question of the attitude of the historian toward the laws of thermodynamics and to seek to find the key of historical development or of *historical degradation.* It is not given to all to bend the bow of Ulysses. I shall attempt a lesser task.[42]

Turner went on to remind his audience that the historian should apply interpretations to history only after having appraised the limitations of his theories in the light of the complexity of human society. To Turner's audience, whether new historians (to whom Turner was something of a patron saint) or old, a thermodynamic theory of history, which doubtless seemed mere satire against Spencerian optimism, was curiously old-fashioned. Although the satire was effective, it came too late to seem pertinent, as Arthur T. Hadley, president of Yale, wrote Adams in responding to his copy of the *Letter.*

> I am constantly astonished to find how much less the younger men of today are caring for a certain kind of scientific romancing than did the men of twenty years ago. Sometime last year an eminent historian gave a lecture to an audience of young men, among whom he spoke of authors with whom intelligent historians were assumed to be familiar and enumerated Herbert Spencer among them. I told him after the lecture that I doubted whether many of his audience read Spencer

41. During the convention of the American Historical Association for 1908 Adams did give a dinner party for Jameson and six other historians of Jameson's selection; on this occasion he may have attended a half day of the sessions; Cater, p. 630.

42. Frederick J. Turner, "Social Forces in American History," *American Historical Review, 16* (1911), 230. Italics mine.

except as a curious phenomenon of morbid egotism. He said he thought I must be mistaken about that, and I said I would inquire. At the club that evening I happened to meet an unusually active group of men of ages varying from twenty-five to thirty-five, and told of my conversation with the lecturer. At the close I said, "Was I right?" There was a moment's silence, and then one of them remarked comprehensively, "Herbert Spencer is as dead as a door nail." [43]

Of course Adams intended the *Letter* as a joke at Spencer's expense, and at the expense of all other nineteenth-century theories of social development more or less tinged with the idea of upward evolution; but he intended much more. If those who received the *Letter* missed its full significance, they were hardly to blame, despite Adams' rueful complaints that the lack of response to his *Letter* proved society, and the universities especially, to be as degraded as he had feared.[44] When the *Letter* was posthumously reissued in 1919 along with the earlier *Tendency* and *Rule* as *The Degradation of the Democratic Dogma*, its symbolic content could be better appreciated. By then the *Education* had appeared as preparation, while even today the *Rule*, with its dramatic metaphor, is more highly regarded than the *Letter*, which is at once more verbose and less decisive. As late as January, 1909, Adams had intended to distribute privately printed copies of the *Education* to teachers, followed after a suitable interval by the *Rule* to "make [his] meaning and method somewhat clearer." [45] Then he scrapped this project, wrote and privately printed the *Letter*, and by March

43. Mar. 14, 1910; unpublished letter in the estate of Henry Adams. In the course of his research for the *Letter* Adams read André Lalande, *La Dissolution opposé à l'évolution dans les sciences physiques et morales* (Paris, Alcan, 1899), which especially attacked the Spencerian concept that evolution represented the development from indefinite and incoherent homogeneity to definite and coherent heterogeneity. Lalande (pp. 6 f.) specifically noted that in setting the term "dissolution" over against Spencer's "evolution" he did not imply degradation in the sense of Clausius' famous aphorism. The tendency of intellectual endeavor toward generalizations was, therefore, for Lalande, an example of dissolution. Adams falsified the meaning of Lalande's book as a whole in lifting bits for citation in the *Letter*. Acknowledging his copy of the privately printed *Letter*, the French philosopher emphasized the dichotomy between physical and biological force which Adams had ignored in his monistic point of view; letter in the estate of Henry Adams, dated Dec. 1, 1910. In his youthful studies Adams apparently imbibed Spencerian ideas at second hand, for, surprisingly, not until 1874 does he seem to have read one of Herbert Spencer's volumes; Ford, *1*, 261; this was *The Philosophy of Style* (New York, Appleton, 1872) with which he disagreed.

44. See especially Ford, *2*, 525, 531, 534, 535, 536, 537, 546. Cater, p. 682.

45. *Ibid.*, p. 783.

of the following year had already distributed some 250 copies.[46] This change of plan was curious. Did he have some reason to feel that the *Education* was too personal or that some of those mentioned in it might object? Did Bumstead's critique of the *Rule* or its refusal by the *American Historical Review* cause him to hesitate; or did he fear that he had been too arbitrary in his graph? Having gone so far in the *Rule*, did he hope to make his evidence even more encyclopedic in the *Letter*, while simultaneously relating history to the evolutionary sciences? Whatever the reason for Adams' change of plan, those teachers who received the *Letter* in 1910 had no way to relate this essay to other aspects of his thinking. No wonder they responded, if at all, so tepidly to his scientific theory, especially when his degradationist scheme eliminated history.

To most of those who first received it the *Letter* must have seemed an elaborate joke out of the middle of the nineteenth century. Too bad, many must have thought to themselves, that so great a historian should perpetrate such nonsense in his eccentric old age.[47]

What else could they think? According to the *Letter* history depended for meaning on science; but the only science with meaning eliminated history. Science, in turn, depended on human reason; but reason was the degradation of instinct.

Of all his straight-line follies, this seemed most foolish. Reason had come late in evolution, when the sun and earth had already cooled to temperatures too low for any creative development. Scholars had never agreed as to what they should call the quality opposing reason; but no matter what the quality, it "slipped readily over to the idea of Energy" and thus came, like history, under the second law of thermodynamics:

46. Ford, *2*, 537.

47. The estate of Henry Adams contains 32 letters, counting two from Bumstead, which may record the professional response to Adams' distribution of at least 250 copies of the *Letter* and perhaps closer to 500 (see above, n. 46 and p. 153, n. 62). Perfunctory "thank you" notes, requests from libraries, and personal requests decrease the total to 19. It would seem doubtful that Adams would have thrown away significant responses if he kept trivial correspondence in connection with the *Letter*. None of the 19 comments was favorable, although some scientists were not so much opposed as the historians. None of the replies was more than a polite discussion of some point raised by Adams. (These letters do not include the response which he may have received from his regular correspondents, or the reply of William James.)

henceforward it mattered little whether the schools, in their rage for nomenclature, called the result "Will," or "Entelechy," or "Dominant," or "Organic Principle," or "Trieb," or "Strebung," or "Intuition," or "Instinct," or just simply "Force" as of old; even the forbidden words "Creative power" became almost orthodox science; in any case the logic of "Will" or "Energetik" imperatively required that every conception whatever, involving a potential . . . [should fall] under the second law of thermodynamics.[48]

Now of course these terms were by no means synonymous. Adams actually spoke in the *Letter* of the instinct of the beast, the "Energetik" and vital force of biological philosophy, the intuition of art, and the will of a people. For convenience only, he finally fixed (but not rigidly) on an overarching "will" like that in Schopenhauer's philosophy as the quality opposing reason.[49] Fortunately his vagueness is sufficient warrant for the avoidance of another technical digression. Suffice it to say, the physiologists whom Adams cited maintained that intelligence stemmed from will, insofar as the individual brain learned by willing its learning.[50] Psychologists demonstrated that instinct possessed a primacy over intelligence, while, when Adams wrote his *Letter*, "instinct" was a vastly more commodious term than it is today. Thanks to James' expanded use of the term, a usage continued and even elaborated during the first quarter of the present century by other psychologists, instinct encompassed such boundless spheres as those of sympathy, hunting, play, curiosity, love, secretiveness, cleanliness, modesty, and a host of others, with Veblen's instinct of workmanship probably the most ambiguous in a catalogue notable for ambiguities.[51] Adams undoubtedly used instinct in this

48. *Degradation: Letter,* p. 194.

49. *Ibid.,* p. 230; although Adams tended to use "will" as the polar opposite to reason throughout the essay.

50. Adams briefly explored the philosophical background for will, *ibid.,* p. 193 (Schopenhauer, Hartmann, and Ciamician), the psychological background, p. 197 (Wundt, Krainsky), finally coming to the physiological, pp. 198–201. Physiologists took one of three approaches to the problem of will. Ostwald, and especially Loeb, reduced the will to physical-chemical reactions, or "mechanical attraction." Dr. William Hanna Thomson asserted that the will creating the "association-fibres" was not "natural, but supernatural." Paul Flechzig attributed will to organic changes. Whether the will was mechanical, supernatural, or organic, Adams brought it under the second law, pp. 201 f., in preparation for the statements by Lalande and Bergson (together with the mention of Reinke and Hartmann), pp. 203 ff., which substantially conclude the chapter, "The Problem."

51. William James, *op. cit., 2,* chap. xxiv. The classic discussion of instinct is

broad sense and with considerable reason for his vagueness. He needed only such philosophers as Schopenhauer, Hartmann, and Bergson to justify completely his undefined use of the active, imaginative quality opposed to reason. One-sided consciousness, amputated intelligence, degraded act, truncated will—with such epithets he showered reason with abuse.[52]

Viewed as allegory, both the *Rule* and the *Letter* extended the final chapters of the *Education*. The inadequacies of reason symbolized the meager accomplishments of modern society with its technological orientation. By the same token reason symbolized the dilemma of that small class of intelligentsia remaining to a collectivized society who were compelled, whether they wished or not, to share in the debased values of their milieu. Reason, then, served as a measure of accomplishment for both the twentieth-century world and its helpless intellectuals as represented by Henry Adams. Both he and his world had made the tortuous journey through thought only to learn at the end the simplest of lessons, yet the most profound, and for intellectuals among the most difficult.

Thought was limited; intuition told more. If science served as Adams' index of twentieth-century thought, it was because his society was wedded to science. As Adams used the phrase, the "limit of thought" depended on its double and opposite meanings. Science was limited if, as those who held out most hope for the ether believed, scientists could substantially discover all that there was to discover. On the other hand, science was also limited if scientists someday reached a point in their investigations where complexities precluded further advance. Adams essentially took the second position, although his despair at the prospect of scientific helplessness owed much of its pessimism to the contrast of this position with the optimism of its opposite. He occasionally lost sight of precisely what he did mean by the limit of thought; or more probably he purposely blurred any precision of meaning. For he toyed with yet a third interpretation for his phrase, less specifically related to his survey of science but doubtless more significant to the whole of his later speculation. This third meaning appeared nowhere more explicitly than in the *Education*, where Adams translated Henri Poincaré, "Doubtless if our means

Luther L. Bernard, *Instinct* (New York, Holt, 1924); see also his article in the *Encyclopaedia of Social Sciences* (New York, Macmillan, 1932), *8*, 82 ff.
52. *Degradation: Letter*, p. 205.

of investigation should become more and more penetrating, we should discover the simple under the complex; then the complex under the simple; then anew the simple under the complex; and so on without ever being able to foresee the last term." [53] In other words, no end appeared in sight for science after all, and the fact that scientists could indefinitely continue their labors would be reason enough for their failure to share in Adams' melancholy. They might even have asked Adams whether the universe was not quite as inexhaustible for the medieval scholastic as for the modern scientist. But this kind of argument is debater's logic. The medieval philosopher could always look up from his momentary task to glimpse the unity which gave meaning to all investigations, whereas the modern scientist looked beyond immediate complexities into the infinite complexity ahead. The limit of thought was the mathematical universe of Arthur Balfour's presidential address, beyond the possibility of models and hence beyond sensory perception. To think was therefore eventually to lose touch with life, or with art which Adams came to identify with life.

Almost too simple a conclusion for such a tortuous journey? Perhaps so, at least for those unsympathetic with the notion of history. The future derived from the past. To touch the future Adams had always detoured, even as a journalist, back through the past. Only the long view—the Comtian view—could provide the sense of inevitable direction which derived from the cumulative weight of events. And only through the unity of history—through the "development of an idea" as Adams had much earlier expressed the same notion [54]—could both he and his world assess their significance. In essence this was his answer to James. Despite the ever-increasing flood of power which man spilled into his society, James would leave open the possibility of achievements as great as those of past societies. Adams would say that the flood must swamp history, if history meant the study of man's humanity. Quality was impossible in a society where the highest aims depended on the exploitation of ever-increasing quantities of power.

Adams' symbol of a power-mad world, continually exploiting its science to uncover new sources for increased power, is by now too familiar to need much attention. More interesting is his conception of his own role—or rather that of intelligentsia like himself—in a world debauched by the energies it unleashed; for true

53. *Education,* p. 455.
54. See above, p. 7.

to his concept of leadership, Adams addressed his *Letter* not to the general public but to a selected group. "Teachers of history" he chose to label his aristocracy, although the *Letter* went to more than historians. History had been his métier and hence served as a professional excuse to gain as large a professional audience as possible. Moreover, if any of his readers took to his proposal, certainly the historian would be most sympathetic. Yet he really addressed not history departments alone but entire universities. To Adams the university served as the repository for all that was worth while in modern culture. Conceived in its broadest sense, history was the essence of all curricula in the university. He envisioned nothing less than

> the University as a system of education grouped about History; a main current of thought branching out, like a tree, into endless forms of activity, in regular development, according to the laws of physics; and to be studied as a single stream, not as now by a multiversal, but by a universal law; not as a scientific but as a historical unity; not as a practise of technical handling, but as a process of mental evolution in history, controlled, like the evolution of any series of chemical or electric equilibria, by one general formula. University education organized on this scheme, would begin by ceasing to compete with technical education, and would found all its instruction on historical method.

Again, to Jameson in 1909 Adams explained that his object in the *Rule* had been "to suggest a reform of the whole University system, grouping all knowledge as an historical stream, to be treated by historical methods, and drawing the line between the University and technology." [55] A unified university, and unified under history! This would parallel the medieval universe of the church. By focusing man's intelligence and his ideals, the university might furnish the only example of unity possible to the twentieth century. True, the odds against attaining any such unity as that of the Middle Ages were great, but without scholarly cooperation even the idea of unity must perish. Narrowly technical training would get no closer to universals than world fairs.

To find unity in the twentieth century the modern university must look toward science as it had once looked toward religion. Scientific concepts alone possessed sufficient generality and pre-

55. Cater, pp. 784, 649 f. (dated Mar. 20, 1909).

cision to enlist the aid and respect of all academic departments. Unless he employed scientific concepts the historian must continue in his passive role of piling datum on datum, petty cores of fact that led nowhere and proved nothing. In a world dominated by science only scientific hypotheses could provide conceptual schemes within which all departments of the university could contribute so as to make otherwise isolated investigations effective in contemporary society. The time was past when a simple society permitted a single individual, like Gallatin, to formulate plans sufficient to guide the destinies of nations. Without the collective effort of an aristocracy of intellect society was doomed.

This dream of the great university was no new one to Adams. He was ever the teacher. Although the pedagogue served as target for some of Adams' sharpest barbs, the persistence with which the archer aimed his shafts betrayed his fascination with this quarry. He addressed all his speculation to teachers. Instinctively he labeled his most autobiographical work *The Education of Henry Adams*. Although the entire volume chronicled what he once called his "career of failure," he branded the chapter on his Harvard teaching with the word itself. Even after leaving Harvard he never abandoned teaching. Time and again his intimates have recalled the pedagogue in Adams, how he stimulated conversation with outrageous pronouncements, then leaned back to listen to the reactions of his audience as he had once listened to Harvard undergraduates, ready with more stimulants should discussion flag.

The great university depended upon just such intellectual stimulation where the teacher in one department challenged his colleague in another, and where both reconciled their differences in cooperation. "In twenty years of search," Adams gratefully, if a little extremely, wrote Bumstead, "you are the only person I have ever found who understood the uses of cooperation, and could cooperate." [56] Much earlier, while acting as secretary in the legation, he had outlined a scheme for education as grand as any envisioned by the colonial leaders. "We want a national set of young men like ourselves or better," he wrote Charles,

> to start new influences not only in politics, but in literature, in law, in society, and throughout the whole social organism of the country—a national school of our own generation . . .
> In England the Universities centralize ability and London

56. Feb. 8, 1910; Cater, p. 677.

gives a field. So in France, Paris encourages and combines these influences. But with us, we should need at least six perfect geniuses . . . spotted over the country and all working together; whereas our generation as yet has not produced one nor the promise of one. It's all random, insulated work, for special and temporary and personal purposes, and we have no means, power or hope of combined action for any unselfish end.[57]

He may have already been reading Comte; if not, he came to Comte with this frame of mind. The Comtian circuit of knowledge remained in memory throughout his life; so did Comtian allusions to the knowledge possible to an aristocracy of enlightened men working together, each contributing his share toward some vast unselfish end. He never came closer to realizing this dream than in the cooperative *Essays in Anglo-Saxon Law*, or his futile attempt to put a coterie of intellectual liberals at the head of an independent political movement, or his effort to measure a century of American thought by obtaining articles from six authorities in as many fields for the January, 1876, issue of the *North American*, or his suggestion that his *History* would serve as the basis for future scholars in their study of the development of American nationalism. And half a century later, in another letter to Charles, he could regret, "We leave no followers, no school, no tradition." [58]

Vanity, to be sure; but again vanity relieved by the idealism of its motivation. Beyond the narrow vocational horizons of other men Adams dreamed of grandiose roles for himself. He was never just a journalist, just a reformer, just a teacher, or just a historian. He finally saw himself in the role of a modern St. Augustine or Aquinas. To William James he confessed, in deprecating the *Education*, that "St. Augustine alone has an idea of literary form,—a notion of writing a story with an end and an object, not for the sake of the object, but for the form." [59] He

57. Nov. 21, 1862; *Cycle, 1,* 196.
58. Nov. 10, 1911; Ford, *2,* 576. For a discussion of the centennial issue of the *North American* see Samuels, pp. 275–278.
59. Feb. 17, 1908; Ford, *2,* 490. In the so-called Editor's Preface to the *Education,* actually written by Adams, he admitted that his "great ambition was to complete St. Augustine's 'Confessions' "; in the Preface he emphasized Rousseau, but not necessarily as his preeminent model. See Cater, p. 615, where he called St. Augustine his "literary model" and p. 623, where he mentioned both St. Augustine and Rousseau; also p. 619, on the problem of "form" in the *Education.*

went on to add that he considered the last chapter of his *Chartres* —the one which had summarized the society of the Middle Ages with the Thomist *Summa*—as "the only thing I ever wrote that I almost think good." Like these saints he would be, as he once mockingly said of himself, "a teacher of teachers." [60] He would undertake to explore the central energies of his society in search of unity, and by his search to chart the way for other scholars.

He carried out his program as fully as possible. When he lost sight of the "object" he continued for the sake of the "form," for his interest lay in "connecting the phenomena." [61] He went as far as reason would take him. Faith, instinct, will, intuition—call it what one would—had carried man much further. But the modern man, like Adams, could not intuit his truths. He must painfully reason his way through scientific data, until he stood at last with the aristocracy of science in a mathematical heaven devoid of significance for humanity. Reason could go no further; nor could Adams, as a reasoning man, who proved the superiority of intuition only by reasoning his conclusion. Having done what he could, he flung his challenge to teachers. Would they take up the quest? Could they do better? If not, then society, or at least everything worth while in society, was lost.

Salvation, however slender its chance, lay in such a program as he had mapped, for it might just happen that there was some way to avoid the debacle. Recall the definition in his most autobiographical work: "education should try to . . . train minds to react, not at haphazard, but *by choice*, on the lines of force that attract their world." [62] By choice—a possible element of free will amidst determinism, a barely possible source of elevation amidst degradation. New England had always kept faith with the teacher.

There was some hope; for, after all, the *Tendency*, the *Rule*, and the *Letter* are challenges, not assertions of fact. Hope seemed dim because the situation was desperate, possibly too desperate for any university to mend. At least teachers in the twentieth century could expect little assistance from an erstwhile Comtist who ended his writing career by turning Comte upside down. Comte had measured progress in terms of thought, while Adams attacked

60. Aug. 6, 1910; Ford, *2*, 546.
61. Feb. 16, 1912; *ibid.*, p. 581.
62. See above, p. 72.

thought as the degradation of instinct. For Comte sociology would predominate over the sciences in the positivistic phase of society, while Adams demonstrated that science had triumphed over man. For Comte mathematics provided the rudiments for all other branches of knowledge, while Adams bewailed mathematics as the phase of ultimate complexity. For Comte the direction and rate of progress in society were beneficent, while Adams found the opposite tendency true. For Comte thought was an activating element in society promising man's steady conquest over the chaotic environment in which he lived, while Adams found instinct the active energy, thought an index of entropy. Not that he sat down to his historical speculations with the avowed purpose of refuting Comte point by point; but the Comtian premises of youth, with all they implied for Adams' life, inevitably comprised the core around which he wound the argument of his valetudinarian speculation. "I don't know," he said of his *Letter*, "that I should see the joke myself if I were not its author. I have to take so much trouble to keep it from being bitter that it has all its nails cut off and can't scratch." [63]

So Adams planned his universe of a scale to match those of St. Augustine or St. Thomas. He meant his universe to serve at once as a critique of conventional history, a guide for university instruction, an appraisal of modern society, a chart of the cosmos, a revelation of self—and all these aims he intended to fuse into an aesthetic unity. Of course his omnibus enterprise failed. James dismissed the result as mere wit and erudition, while others saw even less to commend. But the failure of the teacher was part of the lesson. If Adams' synthesis was mere satire of those by St. Augustine and St. Thomas, then whose fault was that?

63. Jan. 24, 1910; Ford, *2*, 531.

F AILURE is the paradoxical unity in Adams' thought. Imagine his thought without the unifying theme. Loose ends would appear everywhere. How easy to count up the loose ends and conclude that Adams did indeed fail. But by admitting his failure—more precisely by his *method* of admitting it—Adams forestalled this easy conclusion. He failed in his logic; but the logic was mere illustration for a larger pattern. His pattern was faulty; but the pattern allegorized his society. His social views were exceedingly narrow; but his picture of the contemporary world provided a background for self-portraiture. To complete the circle, his autobiography was actually that of modern man whose traditions in knowledge and society had both lost significance. His failure defied precise measurement. It was as though Adams were at one end of an elastic yardstick, stretching or bending the stick whenever measurement threatened. Make any number of measurements; others always remained, each qualifying all. It was in this process of stretching and bending that the unity occurred. Indeed, the lack of fixed points for measurement intensified the sense of multiplicity which was the real measure of failure.

If, however, Adams manipulated the pliable measure of failure in terms of himself, he was always just outside the area measured, while in eluding measurement he asserted his sense of superiority over his measurer. He was the oracle speaking in enigmas; and lest his reader take as fact what he intended as enigma, Adams reinforced the riddle by interlarding his personal account of decline and fall with reminders of his accomplishments. Although he failed as a teacher, the erstwhile professor did not forget to add that President Eliot had commended him; while (in the event that his reader had not come across the volume) John Fiske "went so far in his notice of the family in 'Appleton's Cyclopedia,' as to say that Henry had left a great reputation at Harvard College . . ." As for the *History* which he pretended to disparage, "The 'Life' of Lincoln [by Nicolay and Hay] had been . . . published hand in hand with the 'History' of Jefferson and Madison, so that between them they had written nearly all the American history there was to write. The intermediate period needed intermediate treatment . . ." By implication, less distinguished scholars could chronicle the intermediate period scorned by Adams and his friends. If he were ignorant, he considered himself only as ignorant as the "best-informed statesman." [1] If he were a failure, Adams managed to imply that no one had enjoyed more success. By thus condemning as failure what to most would have seemed success,[2] he chided his society for its standards, while crediting himself not only for his achievement but also for his perception in seeing its limitations. Moreover, the limitations to his success were those of his society rather than himself. So his failure served not only to give form to whatever was formless in his thought, his artistry, his world, and his life; it also served as the device to redeem his wounded vanity. In short, he made his failure heroic.[3]

In the preface to the *Education* he referred to himself as a manikin. If manikins can be heroes, then perhaps he was a heroic manikin in a society which delimited the grandeur of failure quite as rigidly as the magnificence of success. Perhaps recalling Carlyle's *Sartor resartus*,[4] he would make of himself a manikin on which the clothes of twentieth-century education could be draped to ascertain their "fit or misfit," the "object of study" being "the garment, not the figure."

The reader of the *Education* is not supposed to gape at the naked manikin. Autobiography is a more self-conscious medium than the psychiatrist's case study or the genuinely personal diary. The manikin was only a "geometrical figure," a "measure of motion, of proportion, of human condition; it must have the air of reality; must be taken for real; must be treated as though it had life. Who knows? Possibly it had!"

This tension between manikin and life, between a general type and a particular individual, is the fascination of great autobiography. It was this tension which Adams had sought in his history and realized so superbly in the *Education*. Like all superb autobiography, the *Education* conceals in the act of disclosing. It is as though Adams stands behind a plate-glass window which re-

1. *Education*, pp. 305, 325, 392, 462, and Cater, p. 470.
2. See especially Ford, *1*, 349; *Education*, p. 326.
3. Baym, pp. 224 ff.
4. Which he recalled more specifically in chap. xxvii.

flects the surrounding panorama. His presence gives a peculiar
significance to the mirrored landscape; but strain to get a closer
view, and the landscape intervenes. Thus Adams hid behind his
time and class. It is important to realize the scenery behind which
he chose to hide—to see the clothes and not the manikin. But it
is equally important to remember that the manikin had life and
that the landscape took its significance from the figure moving
in the background.

What was the nature of this twentieth-century professor whose
field, like Carlyle's Teufelsdröckh, was Things in General? He
was intensely vain; so much is certain and part of his family heritage. Self-righteous; again even the casual student of American
history will recognize this quality as traditional to the family.
The Adamses were rather sourly right; the world was wrong. And
the Adamses belonged to the elect who knew the magnitude of
error in the world. Ambition, intellect, morality, and idealism—
these attributes too. Taken together they might easily have led to
failure in the America of the nineteenth century. But there was
another quality, rather more personal to Henry Adams than to
his famous forebears, which went far toward insuring the failure
which the other qualities merely suggested. This was his uncertainty, his tendency toward vacillation. While in the legation the
young secretary faced himself more honestly perhaps than at any
time in later life. To Charles he confessed,

> The more I see, the more I am convinced that [to] a man
> whose mind is balanced like mine, in such a way that what is
> evil never seems unmixed with good, and what is good always
> streaked with evil, an object seems never important enough to
> call out strong energies till they are exhausted, nor necessary
> enough not to allow of its failure being possible to retrieve;
> in short, a mind which is not strongly positive and absolute,
> cannot be steadily successful in action, which requires quiet-
> ness and perseverance.[5]

If good was always streaked with evil, it was hardly surprising
that a mind not strongly positive and absolute should perpetually
lose sight of achievement in every line of endeavor by too readily
glimpsing its limitations. To Oliver Wendell Holmes, who had
completed a biography of Emerson in 1885, Adams observed,
"After studying the scope of any mind, I want as well to study

5. Nov. 21, 1862; Cycle, 1, 195.

its limitations. The limitations of [men's] minds would tell me
more than their extensions, so far as relative values are concerned." [6] Biographies, Adams believed, must "belittle the victim
and the assassin equally." [7] Crowing loudly (with perhaps just a
touch of envy) over John Hay's fate at the hands of an eventual
biographer, Adams wrote, "You cannot escape the biographer.
When I read,—standing behind the curtain—these representations of life, flabby and foolish as I am;—when I try to glug-glug
down my snuffling mucous membrane these lumps of cold calves'-
head and boiled pork-fat, then I know what you will suffer for your
sins, and I see President Quiensabe of Columbia avenged." [8] The
History appraised the limits to which localistic opposition could
go in its vain attempt to subvert an inevitable nationalism; while
the limitations of American character, appearing in both the
prologue and the epilogue, recurred within the Education.[9] In this
latter work he set for himself the task of exploring the limits of
thought. Small wonder that in the Education he should invert the
success story traditional for most autobiography.

So much the Education tells, not directly perhaps but hardly
very covertly, about the man. On the other hand, Adams' emotional
nature appears very fleetingly in his autobiographical work. After
all, it could not intrude lest the manikin detract from the clothes.
Where Adams was not himself under scrutiny, or his subject not
intellectualistic, he could disclose his emotional side, if not freely
at least unmistakably, as in Esther and Chartres. Both books, he
told correspondents at different times, meant more to him than
any of his other works.[10] But the Education does give glimpses of
Adams' emotionalism. Consider the agonized passage on the premature death of his oldest sister, Louisa. Or the "overpowering
beauty and sweetness of the Maryland autumn, almost unendur-
able" in the intensity of its colors.[11] Or the silence in the middle
of the volume, the chapter on Harvard teaching followed by
"Twenty Years After." No one can know, or perhaps has any
right to know, how much the interval meant to Adams or how
much he blamed himself for his inability to prevent his wife's suicide. Even his personal letters cautiously skirted topics charged

6. Jan. 4, 1885; Cater, pp. 134 f.
7. Mar. 5, 1900; Ford, 2, 271.
8. Nov. 22, 1903; ibid., p. 416.
9. Pp. 297 f., 319.
10. On Esther see below, p. 278. On Chartres: Ford, 2, 542, 594; Cater, p. 611.
11. Education, pp. 287 ff. (for his tribute to Louisa see also p. 35), 255.

with emotion, although very occasionally the emotion seems about to melt the caution, as when in 1898 Adams returned to the Nile where he and Mrs. Adams had passed part of their wedding trip. "Indeed, the sudden return to the boat came near knocking me quite off my perch," he wrote Elizabeth Cameron, who had known Mrs. Adams and to whom Adams seems to have addressed his most intimate letters in later life.

I knew it would be a risky thing, but it came so suddenly that before I could catch myself, I was unconsciously wringing my hands and the tears rolled down in the old way, and I had to get off by myself for a few minutes to prevent Helen [Hay's daughter], who was with me, from thinking me more mad than usual. She could hardly know what it meant, in any case, and it would not have been worth while to tell her. A few hours wore off the nervous effect, and now I can stand anything, although of course there is hardly a moment when some memory of twenty-five years ago is not brought to my mind. The Nile does not change.[12]

Or again, to Mrs. Cameron in 1916, on the death of Henry James,

Harry's death hits me harder than any stroke since my brother Charles' death a year ago. Not only was he a friend of mine for more than forty years, but he also belonged to the circle of my wife's set long before I knew him or her, and you know how I have clung to all that belonged to my wife. I have been living all day in the seventies. Swallow, sister! sweet sister swallow! indeed and indeed, we really were happy then.[13]

Sweet sister swallow: his farewell to the Theodore Roosevelts on their leaving the White House can stand almost as a symbol. In Owen Wister's words, who had heard of the farewell from Mrs. Roosevelt, he "spoke to them simply." Merely, " 'I shall miss you very much.' " Adams shook hands and went away; but Mrs. Roosevelt never forgot the "sound of his voice in those six words." [14]

Perhaps this need to express emotions which neither shyness nor vanity would permit accounted for his fondness for children. With them the childless "uncle" could lavish his penchant for

12. Feb. 3, 1898; Ford, 2, 149. Hume, pp. 153 f., has commented on the quality of Adams' letters to Mrs. Cameron.

13. Mar. 1, 1916; Ford, 2, 638.

14. Owen Wister, *Roosevelt: The Story of a Friendship* (New York, Macmillan, 1930), p. 149.

fanciful exaggeration and simultaneously exhibit a degree of affection otherwise impossible. Aloof and seemingly disinclined to
encourage new friendships—such was Mrs. Winthrop Chanler's
recollection of her impression of Adams on first meeting him in
Rome; but within a short time he began "rather shyly making
friends with Laura," the Chanlers' eleven-year-old daughter. With
her he would josh about his shortness, a sensitive subject, pretend-
ing that he was her "little boy" and shrinking steadily. He possessed a rare facility for fitting himself into a child's world. It
was at Laura's invitation that he first came to the Chanler home
for lunch.[15]

Certainly his sensitive nature, however fleetingly it appeared
in the *Education*, also played a substantial role in Adams' failure.
There was, then, the family background of success that weighed
on the representative of the fourth generation. There was the smug-
ness, the scrupulosity, the intellectuality, and the introspective
turn of mind setting Henry Adams apart from an age dominated
by more ruthless personalities. There was the negativism, the in-
decisiveness which turned thought round and round on itself. There
was the emotional and aesthetic nature in growing conflict with
his intellectuality as life advanced. There was the vanity of heritage and abilities which either forced Adams in directions unsuit-
able for his talents or destroyed the sense of suitability by demanding more of every situation than the situation normally offered.
Juxtapose this personality against Adams' belief that education
should teach men to act "by choice, on the lines of force that attract
their world." Failure was inevitable.

What lines of force attracted Adams' world? First, a line of
force that led toward the least probable destination for a man of
Adams' endowments: he might have sought wealth. Although he
possessed more than enough income for his needs,[16] his affluence
was modest indeed if measured against the accumulations of others,
and especially in an age of accumulation. Certainly he could not

15. Margaret (Mrs. Winthrop) Chanler, *Roman Spring* (Boston, Little,
Brown, 1934), p. 294. In the *Education* (p. 368) he alluded to his height in an
ironical manner within the well-known epitaph which he composed to commemorate
the pedantries of his *Essays in Anglo-Saxon Law:* "Here lies/ a little man [*ho-
munculus*] writer/ a doctor barbarian/ Henry Adams/ son of Adam and Eve/
who first explained/ Soc/."

16. Cater, p. xcii, has estimated that Adams' annual income was not less than
$25,000.

have followed the path which so many of the idols of his period pursued. Yet the "gilded age" left him not immune. A "pilgrimage to State Street, [to] ask for the fatted calf of his grandfather Brooks and a clerkship in the Suffolk Bank" was unthinkable, but he realized that "the material advantages" lay behind the teller's wicket. In a "banker's world" [17] he had only to accept a banking patrimony to act decisively on his environment. Like a petulant child, who, stamping from the dinner table, disavows his hunger, Henry peeped with wistful envy at the diners feasting on the fatted calf, an envy which may have rankled all the more because his chair stood empty waiting for his change of mind. Of course the mind would never change; but when he sent the first volumes of the *History* to his publisher he could not resist a lengthy and somewhat gratuitous complaint, telling just how much he could have earned had he spent the period of documentary research with more negotiable paper. In the *Education* he recalled this balance sheet: "Adams had given ten or a dozen years to Jefferson and Madison, with expenses which, in any mercantile business, could hardly have been reckoned at less than a hundred thousand dollars, on a salary of five thousand a year; and when he asked what return he got from this expenditure, rather more extravagant in proportion to his means than a racing-stable, he could see none whatever." [18]

Again and again his letters turned bitter with invective against the banker. But his was not the malice of the socialist, for although Adams repeatedly labeled himself a "Conservative Anarchist" [19] in later life, his livelihood depended on the wisdom of his broker. As a cultivated man of substance Adams could afford to scorn the stocks-and-bonds mentality that gave him substance to pursue his cultivation. Wealthy men have often found it easy to condemn materialism, and on the whole such condemnation has ranked among the most laudable uses for wealth. On this score, then, few would condemn Adams' inconsistency. Unfortunately for his own peace of mind, the virulence with which he attacked the capitalist revealed a touch of rancor at the recollection that what he had

17. *Education,* pp. 22, 247.
18. Roger Burlingame, *Of Making Many Books* (New York, Scribners, 1946), pp. 157 f. *Education,* p. 327. Mrs. Chanler, *op. cit.,* p. 296, suggests that Adams may have frequently alluded to the cost of the *History* to his friends.
19. Or occasionally "Christian Conservative Anarchist." From its use this paradoxical label seems to have meant that Adams favored mild reform in opposition to a financial oligarchy, which he identified with Jewish control.

spurned, others grabbed and converted into personal power. Following the advice of his brother Charles, he too had attempted to push his way into a world dominated by finance, not as a banker but as an authority above bankers from whom the entire country might seek advice. Of course he failed in this, one of many lines of force to attract his world.

Social prestige might also have served as a path to power. "Wealth valued social position and classical education as highly as either of these valued wealth," [20] he wrote, cognizant that he had only to develop this triple inheritance for success in his America. It would be foolish to maintain that Henry Adams could have climbed the social ladder with the singleness of purpose required for this kind of eminence, equally foolish to deny that he bristled at the ease with which a parvenu society ignored his family name. On leaving Harvard the retiring assistant professor informed an English friend that he and Mrs. Adams fancied they were "of use" in Washington, "for we distinctly occupy niches which ought to be filled." While working on his *History* he felt that he could easily double as social arbiter in national politics, since "a single house [in Washington] counts for more than half a dozen elsewhere; there are so few of them." Somewhat later, to the same Englishman, he reported the success with which he had filled his niche:

> Socially speaking, we are very near most of the powerful people, either as enemies or as friends. Among others our pet enmity is Mr. Blaine. . . . His overthrow has been a matter of deep concern to us, both politically and personally, for we have always refused him even social recognition on account of his previous scandals, and I assure you that to stand alone in a small society like this, and to cut the Secretary of State for Foreign Affairs, without doing it offensively or with ill-breeding, requires not only some courage but some skill. . . . I trust that Mr. Blaine is blown up for ever.[21]

It was the Adamses who were blown up by the Blaines—and by the Grants, whom Adams had visited shortly after he left the legation with consequences prophetic for his later social aspirations.

> Last evening I went with General Badeau to call for the first time on the President and his wife. . . . At last Mrs. Grant strolled in. She squints like an isosceles triangle, but is not

20. *Education,* p. 348.
21. Nov. 25, 1877; May 30, 1878; Jan. 29, 1882. Ford, *1,* 302, 306, 333.

much more vulgar than some Duchesses. Her sense of dignity did not allow her to talk to me, but occasionally she condescended to throw me a constrained remark. I chattered, however, with that blandness for which I am so justly distinguished, and I flatter myself it was I who showed them how they ought to behave. One feels such an irresistible desire, as you know, to tell this kind of individual to put themselves at their ease and talk just as though they were at home. I restrained it, however, and performed the part of guest, though you can imagine with what an effort.[22]

Snubbed by those whom he felt he should have snubbed, Adams nursed his irritation through literary satire, recalling, as he did, his evening at the Grants' both in *Democracy* and, twenty-seven years later, in the *Education*.

Smile at these social aspirations as we will, can we also smile at the cause which Adams meant to further? He saw his role in no frivolous sense. If he abhorred the social climber, at least his was not the narrow prejudice of those who placed ancestry above virtue and intelligence. Witness Carl Schurz and Jacob Cox—both had risen from relatively humble origins; each gained Adams' support. In the *History* he even admitted that "Burr's conspiracy, like that of Pickering and Griswold, had no deep roots in society, but was mostly confined to a circle of well-born, well-bred, and well-educated individuals, whose want of moral sense was one more proof that the moral instinct had little to do with social distinctions." [23] Hence Adams' idea of society savored rather of Jefferson's ideal of a governing *aristoi* of ability rather than of a governing aristocracy. But if Adams had succeeded as social arbiter, the selection of the aristoi must have proceeded from a group delimited by his conservatism, his family position, his cultivation, and his social fastidiousness. When after 1885 he ceased to long for an active role in politics and viewed with alarm what he considered to be the growing mediocrity of society, his isolation intensified his snobbishness.

In any event, he had not been long in Washington before he realized the naivete of his hope that social ostracism would effect reform. In 1883 he told Hay how he refused to lend the prestige of the Adams name to the Arthur administration: "I do not go

22. Dec. 13, 1860; *ibid.*, p. 176. See also *Democracy*, pp. 85 f.; *Education*, p. 320.
23. *History, 3,* 441.

to the White House because I see and hear things I don't like, but I am quite alone . . ." [24] The Adamses joined with the Hays and Clarence King to form their own little coterie. Meeting frequently for tea during the early years of the eighties, the group extended into real life the urbanity of the *History* in which Adams traced so discerningly the influence of society on diplomacy. The intimate emblem printed on their private note paper,[25] a five of hearts, could well symbolize the futility of Adams' career as social arbiter to the gilded age.

A third line of force: political office. This, too, if not the gift of his heritage, was at least its clear promise. Most critics are convinced that Henry Adams never seriously tried to follow the brilliant precedents established by three preceding generations. Temperament unsuited him for a governmental niche. His was not a positive mind. Nor was he, like Hay, a party regular.[26] Whether Adams could have disciplined his vacillating and independent mind had public office demanded both a policy and party loyalty is a question. Although his was a strategic position for political office through both antecedents and contacts, he never pursued this advantage.

Of course, he always doubted the value of the prize. Few men have realized more keenly than Adams the effect of politics on personality. Even as he studied the Washington of Jefferson's day, he attacked his own Washington in terms of the pompous amorality of Senator Ratcliffe.

[Mrs. Lee asked,] "Have you never refused to go with your party?"

"Never!" was Ratcliffe's firm reply.

Madeleine [Mrs. Lee] still more thoughtfully inquired again: "Is there nothing more powerful than party allegiance?"

24. Mar. 4, 1883; Ford, *1*, 348, 336.

25. Cater, p. xliv. See Tyler Dennett, *John Hay, from Poetry to Politics* (New York, Dodd, Mead, 1934), pp. 157-167, for the best account of the Five of Hearts. On King see David H. Dickason, "Henry Adams and Clarence King," *New England Quarterly, 17* (1944), 229-254.

26. In presidential elections Adams seems to have favored the following: Lincoln, 1864; Grant, 1868; Greeley, 1872 (only because he opposed Grant); Tilden, 1876; Garfield, 1880; Cleveland, 1884 (of whom he soon tired, after originally favoring Cleveland for his free trade platform and his opposition to Blaine); Harrison, 1888. For the elections of 1892 and 1896 Adams' vote is uncertain but probably against Cleveland and for McKinley. He favored Theodore Roosevelt, Taft, and, for a second term, Wilson.

"Nothing, except national allegiance," replied Ratcliffe, still more firmly.

The two allegiances inevitably coincided, as Ratcliffe acknowledged in attempting to mitigate Madeline's censure at his complicity in a corrupt political bargain: "I was a Senator of the United States. I was also a trusted member of a great political party which I looked upon as identical with the nation." [27]

Certainly Adams offered sincere advice when Lodge showed signs of abandoning history for politics. Although Adams had earlier urged his protégé to seek the active life in Massachusetts politics that Lodge desired,[28] he barely expressed regret when Lodge lost an election for state senator in 1881. "I suppose every man who has looked on at the game has been struck by the remarkable way in which politics deteriorate the moral tone of everyone who mixes in them. The deterioration is far more marked than in any other occupation I know except the turf, stock-jobbing, and gambling. I imagine the reason in each case to be the same. It is the curse of politics that what one man gains, another man loses." [29] Adams added that "the moment is one for you to stop and think about [your choice]." Lodge discounted the advice. Fondness for the wife, and later for the son, doubtless preserved a friendship with the husband as Cabot rose to senatorial fame.[30]

Adams never essentially altered the pessimistic view of politics shown in his advice to Lodge. Such a point of view would indicate a repugnance for office; but did it? No one knows, probably not even Adams. During the period in which he had sought an active life, his ultimate ambitions went undefined. He never clearly envisioned a political office, nor did he exclude its possibility. Having withdrawn into semiretirement after 1884, Adams had no chance for office until McKinley called John Hay to the cabinet in 1898. Then the mere thought of office titillated. "Do you blame me for wanting to keep out of the scrimmage? Do you think I ought to ask for office? I am just praying to escape before the snakes bite me." His prayers were answered. To Elizabeth Cameron he had earlier confided in a less extravagant spirit that party considerations, if no other, prevented Hay from offering. Hay had com-

27. *Democracy*, pp. 82, 356.
28. Ford, *1*, 318, 324.
29. Nov. 15, 1881; *ibid.*, p. 331. See too his later analysis of both the evils and duties of public office, *Education*, pp. 364 f.
30. *Ibid.*, pp. 353 f.

plained at his inability to create an efficient diplomatic service; for, according to Adams, the secretary of state was "not allowed to use even the instruments he has at hand—meaning Rockhill and me—and has not a single diplomatic agent who can be utilised to advantage. I believe all this to be true. You will appreciate how glad I am of it. To refuse him my help would be most disagreeable to me; but to accept office would be misery." [31] There is no reason to doubt this statement: it sounds sincere and, again, the letter went to Elizabeth Cameron. Had Hay offered, Adams would probably have reluctantly refused. But even Adams was uncertain. If the snakes had bitten him earlier in life? [32] Who knows? Much would have depended on the circumstances.

Here political office could be dismissed as a line of force in Adams' world—except that he could never quite dismiss the idea. Surely he had abandoned both expectation and desire by the time he wrote the *Education*; but he still nursed the idea. He carefully recorded Secretary Seward's unavailing proposal that his informal position as his father's clerk be converted into an official one as assistant secretary to the legation: "It was the first—and last— office ever offered him . . ." Later, while in Washington in 1868 as an aspiring journalist, he invited Seward to his apartment for a game of whist. "It was the only favor he ever asked of Mr. Seward, and the only one he ever accepted." [33] A card table stood between Adams and the man who might have bowed him into politics; a card table—and the request. The *Education* disclosed Adams' satisfaction that he had never asked. Yet how many times in life had he recalled that game of whist? During these early years he had only to ask. Delicacy doubtless forbade his embarrassing those who did not offer, and pride, too, made it inconceivable that an Adams should seek what did not come unsought. Looking back in the *Education*, he recalled the "handsomest

31. Feb. 26, 1899; Nov. 21, 1898; Ford, *2*, 220, 191. This latter letter seems the more sincere because, after confessing that office would be misery, Adams immediately added words to the effect that Hay might only have been making "pretty speeches." When Adams exaggerated, he rarely weakened the exaggeration with false modesty, unless the modesty in some way heightened the exaggeration as is not the case here. See also *ibid.,* p. 211. Dennett, *op. cit.,* p. 289, credits Adams with laying the foundation for Hay's Far Eastern policy. For a summary of Adams' relationship to Hay see Herbert Edwards, "Henry Adams: Politician and Statesman," *New England Quarterly, 22* (1949), 54–60.

32. He was offered a diplomatic post in Costa Rica in 1882 but did not accept the offer; Thoron, p. 360.

33. *Education,* pp. 145, 247.

formula" as that of "the grandly courteous Southern phrase of Lamar: 'Of course Mr. Adams knows that anything in my power is at his service.' . . . The form must have been correct since it released both parties . . . a bow and a conventional smile closed the subject forever, and every one felt flattered." [34] As a descendant of statesmen and as "stable-companion" [35] to the remnants of statesmanship in the Washington of his day, Adams could never quite reconcile his appraisal of politics with the longing that his appraisal might be different from what it was. Were public service different, he need not have spent a lifetime bemused between fascination and repugnance. It was not lack of office, then, which measured failure so much as his paralysis at the idea.

If Adams never really decided whether or not he would like to be in the government, it was because he preferred to start behind the government as a journalist, perhaps as a publisher, or even as an advisor to the reform wing of a political party. After such a start the decision on political office could come in time. But the start was over before it had fairly begun. Of Adams' failure in a fourth line of force to attract his world—that of reform journalism—there is no doubt whatsoever.

In the *Education* he accused Grant of wrecking his vision of political reform.[36] The dream more properly disappeared when the independent movement split in 1876. After this discouragement the reformer turned historian. Although he invested $20,000 in the *New York Evening Post* in 1881 and suggested to Schurz as late as 1883 that he "would gladly help to organise a free trade party," and during the election of 1884 even referred to politics as "my second interest," [37] the historian never again had the leisure (or perhaps the compelling desire) to make an effective bid as reformer before his life was "cut in halves." Suppose the youthful journalist of 1868 had been young in 1900 when the progressive era afforded a time more congenial to reform? Adams might have started behind the political scene with Theodore Roosevelt. Eventually he might even have accepted an appointive office.

As he longed for a creed, so Adams yearned for a leader. Although he himself could not fight in the market place, he would

34. *Ibid.*, p. 322.
35. See above, p. 25.
36. Pp. 262 f., 333.
37. Citations from letters dated May 20, 1883, and May 18, 1884, respectively. Ford, *1*, 351, 358. Cater, p. 114; for his interest in the editorial policy of the *New York Evening Post* see above, p. 39, n. 52.

willingly have backed such a fighter. "What we want from you now is a lead," he wrote Jacob Cox in 1870. "We will defend you personally wherever defence is needed, but you must lay down for us the great principles of our movement." [38] Without the buffer of leadership between the people and himself Adams could scarcely project his sentiments for reform beyond his own aristocratic set. They appeared for a few years among the pages of the *North American,* the *Nation,* or the *New York Evening Post,* to exercise, as Adams once fondly hoped, "a distinct influence on public opinion by acting on the limited number of cultivated minds." [39] He intended that his enlightened elite should capture the caucus; through the caucus the party; and through the party the people.

Giving serious thought to this program for reform while in Washington at the end of the sixties, he did not forget it at Harvard. The chance came in 1876. Confessing his principal reason for assisting in the organization of the Independents, Adams wrote Schurz, "To attack the caucus system is . . . the end and aim of all my political desires." Adams would attack the caucus without troubling to expend the time and energy required in a political apprenticeship in minor offices; he would start at the top. A junto of Independent intellectuals would force their choice on the Republican convention by threatening a third party candidate. This strategy was certainly inconclusive as reform. Although a junto of liberal intellectuals, who planned to exclude "the most dangerous elements" from their midst, might have had a salutary effect on the Republican party for a brief period, such a nucleus was perilously close to the abhorred caucus. For the steam roller of the machine politicians Adams would have substituted the gentleman's agreement.[40] Even so, a change of leadership would give reform at least temporary impetus. But before any enlightened minority could obtain the power necessary for reform, it must back a leader who boasted not only integrity but popular support as well. Potential leaders with these qualifications refused the risk of antagonizing the established organization; nor could a respectable literary and intellectual quarterly afford to alienate

38. Nov. 11, 1870; Cater, pp. 47, 45.

39. May 17, 1869; Ford, *1,* 159; *ibid., 2,* 459.

40. Feb. 14, 1876; *ibid., 1,* 274 f. Edwards, *op. cit.,* pp. 51–54, emphasizes Adams' attempt to start at the top and perhaps rather overemphasizes Adams' fitness for office. See *Gallatin,* pp. 214 f., for Adams' ideal for the relationship between the statesman and his party.

its subscribers because of the crusading ardor of its editor. As it happened, Adams' resignation from the editorship of the *North American* in 1876 terminated his thwarted career in active reform and serious journalism.

In retrospect it is clear that Adams' concept of reform depended too much on eighteenth-century ideals of stewardship and their confirmation in such nineteenth-century writers as Comte, Mill, Tocqueville. He placed too high a value on personal character, too little on a public platform. As a liberal Republican, he stood first and foremost opposed to political corruption. In their brave denunciations of Grantism and Gouldism the youthful reformers of Adams' sort doubtless saw their radicalism as greater than it was. "They risked something," he noted in the *Education*,[41] recalling how he and Charles had exposed Jay Gould's gold conspiracy in the *Westminster Review*. The risk of libel,[42] of social ostracism, even perhaps of personal injury, is obvious; the courage of the brothers evident. But equally evident from the safe distance of the intervening years are the limitations of their crusade.

Of Henry Adams' entire platform only the plank opposing corruption could possibly have fired the popular imagination. Even when excited by the disclosure of political corruption, the people have all too often regarded the exposé more as a source of diversion than as a cause for indignation. In the energy expended in assailing political rascality it was easy for Adams to forget these limitations to his cause. Above all, he lost sight of its essentially negative character. Clean government is, after all, merely the condition in which more fundamental reforms can best occur, while even corrupt administrations have favored essential reforms where these were to their interest. It was the positive side of Adams' platform which showed the tragic blindness of his class. Once cleansed, what would the federal government do? Adams recommended the resumption of specie payments, civil service, reconciliation with the South, and lower tariffs—in short, the conventional measures recommended by the liberal conservatives of his day, and hardly such as would compel popular enthusiasm. Since business interests favored specie payments, the Grant administration readily obliged. Civil service made some progress during the Hayes administration, when at least the principle was accepted. The same administration saw the last of the Union troops

41. P. 270.
42. Samuels, pp. 197, 199.

recalled from the South, largely because northern investors willingly returned the South to local control in order to obtain the social stability needed for their capital. Finally, the Cleveland administration provided an interval of lowered tariffs. Obviously these measures scarcely remedied the problems faced by Adams' America.

If the decades following the Civil War seem singularly barren of creative political theory, it is because the idealistic intellectuals of the period thought in terms too narrowly political, diplomatic, financial, military, and moralistic, precisely as Adams had done in his *History*. Like them, he sensed the people only vaguely and left largely unexplained what he could not know. Where the impulse toward nationalism had eventually forced the people to take up arms in 1812, so Adams hoped that the "independent intelligence" [43] of the people would eliminate the rascality in the politics of the Grant administration. Although inarticulate in formulating political goals, the people were ultimately right; but they depended on leadership to provide a clear direction. Both as reformer and historian Adams made this premise the basis for his faith in democracy. As a historian he had observed the failure of Jefferson's statesmanship to utilize the "silent pulsations" of American nationalism to guide the United States with a minimum of friction and a maximum of benefit along the necessary path of the future. How ironic that Jefferson's historian, in his earlier career as a political reformer, should be open to the charge that he too failed to tap the silent pulsations driving his America toward its twentieth-century destiny.

Adams viewed the prophetic reform of the post-Civil War period with all the alarm of his class. The fastidious Brahmin deplored the evidences of the crowd which he saw in the late nineteenth century quite as much as he abhorred the capitalist. Both phenomena showed degradation of energy. Of *Das Kapital* he wrote that he had "never struck a book which taught me so much, and with which I disagreed so radically in conclusion." [44] Here in Marx was Adams' youthful faith that the destiny of the people was the destiny of history, but without the restraining hand of benevolent leadership. It was as though history had conspired to move in the general direction which Adams had foreseen, although it had in the process squeezed him from the eminent role which

43. *NAR, 123* (1876), 467.
44. June 18, 1894; Ford, *2*, 49.

he and his class were to play in the measured but steady progression. Where the youth had fancied himself in the vanguard of reform, events had before the turn of the century pushed him to the rear. Disliking the banker and fearing the worker, he revealed his dilemma during the silver election of 1896.

Since he had once viewed the tension of the secession winter as a constitutional crisis, it was not surprising that he missed the human drama behind the booming chant for Bryan. Adams saw the contest as two impersonal energies epitomized by the vast abstractions gold and silver. "As a man of sense," he wrote his brother Brooks, "I am a gold-bug and support a gold-bug government and a gold-bug society. As a man of the world, I like confusion, anarchy and war." Toying with this dilemma for a while, he finally decided that, "As free-silver, in my eyes, means fun . . . j'y suis!" [45] He complicated his fun a little later, telling another correspondent, "Although I—very doubtfully—hold that on the whole the election of McKinley will do more mischief than that of Bryan, and, as a conservative anarchist, am therefore inclined to hope for McKinley's success, while I help Bryan all I can, certainly I cannot make so very complicated a program intelligible to any party." [46] In like manner he embroidered his dilemma through a number of letters, until the dilemma was lost in the interlace of extravagant wit and feigned alarm. Some time after the election was over he returned in a more candid spirit to his uncertainty and in the *Education* confessed,

> Of all forms of society or government, [capitalism] was the one he liked least, but his likes or dislikes were as antiquated as the rebel doctrine of State rights. A capitalistic system had been adopted, and if it were to be run at all, it must be run by capital and by capitalistic methods; for nothing could surpass the nonsensity of trying to run so complex and so concentrated a machine by Southern and Western farmers in grotesque alliance with city day-laborers, as had been tried in 1800 and 1828, and had failed even under simple conditions. [47]

He was opposed to "ineffectual politics" [48]—customary indication of conservatism and a sign that domestic politics had by the nineties essentially passed beyond Adams' comprehension. Again,

45. June 5, 1895; *ibid.*, p. 69.
46. July 27, 1896; *ibid.*, p. 109.
47. *Education*, p. 344.
48. *Ibid.*

paralysis. He was left to his Janus-faced game of "conservative anarchist."

If he could not effect reform, he could pretend to laugh at the goal that had once meant so much. But the laughter choked. "When I think of the formulas of our youth,—when I look at my old set of John Stuart Mill,—and suddenly recall that I am actually a member of the Cobden Club,—I feel that somewhere there is the biggest kind of joke, if I could only see it." [49] Thus in 1894 he recorded his disillusionment. The final volumes of the *History* had come from the press barely three years before. He had completed this work, which owed much to the inspiration of Mill, Tocqueville, and Cobden, even as their inspiration faded. Through its pages glowed the Indian summer of his youthful conviction that in a democracy mankind might reach a happy limit to its possibilities, while he himself might play some significant role in the trend toward this goal. To the end, the idealism of his youthful hopes penetrated the pessimism of later life and, when he was most sincere, left wry bitterness in its wake. The "biggest liar" was the reformer, for he lied "double: to himself and to the public." [50] For all his extravagant denunciations, the old ideals meant too much to permit him to lapse into the cynicism which he frequently affected.

From the first Adams should have followed the course he finally took. He should have ignored reform to hitch his talents to the star of scholarship and literature. As it happened, he came to history as a last recourse, and even then refused to relinquish the idea of active life. Later, after he had resigned himself to the passive role of spectator, even then he could never quite repress his disappointment that no one had sought his performance.

These failures of early life comprised a small part of the larger failure celebrated in old age; but without them perhaps Adams would never have thought of his theme. Failure in active life blended insensibly with the alleged failure in the passive life which began with the teaching at Harvard.

In the sense of social or professional prestige Adams did succeed as a historian. Disappointed as he must have been by the lack of any review of his long labor possessing either the scope or seriousness of his article on Lyell,[51] he knew that society awaited

49. Sept. 27, 1894; Ford, *2*, pp. 55 f., 377, 417; also *Education*, p. 324.
50. Feb. 1, 1903; Ford, *2*, 395.
51. Samuels, pp. 304 ff.

only his permission to accord him emoluments which would spell success beyond the wildest dreams of most gelehrte. But then, he was no ordinary gelehrt. Despite his sojourn at Harvard, he remained the gentleman scholar.[52] Writing his account of the Jefferson and Madison administrations at a time when historians in the United States had begun to set themselves apart from society as a self-conscious guild, Adams belongs among an impressive roster of nineteenth-century Americans—Prescott, Motley, Bancroft, Parkman—who considered history as more than a profession for teaching boys or for training more historians. To them history was a branch of literature. From such history one expected more than honorary degrees and much more than a boost in the academic hierarchy. Such history warranted the prestige accorded to literary men, prestige sufficient to "dazzle and set the world on fire hereafter."

Adams' *History* brought no such fame. Even today the world continues to ignore his nine volumes. He is the historian's historian. Perhaps no history that so successfully buried its grand theme beneath equivocality could have proved a popular success; certainly none that used so rigorously the scientific approach on matter so complex. Like all historians Adams necessarily worked a middle ground between the arts and sciences. Unlike most he was acutely conscious of the tension. The artist can encompass power within a personal expression; the scientist within a general formula. History, to borrow from Adams' vocabulary, must forever dissipate its intensity between personal and impersonal power. In his *History* Adams delineated situations "touch by touch," until their subtle intricacies rivaled those of Henry James. Yet Adams had no real command of the characters he created, since the science of the documents rigidly controlled his hand. The historian might contrive a chronological sequence; he could never, Adams believed, achieve what James and any other novelist could attain, a sequence in which personality and environment interacted purposefully. His Jefferson and Madison seemed mere "grasshoppers . . . kicking and gesticulating" to little purpose in the middle of the Mississippi. Or as he wrote a friend on September 9, 1888, "I can hardly believe my own ears when I say that tomorrow my narrative will be finished; all my wicked villains will be duly rewarded with Presidencies and the plunder of the

52. To the extent of, first, writing letters in faculty meetings and, finally, cutting them altogether; Samuels, p. 213.

innocent; all my models of usefulness and intelligence will be fitly punished, and deprived of office and honors . . ." [53] Even as he wrote the *History* Adams easily convinced himself of its pointlessness.

It seemed even more pointless by the time he wrote his *Education*. The "severest process of stating, with the least possible comment, such facts as seemed sure, in such order as seemed rigorously consequent," simply did not "fix for a familiar moment a necessary sequence of human movement." [54] A necessary sequence: this was the novelist's necessity. Adams believed that the historian could not attain it.

A necessary sequence was even more essential to the natural scientist. Adams told in the *Education* how he had tried a series of sequences. "Satisfied that the sequence of men led to nothing and that the sequence of their society could lead no further, while the mere sequence of time was artificial, and the sequence of thought was chaos, he turned at last to the sequence of force . . ." [55] Of course he had never tried any such experiment, and had he tried, he could never have analyzed this gamut of sequences sequentially. None of these series could be separated from the others as Adams jokingly pretended in the pseudoscientific language of the *Education*. All had appeared intermingled in the *History*. His statement in the *Education* merely indicated the range through which the pendulum of history swung, from personality on one side to impersonal force on the other. As he admired the novelist's ability to make personality purposeful, so he yearned for the scientist's competence to make force equally meaningful. Adams was fascinated by the work of those geologists who began in the late sixties, under King's supervision, to survey the mineral resources in western United States by analyzing a strip of territory centering on the fortieth parallel. "They held under their hammers a thousand miles of mineral country with all its riddles to solve, and its stores of possible wealth to mark. They felt the future in their hands." [56] With a bushel basket of pebbles the geologist might go far in forecasting the power potential of a nation. With many bushels of documents, could the historian demonstrate as certainly the power of its statesmen, the

53. Ford, *1*, 391. *History, 9*, 141 f.
54. See above, p. 13. In the *Education*, p. 363, Adams complained that history showed no "proof of sequence and intelligence in the affairs of man."
55. *Education*, p. 382.
56. *Ibid.*, p. 309.

energy potential of its people, or the impact of any given event
on national destiny? The capacity of science to generalize from
tiny samples never ceased to interest Adams. At the same time
his aesthetic conscience persistently asked whether history could
ever be scientific, in positivistic terms, if Jefferson's personality
"belonged to the controlling influences of American history, more
necessary to the story than three fourths of the official papers,
which only hid the truth." [57]

This inner battle between his aesthetic and his scientific predilections can be traced throughout Adams' life. It is most evident
on the aesthetic side, the almost feminine side of his nature. While
in the midst of his *History*, Adams made his brief excursion into
fiction with *Democracy* and *Esther*. Both novels, as Robert E.
Spiller has pointed out,[58] treat the same basic theme. Both depict
a woman's quest for truth, which in each case is embodied in the
man she loves. Madeleine Lee seeks the truth of democracy in the
person of Senator Ratcliffe; Esther Dudley pursues the truth
of religion as exemplified by the Reverend Mr. Hazard. Both
heroines are ultimately disenchanted. After Madeleine learns of
Ratcliffe's dishonesty she indignantly dismisses the senator's suit
and flees to the Nile [59] to forget the unhappy love affair. *Esther*
is a subtler novel. Here no external situation but her gradual discomfiture at the sham of fashionable religion compels Esther to
leave her clerical fiancé.

These fictional quests for faith parallel in their succession
Adams' own search for belief, first in democracy, then increasingly
in some more personal creed. For the study of his historical mind,
a more interesting aspect of the two novels was Adams' choice of
women to represent the power of intuition. The power of woman
in society had always fascinated him, until the inertia of woman
joined with that of a people to serve Adams as the massive enigma
of history. While on the Harvard faculty he lectured at the
Lowell Institute on the status of woman in various primitive
societies and concluded that woman's function as the creative
energy behind the family had accorded her a degree of prestige
and power in some tribal cultures unrivaled in later and more

57. See above, p. 70.
58. Introduction, *Esther: A Novel* (New York, Scholars' Facsimiles and Reprints, 1938), pp. v–ix.
59. Where Adams went on his wedding trip and where he returned nostalgically
in 1898; see especially Ford, *2*, 149.

complex societies.[60] In the South Sea Islands almost two decades later he met Marau, an old Polynesian chieftess, who recounted the history of her island to the traveler. Returning home Adams wrote and printed a private edition of this account as the *Memoirs of Marau Taaroa, Last Queen of Tahiti*. Unlike American history, which "mentioned hardly the name of a woman," [61] the Tahitian past showed heroines as well as heroes. Yet no Polynesian matriarch, however powerful, had boasted more than temporary fame, which faded even as the last queen told her story. For such a monument as Chartres mankind required the Queen of queens. Unity, intuition, art, woman, Madeleine, Esther, the Virgin, and Mrs. Adams: these formed one pole.[62] The other: multiplicity, logic, science, man, Ratcliffe, Hazard, and finally Henry Adams. Between the poles—the graph of degradation.

After 1885 Adams' world became increasingly feminine. His longest and most intimate letters went usually to feminine correspondents. Constantly surrounded by a bevy of nieces, he complained (but not too strongly) in 1897, "here I am, with an army of nieces . . . but never a man . . ." He admitted occasional visits from two male acquaintances; yet they hardly offset at least six women who vacationed with him at a French chateau he had rented for the summer. Two years later in Washington he confessed to seeing several "old men," but although he had "runners everywhere . . . with orders to seize and bring in every likely young man they hear of," the unsuccessful search left him only "nieces without limit." In 1904 he wrote, "Women are plenty but men very scarce and mostly bores." Four years later he sighed to

60. Published in a revised version in 1891, when Adams included it in his "Primitive Rights of Women," *Historical Essays* (New York, Scribners, 1891), pp. 1–41.

61. *Education*, p. 441. Adams mentioned the ingenuity of Yankee women in the *History, 5*, 18 f., and discussed something of the influence of women on diplomatic society. He observed the "feminine" characteristics of Jefferson, *ibid., 1*, 144, 323 f., and of Randolph, *ibid., 5*, 362. It is significant too that the only member of the Adams family on whom Henry Adams ever seems to have contemplated biographical work was Abigail Adams; see above, p. 65. On Dolly Madison, to whom many historians would have given extensive treatment in a study of the Madison administration, the *History* shows but three mentions—surprisingly brief notice, even within the rigorous narrative which Adams set for himself. *Memoirs of Marau Taaroa, Last Queen of Tahiti;* reprinted, with short title, Robert E. Spiller, ed., *Tahiti* (Scholars' Facsimiles and Reprints, 1947). On the women in Adams' life and on woman as symbol, see Bibliography, Sec. A.

62. For Adams' aesthetic inclination and his use of "intuition" see appropriate items in Bibliography, Secs. A and B. Hume, p. 129, refers to Mrs. Adams, Arii Taimai, and the Virgin as a trinity in Adams' life.

a feminine correspondent, "You bring me charming women in plenty, but when I ask them for men, they look blank . . . they don't know what a man is." [63] According to its preface *Chartres* was intended for nieces rather than nephews, perhaps to show women the power they might possess if, like their predecessors in both primitive society and Christianity, they only chose to use it.[64] "If I were beginning again as a writer," he wrote in 1903, "I think I should drop the man, except as an accessory, and study the woman of the future . . . Contrasts of feminine types are possible. I am not absolutely sure that there is more than one American man." With his conclusion that "The American woman . . . is all that is left to art," [65] it was not surprising that when in 1891 he had dismissed the *History* as belonging to the "*me* of 1870," he added, "I care more for one chapter, or any dozen pages of *Esther* than for the whole history, including maps and indexes; so much more, indeed, that I would not let anyone read the story for fear the reader should profane it." Of his most feminine novel he confessed to Hay, "I will not pretend that the book is not precious to me, but its value has nothing to do with the public who could never understand that such a book might be written in one's heart's blood." [66]

It was as inevitable that the nieces should have flocked about the lonely uncle as that he should have needed and encouraged their affection. Women, moreover, proved both appreciative and available companions for such time-consuming luxuries as vacations at chateaux or pilgrimages to cathedrals. Their husbands (Senators Lodge and Cameron, for example) occasionally traveled with Adams and his predominantly feminine entourage, but definitely as accessories. His later life showed a greater number of artists and literary men among his close acquaintances than there had been prior to 1885. Among the young men there were John Trumbull Stickney and Bay Lodge; [67] among the old, Augustus St. Gaudens and especially John La Farge. The new companions represented Adams' increasing interest in the arts in later life;

63. Aug. 8, 1897 (he mentioned "five girls and Martha Cameron" and seems not to have included Mrs. Cameron in the "five girls"); Jan. 19, 1899 (except for an occasional young man from the British Embassy); Apr. 27, 1904; Sept. 4, 1908. Cater, pp. 418 f.; Ford, *2*, 205, 433, 506.

64. *Education*, especially pp. 384 f., 441–448. *Degradation*, pp. 2–5.

65. Apr. 27, 1903; Cater, pp. 544, 545.

66. Feb. 23, 1891; Aug. 23, 1886; Ford, *1*, 468, 377.

67. For their close relationship in Paris see *Education*, pp. 403, 405. On Bay's death, Cater, pp. 661–664.

moreover, like women, poets and artists were freer than most men to travel, and free in their appreciation of beauty encountered on the way. No wonder that the "artist stood best" in the *Education,* while the statesman, the general, the businessman, and even the scientist failed in Adams' America.[68]

In this aesthetic ambient Adams paid his wistful homage to the Virgin. Together with the poems "Prayer to the Virgin at Chartres" and "Buddha and Brahma," *Mont-Saint-Michel and Chartres* furnishes the supreme testimony to the intensity of Adams' emotional and aesthetic nature. More strikingly than any other of his works this volume bares his inner conflict between art and science. In contrast to the *History, Chartres* was poetry lifted from the documents. To his vastly expanded bevy of nieces the guide affirmed, "we have taken to feel, if not to understand!" To feel, however, Adams needed to understand. "With the irritating demand for literal exactness . . . which lights up every truly American eye, you will certainly ask when [the] exaltation of Mary began, and unless you get the dates, you will doubt the facts. It is your own fault if they are tiresome; you might easily read them all in the 'Iconographie de la Sainte Vierge,' by M. Rohault de Fleury, published in 1878." [69] Doubtless most nieces would find Fleury tedious. It was their guide who wished such data, even as he protested that knowledge threatened emotional intensity.

Adams approached the cathedral with little of the analytical and critical spirit of the historian of art. On sculpture he left the aesthetic problem of form development unmentioned, to concentrate on the predominantly literary question of iconography, where he constantly quoted from authorities.[70] For most of his aesthetic judgments on architecture and glass he relied on the authority of others, particularly the "sacred sources of M. Viollet-Le-Duc." Despite his strictures against the "scientific taste" of art historians, Adams tended to accept their verdicts. His most original work centered in the literary sources of the Middle Ages.

68. *Education,* pp. 326, 341, 346 ff.

69. *Chartres,* pp. 71, 91.

70. In the *Education,* p. 354, Adams specifically saw the French cathedrals as the antithesis of the "German" training of his youth, and when the Lodges, with whom he was traveling in 1901, visited Berlin (p. 410) Adams' "memories" of the city were so unpleasant that he parted company. Note also that in writing of the memorial to his wife Adams asserted (p. 387), that "One sees what one brings," but what one saw was clearly some "meaning" in a literary sense, even if a personal and therefore enigmatic meaning (p. 329). Adams did not discuss the purely formalistic aspects of art.

In the field of art history *Chartres* remained a pastiche of authorities and guidebooks, molded with a tourist's love into what the late nineteenth century was fond of calling an appreciation. Even as he cited his sources Adams continually reminded his nieces that they need not believe the presumptions of authority. "M. Huysmans insists that his sculpture is poor in comparison with his twelfth-century Prodigal Daughter, and I hope you can enter into the spirit of his enthusiasm; but other people prefer the thirteenth-century work, and think it equals the best Greek. Approaching, or surpassing this,—as you like,—is the sculpture you will see at Rheims . . ." [71] In short, the authority Huysmans preferred a certain piece of sculpture, and Adams could not help but hope that the nieces would see as Huysmans saw. Other people, apparently beneath the dignity of designation, disagreed with the authority cited. No matter, for although Huysmans' perceptivity merited respect, qualitative opinion on art could not be absolute. Not that he denied the importance of scholarship on the cathedral; he merely implied that a relatively untutored niece could "feel" the cathedral without bibliographical assistance, while she could never comprehend the Jefferson and Madison administrations except with the impedimenta of professordom.

To this extent art permitted freedom from authority. In fact, only by discarding such art history as she may have acquired and by once more becoming a child of nature could an educated niece really understand Chartres. "Unless you can go back to your dolls, you are out of place here. If you can go back to them, and get rid for one small hour of the weight of custom, you shall see Chartres in glory." [72] For one small hour Adams may himself have seen Chartres in the glory which it showed the innocent; but the weight of custom constantly sent him scurrying to the bookshelf to check his naivete against the printed page.

Of all romantic attitudes few are more patently so than this belief that learning dulls the sharp edge of aesthetic sensitivity. For all his glorification of the rational, Adams was at heart a romantic; or, more precisely, he yearned in vain for the romantic disposition, for that release from hesitation which would permit freedom of either action or feeling. He readily agreed with La Farge's stricture, " 'Adams, you reason too much!' " [73] If in-

71. *Chartres*, pp. 56, 112, 83.
72. *Ibid.*, pp. 90 f.
73. *Education*, p. 370. On Adams as a "romantic" see Max I. Baym, "Henry

nocence gave the nieces an advantage over their guide at Chartres,
so innocence had long ago, in Adams' second novel, accounted for
the vitality of Esther's painting in the mural decoration at St.
John's Church in New York. The artist Wharton had good-
humoredly permitted Esther, little more than student though
she was, to add a St. Cecilia to his procession of Byzantinized
saints, who paraded with academic correctness through the lavish
gloom of their Fifth Avenue setting. Both uninhibited by the dead
hand of knowledge and untainted by the harsh experiences of life
Esther employed her vivacious Colorado cousin as a model for
her Cecilia. The finished work possessed a glow of youth and innocence so out of keeping with the rest of the mural that Wharton
complained, " 'It's not good! It's not handled in a large way or
in keeping with the work round it.' " Still he would leave it. " 'I
can draw better and paint better, but I can't make a young girl
from Colorado as pure and fresh as that. To me religion is passion. To reach Heaven, you just go through hell, and carry its
marks on your face and figure. I can't paint innocence without
suggesting sin, but you can, and the church likes it. Put your
own sanctity on the wall beside my martyrdom!' " [74]

Thus the "American Saint" remained in its dark corner in St.
John's. Perhaps this new order of saint matched the new order of
man in the *History*. As the American saint was a product of intuition, so American nationality seemed to Adams the result of
instinct almost equally inexplicable. When he later despaired of
the efficacy of this popular will to produce a better society, Adams
veiled his disillusionment with the gauze of science, as he had
earlier decreed a shadowed corner for Esther's saint.[75] Lift the
veil; dispel the shadow. The argument stood revealed: Reason was
degradation from intuition. No wonder Adams alternately chuck-
led at the elaborate satire of his historical essays and then turned
wistful to think that he should have to call on science merely to
prove the superiority of art.

If habitual scholarship hobbled escape to pure sensation, escape was doubly difficult for a scholar imbued with Comtian posi-

74. *Esther,* pp. 128 f., also pp. 80 f., 96, 105. A Bostonian, believing, as so many
Bostonians of the late nineteenth century did, in the decadence of Boston, it is
significant that Adams should see the West as a source of vigor, energy, and simplicity. Like Esther's cousin, Senator Ratcliffe also came out of the West.

75. *Ibid.,* pp. 80 f., 73.

tivism; for one nurtured on New England authoritarianism triply so. Hemmed in by cautions quite sufficient to temper emotional and aesthetic intensity, Henry Adams also inherited the introspective turn of mind, the inner check, recorded in the famed ancestral diaries. John and John Quincy had scrutinized their every action as though they stood outside themselves, peering through a darkened pane at their own deficiencies. Although not always quite so honest in his self-analysis as his presidential forebears, Henry gloomily viewed himself with much this same detachment. "I've disappointed myself," he wrote Charles as early as 1862 in a moment of intense honesty, "and experience the curious sensation of discovering myself to be a humbug. How is this possible? Do you understand how, without a double personality, I can feel that I am a failure? One could think that the I which could feel that, must be a different *ego* from the I of which it is felt." [76] If Henry Adams mirrored the introspective nature of his ancestors, he was unlike them in his aesthetic sensitivity. In his writing his aesthetic self stood outside the darkened pane to mock the demon of authority within: "there are three professions—the preacher, the teacher and the speaker,—which inevitably ruin the finest nature in a definite time. I was a pedagogue myself, and blush to this day at the marks I bear of it." [77] He had lampooned the bombast of the preacher in *Esther*, the speaker in *Democracy*, and the teacher in the *Education*. These authoritarian professions may have ruined the finest natures, but the vices they instilled in their practitioners —didacticism, pomposity, intellectuality, positivism—were fatal to literature.

Need we follow the conflict further? Need we wonder why he instinctively refused to labor over the documents left by his dogmatic forebears? [78] Need we ask why he could catch the ambiguities of Jefferson's personality insofar as he could lift them bit by bit from the documents, while leaving Madeleine and Esther as little more than puppets to his didactic intent in fiction? Or be surprised at Adams' fascination with the picturesque primitivism of the South Seas? Or ask why he twisted the charming account of Marau in his correspondence into the ponderous *Memoirs?* A curious chronicle this, of which Adams once complained that his

76. Feb. 14, 1862; *Cycle, 1,* 112 f.
77. Apr. 13, 1902; Ford, *2,* 386.
78. See, for example, Cater, pp. 487, 588; compare with Ford, *1,* 160. Of course he used a few family documents for his volume on New England Federalism.

hand was "too heavy" for the task, precisely as he had earlier found it too heavy to depict the personality of Jefferson: not quite the science of the ethnographer because Adams enhanced the artlessness of Marau's history with the studied naivete of his own style,[79] nor quite the art of the storyteller since he refused to select from the intricate detail in order to achieve an aesthetic unity.

Although Adams rebelled at authority, complete escape for more than "one small hour" he found impossible. He could not even enjoy his querulous forays into "catastrophe." Although he might flaunt his anarchism or curse his failure, his extreme statements are unbelievable because he himself did not believe in their extremity. His balanced mind mocked these attempts at escape into pure sensation. He came to Chartres. Here certainly he could cast off caution. But no, he could glimpse the truth of Chartres only in the truth of authority. The sophistication of the much traveled tourist and much read dilettante would not be downed. He left *Chartres* as a wistful plea for that innocence, that intuition, which enables man to grasp some unity from life.

In reality his vain attempts to find intensity in art symbolized his futile efforts to grasp intensity in life. Reviewed rapidly, his life falls into a kaleidoscope of fragments: documents, coins, stones, objets d'art, the restless panorama of the traveler, tasks picked up and changed, the dead end of paradox, the piecing of research into tottering unities, the life "cut in halves." If he could only scrap the odds and ends to grasp some wholeness out of life! He must have sympathized with his young friend Bay Lodge who far more self-consciously than Adams sought to gain intensity of feeling from a life surfeited with leisure, intellectualism, conventionalism, and—for Lodge—preciosity. Undoubtedly patterned on Henry James' *William Wetmore Story and His Friends*,

79. On the heaviness of Adams' hand see Ford, *1*, 487; above, p. 70. On the impingement of Adams' style on the account given by Arii Taimai and translated for Adams by her son and daughter, Tati and Marau, see Paul Hambruch, introduction to the German translation of Adams' volume on Tahiti, "Denkwürdigkeiten von Arii Taimai *E,* Marama von Eimeo, Teriirere von Tooarai," *Mitteilungen aus dem Museum für Völkerkunde* (Hamburg, Meissners, 1923), *8*. The publication of Adams' volume by an ethnographical museum testifies to the value of *Tahiti* from the point of view of the professional anthropologist. Hambruch praised the volume as coming from a "pure and unfalsified" source, adding that the material had been ordered in preparation for publication so that only in the last chapter did Arii really have her "say." Hambruch believed, however, that the intervention of Adams' style was easily separated from Arii's account in the remainder of the volume.

which Adams so much admired for its demonstration that those
born in Boston could never produce art,[80] *The Life of George
Cabot Lodge* represented his final attempt at letting the documents tell their own story. " 'I found an alley with a dozen jumps
in it,' " Bay Lodge had written his mother from Paris,

> and whisked my old hired horse over the entire lot, with the
> surprising result that he jumped rather well . . . Then I
> came home and read Petrarch and Ronsard, and in the after-
> noon took a boat down a bright blue Seine with white bridges
> spanning it and a Louvre, etc., on either hand. I got off at the
> Ile St. Louis, and for the pure dramatic effect went into the
> "Doric little morgue" and saw two terrible dead old women
> with the lower jaw dropped on the withered breast and the
> green of decomposition beginning about the open eyes. Then
> I came out into the broad sunshine, with that blessed Cathedral
> Apse in front of me, and its little sun-filled garden with the
> old Gothic fountain running pure water, and felt it was very
> good to live.[81]

Not that Adams required the elaborate rituals of his jaded friend
in order to touch the joy of life. The older man was too vital, too
realistic, and too amused with life to need such priming for its
enjoyment. Although he filled his letters with gloomy predictions,
they were usually electric with the humorous exaggeration of
his alarm and even revealed his impatience at a world so slow in
going to smash: "Let's get there quick! I'm for Morgan, McKinley
and the Trusts." [82] Lonely at times, restless, dyspeptic, often
bored, he nevertheless felt that "Truly this world is heaps of
fun!" [83] The trouble lay in the formlessness of the heap. Without form, experience could not become art. To this extent Adams'
problem was Lodge's. Both were thwarted in their ambition to
unify experience in such a manner that a transcendent experience
resulted; both suffered the frustration of the aesthetic temperament, unable through intensity of feeling to fuse the raw materials
of art into the self-sufficient reality of the masterpiece.

80. Ford, *2*, 413 ff. Edmund Wilson, introduction to a reprinting of Adams'
The Life of George Cabot Lodge in Wilson, ed., *The Shock of Recognition* (New
York, Doubleday, Doran, 1943), p. 744, remarks that Adams "turns the poor young
man into a shadow and withers up his verse with a wintry pinch."
81. Henry Adams, *The Life of George Cabot Lodge* (Boston, Houghton Mifflin,
1911), pp. 40 f.
82. Feb. 7, 1896; Ford, *2*, 97.
83. Apr. 8, 1901; *ibid.*, p. 325. Cater, p. 468.

If man could not reason his aesthetic unities, neither could he reason his heaven. *Chartres* invoked a unity both aesthetic and religious. Religious faith provided another—the sixth—line of force in Adams' world. Although his want of a "strongly positive and absolute" temperament [84] obviously blocked this path to inner certainty, Adams wistfully hovered at its entrance, to scan the course as far as he could see.

To one who abhorred dogmatism those creeds which coated dogma with aesthetics made a strong appeal—at least up to the point where one turned dogmatic for further belief or floundered into pensive skepticism. Having denounced society after 1885, Adams, like Bay Lodge, inquired into Buddhism, although, unlike Bay, Adams was hardly serious. In Ceylon he visited the Buddhist temple at Kandy, "the last remaining watchfire of our church, except for Boston where Bill Bigelow and [Ernest Francisco] Fenollosa fan faint embers." Dutifully and whimsically he "went at once to the sacred bo-tree," as he had earlier mused at the church of Ara Coeli. Although he "sat for half an hour, hoping to attain Nirvana," he left the sacred spot "without attaining Buddhaship." [85] To one who "hunger[ed] for annihilation," the passive femininity of his nature which sought "absorption in a higher unity," [86] Buddhism made a poetic appeal but never a religious one. From Japan, where he met Fenollosa, Adams wrote, "He has joined a Buddhist sect; I was myself a Buddhist when I left America, but he has converted me to Calvinism with leanings towards the Methodists." [87]

He could pursue Buddhism until its dogmatism interfered with the pure beauty of the oriental objets d'art in the house on Washington Square. He could make "a pilgrimage to Assisi" for "an interview with St. Francis, whose solution of historical riddles seemed the most satisfactory—or sufficient—ever offered," [88] so long as St. Francis stayed in frescoes. He could worship the Virgin if Viollet-le-Duc were her catechism. So he memorialized his wife with a monument barren of inscription and stripped of conventional religious symbolism—a hooded figure testifying by its symbolic ambiguity to both the intimacy of a husband's bereavement and to the uncertainty of his belief. His was the religion of the

84. See above, p. 258.
85. Sept. 10 and 13, 1891; Ford, *1*, 524, 526.
86. Mar. 17, 1909; May 7, 1901; Cater, pp. 647, 510.
87. July 27, 1886; Ford, *1*, 372.
88. *Education*, p. 367.

aesthete, a substitute for the faith of the believer. "Truth, indeed, may not exist; science avers it to be only a relation; but what men took for truth stares one everywhere in the eye and begs for sympathy." [89] He could feel truth in the cathedral; but "what men took for truth" begged for more than sympathy. It also pled for that believing which Adams could not give.[90]

He took the course that remained. Seeking his unity within the unity of history, he would give his own experience meaning within the transcendent experience of the human past. As he had once located the source of democracy in the forests of medieval Germany, so Adams eventually fixed in medieval France the point of highest intensity for history, when the people had hauled stones for Chartres.[91] He chose a time when the "Pastrycooks and Turners [looked] across at the Weavers and Curriers and Money-Changers," while these tradesmen mingled in the stained-glass society of nobility. The Virgin welcomed all to her presence regardless of earthly station. In the aesthetic democracy of Chartres each recognized and took pride in his station, for all had cooperated in creating the cathedral as a monument to their culture and its aspirations.[92] It was a time, too, when reason erected its own cathedral beside that of intuition. The line of St. Thomas' argument paralleled the soaring lines of the cathedral, the thrust of doubt countered by the thrust of conviction, the nicety of scholastic logic matched by the precision of the engineering vision of Viollet-le-Duc. An engineer's Gothic readily lent itself to translation in terms of energy, and in the final chapter of *Chartres* Adams brought the architectonics of both the *Summa* and the cathedral into his metaphor of energy. If the Virgin was primarily responsible for the aesthetic expression of the Middle Ages, God served as

89. *Chartres,* p. 382.
90. Baym, p. 203, raises the question of Adams' conversion to Catholicism, although there is little question but that he remained outside the church; see especially Ford, *2,* 630. Mabel La Farge, "Henry Adams," *Commonweal, 18* (May 19, 1933), 74 f., vaguely suggests that Adams may have come to the Church but more in spirit than formally. Another close Catholic friend, Mrs. Winthrop Chanler, *Roman Spring* (Boston, Little, Brown, 1934), p. 299, definitely states that "There was never a moment's serious thought that Henry Adams might enter the Church." Last rites for Adams were conducted from St. John's Episcopal Church, Washington, D.C.
91. Although there is evidence of popular participation for a short period in the actual construction of Chartres, this practice was rare. On the master mason tradition see, for example, the last two items mentioned on p. 140, n. 44.
92. *Chartres,* pp. 181 f.

the "prime motor" for the masculine expression of unity in St. Thomas' reasoning. God radiated lines of force of which

> a certain group ran to the human race, and, as long as the conduction was perfect, each man acted mechanically. In cases where the current, for any reason, was for a moment checked, —that is to say, produced the effect of hesitation or reflection in the mind,—the current accumulated until it acquired power to leap the obstacle . . . The apparent freedom [of men's will] was an illusion arising from the extreme delicacy of the machine, but the motive power was in fact the same—that of God.[93]

Free will was equivalent to the moment of hesitation in human thought; but as long as the moment of hesitation involved the reconciliation of man's world with the intuited faith of religion, just so long could man give unity to his society, his works, and his hopes. If the moment of hesitation merely involved some adjustment to technological improvement, then unity must disappear in the multiplicity which a blind technology had brought.

When he later challenged teachers of history to dispute his conclusion he had pretty much made up his own mind. The drift of his thought is clear as he wrote Henry Osborn Taylor in 1901 that

> it was really La Farge and his glass that led me [to an aesthetic appreciation of the Middle Ages]; not any remembrance of my dreary Anglo-Saxon Law which was a *tour-de-force* possible only to youth. Never did any man go blind on a career more virtuously than I did, when I threw myself so obediently into the arms of the Anglo-Saxons in history, and the Germans in art. The reaction, it is true, has been the more violent. Between Bishop [William] Stubbs and John La Farge the chasm has required lively gymnastics. The text of Edward the Confessor was uncommonly remote from a twelfth-century window. To clamber across the gap has needed many years of La Farge's closest instruction to me, on the use of eyes, not to say feet.[94]

However clear the drift of Adams' thought, the trend from rationality toward intuition did not represent conversion so much

93. *Ibid.*, p. 375.
94. May 4, 1901; Ford, *2*, 332 f.

as a progressive revelation, until he eventually confronted the full complexity of what he wryly termed his "balanced mind." Decisiveness, even had it been possible, would have disturbed this balance. For his final unity he sought a synthesis which would tax every facet of his mentality and bring all to an enigmatic equilibrium, while yet suggesting the primacy of feeling over intellect. History has frequently tempted the man whose interests encompass aspects of literature, social theory, science, and philosophy. The fascination of the historical classic depends on the resulting tension—a tension so balanced that a plausible and consistent past results with enough resemblance to the mythical "real" past seemingly to exist as a self-sufficient sequence independent of the historian who created it. So Adams, who had always viewed his own role in the light of history, eventually gave his life significance by paralleling his experience with that of the whole of the human past.

The result was not decision but tension, not solution but challenge. "The *auto*," he sighed to a correspondent shortly after he had purchased one in 1904, "is a great tyrant. I have to invent space for it." [95] Just so for his imagination. He enjoyed the sense of "going—going—going," whirling from one cathedral to the next, the centuries dropping "like autumn leaves" before this twentieth-century source of power. A tourist of the imagination, he bundled his readers beside the nieces in the tonneau and set off on a quest part whimsical and part serious, part rational and part aesthetic, part comic and part tragic. The journey, not the destination, was important, although in travel as in life direction suggests destination, while becoming may suffice for arrival. But suppose the sense of direction was only apparent? Suppose it was mere movement? The motion of the dynamo, of molecules, of society through time, of the tourist through space, and of thought through both: suppose movement without direction summarized personal and historical experience? Such was the challenge of the disillusioned Comtist, whose Mercedes brought him and his passengers to a phase where he, for one, could travel no further.

95. Aug. 19, 1905; *ibid.*, p. 458. Citations immediately following: Aug. 27, 1904; *ibid.*, p. 438, and *Education*, p. 470.

A Short Chronology of Adams' Life

Childhood and Youth (*Education,* chaps. i–vii)

1838 Born February 16.

1854–58 Harvard.

1858–60 Civil law in Berlin; grand tour of Europe. Writings: letters to the *Boston Daily Courier.*

1860–61 Brief period of law study in Quincy; private secretary to his father in Washington; return to Quincy.
Writings: letters to the *Boston Daily Advertiser;* "The Great Secession Winter."

American Legation (*Education,* chaps. viii–xv)

1861–68 Private secretary to his father in London; secret correspondent for the *New York Times* (1861–62).
Writings: "A Visit to Manchester" (1861); article on John Smith (1867); "British Finance in 1816" (1867); "The Bank of England Restriction" (1867); review of Sir Charles Lyell's *Principles of Geology* (1868).

Reform Journalism (*Education,* chaps. xvi–xix)

1868–70 Free-lance correspondent in Washington for the *North American Review, Nation, New York Post;* articles in *Edinburgh Review* and *Westminster Review.*

"Professordom" (*Education,* chap. xx, covering only 1871)

1870–77   Assistant professor of medieval and American history at Harvard; editor of *North American Review;* marriage to Marian Hooper; one year's leave of absence for European trip; active interest in Independent party in 1876; access to the Gallatin papers acquired in 1877.

Writings: articles and reviews for the *North American Review; Essays in Anglo-Saxon Law* (1876); *Documents Relating to New England Federalism* (1877).

The *History* (omitted from the *Education*)

1877–92   Residence in Washington; trip abroad for documents in European archives; Mrs. Adams' suicide; trip to Japan with La Farge; trip to the South Sea Islands, Australia, Java, Ceylon, India, and return via Europe.

Writings: *Gallatin* (1879); *Democracy* (1880); *Randolph* (1882); *Esther* (1884); *History* (1889–91).

The Later Years (*Education,* chaps. xxi–xxxv, to 1905)

1892–1918   Extensive travel; stroke (1912); research in medieval music.

Writings: *Tahiti* (1892, 1901); *Tendency* (1895); *Chartres* (1904, 1913); *Education* (1907, 1918); *Rule* (1909); *Letter* (1910); *The Life of George Cabot Lodge* (1911).

1918   Died March 26.

SELECTED BIBLIOGRAPHY

M ANY titles which might have been included here appear in existing bibliographies. For example, Samuels gives the bibliography on Adams' early life, Hume an extensive list of periodical articles, and Baym a cosmopolitan bibliography centering on French influences. I have limited this bibliography to three major divisions: works dealing with aspects of Adams' life, writing, and thought; history; and science. The first of these major divisions is subdivided into six sections: (A) appraisals of Adams' life and thought as a whole or of aspects of his life and thought of particular relevance for this study; (B) critiques centering in the *Education;* (C) the *History* and Adams' historical career as a whole; (D) reviews of the *History* and alterations by subsequent scholars; (E) the *Tendency, Rule,* and *Letter;* (F) Adams' other writings. The second major division on history is subdivided into three subsections: (G) Comte and positivism, institutional history and the idea of race; (H) scientific history and the nature of history; (I) the "new" history. The third major division on science parallels the order of topics considered in the text. A † preceding books in this final division indicates that either the designated volume or the position represented by the volume played a part in the development of Adams' speculation.

I. ASPECTS OF ADAMS' LIFE, THOUGHT, AND WRITING

GENERAL APPROACHES TO ADAMS' LIFE AND THOUGHT

(On Adams' early life, up to 1877, see notes and bibliography in Samuels.)

A. Appraisals of Adams' life and thought as a whole or of aspects of his life and thought of particular relevance for this study. Robert E. Spiller, "Henry Adams," *Literary History of the United States,* ed. R. Spiller, W. Thorp, T. Johnson, H. Canby (New York, Macmillan, 1948), *2,* 1080–1103, discusses Adams' life in terms of his belated discovery of his aesthetic nature after he had finally overcome two inhibitions which hindered his literary development, namely, that thought without action is void and that thought without emotion is valid. Like Spiller, Charles I. Glicksberg, "Henry Adams and the Repudiation of Science," *Scientific Monthly, 64* (1947), 63–71, sees Adams' development as tending away from rationalism toward intuition, as does Van Wyck Brooks, "The Miseducation of Henry Adams," *Sketches in Criticism* (New York, Dutton, 1932), pp. 197–210, and Brooks, *New England: Indian Summer* (New York, Dutton, 1940), pp. 250–275, 354–372, 474–490. Bernard Smith, "The Quest for Beauty," *Forces in American Criticism* (New York, Harcourt, Brace, 1939), pp. 220–228, substantially ignores the rational side of Adams' personality to concentrate on Adams' aesthetic nature by contrasting his "quest for beauty" through "idealism" with similar quests by Poe through "romanticism" and by Henry James through "realism." Ludwig Lewisohn, *Expression in America* (New York, Harper, 1932), pp. 278 f., 342–347, likewise emphasizes the aesthetic-critical side of Adams' nature as the more important side, and particularly important in that Adams sensed the degree to which America had "cut itself off from access to those forces which might have opposed materialism" whether through social idealism or aesthetic creation. M. Maurice Le Breton, "Henry Adams et la France," *Harvard et la France* (Paris, La Revue d'histoire moderne, 1936), pp. 74–96.

Adams is seen more as a social commentator by Ralph H. Gabriel, "Frederick Jackson Turner versus Henry Adams," *The Course of American Democratic Thought* (New York, Ronald, 1940), pp. 251–268; Henry S. Commager, "Henry Adams," *South Atlantic Quarterly*, *26* (1927), 252–265; Commager, *The American Mind* (New Haven, Yale University Press, 1950), *passim*. On Adams' social prophecies, Commager, "Henry Adams, Prophet of Our Disjointed World," *New York Times Magazine*, Feb. 20, 1938, p. 11; Herbert Edwards, "The Prophetic Mind of Henry Adams," *College English*, *3* (1942), 708–721. Social criticisms of special aspects of Adams' career are Richard P. Blackmur, "Henry and Brooks Adams: Parallels to Two Generations," *Southern Quarterly Review*, *5* (1939), 308–334, who contrasts Brooks Adams' legalistic view of society with Henry Adams' imaginative view; Maurice F. Neufeld, "Crisis in Prospect; Henry Adams and the White City," *American Scholar*, *4* (1935), 397–408; William H. Jordy, "Henry Adams and Walt Whitman," *South Atlantic Quarterly*, *40* (1941), 132–145. Herbert W. Schneider, *A History of American Philosophy* (New York, Columbia University Press, 1946), pp. 396–415, relates the "desperate naturalism" of Henry Adams to that of William Graham Sumner, Edward Arlington Robinson, and George Santayana. Robert C.

Le Clair, *Three American Travellers in England* (Philadelphia, University of Pennsylvania Press, 1945), pp. 61–122, contrasts James Russell Lowell, who was content with his native country, and Henry James, who became an expatriot, with Henry Adams, whose restless voyaging between two continents left him at home in neither; Philip Rahv, "Henry Adams," *Discovery of Europe* (Boston, Houghton Mifflin, 1947), p. 322, contrasts the views of European civilization held by Adams and Henry James. John Lydenberg, "Henry Adams and Lincoln Steffens," *South Atlantic Quarterly*, *48* (1949), 42–64.

Women in Adams' life and woman as symbol. General discussions are Richard F. Miller, "Henry Adams and the Influence of Woman," *American Literature*, *18* (1947), 291–298; Ferner Nuhn, "Henry Adams and the Hand of the Fathers," *The Wind Blew from the East* (New York, Harper, 1942), pp. 164–194. On Mrs. Adams see Katherine Simonds, "The Tragedy of Mrs. Henry Adams," *New England Quarterly*, *9* (1936), 564–582, which is still the best analysis of Mrs. Adams' suicide; Susan La Follette, "Henry Adams' Wife," *New Republic*, *89* (1936), 278; Richard P. Blackmur, "The Letters of Marian Adams," *The Expense of Greatness* (New York, Arrow Editions, 1940), pp. 245–252. On the role of woman in Adams' novels, Blackmur, "The Novels of Henry Adams," *Sewanee Review*, *51* (1943), 281–304; Robert E. Spiller, Introduction to Adams, *Esther* (Scholars' Facsimiles and Reprints, 1938), pp. iii–xxv. On Tahiti, Spiller, Introduction to Adams, *Tahiti* (Scholars' Facsimiles and Reprints, 1947), pp. iii–viii. On the Virgin, Geraldine P. Dilla, "The Religious Appeal of Architectural Masterpieces," *South Atlantic Quarterly*, *36* (1937), 180–188, compares Renan's poem to Athena with Adams' *Prayer to the Virgin of Chartres*, which is more completely discussed by Baym, pp. 81–89.

The warmer side of Adams' personality, as seen by intimate friends. See especially Cater, Introduction, pp. xv–cxix; Margaret (Mrs. Winthrop) Chanler, "Friendship of Henry Adams," *Roman Spring* (Boston, Little, Brown, 1934), pp. 291–308; Stephen Gwynn, *The Letters and Friendships of Sir Cecil Spring Rice* (London, Constable, 1939), *1*, 51–102 *passim*, 367 f., 380 ff.; *2*, 168 f., 180–185; Owen Wister, *Roosevelt; the Story of a Friendship, 1880–1919* (New York, Macmillan, 1930), pp. 147–153; Mabel La Farge, Introduction, *Letters to a Niece and Prayer to the Virgin of Chartres* (Boston and New York, Houghton Mifflin,

1920), pp. 3–27; La Farge, "Henry Adams," *Commonweal, 18* (1933), 74 f.

CRITIQUES CENTERING IN THE *Education*

(The following divisions for criticisms of the *Education* suggest divergent emphases rather than rigid categories.)

B. Adams the enigma. Seldon P. Delany, "Man of Mystery," *North American Review, 216* (1922), 694–704; Mark A. D. Howe, "Elusive Henry Adams," *Saturday Review of Literature, 7* (1930), 237 ff. Huntington Cairns, Allen Tate, and Mark Van Doren, with Richard P. Blackmur as guest, "The Education of Henry Adams," *Invitation to Learning* (New York, Random House, 1941), pp. 121–132, pose more questions than answers; so does Carl L. Becker, *American Historical Review, 25* (1920), 480–482, and *Everyman His Own Historian* (New York, Crofts, 1935), pp. 143–168. In the latter volume Becker asserts that Adams confused the term "education" by using it in the double sense of obtaining worldly power and of discovering eternal verities; this observation was made earlier by Henry H. Williams, "The Education of Henry Adams," *Monist, 31* (1921), 149–159.

The irresponsible and sour egotist. Gamaliel Bradford, "Henry Adams," *American Portraits, 1875–1900* (Boston and New York, Houghton Mifflin, 1922), pp. 31–57, is representative of hostile criticism which finds the *Education* the product of an effete, perverse egotist who perverted truth for sardonic amusement, lacked passion, and blamed society for his own deficiencies. Other hostile critiques comparable to Bradford's are those by H. T. J. Coleman, "Henry Adams: A Study in Multiplicity," *Queen's Quarterly, 28* (1920), 1–14; C. Lewis Hind, *Authors and I* (New York and London, Lane, 1921), pp. 13–18; Samuel McChord Crothers, "Education in Pursuit of Henry Adams," *The Dame School of Experience* (Boston and New York, Houghton Mifflin, 1920), pp. 186–213; Mark A. D. Howe, *John Jay Chapman and His Letters* (Boston, Houghton Mifflin, 1937), pp. 360, 419, where Chapman remarks on the "equanimity and patience" displayed in the *History* as opposed to the "odious" conceit of intellectual pretense in the *Education*. Charles F. Thwing, *Guides, Philosophers and Friends* (New York, Macmillan, 1927), pp. 222–236, 284–287, considers the *Education* mere "raillery" but attributable to "intellectual exuberance" rather than perversity.

Social criticism. Odell Shepherd, "The Ghost of Henry Adams," *Nation, 147* (Oct. 22, 1938), 419, takes as a springboard for social criticism the theme of the "tired and hypersensitive mind turning away from the weight and complexity of modern thought toward the puerile *élan vitale* of Bergson." Louis Kronenberger, " 'The Education of Henry Adams,' " *Books That Changed Our Minds*, ed. Malcolm Cowley and Bernard Smith (New York, Doubleday, Doran, 1939), pp. 45–57, sees the *Education* as a manifestation of futilitarian attitudes prevalent in the 1920's. Other social critiques of the *Education* are Edgar Johnson, "An Old Man in a Dry Month," *A Treasury of Biography* (New York, Howell Soskin, 1941), pp. 396–398, which also views the *Education* as a futilitarian document of the twenties; and Johnson, "Henry Adams: The Last Liberal," *Science and Society, 1* (1937), 362–377, which shows Adams as the sterile end of "upper middle class liberalism." Granville Hicks, *The Great Tradition* (New York, Macmillan, 1933), pp. 68–74, 131–139, takes the Marxist position that the *Education* reveals the breakdown of capitalism. Vernon L. Parrington, "The Skepticism of the House of Adams," *Main Currents in American Thought* (New York, Harcourt, Brace, 1930), *3*, 212–236, also relates Adams to the breakdown of the Jeffersonian agrarian tradition but does go on to note the contrast between the rationalism of the *History* and the "pantheistic mysticism" of *Chartres*. Roger V. Shumate, "Political Philosophy of Henry Adams," *American Political Science Review, 38* (1934), 599–610, criticizes Adams' political and historical views in the *Education*. Harry Slochower, "Henry Adams and T. S. Eliot on Unity," *No Voice Is Wholly Lost* (New York, Creative Age, 1945), pp. 371–375, 378 f., shows Adams, like Eliot, adrift in society and therefore unable to create any unity save one where metaphysical, religious, and cultural factors lack social and economic meaning.

The Puritan theme. Dixon Wector, "The Harvard Exiles," *Virginia Quarterly Review, 10* (1934), 224–257, compares Adams to other "Harvard exiles" from the American scene around 1900, like Henry James, George Santayana, and T. S. Eliot, to find that all these writers transformed the Puritan quest for religious perfection into a bookish quest for aesthetic perfection, while meeting the Puritan's need for universality by an appeal to monarchy and/or Catholicism. Other essays relating Adams to the frustration of the Puritan ideal are Robert M. Lovett, "The Betrayal of Henry Adams," *Dial, 65* (1918), 468–472; Regis

Michaud, "Un Amateur de décadence: 'L'Éducation' de Henry Adams," *Autour d'Emerson* (Paris, Bossand, 1924), pp. 201–215; Paul E. More, "Henry Adams," *A New England Group and Others*, Shelburne Essays, 11th Ser. (Boston and New York, Houghton Mifflin, 1921), pp. 117–140; Yvor Winters, *The Anatomy of Nonsense* (Norfolk, Conn., New Directions, 1943), pp. 23–87, which sees the nonsense in Adams' later work as a perversion of the Puritan ethic and psychology in contrast to the merit of his *History*; Nathalia Wright, "Henry Adams's Theory of History: A Puritan Defense," *New England Quarterly, 58* (1945), 204–210.

The family theme. Stuart P. Sherman, "Evolution in the Adams Family," *Americans* (New York, Scribners, 1924), pp. 288–315, is an early example of viewing the *Education* as the "continued story" of the Adams heritage, of which James T. Adams, *The Adams Family* (Boston, Little, Brown, 1930), is a later installment and Brooks Adams, Introduction, *The Degradation of the Democratic Dogma* (New York, Macmillan, 1919), pp. 1–122, an earlier.

The romantic. John Cournos, "Henry Adams—Another 'Failure,'" *A Modern Plutarch* (Indianapolis, Bobbs-Merrill, 1928), pp. 275–284; in another chapter, "The Comparison of Amiel with Adams," pp. 285–287, Cournos compares the "romantic failure" of Henri-Frederick Amiel with that of Adams; Max I. Baym, "Henry Adams and the Critics," *American Scholar, 15* (1945–46), 79–89, and later in his *The French Education of Henry Adams*, has developed this idea of "romantic failure" furthest.

The man of action and reason to the man of contemplation and intuition. Charles I. Glicksberg, "Henry Adams and the Modern Spirit," *Dalhousie Review, 27* (1947), 299–309; Glicksberg (see Sec. A); Robert E. Spiller, "Henry Adams: Man of Letters," *Saturday Review of Literature, 30* (Feb. 22, 1947), 11 f.; Spiller, *Literary History of the United States* (see Sec. A); Nuhn (see Sec. A), who makes the contrast by comparing the public man of reason with the private man of intuition; Richard P. Blackmur, "The Expense of Greatness: Three Emphases on Henry Adams," *The Expense of Greatness* (see Sec. A), pp. 253–276, shows Adams as a young man attempting to work directly in society, his later attempt to define worth-while goals by working outside his society beginning with the *Gallatin*, and his valetudinarian "failure" to unify the diversified experience of life where the "greatness is in the effort itself . . . and failure is the expense of greatness."

Finally, at a pole almost diametrically opposed to the hostile critics who have viewed the *Education* primarily in autobiographical terms is Gerrit H. Roelofs, "Henry Adams: Pessimism and the Intelligent Use of Doom," *Journal of English Literary History, 17* (1950), 214–239, who minimizes the autobiographical aspect of the *Education* in identifying his own point of view with that of Blackmur (immediately above); Roelofs' essay, however, seems to go further than Blackmur's in making Adams' life an incidental focus for the *Education* which was designed as a challenge to the twentieth century.

Miscellaneous emphases on aspects of the *Education*. Charles I. Glicksberg, "Henry Adams on Education," *Educational Record, 31* (1940), 177–187, uses the *Education* to elicit Adams' principles of the ideal education. Robert A. Hume, "The Style and Literary Background of Henry Adams, with Attention to *The Education of Henry Adams*," *American Literature, 16* (1945), 296–315.

ON ADAMS' HISTORICAL CAREER

(For the major bibliography on Adams' teaching career see Samuels, p. 339, n. 3.)

C. The *History*. Michael Kraus, "Henry Adams," *A History of American History* (New York, Farrar & Rinehart, 1937), pp. 321–335, is a summary of the *History* together with an analysis of some of its merits and deficiencies; this chapter is most significant when read in conjunction with the preceding chapter on the rise of scientific history in America. Gabriel (see Sec. A) compares Adams and Frederick Jackson Turner. Henry S. Commager, "Henry Adams," *The Marcus W. Jernegan Essays in American Historiography* (Chicago, University of Chicago Press, 1937), pp. 191–206, suggests that the *History* was written to display the achievements of the Adams family and to analyze American character. Commager, Introduction to Henry Adams, *History* (New York, Boni, 1930), *1*, vii–xviii, comments on the dichotomy between Adams' desire to portray social history and his political and diplomatic approach to history; he ponders the meaning of the *History* and is especially cogent on Adams' style. William R. Taylor, "Historical Bifocals on the Year 1800," *New England*

Quarterly, 23 (1950), 172–186, contrasts the approaches of
Adams and John Bach McMaster to social history; for a com-
parison of the social history of Adams and Edward Channing see
David S. Muzzey, review of William Channing, *A History of the
United States, 5,* in *Political Science Quarterly, 37* (1922), 300.
W. Stull Holt, "The Idea of Scientific History in America,"
Journal of the History of Ideas, 1 (1940), 352–362, examines
Adams in relation to the movement for scientific history in America
toward the end of the nineteenth century.

SOME REVIEWS AND CORRECTIONS OF THE *History*

D. Representative reviews of the *History* arranged alphabet-
ically by periodical. Most of the longer reviews summarized Adams'
argument; practically all praised his style and impartiality, although opinions differed as to the degree of monotony in the
events depicted. The topics indicated in the list below refer only
to those critical remarks of particular interest. In this country the
History usually appeared in the lead position in book review sections, although few periodicals reviewed every installment of the
volumes. In the following list no attempt has been made to indicate
the particular volumes under review except where comments make
their mention necessary. Reviews are anonymous unless an author
is indicated. *Atheneum* (London), *64*[2] (1891), 253, comments on
the curious numbering of the volumes; vaguely critical of Adams'
style. (*Ibid.*, *65*[1] [1892], 148, on Adams' *Historical Essays*
[New York, Scribners, 1891], is decidedly critical of Adams'
style; contrasts his essays on finance with the clarity of those by
Walter Bagehot; considers the *Rights of Women* and *The Session,
1869–70* as least significant.) *Ibid.*, *66*[1] (1893), 669; *67*[1] (1894),
507. *Atlantic Monthly, 65* (1890), 274–278, *History* "overmuch
expected"; studies of the society of New England and the Middle Atlantic States are too critical, gentler on the South; carping
negativism of his style which lacks color; paradoxical treatment
of Jefferson; dislike of Hamilton; Madison and Gallatin are life-
less, Randolph and Marshall more successful; unfavorably contrasts Adams' treatment of Judge Chase with Macaulay's treatment of Warren Hastings. *Boston Evening Transcript*, Mar. 21,
1891, p. 10. Henry Coppée, *Church Review, 57* (1890), 253 ff.
Critic (London), new ser., *13* (1890), 164; new ser., *14* (1890),
229; new ser., *15* (1891), 106. *Dial, 11* (1890), 33 f.; *12* (1891),
307 f. J. A. Doyle, *English Historical Review, 8* (1893), 802–

806, too partisan to Jefferson in the Callender incident, too much inclined to believe that the opinions of English newspapers and leaders necessarily represented popular opinion, Gallatin the hero. *Harper's Monthly, 80* (1890), 968 f., fairness to Jefferson even though Adams "probably" doesn't like him; Burr story is the best part of Vols. 1 and 2. *Overland*, 2d ser., *16* (1890), 547–551, Adams impartial, Gallatin the hero. *Nation, 50* (1890), 376 ff., 395 ff., Vols. 3 and 4 show greater fluency and certainty than Vols. 1 and 2 where Adams had seemed doubtful as to how to interpret the "glamor" of Jefferson's political fame which Adams "could not substantiate to himself"; fails to show how the erstwhile democratic North and aristocratic South reversed their positions; the importance of Gallatin; Jefferson blamed for failures more the fault of events than of his policy; criticizes Adams' analysis of the Bravo River situation, his treatment of Jefferson's case against Burr, his neglect to ascertain specifically the cost to the South of the embargo, and his tendency to ascribe to all supporters of the Federalist party the opinions of their leaders. *Ibid., 51* (1890), 405 ff., 424 ff., monotony of Vol. 5 owing to events discussed, too harsh on Madison despite his incapabilities, more harsh on Madison in the *History* than in the *Gallatin*, omissions in respect to the revocation of the French decrees, Randolph in the role of the chorus in a Greek tragedy although Adams records too much of Randolph's trivia. *Ibid., 52* (1891), 322 ff., 344 ff., dullness of the War of 1812 save for a few actions, observed Adams' comparison of the southern policy of embargo during both the War of 1812 and the Civil War, believes Adams exaggerates the collapse of the American government during the War of 1812, Gallatin the hero of the Treaty of Ghent, further contributions to the period will be "rather in the interpretation of the facts than in the discovery of new facts." *New York Times*, Oct. 27, 1889, p. 19, Adams' portrait of Jefferson is that of a "temporizing, inconsistent, and perhaps somewhat selfish person, a little of the casuist too," Adams failed to "put himself in [Jefferson's] place." *Ibid.*, Feb. 9, 1890, p. 19, best political history ever written on the United States except possibly for Von Holst's first volume; the best written American history except for Parkman; want of sympathy for Jefferson borders on prejudice, for example, Adams' criticism that Jefferson did not use the steamboat during the War of 1812 as though Jefferson should have been more enlightened than the vast majority of his contemporaries in this respect; too harsh on Jefferson's compromising with the British after the *Chesapeake-Leopard* affair; Jefferson's retention of the embargo was not necessarily due to his desire for popularity; Gallatin the hero, but Adams gives Gallatin too much credit for Jefferson's popular support since an administration with a far-sighted financial policy does not invariably possess popular appeal; Adams failed to observe that Burr's "treason" at a time when the idea of American nationality was not firmly established was quite a different matter than would have been the case had his activities occurred sometime after the War of 1812. *Ibid.*, Mar. 1, 1891, p. 19, contrasts Adams' work with George Bancroft's ultra-patriotism and "ornate" style; finds the policies of Jefferson and Madison contemptible; Adams as a New England historian but fair to Virginia; Gallatin the hero of the Treaty of Ghent; Adams' unheroic statesmen; naval battles especially good. *New York Tribune*, Dec. 8, 1889, p. 14, paradoxical nature of the period; Virginia unconsciously perpetrates a revolution; excellent description of Adams' style. *Ibid.*, Feb. 23, 1890, p. 14, exaggerates Canning's desire to ruin American commerce; Jefferson gets just deserts. *Ibid.*, Oct. 5, 1890, p. 14, Gallatin as hero, the mystery of American skill in gunnery during the War of 1812 remains mysterious. *Ibid.*, Jan. 25, 1891, p. 14, a lengthy discussion of the paradoxical aspects of the War of 1812 together with mention of some events fortuitous for the Americans. Worthington Ford, *Political Science Quarterly*, 5 (1890), 541 ff., 697 ff., the "advocate" is more apparent in Vols. 5 and 6 than in earlier volumes; Gallatin the "balance wheel" of the Jefferson administration. *Spectator* (London), *66* (1891), 726 f.; *68* (1892), 126 f.

Subsequent criticisms and discussions of the factual data and conclusions of the *History*. An extensive search of relevant articles from Grace G. Griffin, *et al.*, ed., *Writings on American History* (New York, Macmillan, 1906–40), and a search of bibliographies and articles in American historical periodicals subsequent to 1940 has uncovered the following items in which a specific criticism was made of Adams' *History*, or a specific comparison with the opinions of other historians. On the embargo, Walter W. Jennings, "The American Embargo, 1807–1809," *University of Iowa Studies in the Social Sciences* (Iowa City, University of Iowa Press, 1921), *8*, 200; Gilbert Chinard, *Thomas Jefferson, the Apostle of Americanism* (Boston, Little, Brown, 1929), pp. 459 f., 464; p. 453 criticizes Adams' exaggerated regard for the caliber of Perceval and Canning; p. 408 on the Louisiana Purchase. Also on the Louisiana Purchase, Everett S. Brown, *The Constitutional History of the Louisiana Purchase, 1803–1812* (Berkeley, University of California Press, 1920), p. 101; R. A. D. McLemore, "Jeffersonian Diplomacy in the Purchase of Louisiana, 1803," *Louisiana Historical Review, 18* (1935), 346; Adrienne Koch, *Jefferson and Madison, the Great Collaboration* (New York, Knopf, 1950), p. 239. Isaac C. Cox, "The American Intervention in West Florida," *Proceedings of the Mississippi Valley Historical Association, 4* (1910), 47 f., accuses Adams of being overly harsh to Jefferson and Madison in respect to American policy in Florida. On the Treaty of San Lorenzo, Arthur P. Whitaker, "New Light on the Treaty of San Lorenzo; an Essay in Historical Criticism," *Mississippi Valley Historical Review, 15* (1929), 439 f. On impressment as a cause of the War of 1812, John W. Foster, review of Frank A. Updyck, *The Diplomacy of the War of 1812,* in *American Journal of International Law, 9* (1915), 764; Alfred L. Burt, *The United States, Great Britain, and British North America* (New Haven, Yale University Press; Toronto, Ryerson; London, Oxford University Press, 1940), p. 288; p. 274 on Erskine's dismissal; p. 284 on Cadore's note on the revocation of Napoleonic decrees against American shipping. On the role of the West in the War of 1812, Christopher B. Coleman, "The Ohio Valley and the War of 1812," *Mississippi Valley Historical Review, 7* (1920), 40; Warren H. Goodman, "The Origins of the War of 1812, a Survey of Changing Interpretations," *Mississippi Valley Historical Review, 28* (1941), 171–186, finds Adams a pioneer in suggesting the influence of the West as a cause of the War of 1812. On Adams' unfairness to the Federalists, Housatonic (pseudonym, identified as William Henry Smith on copy in the New York Public Library), *A Case of Hereditary Bias. Henry Adams as an Historian,* privately printed pamphlet of articles originally appearing in the *New York Tribune,* Sept. 10 and Dec. 15, 1890 (Washington, 1891). Morris Zucker, *The Philosophy of American History* (New York, Arnold-Howard, 1945), *1,* 20, 48, 52, 100; *2,* 347 f., 899 f., takes a Marxist point of view in opposing Adams' exaggeration of the isolation of the American people and criticizes his notion of fixity for national character after the War of 1812, while praising Adams' awareness of change in history and his portrayal of American society as too "simple" to be torn by the capitalism versus democracy argument which many historians have made of the

Hamilton-Jefferson conflict. Muzzey, review of Channing (see Sec. C), gives a brief comparison of the social history of Channing and Adams.

Subsequent criticisms of Adams' appraisal of individual statesmen. Definitive critiques of Adams' appraisal of the statesmanship and character of either Jefferson or Madison have not appeared; only David Muzzey, *Thomas Jefferson* (New York, Scribners, 1918), p. 272, on Jefferson's attitude toward the collapse of his embargo policy seems worth mentioning; minor criticism of Adams on Jefferson appears in Francis W. Hirst, *Life and Letters of Thomas Jefferson* (New York, Macmillan, 1926), pp. 388 f., 434. Jay C. Heinlein, "Albert Gallatin: A Pioneer in Public Administration," *William and Mary Quarterly*, 7 (1950), 76 f., summarizes historical scholarship on Jefferson's indecision in respect to the antagonism between William Duane and Albert Gallatin. On Monroe, George Morgan, *The Life of James Monroe* (Boston, Small, Maynard, 1921), pp. 210, 230, 238, 280, 285, 290, 298, 308, 311, 340, who especially indicates instances of Adams' overly harsh and satirical pronouncements; anonymous review of this volume in *Tyler's Quarterly Historical and Genealogical Magazine*, 3 (1922), 238 f., concurs in Morgan's judgment, consigning Adams among the "Northern" historians prejudiced against Virginian statesmanship. Claude Bowers, *Jefferson in Power* (Boston, Houghton Mifflin, 1936), p. 98, believes that Adams' "anti-Virginian interpretation" led him to minimize the abilities of William Giles; p. 398 on Burr. On John Randolph, William C. Bruce, *John Randolph of Roanoke, 1773–1833* (New York, Putnam, 1922), *1*, v-vi, and footnotes throughout; reviewed by D. R. Anderson, *American Historical Review*, 29 (1924), 348. Aaron Burr has thus far proved the focus for the most extreme controversy with Adams' conclusions; Julius W. Pratt, "Aaron Burr and the Historians," *New York History*, 26 (1945), 447–470, summarizes the controversy and gives bibliography. Gabriel E. Manigault, "General George Izard's Military Career; a Reply to Mr. Henry Adams," *Magazine of American History*, 26 (1891), 457–462, defends Izard's reputation against Adams' interpretation.

ON *Tendency, Rule,* AND *Letter*

E. Adams' scientific speculation on history. Charles A. Beard, Introduction to Brooks Adams, *The Law of Civilization and Decay* (New York, Knopf, 1943), pp. 3–53, refutes the idea that Henry

Adams contributed substantially to Brooks' *Law* and credits Brooks with initiating Henry's interest in scientific theories of history. Brooks Adams (see Sec. B), relates Henry Adams' interest in science to the similar interest of John Quincy Adams. Robert Shafer, "Science and History," *Progress and Science* (New Haven, Yale University Press, 1922), pp. 155–193, also emphasizes the influence of John Quincy and Brooks Adams on Henry Adams' monistic view of the universe, which did not rise above the materialism that Adams scorned. James T. Adams, "Henry Adams and the New Physics," *The Tempo of Modern Life* (New York, Boni, 1931), pp. 214–239, and Roy F. Nichols, "The Dynamic Interpretation of History," *New England Quarterly, 8* (1935), 163–178, criticize the *Rule* in the light of modern physics, although with sympathy for Adams' purpose. Robert A. Hume, "Henry Adams' Quest for Certainty," *Stanford Studies in Language and Literature* (Stanford, Stanford University Press, 1941), pp. 361–373, indicates in more detail than either J. T. Adams or Nichols a number of flaws in Henry Adams' reasoning; Winters (see Sec. B) indicates others, and very vitriolically. George H. Sabine, "Henry Adams and the Writing of History," *California University Chronicle, 26* (1924), 31–46, concludes that Adams' problem ultimately became a search for a principle underlying historical change. James Stone, "Henry Adams's Philosophy of History," *New England Quarterly, 14* (1941), 538–548, finds that Adams' use of science (reason) to approach mystery was akin to that of other intellectuals of his period.

ON ADAMS' OTHER WORKS

F. Samuel F. Bemis, *John Quincy Adams and the Foundations of American Foreign Policy* (New York, Knopf, 1949), pp. 575 f., discusses an important document on the relation of John Quincy Adams and the Federalist party either ignored by or more probably unknown to Henry Adams when he edited *Documents Relating to New England Federalism.* Evelyn Page, "The Diary and the Public Man," *New England Quarterly, 22* (1949), 147–172, believes that Adams is the author of the anonymous "Diary of a Public Man." Morris E. Speare, *The Political Novel; Its Development in England and in America* (New York, Oxford University Press, 1924), pp. 287–306, terms *Democracy* the "first true political novel written in America." Edmund Wilson, "A Novel of Henry Adams," *New Republic, 44* (Oct. 14, 1925),

203, contrasts the more attractive Adams of *Democracy* with the despairing Adams of the *Education* and relates *Democracy* to Henry James' *The Bostonians*. Blackmur, *Sewanee Review* (see Sec. A) notes the parallels between Adams' life and those of the heroines in *Democracy* and *Esther* who escaped from action when their respective quests for faith ended in disaster; he also relates *Esther* to Hawthorne and Petrarch. Spiller, Introduction to *Esther* (see Sec. A), compares this novel with *Democracy*, with the feminine theme in Adams' life, and with the intuitional bent of his later writing. Nuhn (see Sec. A) and Dilla (see Sec. A) discuss the *Prayer to the Virgin of Chartres*, the latter comparing Adams' prayer with Renan's prayer to Athena. Oscar Cargill, "The Medievalism of Henry Adams," *Essays in Honor of Carleton Brown* (New York, New York University Press, 1940), pp. 296–329, discusses the *Essays in Anglo-Saxon Law* and sees *Chartres* as an expiation for *Esther*, which he considers a key to the suicide of Mrs. Adams. On this latter point, Simonds (see Sec. A). Herbert L. Creek, "The Medievalism of Henry Adams," *South Atlantic Quarterly, 24* (1925), 86–97, believes that Adams found in the "lawlessness" of the Virgin an escape from Puritanical conscience. For Catholic opinions of *Chartres* see Anonymous, "Medieval Democracy in the Cathedral of Chartres," *Catholic World, 124* (1926), 252 f.; Hugh F. Blunt, "The Mal-Education of Henry Adams," *Catholic World, 145* (1937), 46–52; Frances Quinlivan, "Irregularities in the Mental Mirror," *Catholic World, 143* (1946), 58–65; the first favorable, the second hostile, the third stating that Adams' Puritanism led him to the error of imagining the Virgin as a conspirator with man against Calvinistic judgments rather than as an intercessor between man and God. Edmund Wilson, Introduction to Henry Adams, *The Life of George Cabot Lodge*, reprinted in Wilson, *The Shock of Recognition* (New York, Doubleday, Doran, 1943), pp. 742–746, analyzes the manner in which Adams blights the reputation of the man whom he memorialized.

II. History

POSITIVISM AND INSTITUTION HISTORY

G. Comte and positivism. Auguste Comte, *The Positive Philosophy of Auguste Comte*, tr. and condensed by Harriet Martineau (1st ed., London, Trübner, 1853; edition used, New York,

Blanchard, 1855), Bk. VI, is the basis for positivistic theories of history. John Stuart Mill, *Auguste Comte and Positivism* (London, Trübner, 1865), and Émile Littré, *Auguste Comte et la philosophie positive* (Paris, Hachette, 1864), are classic analyses. For a more recent appraisal see Lucien Lévy-Bruhl, *The Philosophy of Auguste Comte*, tr. F. Harrison (New York, Putnam; London, Sonnenschein, 1903), especially Bk. IV on social ethics. Historical theory much influenced by Comte appears in Louis Bourdeau, *L'Histoire et les historiens* (Paris, Alcan, 1888). Among the excellent shorter essays on positivism are Ernst Cassirer, *The Problem of Knowledge* (New Haven, Yale University Press, 1950), chap. xiv; Frederick J. Teggart, *Theory and Processes of History* (Berkeley and Los Angeles, University of California Press, 1941), Pt. 2, chaps. ix, x; Basil Willey, *Nineteenth Century Studies* (New York, Columbia University Press, 1949), chap. vii; Giorgio de Santillana, "Positivism and the Technocratic Ideal in the XIXth Century," *Studies and Essays in the History of Science and Learning in Honor of George Sarton* (New York, Schuman, 1947), pp. 249–259.

Institutional history and the idea of race. Herbert B. Adams, *The Study of History in American Colleges and Universities*, United States Bureau of Education, Circular of Information No. 2 (Washington, Government Printing Office, 1887), emphasizes the institutional approach in a survey of university teaching methods toward the end of the nineteenth century; William Stubbs, *Lectures on Early English History*, ed. A. Hassal (London and New York, Longmans, Green, 1906), especially Essays 10, 13, 18, 19; Edward Freeman, "The English People in Its Three Homes," *Lectures to American Audiences* (Philadelphia, Porter & Coates, 1882); Robert H. Lowie, *The History of Ethnographical Theory* (New York, Farrar & Rinehart, 1937), chaps. v, vi, vii. On Adams' view of race see Edward N. Saveth, *American Historians and European Immigrants, 1875–1925* (New York, Columbia University Press, 1948), chap. iii; an unpublished paper by Joseph W. Keena, Yale University, was extremely helpful on the relationship between theories of race and English historiography of the nineteenth century.

THE NATURE OF HISTORY

H. The nature of history with particular respect to the degree of absolutism possible to history. For scientific history in America and its relation to Adams, Holt (see Sec. C). For brief, sympathetic statements on Ranke's significance consult Hajo Holborn, "The Science of History," *The Interpretation of History*, ed. J. R. Strayer (Princeton, Princeton University Press, 1943), pp. 61–83, and Cassirer (see Sec. G), chap. xiii. On various approaches to the problem of scientific history: John Fiske, "The Laws of History," *NAR*, *109* (1869), 197–230, a review of John W. Draper's *A History of the Intellectual Development of Europe* and Sir Henry Maine's *Ancient Law;* Herman Ausubel, *Historians and Their Craft: A Study of the Presidential Addresses of the American Historical Association, 1884–1945* (New York, Columbia University Press, 1950), especially chaps. vi, vii, on presidential addresses dealing with science and history; Hugh Miller, *History and Science* (Berkeley, University of California Press, 1939); John B. Bury, "The Science of History," *Selected Essays* (Cambridge, Cambridge University Press, 1930), pp. 3–22; the following essay, "Darwinism and History," pp. 23–42, is also helpful; Ernest Scott, *History and Historical Problems* (Melbourne and London, Oxford University Press, 1925), chap. v, on history and the physical sciences; Edmund S. Meany, "History and Science," *Washington Historical Quarterly*, *19* (1928), 83–89, with additional bibliography suggested in the text; Edward P. Cheyney, *Law in History, and Other Essays* (New York, Knopf, 1927), chap. i; Edgar Zilsel, "Physics and the Problem of Historico-sociological Laws," *Philosophy of Science*, *8* (1941), 567–579; James B. Conant, *Science and Common Sense* (New Haven, Yale University Press, 1951), chap. x; W. E. Hocking, "On the Law of History," *University of California Publications in Philosophy*, *2* (1909), 45–65; Charles O. Paullin, "Historical Predictions," *South Atlantic Quarterly*, *25* (1926), 361–369, discusses the predictions of famous men, mentioning Adams along with others of his contemporaries who foresaw World War I. Douglas G. Haring, "Science and Social Phenomena," *American Scientist*, *35* (1947), 351–363, specifies the ways in which science and society are incomparable. For attacks on various scientific approaches by historical relativists see Benedetto Croce, *Theory and History of Historiography*, tr. D. Ainslie (London, Harrap, 1921), also published as *On History* (New York, Harcourt Brace, 1921), especially Pt. 2, chaps. v–viii, which contrast the historiography of the enlightenment, romanticism, and positivism with the "new historiography." Robin G. Collingwood, *The Idea of His-*

tory (Oxford, Clarendon Press, 1946) ; Becker, *Everyman His Own Historian* (see Sec. B), pp. 233–255; Charles A. Beard, "That Noble Dream," *American Historical Review, 41* (1935), 74–87, who summarizes the argument against the Rankean position very clearly and succinctly, with bibliography; Beard, "Written History as an Act of Faith," *American Historical Review, 39* (1934), 219–229, and Beard and Alfred Vagts, "Currents of Thought in Historiography," *American Historical Review, 42* (1937), 460–483, give similar points of view. Lucy M. Salmon, *Why Is History Rewritten?* (New York, Oxford University Press, 1929), discusses a major contention of the relativists. For the opposition to the relativists see Maurice Mandelbaum, *The Problem of Historical Knowledge* (New York, Liveright, 1938), and Chester McA. Destler, "Some Observations on Contemporary Historical Theory," *American Historical Review, 55* (1950), 503–529, the latter providing an excellent introductory bibliography on the argument between historical subjectivists and objectivists.

Books of a more general nature on history of particular value for this study include Bertrand Russell, *Power, a New Social Analysis* (New York, Norton, 1938), a classic on the role of power in history and society. George P. Gooch, *History and Historians in the Nineteenth Century* (London and New York, Longmans, Green, 1935), is the standard work in English in its field. Ernst Bernheim, *Lehrbuch der historischen Methode* (Leipzig, Duncker und Humblot, 1889), chap. i, was helpful on the relation of history to other fields. Charles A. Beard, *The American Spirit* (New York, Macmillan, 1942), chaps. i–iii, presents an excellent survey of the development of the idea of civilization in history. Finally, two books generally helpful for bibliographies as well as content, Fred M. Fling, *The Writing of History* (New Haven, Yale University Press, 1920), and *Theory and Practice in Historical Study: A Report of the Committee on Historiography*, Bulletin 54 (New York, Social Science Research Council, 1946).

THE NEW HISTORY

I. An excellent introduction to the movement is Morton G. White, *Social Thought in America; the Revolt against Formalism* (New York, Viking, 1949), chap. iv, which relates new history to the revolt against formalism in other fields. The prolegomenon of the movement is James Harvey Robinson, *The New History* (New York, Macmillan, 1912), while Arthur M. Schlesinger, Sr.,

New Viewpoints in American History (New York, Macmillan, 1922), is a typical product. The works of Harry Elmer Barnes have provided the most extensive analysis of historical and social scientific theory from the perspective of the new historian: *The New History and Social Studies* (New York, Century, 1925), *A History of Historical Writing* (Norman, University of Oklahoma Press, 1947). Gaetano Salvemini, *Historian and Scientist* (Cambridge, Harvard University Press, 1939), and Fred L. Rowse, *Science and History* (New York, Norton, 1928), are typical of those who have used "science" in connection with history in a manner akin to that of the new historians; but see also certain of the volumes in Sec. H. Other articles of interest are Alexander A. Goldenweiser, "A New Approach to History," *American Anthropologist*, new ser., *22* (1920), 26–47; Ross L. Finney, "A Course in General History from the Sociologist's Standpoint," *Historical Outlook*, *11* (1920), 221–227, characteristic of the teaching programs recommended by the new historians; H. E. Barnes, "The Significance of Sociology for the 'New' or Synthetic History," *Historical Outlook*, *13* (1922), 277–299, with a discussion pp. 300–306; James H. Robinson, "The Newer Ways of Historians," *American Historical Review*, *35* (1930), 245–255; Crane Brinton, "The New History: Twenty-five Years After," *Journal of Social Philosophy*, *1* (1936), 134–147, an appraisal of the movement in a criticism of H. E. Barnes, *The History of Western Civilization*, with a reply by Barnes, "The New History and Common-Sense," *Journal of Social Philosophy*, *1* (1936), 148–153; Brinton, "The 'New History' and 'Past Everything,' " *American Scholar*, *8* (1939), 144–157; Esmond Wright, "History: The 'New' and the Newer," *Sewanee Review*, *49* (1941), 479–491.

III. SCIENCE

GENERAL HISTORIES OF SCIENCE

J. Perhaps the most helpful volume for this study was the well-known John T. Merz, *A History of European Thought in the Nineteenth Century* (Edinburgh and London, Blackwood, 1903), especially Vol. 2, which devotes a chapter to the development of each of seven ways of viewing nature—the kinetic or mechanical, the physical, the morphological, the genetic, the vitalistic, the psychophysical, and the statistical. Another standard work, Sir William Dampier, *A History of Science* (4th ed., Cambridge, Cambridge University Press; New York, Macmillan, 1949), was helpful, as especially was A. d'Abro, *The Decline of Mechanism* (New York, Van Nostrand, 1939). For their more philosophical points of view, Cassirer (see Sec. G), Pt. 1, and Alfred Whitehead, *Science and the Modern World* (New York, Macmillan, 1925; Mentor ed., 1948), were also valuable. For historical material in volumes less specifically historical in their intention see Sec. W.

THERMODYNAMICS

K. The second law is discussed, together with certain scientific and speculative problems which it poses, by Percy W. Bridgman, *The Nature of Thermodynamics* (Cambridge, Harvard University Press, 1941); Roderick Seidenberg, *Posthistoric Man* (Chapel Hill, University of North Carolina Press, 1950); †Wilhelm Ostwald, *L'Énergie*, tr. E. Philippi (Paris, Alcan, 1909); †Bernhard Brunhes, *La Dégradation de l'énergie* (Paris, Flammarion, 1908). For a clear account of the early history of thermodynamic theory see Hermann von Helmholtz, "On the Interaction of Natural Forces" and "On the Conservation of Force," *Popular Lectures on Scientific Subjects*, 1st ser., tr. E. Atkinson (London, Longmans, Green, 1873). †Alexander Findlay, *The Phase Rule and Its Application* (London, Longmans, Green, 1906), chaps. i–iv, and D'Abro (see Sec. J), chap. xxi, discuss the phase rule; the latter is exceptional in its clarity and succinctness. On Willard Gibbs see Muriel Rukeyser, *Willard Gibbs* (New York, Doubleday, Doran, 1942), and Lynde P. Wheeler, *Josiah Willard Gibbs, the History of a Great Mind* (New Haven, Yale University Press, 1951), both containing bibliography on thermodynamics. L. Brillouin, "Life, Thermodynamics, and Cybernetics," *American Scientist*, *37* (1949), 554–568, emphasizes the limitations of the second law. †Gustave Le Bon, *The Evolution of Forces* (London, Paul, Trench, Trübner, 1908), is a vividly written, somewhat unreliable study of energy in relation to the ether and atomic theories which influenced Adams.

GEOLOGY AND RELATED FIELDS

L. The uniformitarian-catastrophist controversy. †Sir Charles Lyell, *Principles of Geology* (London, Murray), *1;* chaps. ii–v present a brief history of geological theory; chap. xiv is the best statement of Lyell's own uniformitarian convictions. Sir Archibald Geikie, presidential address, *Report of the British Association for the Advancement of Science* (Edinburgh meeting, 1892), pp. 3–26, is a classic statement of the uniformitarian position. †Clarence King, *Catastrophism and the Evolution of Environment* (no place, presumably New Haven, 1877), a short address vigorously attacking the uniformitarian position. Jules Marcou, *The Life and Letters of Louis Agassiz* (New York and London, Macmillan, 1896), *2*, chap. xviii, discusses the spread of the catastrophist position during the nineteenth century. Also helpful are Sir Archibald Geikie, *The Founders of Geology* (London, Macmillan, 1905) ; Thomas G. Bonney, *Charles Lyell and Modern Geology* (London, Cassell, 1901), especially chap. v; Carroll L. Fenton and Mildred A. Fenton, *The Story of the Great Geologists* (London, Doubleday, Doran, 1945) ; Karl A. von Zittel, *History of Geology and Paleontology to the End of the Nineteenth Century*, tr. M. M. Ogilvie-Gordon (London, Walter Scott Publishing Co., New York, Scribners, 1914).

M. Geological climates. Richard F. Flint, *Glacial Geology and the Pleistocene Epoch* (New York, Wiley; London, Chapman & Hall, 1947), chap. i, provides a brief history of glacial theories; chap. xxii, an excellent survey of all theories on climatic fluctuations throughout geological time with an evaluation of their present status. Charles E. P. Brooks, *Climate through the Ages* (New Haven, Yale University Press, 1928), in his introduction contrasts the "abnormal" climates of the present with the presumably more "normal" climates of past geological periods. George Gamow, *Biography of the Earth* (New York, Viking, 1941 ; Mentor ed., 1948), chap. vii, briefly summarizes knowledge of past climates; Arthur P. Coleman, *Ice Ages, Recent and Ancient* (New York, Macmillan, 1926), is a standard work on pre-Pleistocene glaciation. Other sources are †Lyell (see Sec. L), *1*, chaps. x–xiii; †Oswald Heer, *The Primaeval World of Switzerland*, ed. and tr. James Heywood (authorized English ed. London, Longmans, Green, 1876), *2*, 262–274; †Louis Saporta, *Le Monde des plantes avant l'apparition de l'homme* (Paris, Masson, 1879) ; †Albert de Lapparent, *Traité de géologie* (5th ed., Paris, Masson, 1906), *3*, 1951–1961; James Croll, *Climate and Time* (New York, Appleton, 1885), especially chaps. xvii and xviii, on evidences of pre-Pleistocene glaciation; James C. Irons, *Autobiographical Sketch of James Croll* (London, Stanford, 1896), chaps. vii, viii, xvii, and xxv, on Croll's theory of glacial ages; †Robert Ball, *The Cause of an Ice Age* (New York, Appleton, 1891), a revision of the Croll hypothesis.

N. The age of the earth. For catastrophic estimates significant for the *Letter*, †Clarence King, "The Age of the Earth," *American Journal of Science*, 3d ser., *45* (1893), 1–20; †Lord Kelvin, "The Age of the Earth as an Abode Fitted for Life," reprinted in *Annual Report of the Smithsonian Institution, 52* (1897), 337–357. For the uniformitarian rebuttal see Thomas C. Chamberlin, "On Lord Kelvin's Address on the Age of the Earth as an Abode Fitted for Life," *Annual Report of the Smithsonian Institution, 54* (1899), 223–246; John Joly, "An Estimate of the Geological Age of the Earth," *Annual Report of the Smithsonian Institution, 54* (1899), 247–288, is especially interesting because Joly defends uniformitarianism while simultaneously attacking its excesses. †Joly, *Radioactivity and Geology* (London, Constable; New York, Van Nostrand, 1909), gives a rather technical summary of early research on radioactive substances in rocks; the title essay in Joly, *The Birth-Time of the World* (London, Unwin, 1915), presents a particularly lucid account of the methods by which the age of the earth has been estimated. Adolph A. Knopf, "Time in Earth History," *Genetics, Paleontology, and Evolution*, ed. G. L. Jepsen, *et al.* (Princeton, Princeton University Press, 1949), summarizes the present position.

O. General background in geology. †Lyell (see Sec. L); †James D. Dana, *Manual of Geology* (4th ed., New York and Cincinnati, American Book Co.; London, Trübner, 1895); Gamow (see Sec. M); George A. Baitsell, ed., *The Evolution of Earth and Man* (New Haven, Yale University Press, 1929).

PALEONTOLOGY AND BIOLOGICAL EVOLUTION

P. Genetics and evolutionary leaps. †Louis Dollo, "Les Lois de l'évolution," *Bulletin de la Société Belge de Géologie, 7* (1893), 164 ff. †Charles Darwin, *Origin of Species*, especially chap. x, on the imperfection of the geological record. †Edward D. Cope, *The Origin of the Fittest* (New York, Appleton, 1886), especially Pt. 1, presents a particularly good discussion of the Darwinian dilemma. Richard Goldschmidt, *The Material Basis of Evolution* (New Haven, Yale University Press, 1940), especially chaps. i, ii, and pp. 199–291, for a technical discussion of quasi-catastrophist theory based on genetics, which is nevertheless comprehensible to the layman in scattered passages. Tracy M. Sonneborn, "Beyond the Gene," *American Scientist, 37* (1949), 33–59, summarizes the present state of genetic theory. George G. Simpson, *Tempo and Mode in Evolution* (New York, Columbia University Press, 1944), especially pp. 206–217, for his quantum theory of evolution.

Q. Irreversibility in evolution. Joseph Needham, "Evolution and Thermodynamics," *Time: The Refreshing River* (London, Allen & Unwin; New York, Macmillan, 1943), a popular discussion of the problem. Needham, "Contributions of Chemical Physiology to the Problem of Reversibility in Evolution," *Biological Reviews of the Cambridge Philosophical Society, 13* (1938), 225–251, a technical discussion containing interesting detail on Dollo, together with a bibliography of Dollo's writings on the subject. Hermann J. Muller, "Reversibility in Evolution Considered from the Standpoint of Genetics," *Biological Reviews of the Cambridge Philosophical Society, 14* (1939), 261–280, an extremely technical article demonstrating that slight reversibility can occur in biological evolution. Harold F. Blum, "A Consideration of Evolution from a Thermodynamic View-Point," *American Naturalist, 69* (1935), 354–369, and Alfred J. Lotka, *Elements of Physical Biology* (Baltimore, Williams & Wilkins, 1925), chaps. i–v, present views of irreversibility in evolution particularly congenial to Adams' point of view. Seidenberg (see Sec. K) considers all the above-mentioned authorities in developing a theory of history very similar to Adams'. Edwin H. Colbert, "Some Paleontological Principles Significant in Human Evolution," *Studies in Physical Anthropology No. 1; Early Man in the Far East,* symposium of the American Association of Physical Anthropologists (Philadelphia, Press of the Wistar Institute, 1949), pp. 117–130, and William K. Gregory, "On the Meaning and Limits of Irreversibility of Evolution," *American Naturalist, 70* (1936), 517–528, emphasize the limitations of the principle of irreversibility, the former in a less technical manner than the latter.

R. The decrease of mammals during the Pleistocene. Edwin H. Colbert, "The Association of Man with Extinct Mammals in the Western Hemisphere," *Proceedings of the Eighth American Scientific Congress* (Washington, Department of State, 1940), *2,* 17–29, and Alfred S. Romer, "Pleistocene Vertebrates and Their Bearing on the Problem of Human Antiquity in North America," *The American Aborigines,* ed. D. Jenness (Toronto,

University of Toronto Press, 1933), pp. 49–83, give lucid accounts of the disappearance of Pleistocene mammals, while Colbert touches on the various explanations which have attempted to account for the phenomenon. William B. Scott, *A History of Land Mammals in the Western Hemisphere* (New York, Macmillan, 1937), especially pp. 112, 259 ff., 727, 745, is helpful. E. H. Sellards, "Early Man in America," *Bulletin of the Geological Society of America, 51* (1940), especially p. 410, is less helpful than the other authorities for the problem which Adams raises but gives an exhaustive bibliography (pp. 412–431) on this and related problems.

S. General information on evolution, paleontology, and genetics. George G. Simpson, *The Meaning of Evolution* (New Haven, Yale University Press, 1949), is an exceedingly interesting and authoritative account by a paleontologist of evolution and its implications for philosophy. †Charles Depéret, *The Transformations of the Animal World*, tr. F. Legge (New York, Appleton, 1909), provides a compact introduction to the history of paleontological theory during the nineteenth century, as does Von Zittel (see Sec. L). Lawrence J. Henderson, *The Fitness of the Environment* (New York, Macmillan, 1924), is a classic on its subject. Julian S. Huxley, *Evolution, the Modern Synthesis* (New York, Harper; London, Allen & Unwin, 1943), although rather chaotic in organization and technical in detail, is a standard work on the interrelations between evolution and genetics. Glenn L. Jepsen, Ernst Mayr, and George G. Simpson, eds., *Genetics, Paleontology, and Evolution* (Princeton, Princeton University Press, 1949), gives present opinions in related evolutionary sciences through a collection of technical essays, parts of which are comprehensible to the layman. Henshaw Ward, *Evolution for John Doe* (Indianapolis, Bobbs-Merrill, 1925), especially pp. 267–336, for a very simple account of the history of major concepts in evolutionary theory. Baitsell (see Sec. O) and J. B. S. Haldane, *The Causes of Evolution* (New York and London, Harper, 1932), were generally helpful. Colbert (see Sec. Q), pp. 103–147, clarifies some of the major concepts in paleontology. William K. Gregory, *Evolution Emerging* (2 vols., New York, Macmillan, 1951), was published too late to be of extensive use in this investigation, but it should be consulted in further explorations of Adams' use of paleontological data.

ANTHROPOLOGY, PSYCHOLOGY, AND THE SOCIAL SCIENCES

T. Physical anthropology and eugenics. For a discussion of the biological deterioration of man see Earnest R. Hooton, *Apes, Men, and Morons* (New York, Putnam, 1937), especially pp. 229–295; Hooton, *Twilight of Man* (New York, Putnam, 1939), especially pp. 214–226, 278–305; George H. Estabrooks, *Man, the Mechanical Misfit* (New York, Macmillan, 1941); †John H. Kellogg, *Are We a Dying Race?*, reprinted from *Good Health* (no place, presumably Battle Creek, Mich., 1897); Frederick Osborn, *Preface to Eugenics* (New York and London, Harper, 1940); A. Kroeber, *Anthropology* (New York, Harcourt, Brace, 1948), chaps. ii, iii, and Earnest Hooton, *Up from the Ape* (rev. ed., New York, Macmillan, 1946), for general background.

U. Sociological theory. For Gustave Le Bon's theory of the "collective mind" and the crowd psychology of the proletariat see his †*The Crowd* (New York, Macmillan, 1907) and †*The Psychology of Socialism* (New York, Macmillan, 1899). Criticism of Le Bon appears in Everett D. Martin, *The Behavior of Crowds* (New York and London, Harper, 1920), especially chaps. ii, iii. †Émile Durkheim, *Le Suicide* (Paris, Alcan, 1897), a classic study of the influence of society on behavior, is discussed by Talcott Parsons, *The Structure of Social Action* (New York and London, McGraw-Hill, 1937), Pt. 2, chaps. viii–xi. Wilhelm Wundt's approach to society through the study of folk psychology, as summarized in *Elements of Folk Psychology*, tr. E. L. Schaub (London, Allen & Unwin; New York, Macmillan, 1916), may have influenced Adams, as Wundt's psychological studies certainly did. The *Letter*, p. 251, shows that Adams knew something of Lamprecht's psychological theory of history; †Karl Lamprecht, *What Is History?*, tr. E. A. Andrews (New York and London, Macmillan, 1905). A critique and further bibliography on Wundt, Lamprecht, and psychological theories as related to history appears in Barnes, *New History and Social Studies* (see Sec. I), chap. iii. On social Darwinism see especially †Herbert Spencer, *Social Statics* and †*First Principles*. †André Lalande, *La Dissolution opposé à l'évolution dans les sciences physiques et morales* (Paris, Alcan, 1899), especially attacked the Spencerian notion that evolution represented the development from indefinite and incoherent homogeneity to definite and coherent heterogeneity. Discussions of social Darwinian theories appear in Richard Hofstadter, *Social Darwinism in American Thought, 1860–1915* (Philadelphia, University of Pennsylvania Press, 1944), and Stow Persons, ed., *Evolutionary Thought in America* (New Haven, Yale University Press, 1950), both with copious bibliographies. For a general history of sociological thought see Floyd N. House, *The Development of Sociology* (New York and London, McGraw-Hill, 1936). See also references to sociological thought in the following section.

V. Instinct, will, intuition and their relation to intelligence and society. For Adams' point of view see †William James, *Psychology*, especially Vol. 2, chaps. xxiv, xxvi; Max I. Baym, "William James and Henry Adams," *New England Quarterly*, 10 (1937), 717–742; †Arthur Schopenhauer, *The World as Will;* Eduard von Hartmann, *Philosophy of the Unconscious*, tr. William C. Coupland (3 vols., London, Paul, Trench, Trübner) ; †Henri Bergson, *Creative Evolution*, tr. A. Mitchell (New York, Holt). Graham Wallas, *The Great Society* (New York, Macmillan, 1932), especially chap. xii, discusses the will of society, as does Edwin A. Hayden, "The Social Will," *Psychological Review*, 10 (April, 1909), entire issue. Archibald Alexander, *Theories of the Will in the History of Philosophy* (New York, Scribners, 1898), especially chaps. v and vi, provides convenient summaries and comparisons of varying theories. On will as variously applied to physiological theory: †Wilhelm Ostwald, *Natural Philosophy*, rev. and tr. T. Seltzer (New York, Holt, 1910), Pt. 4, and †Jacques Loeb, "Les Tropismes et la psychologie," *La Revue des idées*, 2d ser., 6 (1909), 249–272, relate the will to physical-chemical and mechanical reactions; †William H. Thomson, *Brain and Personality* (New York, Dodd, Mead, 1906), to the connection of new association fibers through an unknown agency; †Paul Flechsig, "Hirnphysiologie und Willenstheorien," *Atti del V Congresso Internazionale di Psicologia* (Rome, Forzani E. C. Tipografi del Senato, 1905), pp. 74–89, to organic changes. For present knowledge on the brain see John Fulton, *Physiology of the Nervous System* (London and New York, Oxford University Press, 1943). Typical theories of instinct for society are William Trotter, *Instincts of the Herd in Peace and War* (London, Unwin, 1916), and William McDougall, *The Group Mind* (New York and London, Putnam, 1920). Seidenberg (see Sec. K), chaps. ii and iii, contrasts the society dominated by instinct with that dominated by the intellect. The

classic critique of theories of instinct as related to society is Luther
L. Bernard, *Instinct* (New York, Holt, 1924), with copious bibliography.

PHYSICAL ETHER

W. The physical ether, atomic theory, and the nature of physical reality. †Lucien Poincaré, *The New Physics and Its Evolution* (London, Paul, Trench, Trübner, 1907), provides a succinct
and rather difficult summary of the state of physics about 1907.
†Sir Oliver Lodge, *Modern Views on Electricity* (London and New
York, Macmillan, 1889), is a compact popularization but again
not easy reading for the layman. †Karl Pearson, *The Grammar of
Science* (2d ed., London, Black, 1900), presents a lucid account
of the ether (in chap. vii with an excellent bibliography) in the
course of developing his positivistic view of physical reality.
†Henri Poincaré, *Science and Hypothesis* (London, Walter Scott
Publishing Co., 1905), reprinted in a collection of translated writings under the title *The Foundations of Science* (New York, Science Press, 1913), is, like Pearson, a classic on the nature of scientific conceptualization. †John B. Stallo, *The Concepts and
Theories of Modern Physics* (2d ed., New York, Appleton, 1881),
an attack on the "metaphysical errors" of mechanistic physics of a
more abstract and professionally philosophical nature than the
criticisms of Pearson and Poincaré. †Ostwald (see Sec. V), a survey of the relationships existing among the various fields of the
natural and physical sciences, together with an analysis of scientific conceptualization. Carlton B. Weinberg, "Mach's Empirio-
Pragmatism in Physical Science" (Ph.D. dissertation, Columbia
University, 1937), a convenient summary of Mach's theory. Sir
Oliver Lodge, *Ether and Reality* (London, Hodder & Stoughton,
1925), is designed for the layman, while the discussion of the ether
by the same author for the *Encyclopaedia Brittanica* (14th ed.)
also provides an excellent introduction to the subject. †G. John-
stone Stoney, "How Thought Presents Itself in Nature," *Proceedings of the Royal Institution, 11* (1885), 178–196; †Stoney,
"Studies in Ontology, from the Standpoint of the Scientific Student of Nature," *Scientific Proceedings of the Royal Dublin Society,* new ser., *6* (1890), 475–524; †Stoney, "Survey of That
Part of the Range of Nature's Operations Which Man Is Competent to Study," *Scientific Proceedings of the Royal Dublin Society,*
new ser., *9* (1899), 79–96, reprinted in *Annual Report of the*

Smithsonian Institution, 54 (1899), 207–222; three essays which Adams read (*Letter*, p. 274) on the nature of scientific reality and the limits possible to scientific investigation. †Arthur J. Balfour, "Reflections Suggested by the New Theory of Matter," *Report of the British Association for the Advancement of Science* (Cambridge meeting, 1904), pp. 3–14, is a very important source for Adams' conviction that the development of the ether theory into an electrical basis for matter meant that science was based on irrational conditions; also Le Bon (see Sec. K). Ernest Rutherford, presidential address of Section A, *Report of the British Association for the Advancement of Science* (Winnipeg meeting, 1909), pp. 373–385, provides an excellent summary of the knowledge of the atom at the time that Adams wrote his *Rule* and *Letter*. Henry Margenau, *The Nature of Physical Reality* (New York, McGraw-Hill, 1950), is especially valuable as a presentation of physical reality in the light of contemporary physics. Warren Weaver, "Science and Complexity," *American Scientist, 36* (1948), 536–544, discusses the kind of complexity which science has successfully investigated and that which has substantially resisted investigation. Ralph B. Perry, *Present Philosophical Tendencies* (New York, Longmans, Green, 1912), Pt. 2, and A. Cornelius Benjamin, *An Introduction to the Philosophy of Science* (New York, Macmillan, 1937), make cogent criticisms of the phenomenalist position. Also helpful on the nature and limits of science are Conant (see Sec. H); Cassirer (see Sec. G), Pt. 1; D'Abro (see Sec. J); Bertrand Russell, *Human Knowledge, Its Scope and Limits* (New York, Simon & Schuster, 1948); John Macmurray, *The Boundaries of Science* (London, Faber & Faber, 1939); J. W. N. Sullivan, *The Limitations of Science* (New York, Viking, 1933; Mentor ed., 1949).

Adams, Henry, TRAITS (*continued*)
266; positivism, 163 f., 170, 176 f., 199,
218, 219, 228 f. and n., 232 f., 237; restraint, 52, 58 f., 260; as romantic,
280 f.; skepticism, 16, 80 (*see also*
pessimism); snobbishness (*see* aloofness); summary of traits, 258, 261;
timidity, 26, 88; urbanity, 6, 45; vanity
(*see* conceit); vacillation, 122 ff.,
258 f., 265
    WRITINGS: see under short title used
in footnotes. For all work in the *North
American Review,* see *NAR*
Adams, Herbert Baxter, 37
Adams, John, 23, 48, 60, 69, 70, 73, 74,
88, 213, 282
Adams, John Quincy, 23, 46, 48, 60, 62,
67, 74, 91, 213, 282
Adams, Louisa, 259
Adams, Marian (Mrs. Henry), 43, 44,
126, 259 f., 263, 285; suicide, 42, 124
Agassiz, Louis, 91, 135, 173 f., 178, 188,
190, 197 f.
Alfred the Great, 76, 105
American Historical Association, 4, 124,
129 and n., 243 ff. and n.
American Historical Review, 247;
"Count Edward de Crillon," 23, 125,
129 ff.
"American Statesmen Series," 71
Ancient Law. See Maine, Sir Henry
Appleton's Cyclopedia, 256
Arthur, Chester, 264
Atlantic Monthly, 27, 28, 61, 174
"Atlantic system," 160
Atomic bomb, 154 and n.
Augustine. *See* St. Augustine
Austin, John, 7, 36

Bacon, Francis, 143
Badeau, Adam, 263
Balfour, Arthur J., 231, 250
Ball, Sir Robert, 181 f.
Bancroft, George, 6, 8, 18, 50, 122, 274;
assistance on *Gallatin* papers, 90 n.;
criticizes *History,* 30 and n.
Bancroft, Hubert H., 50
Barlow, Joel, 93
Baym, Max I., 65
Beard, Charles A., 13 n., 14 and n., 242 f.
and n.; on Brooks Adams, 131 n.
Beaumarchais, Pierre de, 70
Becker, Carl L., 14, 243
Bergson, Henri, 155, 248 n., 249
Bigelow, John, 161 n.

Bigelow, William, 285
Blaine, James G., 213, 263
Boer War, 160
Bohr, Niels, 228
Boltzmann, Ludwig, 166 f., 206, 216 n.
Bonnington, Richard P., 44
Boston Art Museum, 44
Boston Daily Advertiser, 26, 39, 123
Boston Daily Courier, 26, 28, 88, 99
Boston Post, 39, 40
Bourne, Edward, 9
Branca, Wilhelm, 209, 210
Bright, John, 99
British Association for the Advance-
ment of Science, 231
Brunhes, Bernhard, 204, 209
Bryan, William J., 272
Buckle, Henry T., 1, 2, 66, 97
"Buddha and Brahma," 279
Bulwer, Edward, Baron Lytton, 24
Bumstead, Henry A., 152 and n., 153 n.,
169 n., 237, 247; criticizes Adams' use
of second law, 216 n.; on ether, 225,
239 f.; on the *Letter,* 139 n.
Burgess, John W., 37 n.
Burke, Edmund, 27, 30, 101
Burr, Aaron, 52 and n., 65, 264; Adams'
presumed biography of, 48 f. and n.
Byron, George Lord, 10

Caesar, Gaius, 36
Calhoun, John C., 75
Callender, James T., 60 f.
Cameron, Don, 68 n., 126, 278
Cameron, Elizabeth, 260, 266 f.
Canning, George, 58
Carboniferous, warmth of. *See* Climate,
prehistoric
Carlyle, Thomas, 24, 257 f.
Carnegie Institution, 152
Catastrophism. *See* Evolution
Cause of an Ice Age, The. See Ball, Sir
Robert
Cecil, Robert, 33
Chamberlin-Moulton hypothesis, 211 n.
Chanler, Laura, 261
Chanler, Margaret (Mrs. Winthrop),
261
Chartres, 107, 120, 127, 189, 277 f., 279 f.,
283, 285, 286 f. and n.; Adams' fond-
ness for, 254, 259; final chapter com-
pared to *Letter,* 214, 254
Chase, Samuel, 57
Chateaubriand, François de, 9
Chesapeake, 93 f.